GRAPHIC
COMMUNICATIONS

GRAPHIC
COMMUNICATIONS

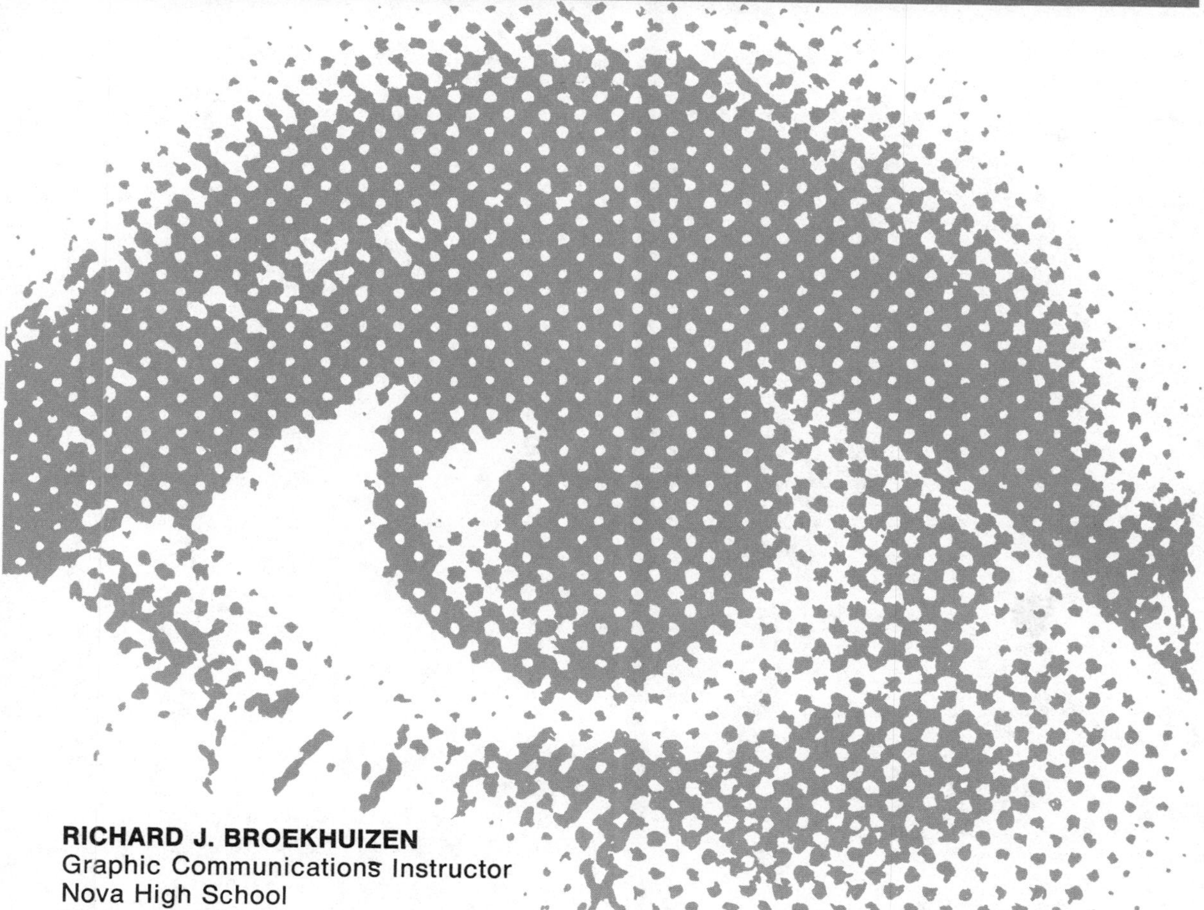

RICHARD J. BROEKHUIZEN
Graphic Communications Instructor
Nova High School
Ft. Lauderdale, Florida

A McKNIGHT PUBLICATION

PUBLISHING COMPANY/BLOOMINGTON, ILLINOIS 61701

SECOND EDITION

Lithographed in U.S.A.

**Library of Congress
Card Catalog Number: 78-57611**

SBN: 87345-246-1

Item No. 7174

PREFACE

Graphic communications—books, magazines, reports, signs, advertisements, documents, printed T-shirts, and many other messages—are produced in huge numbers every day. Many different kinds of processes are used to produce them. Many people in different kinds of jobs play a part in creating and producing these graphic messages. You can be one of those people.

GRAPHIC COMMUNICATIONS is designed to help you manage, plan, design, prepare, and produce graphic messages. It explains how quality, quantity, cost, and time required will determine the materials, equipment, and processes used.

This book is organized so that you can study those processes that best suit your needs or interests. It is divided into sections, chapters, and units. Sections explain the main concepts of graphic communication. Section I is an overview of communications. As you can see in the chart on page vi, Sections II through V explain design, image generation, preproduction and production, and finishing, binding, and packaging. Section VI is a final overview.

Read the section material to understand a major graphic arts concept. Then, for a description of specific processes, read the chapters. They help you determine which method of production is best for a particular message. The units explain how to do specific tasks. Study the unit or units which fit your needs. By using the chart, you can direct yourself in the course of instruction that best suits your purposes. It will help you design your own individualized instruction to learn what you want to know about graphic communication.

Producing good graphic products is a challenge. This book will help you learn to make production decisions to meet this challenge. Your experience in this course may also help you find the kind of work you want to make your career.

The Publisher

GRAPHIC COMMUNICATIONS

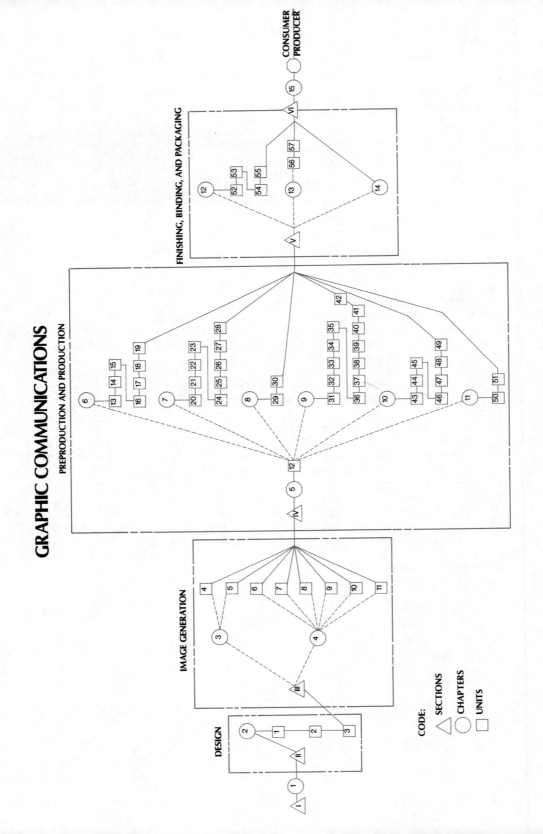

PREPRODUCTION AND PRODUCTION

FINISHING, BINDING, AND PACKAGING

IMAGE GENERATION

DESIGN

CONSUMER
PRODUCER

CODE:

△ SECTIONS

◯ CHAPTERS

☐ UNITS

ACKNOWLEDGMENTS

The author wishes to express sincere thanks and appreciation to **Pat** and **Kristi** for their cooperation, assistance, and understanding. Appreciation is also expressed to **Mr. Sanford E. Rich** of Central Connecticut State College for his many suggestions and his assistance in the preparation of the manuscript for this edition. Appreciation is extended to the many friends, relatives, and colleagues who have assisted in the preparation of this textbook.

A special note of thanks is extended to **Mr. James Rehrer** for assistance in the creation and preparation of many of the drawings and photographs which appear in this textbook.

The author also extends sincere thanks to the following companies for their cooperation and courtesy in supplying illustrative materials used in this textbook.

Acme Stapling Company
Addressograph-Multigraph Company
  Bruning Division
  VariTyper Division
Advance Process Supply Company
Allen Hollender Company
Alepha Machine Corporation
Alphatype Corporation
American Engineering and Design Corporation
American Type Founders
Beamer, Curt
Beck Engraving Company, Inc., The
Bell and Howell Baumfolder Division
Bell and Howell Ditto Division
Beseler Photo Marketing Co., Inc.
Borden, Inc.
Bostitch Division of Textron, Inc.
Brandtjen and Kluge, Inc.
Braun North American Corporation
Brown Manufacturing Company
Bruning, Charles Company
ByChrome Company, Inc.
California Redwood Association
Caprock Developments, Inc.
Caterpillar Tractor Company
Challenge Machinery Company, The
Chandler & Price Company
Chartpak, Rotex
Clopay Corporation

Compugraphic Corporation
C-Thru Ruler Company
Dick, A. B. Company
Didde-Glaser, Inc.
Dimco Gray Company
Dow Chemical U.S.A.
Dynamic Graphics, Inc.
Eastman Kodak Company
Ehrenreich Photo Optical Instruments, Inc.
Felins Tying Machine Company
FilmFair, Inc.
Filmotype Corporation
Fototype, Inc.
Friden Division, Singer Company
General Binding Corporation
Gorman's Typesetting
Graflex Division, Singer Company
Graphic Products Corporation
Halvorford Kwikprint Company
Hamilton Manufacturing Company
Heidelberg Eastern, Inc.
Honeywell, Inc.
Hunt Manufacturing Company
Itek Business Products
Instantype, Inc.
International Business Machines Corporation
Intertype Company
Kellogg Company ("Tony the Tiger")
Kenro Corporation

Keuffel and Esser Company
Ludlow Typograph Company
Mergenthaler Linotype Company
Naz-Dar Company
Northwestern Colorgraphics
Nu Arc Company, Inc.
Photo Materials, Inc.
Pitney-Bowes, Inc.
Polaroid Corporation
Prestype, Inc.
Printing Management
Quartet Films, Inc. and Leo Burnett Company
   ("Tony the Tiger")
Rapidesign, Inc.
Reader's Digest
Robertson-Photo-Mechanix, Inc.

Rosback, F. P. Company
Rouse, H. B. and Company
Seal, Incorporated
Simmon Omego, Inc.
StripPrinter, Inc.
SCM Corporation
3M Company
Typographic Sales, Incorporated
U. S. Forest Service
Valdes Associates, Inc.
Varityper Corporation
Visual Graphics Corporation
Weldotron Corporation
Wood-Regan Instrument Company, The
Xerox Business Products Group
Yankee Photo Products, Inc.

The following individuals are gratefully acknowledged for their helpful suggestions during the planning stages of this revision:

James B. Barrett
E.C. Hollenbach
Bill McLennan
Phillip J. Marron
Vincent S. Mordeno

David Pasco
John R. Schmidt
Neill C. Slack
O. Ray Smith

Jim Stinson
Dale Stonek
David Tripp
John A. Woolley

TABLE OF CONTENTS

COMMUNICATIONS

Communication is the act of transferring information from creature to creature, person to person, and point to point. Communicating is an important activity during every waking hour in every day of our lives. Often, we do not realize that, as individuals, we are communicating by one process or another at all times. Many aspects of communication are taken for granted because they have become natural activities in our daily habits.

One of the simplest forms of communication is the facial expression or gesture. A smile communicates a feeling of happiness, while a frown communicates a feeling of sadness or discontent. The traffic officer uses gestures to communicate to automobile drivers, Fig. I-1. Traffic lights, the painted center line on a busy highway, raising your hand in class, the slap of a beaver's tail on water, the bark of a dog, and the scream of a fire truck siren are all simple forms of communication.

We **talk** each day to express our own ideas, and we **listen** to hear the ideas of others. We also use our sense of **sight** for reading and interpreting visual forms of communication. Many blind people have developed their sense of **touch** so that they may read by running their fingers over raised patterns of symbols. Those who are deaf or unable to speak use their fingers to communicate in sign language, Fig. I-2. We also use our sense of **smell** to give us information. Therefore, it is important that we learn to use the natural devices we have for communicating by (1) talking, (2) listening, (3) seeing, (4) touching, and (5) smelling.

Since the beginning of time, people have developed communication systems that will help fulfill their needs. The members of early civilizations did not have a language as it is known today. However, they were able to communicate by using sounds, such as growls, cries, and screams. They also expressed their feelings with body motions. A hand wave meant hello or goodbye while waving a club showed feelings of anger.

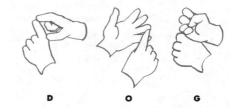

D   O   G

Fig. I-2. Communicating with finger sign language

Fig. I-1. Gestures are used to communicate messages

Fig. I-3. Actions communicate messages

A gliding hand and arm motion meant "snake." As you can see, we are still using many of these early gestures of communication, Fig. I-3. People also communicated by recording their thoughts, feelings, and experiences with crude figures drawn on bark, animal skins, or cave walls, Fig. I-4.

As early civilizations began to expand, larger numbers of people needed to communicate over longer distances. The development of tribal languages accomplished only part of the need for expanded communications. With fire and smoke signals and the beating of drums, communication from one point to another was possible, Fig. I-5. Later, by setting up a series of signaling stations, messages could be sent over longer distances.

As people became skilled in drawing, they began developing a standardized alphabet. Drawn symbols represented specific sounds in the tribal language. These drawn symbols made up an alphabet with which people could communicate. Messages were generally carved in stone tablets, a task that was long and difficult, Fig. I-6. The weight of the tablets, however, discouraged sending messages any great distance.

Fig. I-5. The beating of drums allowed communication over long distances

Fig. I-4. Experiences were often recorded by crude drawings

Fig. I-6. Written communications were carved in stone tablets

It is recorded that the early Egyptians developed a material known as **papyrus** which could be written on. It was made by hammering the stems of the papyrus plant together as they dried. Ink made from cuttlefish and writing pens made from hollow reeds, bamboo, or feathers were used to record the symbols on the papyrus. Later, paper was invented by the Chinese, and it has been improved greatly throughout the years as has the pen.

For a long time messages were written by hand on paper or animal skin so they could be saved or carried over long distances to other people. Writing by hand was too slow a process especially if more than one copy of the message was desired. For many years, people searched for a method of casting a message in one form so that several copies could be made without the need to rewrite each time. Although unaware of it, people were searching for **graphic communications** — ways of using **printed** images to convey a message.

With the increased demand for several copies of a message came the development of the techniques of **printing**. One early attempt involved the use of wood blocks. The message was carved in the wood and then inked and printed on the paper. This procedure proved inadequate because the carving was slow and each new message required carving a new block of wood. Johann Gutenberg is credited with the use of movable metal type that could be reused several times. Movable type was easier and faster to assemble into new messages than hand-carved wood blocks. Early printing was performed on hand-operated presses, Fig. I-7. It is interesting to note that at one time Gutenberg converted a wine press (used to squeeze grapes or other food) into a printing press.

Even though the new process of printing improved the quality of a prepared message, it still took a long time to transport it over long distances. Many years later, the pony express rider was one solution to this problem, but it often took several days or more to relay a message from one area of the country to another. The search for a faster method of **sending** messages continued.

The invention of the **telegraph** made it possible to send messages over great distances by using a series of electrical impulses in the form of dots and dashes. A standard system of electrical impulses was needed so the telegraphed messages could be understood everywhere. Samuel Morse standardized the dots and dashes to represent the alphabet. This is called the Morse Code. The message to be sent is tapped out in the dot-dash code for each individual letter. The received message is written into words by the operator who decodes the electrical impulses, Fig. I-8.

The **telephone,** an invention of Alexander Graham Bell, made it possible to send voice messages from one point to another. Although the first telephone system had limited capabilities, it was possible to talk over wires covering hundreds of miles. Today it is possible to talk to others anywhere in the world using the telephone systems. Now it is also possible to transmit visual images

Fig. I-7. Early hand-operated printing press

as well as sounds over the telephone network, Fig. I-9.

Spurred on by the invention of the telegraph and telephone, scientists soon began experimenting with other forms of electrical communication devices. The development of **radio** made it possible to communicate over long distances to a large listening audience in different locations. The radio, first called the **wireless**, sends electrical impulses through the air without the use of wire. Soon after the development of the radio, it was discovered that not only sound but visual images as well could be sent from point to point using a principle similar to radio broadcasting. This led to the development of **television**.

Since the first communication system was developed, many different systems have been developed and improved. Now we can communicate directly with most parts of our world and even into outer space. Modern technology has developed electronic communication **satellites** that make it possible to view events as they take place in any part of the world or even on the surface of the moon, Fig. I-10.

As you can see in this brief history of communication systems, we communicate by (1) verbal, (2) written, and (3) visual methods. Verbal communication uses the spoken word. Written methods use signs and symbols such as the letters of the alphabet. Visual methods also use signs and symbols for communication purposes. This method, however, is generally thought of as an association of one or more words with an object that is viewed. For instance, when you see (or visualize) a three-sided object,

Fig. I-9. Video-telephones transmit visual and verbal messages

Fig. I-8. Telegraph messages are sent by Morse Code

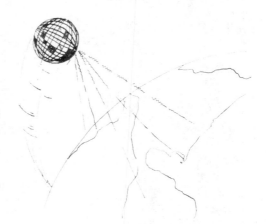

Fig. I-10. World-wide communication systems use satellites

Fig. I-11. Visual images are associated with words

Fig. I-12. Printed communications stimulate reactions

you may associate the object with the word "triangle," Fig. I-11.

Communicated messages may have different purposes, depending upon the need of the individual or organization that is communicating. These messages are used to inform, question, stimulate, provoke, persuade, influence, enhance knowledge, or entertain, Fig. I-12. The method used to communicate a message is often dependent on (1) the situation, (2) the nature of the message, and (3) the number of people receiving the message. For example, if you are giving away puppies, it may only be necessary to **talk** with a few classmates. To present the message to the entire school body, however, may require preparation and presentation of the same message over the school **public address system**. To reach an even larger audience, you could advertise in the local **newspaper**, Fig. I-13.

Methods of communicating range from the very simple to the very complex — from gestures such as a wave of the hand to electronic systems such as television or satellite. The great variety of methods of communicating that lie somewhere between these two extremes are often part of your everyday life: newspapers, books, catalogs, letterheads, greeting cards, advertising and sales literature, business forms, tickets, labels, and so on; these examples, incidentally, are all printed images and therefore are examples of graphic communication. The methods of communicating graphically will be explored in this textbook so that you will understand the graphic communications industry. Eventually, you may want to study the communications industries of telephone, radio, or television. You will find that your understanding of all other communication systems will depend to some degree upon your understanding and knowledge of the graphic communications industry. After your study of each of the sections, chapters, and units of this book, you will appreciate the many talents of people required to (1) prepare, (2) produce, and (3) distribute graphic communications.

A. Conversation with friends

B. Public address system

C. Newspaper ad

Fig. I-13. Different methods may be used to communicate the same message

1 CHAPTER

GRAPHIC COMMUNICATIONS

Graphic communication deals with printed images in such forms as newspapers, books, printed T-shirts, signs, photographs, soda cans, wallpaper, or stationery (letterheads). We are continually acting and reacting as a result of printed communications in one form or another, Fig. 1-1. We look at calendars to check today's date, use road maps to locate routes to our destination when traveling, buy goods and services as a result of printed advertisements, use printed postage stamps for mailing letters and packages, and pay bills with printed money and checks. These examples and many others that you can think of are all forms of graphic communication.

There are four stages of work in the development of a message that is to be communicated graphically. These four stages are:

Fig. 1-1. People react differently to the same message

1. **Design** — the stage of planning the message so that it will be a useful communication device.
2. **Image Generation** — the stage of preparing the exact form of the words, symbols, or pictures that express the message as it was planned in the design stage.
3. **Preproduction and Production** — the stage of (a) preparing the message to "fit" the method of printing that was selected and (b) actually printing the message as planned so that it will fit the distribution system of mailing or shipping to the consumer.

4. **Finishing, Binding, and Packaging** — the stage of forming the printed message into the size or shape that was selected in the design stage for shipping, handling, or use of the product.

DESIGN

The desire to communicate graphically stems from the need of an individual or group of individuals to prepare, produce, and distribute a printed message. The design stage is the planning operation that formulates the message into a pleasing arrangement of words, sentences, pictures, and colors. The message must be carefully analyzed in terms of:

1. **Content** — What is to be communicated and why?
2. **Purpose** — What will the message stimulate in the reader? New knowledge or information? Will it result in some type of action (for instance, a desire to buy)?
3. **Nature of the Audience Receiving the Message** — Is the reader old or young, man or woman, buyer or seller, a leader or a follower, one person or several people?
4. **Location of the Reader** — Is the reader at home, in an office, or in a factory; driving down a highway; located in a theater, television, or radio audience?

If you are responsible for communicating the message to a selected audience, then you must plan the design and the production of your message so that it will perform the function you identified in the above categories of anaylsis. If your audience is only five people, then you should plan the design and production for a small group. For example, if you are selling concrete blocks, you may have only a few customers in a city. Therefore, you may send letters or make personal visits or telephone the contractors or lumberyards. However, if you are selling houses, you will want to contact every potential house buyer in the city. As you can see, you must analyze (1) the content, (2) the purpose, (3) type of audience, and (4) location of the audience before you decide how you will communicate.

The design of the message should be planned to give the best results. This requires considering such factors as:

1. **Cost** — How much will the design, the production, the handling, the packaging, and the shipping of the message cost the communicator?
2. **Quantity** — How many people will receive the message and what type of production equipment will be used to create the number of messages required?
3. **Quality** — Do you need to impress the customer with unique design, several colors, high grade of paper or material, or usefulness of the product?

As these factors are considered, the person wishing to communicate and the designer can decide how the message can be best presented to the receiver. That is, will the message contain photographs, line drawings, graphs, reading matter or a combination of any or all of these? These elements must be considered when the method of production is chosen. For example, a business card, instructions for appliance maintenance, and a catalog of holiday merchandise each requires special consideration as to what production methods to use. The design for each of these, then, is prepared with a particular production method in mind. In other words, the design is "thought through" to the finished message.

Now you can see that the communicator must analyze many items before the design is prepared, before the production methods are selected, before the message is packaged, and before the message is delivered to the audience. The people in the graphic arts industry who are usually responsible for making decisions concerning message design are artists, designers, editors, buyers, and advertisers. These people must be creative and aware of good business practices such as how much money to spend and who to select to work on further preparation of the message.

Section II (including Chapter 2 and Units 1 through 3) is devoted to design considerations.

IMAGE GENERATION

After the design is ready, the message must be prepared or composed. This is the process of generating an image for graphic reproduction.

Images for graphic reproduction can be generated in several ways. An image can be an alphabetical letter, a number, a symbol, an artist's sketch, a photograph, or any other form that communicates a message. An artist can use colors or simple lines on a piece of paper to convey a message. A photographer can use a camera and light-sensitive film to capture an image in a photograph. A typist or compositor (one who sets type) uses a machine to assemble characters in an organized manner to form the content of the message. The communicator and the designer should plan the best method or combination of several methods of image generation to convey the message to the reader.

For example, what information would the communicator and the designer need to know before selecting a method to generate an image prepared by a typist or a compositor? The following two paragraphs will give you a general idea.

Each character for image generation is prepared by either (1) a hot composition method or (2) a cold composition method. The compositor can assemble type by hand or use a machine to organize the message as planned by the designer. The hot composition methods of image generation employ **molten metal that is cast into relief printing type characters**. Hand-set foundry type and machine-set type are both examples of hot composition methods, Fig. 1-2.

Cold composition methods of image generation include those methods **using other than molten metal type forms**. The types of cold composition methods that you will study in this book include **linoleum block carving, technical illustration, clip art and preprinted type, strike-on** (typewriter), **photocomposition,** and **continuous tone photography**, Fig. 1-3. A designer may specify the use of several image generation methods in the preparation of a single communication such as a magazine or book.

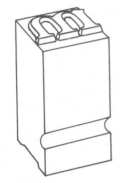

A. Hand-set foundry type

B. Machine-set type

Fig. 1-2. Hot composition

It is important that you understand that any method of generation can be used to create the image for any type of production process or equipment. But, for reasons of cost or time involved, one method of generating the image may be more efficient or practical than another. Therefore, the best generation method must be selected so that the image produced will (1) communicate the message, (2) please the reader, and (3)

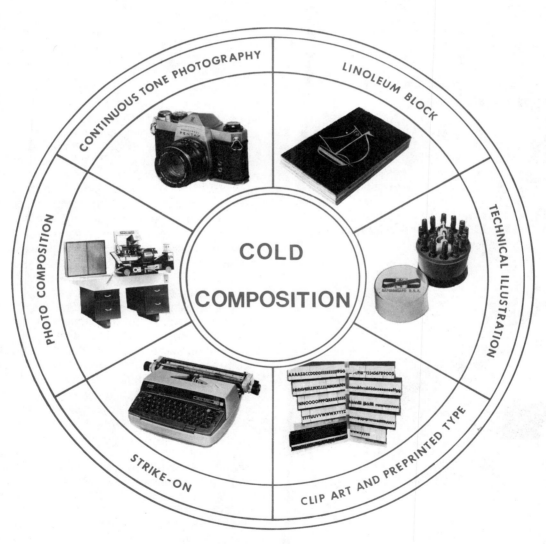

Fig. 1-3. Methods of cold composition

save production costs where possible. For this reason, it is important that you learn which method of image generation is best for a specific type of production process. Printing managers, editors, and artists must know how to prepare messages so the cost of production is acceptable. Section III (including Chapters 3 and 4 and Units 4 through 11) presents the information necessary for a thorough understanding of image generation. After you study this book, you will have a better understanding of the problems of planning, preparing, and producing printed products.

PREPRODUCTION AND PRODUCTION

There are six commonly used production processes in the field of graphic communications. These are:
1. Relief printing (letter press)
2. Screen process printing
3. Gravure (intaglio) printing
4. Planographic printing (lithography)
5. Continuous tone photography
6. Office copying and duplicating

Fig. 1-4. Relief printing

Each production process has certain characteristics which distinguish it from each of the other processes.

RELIEF PRINTING

In the relief printing process, pieces of type are cast with the printing image raised above the supporting body. The raised surface has a symbol or character on it which is cast "wrong reading" or backwards, and this surface carries the ink to the paper being printed, Fig. 1-4. As the piece of type is pressed against the paper, the printing image is transferred to the paper so that it is "right reading." Relief printing is also referred to as **letterpress printing**.

The image generation methods of hand-set foundry type, machine-set type, and linoleum block carving result directly in relief printing images. Other image generation methods may also be employed; however, each requires several intermediate steps to prepare a letterpress plate. Therefore, a designer would specify a form of relief image generation that would reduce the cost of preparation time on a letterpress.

Detailed information concerning relief printing is given in Chapter 6 and Units 13 through 19.

SCREEN PROCESS PRINTING

Screen process printing is one of the most versatile of all production processes in graphic communications. It may be used for printing on a wide variety of materials such as cloth, wood, glass, plastic, and metal as well as many other surfaces. Because of the nature of this method, screen process printing allows a much heavier deposit of ink to be applied to the receiving surface than any of the other production methods. Screen process printing may be accomplished on flat as well as irregularly shaped surfaces such as cans and bottles.

In the screen process printing method, a stencil which carries the design in open areas is prepared. The stencil is adhered to an open weave material (usually cloth) that has been stretched tightly across a printing frame. Open areas in the stencil allow the ink to be forced through the open weave material and onto the surface being printed, Fig. 1-5. Stencils for screen process printing may be prepared by:

1. hand lettering or drawing directly on the screen,
2. hand-cutting paper or film, and
3. photographic processing of copy that has been prepared by any of the image generation methods.

Chapter 7 and Units 20 through 28 give a thorough presentation of screen process printing.

GRAVURE (INTAGLIO) PRINTING

In gravure printing (also known as **intaglio** printing), the printing plate has image areas that are **cut below or into the surface**, Fig. 1-6. During the production process, the entire surface of the plate is inked. Before actual printing, however, the surface of the plate is wiped clean which **leaves the ink in the depressions of the plate**. The ink in the depressed areas is transferred to the paper when it is placed against the plate under pressure, thus printing the image from below the surface (intaglio, pronounced **in-tal-yo**).

Gravure printing plates are prepared by engraving or etching or a combination of both operations. **Engraved** plates are pre-pared by scratching the image into the surface of the metal plate that is generally copper. **Etched** plates are prepared by first coating the entire plate with an **acid resist**. The image is then scratched in the resist to expose bare metal. The plate is then placed in an acid bath which dissolves the bare metal in the image areas, creating the printing depressions or ink wells. Although any image generation method may be used in preparation for gravure printing, none results directly in an intaglio surface.

For a more detailed study of gravure printing, see Chapter 8 and Units 29 and 30.

PLANOGRAPHIC PRINTING

Planographic (lithographic) production processes use flat surface printing plates. Basic to this type of printing process is the fact that grease (ink) and water do not mix. The printing image areas of the plate have a grease base. When water is applied to the plate, it is repelled by the image areas

Fig. 1-6. Gravure (intaglio) printing

Fig. 1-5. Screen process printing

but forms a thin moisture coating over the non-image areas. The ink, when applied to the plate, will stick to the grease image areas but will be repelled by the moisture coating in the non-image areas.

During planographic production, the image on the plate is **offset** (transferred) to a rubber blanket. The paper receives the image as it passes between the blanket cylinder and the impression cylinder, Fig. 1-7. The paper being printed **does not** make contact with the printing plate, but receives the image from the blanket. Chapter 9 and Units 31 through 42 deal with the planographic (lithographic offset) production methods.

Offset printing is usually capable of providing high-quality, finely detailed printing impressions. Designers select this printing process when large quantities of printed materials are needed for distribution, because offset printing is a high-speed production process. All methods of generation can be used to create images for offset printing. The type in this book was set by hot-metal linotype machines, and the proofs were then photographed for making the offset plates. The drawings in this textbook were drawn first on paper and then photographed in negative form to make plates. The photographs were generated by continuous tone photography, and then they were shot as halftone (dots) negatives to make plates.

CONTINUOUS TONE PHOTOGRAPHY

Continuous tone photography can be considered as both an image generation method and a production process. A light-sensitive material known as **film** is placed in a camera which is light-tight, Fig. 1-8. When the lens shutter is opened, a small amount of light (which is reflected from the object being photographed) strikes the light-sensitive **emulsion** of the film and produces a negative image. The light areas of the object being photographed reflect more light than the dark areas and therefore register as dark areas on the film. The negative image is not visible until after the film has been developed. Since the photographic process

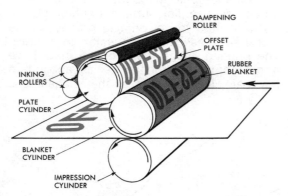

Fig. 1-7. Planographic (lithographic) printing

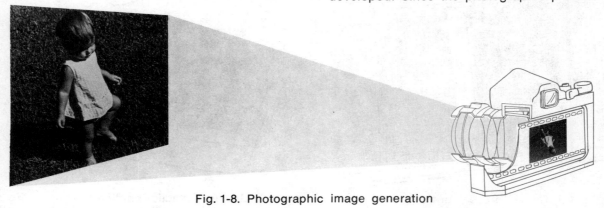

Fig. 1-8. Photographic image generation

is capable of recording an image that can be understood, it is a method of "image generation," as detailed in Unit 11. Also, since the film negative can be used several times to print on sensitive paper, it is a production process.

The negative can be used for the production of photographic pictures called **prints** or **enlargements**. The negative is placed in an **enlarger** between a light source and a lens, Fig. 1-9. The light passes through the negative and the lens and is projected onto the surface of light-sensitive **enlarging paper**. The clear areas of the negative (those parts you can easily see through) allow more light to be projected through them than the dark areas. Therefore, the more light passing through the negative, the darker these areas are on the enlarging paper. The dark areas, which allow less light to be projected, appear as light areas on the paper. The positive image that is projected onto the enlarging paper is not visible until after it has been developed.

Any number of photographic enlargements may be produced from a single negative. Photographic prints may be used in conjunction with text material to explain a topic (as do the pictures in this book). Pictures may be used with any of the printing processes, but they must be prepared for the particular production method being used.

To summarize, continuous tone photography is used to generate images by registering light reflection on film. The resultant film negatives can be used to produce photographic enlargements by the continuous tone photography production process. (See Chapter 10 and Units 43 through 49.) The pictures can also be considered "generated images" for any of the other production processes in graphic communications.

OFFICE COPYING AND OFFICE DUPLICATING

Office copying and office duplicating is a general production process classification that includes a variety of methods. **Office copying** refers to methods that do not use an intermediate image carrier. The image is copied directly from the original to another sheet of paper. The **office duplicating** production processes are those that require an intermediate image carrier such as a stencil, Fig. 1-10.

Office copying and office duplicating systems are used in many offices for the following reasons:

1. The copy for the message can usually be prepared by a typewriter.
2. Offices generally need only a few copies of letters or articles.
3. The equipment is easy to operate and does not require a highly skilled operator.

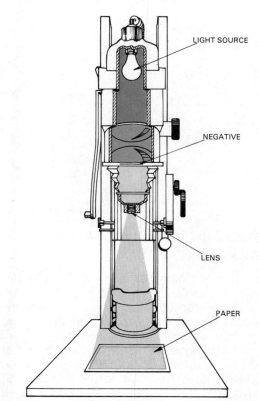

Fig. 1-9. An enlarger is used to make photographic prints from negatives

4. It does not require much time to print.
5. The equipment is not as expensive to purchase, rent or maintain as high-quality printing equipment.

A detailed description of some of the office copying and office duplicating methods will be presented in Chapter 11, "Office Copying and Office Duplicating." Many offices that do a large volume of duplication are using duplicating systems that consist of automatic master makers, offset duplicators, and collators. These systems generally require a full-time or a "dedicated operator." Therefore the duplication systems are not included in Chapter 11. They are included in Chapter 9, "Planographic Printing."

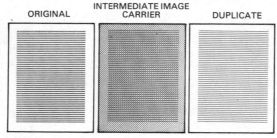

Fig. 1-10. Office copying — office duplicating

FINISHING, BINDING, AND PACKAGING

The finishing, binding, and packaging stage is the final step in the graphic communication reproduction process. These operations vary with the nature of the printed message. Some printed messages are ready to be packaged as soon as they come off the press. Items such as tickets and posters generally do not require finishing or binding. However, other items, such as this book, require specific finishing and binding operations before they can be packaged for shipment or delivery and eventual distribution to the message receiver.

The nature and purpose of the printed communication often dictate the finishing and binding operations that must be performed, Fig. 1-11. Desk note pads, for example, are generally adhered at one end. This holds the individual sheets together but also makes it possible to easily tear the sheets from the pad. The three remaining edges are usually trimmed after the first edge is adhered.

Newsletters (school, industrial, and business informative publications) require

Fig. 1-11. The method used to bind a printed message depends upon its nature and purpose

Fig. 1-12. Direct mail magazine packaging

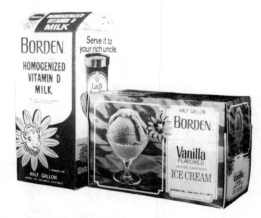

Fig. 1-13. Messages are often printed on product containers

a much different method of binding. The individual pages, after printing, must be collated into page sequence. The individual pages are then bound together by stapling or sewing.

Printed pages or sheets that are to be placed in ring notebooks are generally drilled after all the pages are put in sequence. Pages to be bound by plastic spiral bindings must be collated and punched before the plastic spiral can be inserted.

Books, such as this one, require much more elaborate finishing and binding operations. Four, eight, sixteen, or thirty-two pages of a book are printed on a large sheet of paper. (Later the same number of pages is printed on the reverse side.) This group of pages is called a **signature.** The pages must be positioned on the front and back of the sheet in such a way that, when folded, the sheet forms a signature with the pages in proper sequence. Each signature is sewn to hold the pages together. Then all the signatures for the book are gathered in proper order and sewn together, and the book is trimmed. Finally, the cover is attached to the book.

The packaging operation often depends upon the method that was selected for distributing the printed message. Many printed messages are sent as direct mail. In this case, the message may be automatically stuffed in an envelope, addressed, and stamped for mail distribution. Frequently, direct mail messages are sealed with a small tape tab on one edge, addressed, and mailed without being inserted in an envelope. Printed communications such as magazines are often wrapped with a single wrapper band, addressed automatically, and distributed as direct mail, Fig. 1-12. Calendars, charts, and maps are often direct-mailed in mailing tubes.

Packaging also takes other forms. Many times, the printed message is produced directly on the product container, Fig. 1-13. In packaging of this type, the

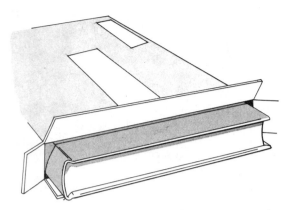

Fig. 1-14. Single copies of books are packaged in boxes for shipment

containers can be assembled into groups for display purposes. Single copies of books are packaged in boxes which are specially constructed for the size of book, Fig. 1-14. Newspapers are usually tied or banded together for distribution to key locations for further distribution to homes by paper carriers. Bags are also used for packaging printed messages. The message is inserted in a plastic bag and sealed. Shrink-wrapping also provides a protective coating and allows the printed product to be seen, Fig. 1-15.

Books and other printed materials in large quantities can be boxed for shipment. Each box holds a specific number of books. At the time of shipment, a number of boxes can be loaded on skids or pallets, and a fork-lift truck will place the skids on trucks. Large quantities of material placed on skids and pallets can be distributed to other locations by air and by train, Fig. 1-16.

Fig. 1-15. Printed communications may be sealed in plastic

Fig. 1-16. Large quantities of printed material are often shipped by rail to central distribution locations

SECTION II

DESIGN

To be an effective communicating device, the message must be presented so that:

1. It attracts the attention of the reader,
2. It is easily read and understood, and
3. It makes a lasting impression on the reader.

The human eye reacts favorably to objects or printed messages that are well-designed; but it quickly rejects those that are not pleasing. Although there are few set rules regarding design, there are basic principles and fundamentals that should be understood.

One of the most important design considerations is **function**. A printed message has little value unless it satisfies the purpose (function) which the communicator intended.

When an individual or organization identifies a need to communicate graphically, the specific purpose or function of the message is also identified. How the printed communication is designed will depend on its function. As an example, companies often need business cards for their salesmen and other representatives. The business card is a communicating device that supplies such basic information as the company name, address and telephone number, the repre-sentative's name and position, and possibly the services rendered by the company. Business cards must be designed to a convenient size that is functional (a size that makes them easily carried in a wallet or shirt pocket). Business cards of great size would not be functional and therefore would not meet the need of the individual or organization, Fig. II-1.

According to need, therefore, printed communications take different shapes and sizes to render the full message. The individual or organization must carefully analyze the message to be communicated to other people (the audience). After the message is determined, the product to be printed is planned and developed. Often, as in the case of businesses such as the Holiday Inn, many printed products are needed and used. In this example, some products are used by motel personnel, while other ones are designed for the convenience of the guests.

When someone mentions "Holiday Inn," what picture comes to mind? Do you think of the Holiday Inn symbol and the name in type form? This is called a logotype (or, in short, logo). A **logo** is a mark that is

Fig. II-1. Printed communications must be designed to a functional size

Fig. II-2. The logo serves as a beacon

designed to represent the products or services produced or rendered by a business, Fig. II-2. To those familiar with Holiday Inn, the general shape of the marquee alone serves as a beacon for locating the motel and immediately communicates the complete scope of services that are available. To those people not familiar with this motel chain, the shape of the marquee really does not communicate a full message; but with the addition of color, lines, and shape as well as words, the marquee presents a more complete message. The total message, however, will not be recognized until the motorist uses the services offered by the Holiday Inn. Therefore, the logo is only a **symbol** of a service organization.

Many printed communications serve the guest's needs once he is inside the motel. He is asked to complete a guest registration card by filling in his name and address as well as other information needed by Holiday Inn. This card is also used to record the guest's room number, room rate, and length of stay, Fig. II-3. As a reminder to the guest and for the convenience of the Holiday Inn personnel, the key ring is printed with the room number.

Other printed communications prove useful and convenient to the guests, Fig. II-4. These include matchbooks, area entertainment listings, maps of the area, brochures on local points of interest, and booklets listing addresses of other Holiday Inn locations.

Inside his room, the guest encounters more printed communications. On the back of the door, for example, is a printed message which lists the guest's responsibilities such as checkout time and the responsibilities of Holiday Inn to the guests.

A Holiday Inn Service Directory may also be found in the room. This convenient and informative pamphlet lists services that are available to guests: room service, swimming pool, restaurant, and baby sitting arrangements. Another printed communication placed in the room for customer convenience is the door knob sign, Fig. II-5,

Fig. II-4. Printed guides provide convenience for guests

Fig. II-3. Printed guest registration card and key ring satisfy needs of guests and management

Fig. II-5. Door knob signs are a useful item

Fig. II-6. Convenient items for customer use

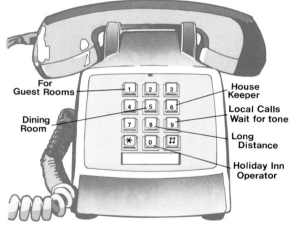

Fig. II-7. The telephone dial communicates messages

Fig. II-8. Attractive printed material serves the dual purpose of identifying the organization and decorating a table

Fig. II-9. Signs are a necessary graphic communication

which permits the guest to express his desires by simply hanging the sign on the outside of the door. Other convenience items are postcards, stationery and envelopes, and plastic bags for carrying wet bathing suits, Fig. II-6.

A printed communication on the guest's telephone tells him how to dial outside the motel and how to obtain room service. It also gives the telephone number from which he is calling should he wish a call returned, Fig. II-7.

Printed messages are also useful in the restaurant. Items such as placemats, napkins, menus, and the waitresses' guest checks are all forms of graphic communications, Fig. II-8. Signs "This Section Closed," "Caution, Wet Floor," and "Exit" are also used to communicate graphically with the motel customers, Fig. II-9.

This example of the printing needs for only one type of business should help you see the variety of communications needs in the business world. At this point you are probably aware that there are many interesting careers in the graphic communication industry, some of which you may want to consider as a vocation.

The following chapter will help you understand the need for careful planning of a communicated message. A designer or a buyer of graphic production should have some knowledge of the various methods of designing, preparing images, producing informative materials by printing, and packaging the products. A large amount of money can be wasted if:

1. The design is not appealing.
2. The design is high quality, but the production method is low quality.
3. The design is low quality, and the production method is high quality.

Many decisions must be made to produce a printed product. The more you know about the variety of printing techniques, the better able you will be to plan and design attractive, functional graphic messages.

2 CHAPTER

MESSAGE ANALYSIS

A graphically communicated message that is to fulfill a specific need and accomplish a specific purpose requires careful planning and preparation. The thoughtful approach to arriving at the purpose of a communication is called **analyzing the message**. Factors that must be considered in this analysis include the age, sex, social status, economic level, personality, intelligence, reading ability, attitude, and interest of the audience receiving the message. For example, a message to be distributed to elementary school children must be prepared to a level that can be easily read and understood at that age. The same message, however, when being designed for distribution to an older group such as high school students, may assume an entirely different appearance, Fig. 2-1.

The readability of the message is often dependent upon the typeface (style of type) that is used. Messages for young children as well as elderly persons are most often set in a legible typeface that is large and bold. Messages that contain a large amount of type, such as this book, must be presented in a typeface that is simple, free of **decorative** lines, and easy to read.

The size, shape, and material that the message will be printed on must also be considered. Size and shape are sometimes determined by the method that will be used for distributing the printed communication. Business cards, as previously mentioned, are designed to a functional size that is easy to carry in a wallet or shirt pocket. Communications that will be displayed in store windows or on the walls of a school corridor, on the other hand, must be designed to a larger size that is readily noticeable and easy to read at a distance. When the message is analyzed in terms of material to be

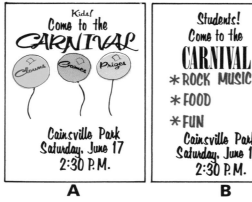

Fig. 2-1. The message must be designed for the level of the receiver
A. Elementary school children
B. High school students

Fig. 2-2. The function of the product must be analyzed before selecting the material

Fig. 2-3. The message should be free of unnecessary wording

selected, the function of the printed product is very important. For example, a printed product produced of **paper** would not be a functional item for carrying a bowling ball, Fig. 2-2. Likewise, a stationery letterhead printed on heavy paper, such as poster board, would not be functional because of the mailing weight.

The selections of ink and paper color depend upon the audience and the purpose of the message. If the message is being designed for high school and college students, what colors do you think would be most appropriate? Would the colors be different if the group were older?

Colors are classified as either **cool** or **warm**. Because they present a cool sensation to the message reader, violet, blue, and dark green are classified as **cool** colors. Red, yellow, and orange, due to the association with fire or sunlight, are considered **warm** colors. The warm colors are more striking and eye-catching than the cool colors, and they are often used for emphasizing portions of printed messages.

The color of the ink and paper must be planned to work together Black ink on

yellow paper is the most effective combination of colors for messages such as posters if they are to be read from a distance. Printed material to be read at arm's length such as books, brochures, and pamphlets are most effective when printed in a dark-colored ink on a highly contrasted paper color. The most used combination is black ink on white paper.

Color in itself communicates. Red, for example, is a very bold and powerful color which easily attracts the attention of the reader. Orange is often associated with gold and wealth, while green generally suggests peace, calmness, and a sense of nature. Blue portrays a feeling of the stillness and quiet associated with sky and water. Royalty is expressed in the use of violet, while yellow symbolizes brightness because of its association with sunlight.

The message itself must also be carefully analyzed in terms of **content**. In this day of fast-paced activity, people often reject lengthy messages. Therefore, the message to be communicated should be concise, complete, and to the point, Fig. 2-3. This calls for a careful analysis of the purpose, content, and wording of a message as well as color, shape, size, and type styles necessary in the planning of a printed communication.

Other factors such as cost, quantity, and quality of the printed message must also be analyzed. The methods of image generation, production, binding, finishing, and packaging, as well as the method of product distribution, are also to be considered in the analysis of the message. **These factors, however, can only be considered after a COMPLETE UNDERSTANDING of the graphic communications industry is obtained.**

DESIGN PRINCIPLES

When designers are working in printed communications, they follow guidelines rather than strict rules. The design principles of **balance, contrast, rhythm, proportion,** and **unity** serve as the guidelines. All of these principles must work together to provide for a successful message presentation.

BALANCE

There are two types of balance: (1) formal and (2) informal. Formal balance is achieved by placing all the elements of a layout on the vertical center of the page. If a vertical line were drawn through the exact center of the page, it would divide the individual message elements in half, Fig. 2-4. This type of balance is often used on layouts that are prepared for formal organizations such as banks, professional associations, and institutions, and for events such as weddings and other special ceremonies.

Formal balance gives a sense of dignity, orderliness, strength, and security.

Informal balance allows for more flexibility in the placement of the message elements on the layout. The elements are **not symmetrically centered** (equal halves of balance), but must be placed so that a state of equilibrium does exist, Fig. 2-5. To create

Fig. 2-4. Formally balanced layout

this feeling of equilibrium, other design principles are used.

CONTRAST

To relieve monotony and to provide variety, the design principle of contrast is employed. The use of contrast allows for the **emphasis** of portions of a printed message. The use of underscoring, *italic typefaces,* **bold typefaces,** and

LARGER TYPEFACES

adds contrast and serves to emphasize areas or words of the message.

The use of color also provides contrast and emphasizes key words or phrases. Color can also be used to attract the attention of people and make the overall design more appealing to the message receiver. The **pri-**

Fig. 2-5. Informally balanced layout

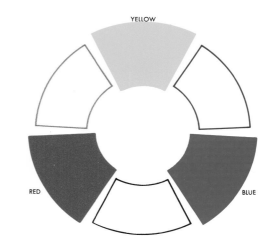

Fig. 2-6. Primary colors of the color wheel

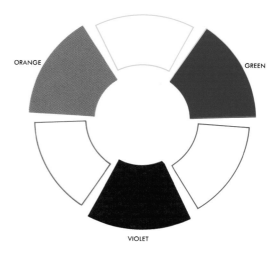

Fig. 2-7. Secondary colors of the color wheel

mary colors (red, blue, and yellow) are the three colors from which all others can be made, Fig. 2-6. These are the only ones that cannot be made by mixing other colors. Children find primary colors attractive. **Secondary colors** (orange, green, and violet) are made by mixing equal parts of two pri-

mary colors. Red and yellow make orange, yellow and blue make green, and blue and red make violet, Fig. 2-7. **Complementary colors** are directly opposite one another on the color wheel. Maximum contrast is achieved by using combinations of these, Fig. 2-8A.

Fig. 2-8A. A complementary color combination

Fig. 2-8B. A monochromatic color combination

Fig. 2-8C. An analogous color combination

Fig. 2-8D. A triadic color combination

A feeling of harmony in a design can be created through the use of color. **Monochromatic** harmony is achieved by printing a color in combination with a shade or a tint of the same color. For example, a blue may be printed with a lighter or a darker blue. The lighter blue is a **tint:** the primary blue has been added to white. The darker blue is a **shade:** black has been added to the primary blue, Fig. 2-8B. Another way to achieve a monochromatic combination is to print a blue ink on a lighter blue paper.

Analogous colors are next to one another on the color wheel. Analogous color harmony is created by using colors, such as red and orange, when printing a two-color design, Fig. 2-8C.

Triadic color harmony is achieved by using any three separate colors on the color wheel that would occur at the angles of an equilateral triangle. (An equilateral triangle is one that has all three sides equal in length.) For example, if straight lines were drawn between the three primary colors, an equilateral triangle would be formed. The primary colors are triadic colors, Fig. 2-8D. The secondary colors would also be a triadic color combination.

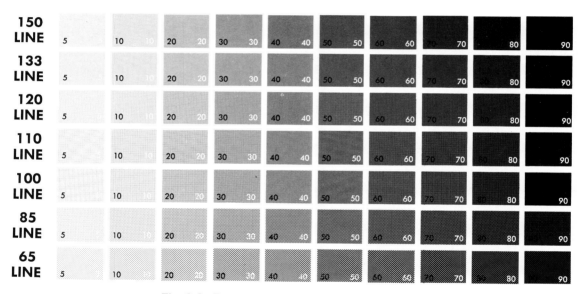

Fig. 2-9. Percentage-calibrated screen tints

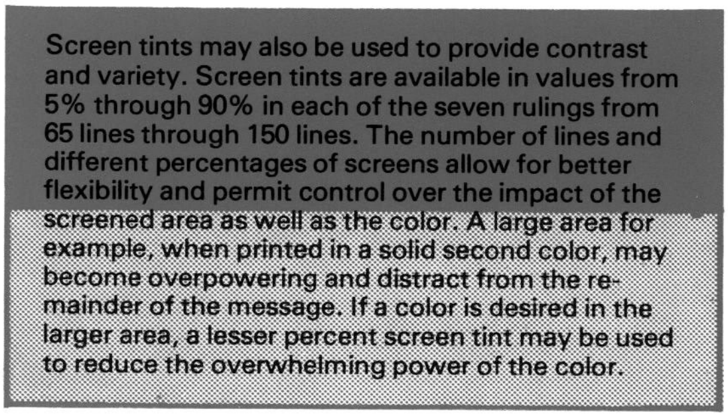

Screen tints may also be used to provide contrast and variety. Screen tints are available in values from 5% through 90% in each of the seven rulings from 65 lines through 150 lines. The number of lines and different percentages of screens allow for better flexibility and permit control over the impact of the screened area as well as the color. A large area for example, when printed in a solid second color, may become overpowering and distract from the remainder of the message. If a color is desired in the larger area, a lesser percent screen tint may be used to reduce the overwhelming power of the color.

Fig. 2-10. Screen tints reduce the power of the color

Screen tints may also be used to provide contrast and variety. Screen tints are available in values from 5% through 90% in each of the seven rulings from 65 lines through 150 lines, Fig. 2-9. The number of lines and different percentages of screens allow for better flexibility. It also allows control over the impact of the screened area as well as the color. A large area, for example, when printed in a solid second color, may become overpowering. This distracts from the remainder of the message. If a color is desired in the larger area, a lesser percent screen tint may be used to reduce the overwhelming power of the color, Fig. 2-10.

Screen tints are often used to create contrast and emphasize areas in a type form.

JOB TICKET	DATE_____ ACCOUNT NO._____ DEADLINE_____

STOCK REQUIREMENTS

NO. OF SHEETS _____TRIM SIZE_____
TYPE:
WEIGHT _____FINISH_____
COLOR
SUPPLIER (If Special Order)_____

INK AND COLOR REQUIREMENTS

NO. OF COLORS_____ ☐PRESS BLACK

☐ PROCESS COLOR
☐ SPECIAL RUN
  COMMENTS:_____

☐ PRESS PROOF REQUIRED

PRODUCT INFORMATION

Fig. 2-11. Screen tints can be used to emphasize areas and provide contrast

This may be done by using screen tint backgrounds which are overprinted with type to create bands or lines, Fig. 2-11. As a general rule, the type should be twice as dark as the screen tint background which it overprints. The use of screen tints can also create contrast by adding a feeling of dimension or weight to line drawings, Fig. 2-12.

Monochromatic harmony is often achieved by using screen tints. In Fig. 2-8B, it appears that two different blue inks were printed. This would require two separate press runs. Actually, only one color ink was printed in one press run. The lighter color blue was created by using a screen tint where the lighter color was desired. The screen tint allowed a lesser percentage of ink to be placed on the paper than in the darker blue areas of the design.

Fig. 2-12. The use of screen tints in line drawings

Reverse image lettering is also an effective means of providing contrast in a printed message, Fig. 2-13, as well as combining several of the methods in one application. For example, reverse lettering of *italic type,* using a second color with a **bold face** or underscoring italic lettering printed in complementary colors, compounds the contrast effect. Changing the size and shape

Fig. 2-13. Reverse image lettering provides contrast

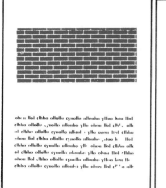

Fig. 2-14. Element size and shape can produce contrast

of element areas of a layout also produces eye-catching contrast, Fig. 2-14.

RHYTHM

Rhythm is associated with eye movement. It leads the reader's eye in the desired direction. Vertical positioning of the message elements on a layout leads the eye upward or downward, while horizontal element positioning suggests either left, right, or angular movement, Fig. 2-15. Numbers are also employed to guide the reader from one layout element to the next in a desired sequence, Fig. 2-16. Rhythm is also enhanced by the effective use of contrast. The position and size of the layout elements also cause the eye to move in the desired direction, Fig. 2-17.

PROPORTION

A sheet size that has good proportion is one known as a **regular oblong**. The regular oblong sheet size is two parts wide by three parts long, Fig. 2-18.

To achieve good proportion in a layout, the designer must regulate the dimensions of the element area so that mathematical relationships are not readily observed by

Fig. 2-15. Element positioning suggests eye movement

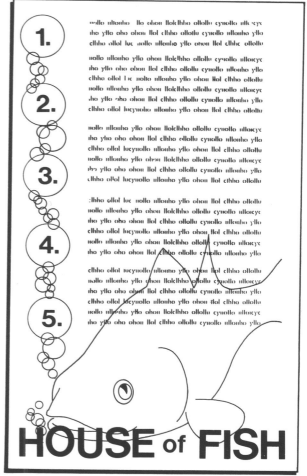

Fig. 2-16. Numbers suggest eye movement

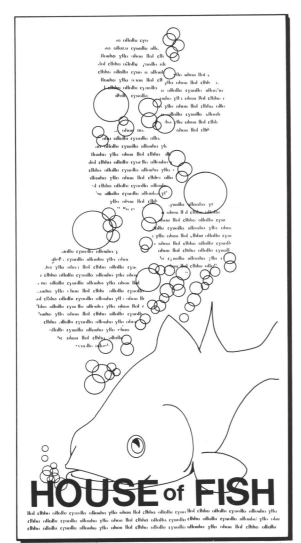

Fig. 2-17. Element size and position suggest eye movement

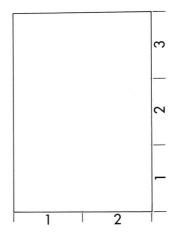

Fig. 2-18. Regular oblong sheet size

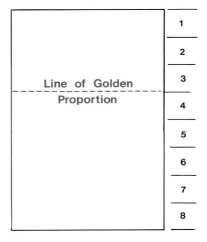

Line of Golden
Proportion

Fig. 2-20. Placement of single words or small groups of words

the reader. When mathematical relationships are apparent, the layout appears dull and static. By regulating the dimensions, the designer can make the layout of elements become alive and interesting, Fig. 2-19.

A single word or small group of words should be placed at the **line of golden proportion**. The line of golden proportion is found by **dividing the height of the page** into eight equal sections. The **third line** from the top is the line of golden proportion. The single word or small group of words should be placed so that one-half of the area extends above and below this line, Fig. 2-20.

The arrangement of a page determines the page margins. On a page set in small typeface, the margins should be narrow to achieve good marginal proportion. Wider margins are recommended for pages set in larger typefaces, Fig. 2-21. The most pleas-

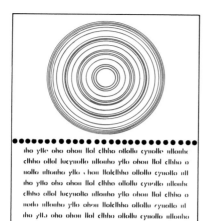

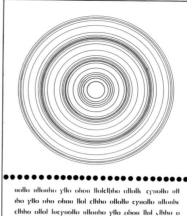

A. Dull and static

B. Alive and interesting

Fig. 2-19. Proportion is regulated by the positioning of the element areas

Fig. 2-21. Page margins are determined by the size of the type used

ing marginal proportion for a **single page** is to have (1) the two side margins narrowest and equal, (2) the top margin a little wider, and (3) the bottom margin the widest, Fig. 2-22.

A sheet of paper that is folded in the center to form two facing pages is called a **book page.** Margins for book pages are regulated so that the inside margin (on either side of the center fold) is the narrowest, the top margin slightly wider, the outside margin the next widest, and the bottom margin the widest, Fig. 2-23.

Book page margins are determined in the following manner:

1. Make a center fold in the paper that will represent two facing pages.
2. Draw vertical lines on the outsides of the pages at the desired width.
3. For the inside margins, draw a second pair of vertical lines at one-half the width of the outside margins.
4. Draw diagonal lines from the top of the center fold of the sheet to the bottom outside corners of the sheet.

The point at which the diagonal lines cross the inside and outside margin lines determines the top and bottom margins, Fig. 2-24.

UNITY

Unity is the most important of all the principles of design. It is the quality that holds the layout together in a harmonious design. Unity in a layout is achieved by regulating the number of typefaces used and by employing similarly shaped element areas.

Using several different type sizes and styles in a layout causes it to appear confusing and disorganized. The layout is more unified if not more than two different type styles are used, Fig. 2-25. Beginning design work should be limited to the same type family. (See Unit 2 for a detailed presentation of type styles.)

Using a variety of different shapes may also cause the layout to appear unorganized and poorly planned, Fig. 2-26. To achieve unity, the relationship of one element to

Fig. 2-22. Single page margin proportions

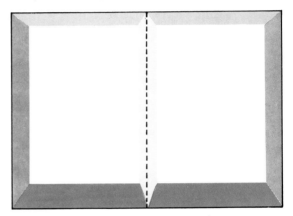

Fig. 2-23. Book page margins

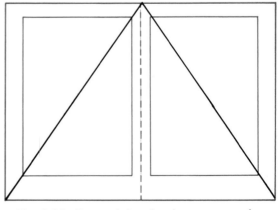

Fig. 2-24. Determining book page margins

JUNIOR CLASS BAR·B·QUE
Saturday, *September 20*
at **FLAG PARK**
11:00 A.M. **to** 4:00 P.M
$2.50 per person   children under 12 $1.00

JUNIOR CLASS BAR-B-QUE
Saturday, September 20th
at Flag Park

11:00 A.M.	$2.50 per person
to	children under 12
4:00 P.M.	$1.00

Fig. 2-25. Unity is achieved by using not more than two different type styles

another in placement must be considered. Each element needs to be placed on the page in a pleasing relationship with the other elements. An organized layout may also be achieved by using a basic shape which may be varied in the design of the elements.

UNIT 1 — TERMS FOR DISCUSSION AND REVIEW

balance	secondary colors
formal	color wheel
informal	complementary
contrast	shade
rhythm	tint
proportion	monochromatic
unity	adjacent
dignity	analogous
symmetrical	equilateral triangle
centered	triadic
underscoring	regular oblong sheet
typefaces	element areas
italic	mathematical
bold	line of golden proportion
color	margins
screen tints	single page
reverse image	book page
primary colors	layout

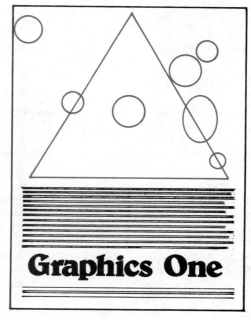

A. Poor

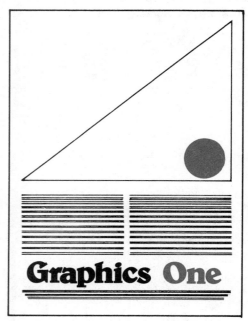

B. Good

Fig. 2-26. Unity is achieved by using the same basic shape

UNIT 2

TYPOGRAPHY

Hand-set foundry type is cast with single characters on individual bodies, Fig. 2-27. The standard height of type in the United States is .918″ (22.95 mm). All relief printing or proofing equipment is designed to use this height.

Type is sold in **fonts** (or separately). Fonts are complete assortments of any one size and style of type, Fig. 2-28. Each font includes capital letters, lowercase letters, figures, and punctuation marks. The number of each of the characters in a font varies with their frequency of use in printing. More letter e's, for example, are supplied in a type font than y's, as e's are more frequently used. Ligatures (ffi), fractions (¼), diphthongs (æ), and special characters are also included in some type fonts.

FONT ARRANGEMENT

A B C D E F G H I J K L M N O P
Q R S T U V W X Y Z a b c d e f g
h i j k l m n o p q r s t u v w x y z
1 2 3 4 5 6 7 8 9 0 $! ? & ¢

Fig. 2-28. A font of type

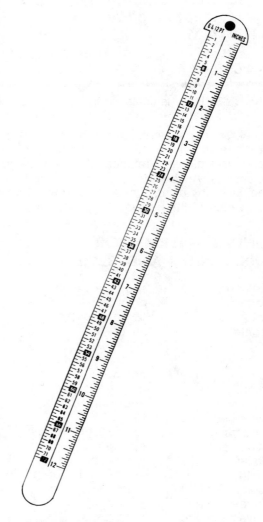

Fig. 2-29. Line gauge

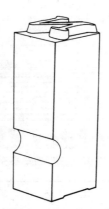

Fig. 2-27. A piece of hand-set foundry type

THE PRINTER'S POINT SYSTEM

The **line gauge** is the printer's rule, Fig. 2-29. The line gauge most comonly used has inch graduations along one edge and pica divisions along the other edge. The **pica** is the standard unit of measure of the printer's point system and is equal to approximately ⅙″ or 4 mm. The pica can be subdivided into twelve equal parts called **points.** The printer's measure is shown in Fig. 2-30.

Type is measured in points from the **nick side** to the **back,** Fig. 2-31. Type sizes larger than 72 point are measured in **lines.**

Each line is equal to 1 pica or 12 points. A six-line type, for example, is equal to 6 picas or 72 points.

Typefaces that measure 12 points or smaller are called **text** or **body type.** Text types are used for composing general reading material such as newspapers, magazines, and book pages. The typeface you are now reading is a text typeface. Typefaces that are larger than 12 points are known as **display types.** The typeface used to identify the chapter and unit headings in this book are considered display typeface sizes.

The most commonly used type sizes are 6, 8, 10, 12, 14, 18, 24, 30, 36, 42, 48,

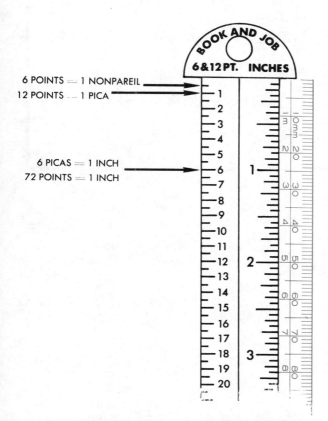

Fig. 2-30. The printer's point system

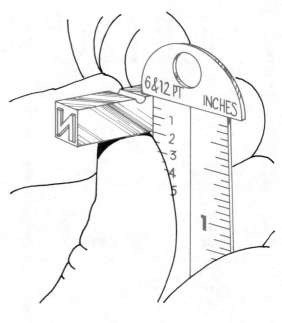

Fig. 2-31. Measuring type from the nick side to the back

ABCDEF
72 point

ABCDEF(
60 point

ABCDEFG
54 point

ABCDEFGH
48 point

ABCDEFGHI
42 point

ABCDEFGHIJK
36 point

ABCDEFGHIJKLI
30 point

ABCDEFGHIJKLMN
24 point

ABCDEFGHIJKLMNOPQ
18 point

ABCDEFGHIJKLMNOPQRSTUV
16 point

ABCDEFGHIJKLMNOPQRSTUVW
14 point

ABCDEFGHIJKLMNOPQRSTUVWXYZ
12 point

ABCDEFGHIJKLMNOPQRSTUVWXYZ
10 point

ABCDEFGHIJKLMNOPQRSTUVWXYZ
8 point

ABCDEFGHIJKLMNOPQRSTUVWXYZ
6 point

Fig. 2-32. A series of type

60, and 72 point. The complete size range of one type design is called a **series,** Fig. 2-32. A **family** of type consists of two or more series, each having the same general characteristics. The type of one family bears the same name, but varies slightly in printed design. The **Century family** includes:

1. Century
2. *Century Italic*
3. **Century Bold**
4. Century Expanded
5. *Century Expanded Italic*
6. Century Schoolbook
7. *Century Schoolbook Italic*
8. **Century Schoolbook Bold**
9. Century Schoolbook Expanded

PARTS OF A HAND-SET FOUNDRY TYPE CHARACTER

The names of the parts of a type character are illustrated in Fig. 2-33. The **face** is the part of the type character that is printed on the paper. The typeface may be made up of varying line thicknesses. The thick stroke of the typeface is referred to as the **stem** while the thin strokes are called

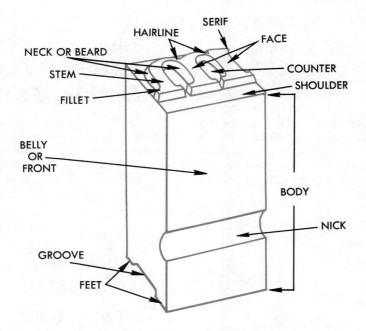

Fig. 2-33. Parts of a hand-set foundry type character

hairlines. **Serifs** may also appear on the typeface. The serif is a short cross line at the end of each unconnected line of the typeface.

The **body** makes up the largest portion of the type and supports the typeface. The **belly** or **front** of the type body has a groove across its surface which is called a **nick**. The nick serves as a guide when type is set and shows that all the characters are from the same font and positioned right side up.

At the base of the type body are the **feet**. The feet are flat surfaces on which the type stands. The recessed area between the feet is known as the **groove**. The flat area at the top of the type body is called the **shoulder**. The shoulder supports the relief typeface. The beveled portion extending from the shoulder to the face is called the **neck** or **beard**. The **counter** is the depressed area that is enclosed by the lines of the typeface. The **fillet** is the rounded corner connecting the letter strokes of a typeface and the serifs. Fillets do not appear

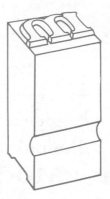

Fig. 2-34. A kerned piece of hand-set foundry type

on all typefaces. Any portion of a typeface that extends over the edge of the type body is known as a **kern**, Fig. 2-34. A kern is sometimes found on such characters as the italic letters *f* and *j*.

CLASSIFICATIONS OF TYPEFACES

Typefaces can be grouped into seven classifications: Old Style, Modern, Sans Serif, Square Serif, Text, Cursive, and Occasional. Each type classification has unique design features. Being able to recognize these classifications is necessary before the most appropriate type can be selected for a particular need. Type specimen books, illustrating faces and sizes of type, can be obtained from composition (typesetting) houses and type founders.

OLD STYLE TYPE

Caslon   Goudy
Century
Garamond

Old Style typefaces are generally used when legibility and readability are important factors of design, which is the reason they are often used for text composition. Old Style typefaces have only slight variations in the thick and thin strokes of the letter. Rounded serifs and fillets are also common characteristics of this classification.

MODERN TYPE

Bernhard Modern Roman
Bodoni
Craw Modern

Modern typefaces have considerable contrast between the thick and thin strokes of the letter and are identified by fine serifs with no fillets. The modern types are used in advertising, book composition, and commercial printing.

SANS SERIF TYPES

Univers   Spartan
GOTHIC, BERNHARD
Gothic, Franklin

"Sans" is a French word which means without. Sans serif type, therefore, is type that does not have serifs. These typefaces have little or no variation in the thickness of the letter strokes. They are often used for display advertising, headlines, and captions in books and magazines.

SQUARE SERIF TYPES

Barnum, P. T.
Hellenic Wide
Tower   Beton   Stymie

Square serif types can easily be identified by the square serif. The serifs have the same weight or thickness as the letter strokes. The letter strokes of square serif types have little or no variation in thickness. Square serif types are durable and are used mainly for display composition, headlines, and short pieces of text material.

TEXT TYPES

Engravers Old English
Goudy Text   American Text
Cloister Text   Wedding Text

Text typefaces are sometimes referred to as Old English. The letters resemble those used by the scribes and are patterned after the earliest types used by Gutenberg. Text types are difficult to read because of the complex design of the letter strokes. These types are used primarily for announcements of special occasions and for Christmas greeting cards. Text types should not be composed in forms of all uppercase (capital) letters.

CURSIVE TYPE

Bank Script **Brush**
Lydian Cursive
Murray Hill

Cursive types resemble handwriting and are often called script types. Many cursive types have uniform line weight while others have both thick and thin letter strokes. Cursive types are used for special effects in advertising and for announcements and invitations. Because they are sometimes difficult to read, cursive type forms should not be composed in all capital letters.

OCCASIONAL TYPE

Dom Casual...

EMPIRE* ...... HUXLEY .... **Onyx** ...

Occasional types are also called decorative or novelty types. These are the attention-getters used in advertising. Each typeface in this classification has individual and distinct characteristics for ex—pressing a particular mood.

point
pica
SI Metric
nick side
back
body type
display type
series
family
face
stem
hairline
serif
body
belly or front
nick
feet
groove

Old Style type
modern type
sans serif type
square serif type
text type
cursive type
occasional type
Caslon
Bodoni
Franklin Gothic
Wedding Text
Brush
Stymie
Dom Casual
Century
Bernhard Gothic
Bernhard Modern
Roman

UNIT 2 — TERMS FOR DISCUSSION AND REVIEW

hand-set foundry type
font
ligature
line gauge
printer's measure

shoulder
neck or beard
counter
fillet
kern

UNIT 3

LAYOUT

A **layout** is a drawing which shows the placement of all the message elements in position for the product to be printed. There are four types of layouts. These are (1) **thumbnail sketches,** (2) **rough layouts,** (3) **comprehensive layouts,** and (4) **mechanical layouts.** The name of each type of layout indicates the amount of care that is exercised in preparation.

THUMBNAIL SKETCHES

The first step in the preparation of a printed product is that of making several thumbnail sketches. By making several sketches, the various layout possibilities may be explored. Even though there is little concern for detail in these sketches, the proposed printed product can be visualized.

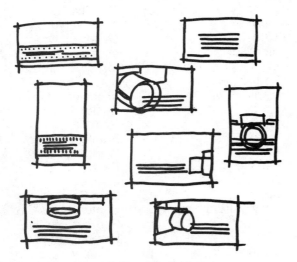

Fig. 2-35. Several thumbnail sketches are prepared

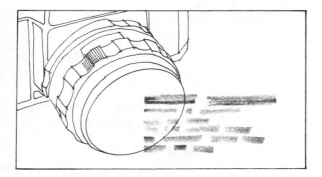

Fig. 2-36. A rough layout

The element areas are simply sketched in as shapes. In some cases, such as headlines, the words may be quickly lettered into place. Text material, however, is usually indicated by lines while pictures, diagrams, and other illustrations are quickly drawn in outline shape. The thumbnail sketches can be prepared in a size smaller but in proportion to the actual size of the printed product, Fig. 2-35.

ROUGH LAYOUT

When the most pleasing thumbnail sketch has been selected, it must be refined and prepared to actual size. This preparation is called **rough layout.** The rough layout is considerably more accurate in size and location of the type and layout of other element areas. Dark, shaded areas are used to indicate the use of bold type, while light areas are used to denote the use of light or smaller type. The pictures, diagrams, and other illustrations must also be prepared with more detail and accuracy, Fig. 2-36.

COMPREHENSIVE LAYOUT

The comprehensive layout is regarded as the prototype for the printed communication. For this reason extreme accuracy is necessary for a true representation of the final printed product.

At this stage in layout development, the artist must use basic drafting equipment. This generally consists of a draftman's drawing board, a T-square and triangles, drafting instruments, a variety of colored pencils, erasers, a scale or ruler, and a printer's line gauge. In addition, the artist must be skilled in the use of an airbrush, felt tipped markers, colored papers, copy-fitting tables, type specimen books, ink charts, and a proportional scale for computing enlargements and reductions, Fig. 2-37.

The comprehensive layout should be prepared to actual size on paper larger than the finished product. The margin areas of the paper provide space for making notations of layout specifications. If the finished product will be printed in two or more colors, the comprehensive layout should be prepared using overlay sheets. Each overlay sheet would contain the copy that is to be printed in one color. The sheets should be labeled with the printing color. Generally, the base sheet is one of heavier white paper. The overlays are often translucent sheets of paper which have been taped to the base

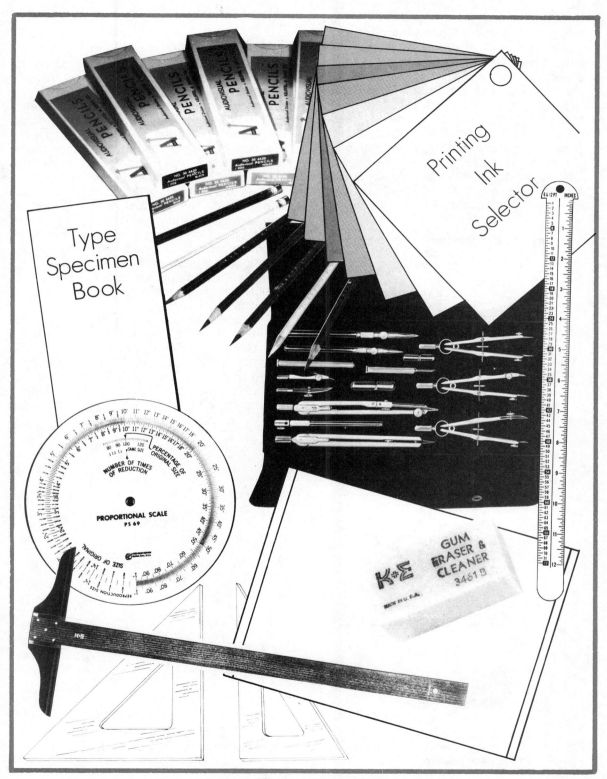

Fig. 2-37. Basic drafting equipment

sheet on one side. This permits the overlay sheets to be folded down over the base sheet. In this way, the product can be seen with all the copy elements in place. Even though the overlay sheets may represent color areas such as red or blue, they are prepared in black ink. Registration marks are generally placed on each of the overlays as well as the base sheet to indicate position-ing. The registration marks should be placed in a triangular pattern, Fig. 2-38.

Fig. 2-38. Place the registration marks in a triangular pattern

The layout paper is taped squarely to the surface of the drawing board. To ac-complish this, first the paper is placed in the center of the board. Then, the T-square, with the head held tightly against the side of the board, is placed on top of the paper. The bottom edge of the paper is aligned with the lower edge of the T-square and (by using small pieces of masking tape) the top cor-ners of the paper are taped to the board, Fig. 2-39A. The bottom of the paper is secured by lowering the T-square and plac-ing masking tape across each corner. The paper must be flat and stretched tightly before the bottom corners are taped, Fig. 2-39B. The squareness of the paper is double checked with the T-square before any drawing is begun.

The actual size of the printed product is then drawn in the center of the paper. **Horizontal lines** are drawn from left to right by right-handed persons, or right to left by those who are left-handed. The head of the T-square should always be held tightly against the edge of the drawing board. When

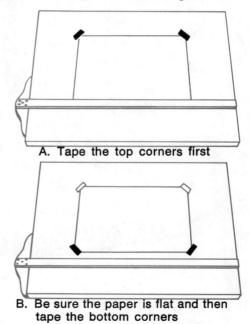

A. Tape the top corners first

B. Be sure the paper is flat and then tape the bottom corners

Fig. 2-39. Tape the corners of the paper to the board

horizontal lines are drawn, the top of the T-square is used as a drawing edge. This permits the use of the T-square as a hand rest and avoids smudges caused by the artist's hand rubbing previously drawn lines, Fig. 2-40. Smudging can also be prevented by beginning the drawing procedure at the top of the paper and progressing toward the bottom. The pencil should be moved from the beginning point of the line to the end point of the line in one continuous motion.

Vertical, 30°, 45°, or 60° lines are drawn with the combined use of the T-square and triangles. The T-square head must be held tightly against the board edge, and the triangle then placed against the top edge of the T-square. The triangle should be positioned so that it will provide a hand rest. When a **vertical line** is drawn, the triangle is placed so that it forms a 90° angle with the T-square. The vertical line is drawn by beginning at the point nearest the T-square and moving the pencil along the edge of the triangle in an upward direction, Fig. 2-41.

Standard drafting triangles are known as 45°-90° and 30°-60°-90° triangles. **Angular lines** of 30°, 45°, and 60° may be drawn in the same manner as a vertical line. The triangle, however, is placed on the top edge of the T-square in a position that will produce the desired angle, Fig. 2-42. Angular lines other than this may be drawn by using an adjustable triangle. The triangle is adjusted for the desired line angle and then placed against the T-square. The line is then drawn, Fig. 2-43. Drafting ma-

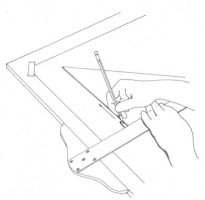

Fig. 2-41. Drawing a vertical line

Fig. 2-42. Drawing an angular line with a standard triangle

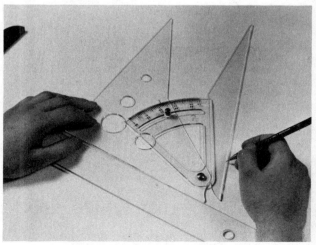

Fig. 2-43. Using an adjustable triangle

Fig. 2-40. Drawing a horizontal line

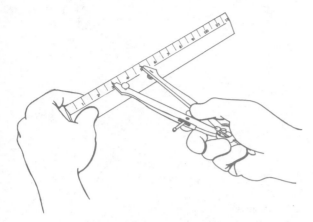

Fig. 2-44. Set the compass to the radius of the circle to be drawn

Fig. 2-45. Tilt the compass in the direction the pencil lead will be moved

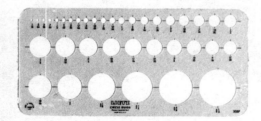

Fig. 2-46. Many sizes of circles are provided on this template

chines are usually used because they are convenient.

Arcs and **circles** are drawn with a draftsman's compass. The compass is set to the radius of the desired circle by adjusting the distance between the pencil lead and the center point of the compass. An accurate setting can be obtained by holding the compass to a ruler, Fig. 2-44. The metal point of the compass is gently pressed into the paper at the previously marked center of the circle to be drawn. The compass is tilted slightly in the direction that the pencil lead will be moved, and the compass is turned to draw the desired line, Fig. 2-45. For most general needs, a template can be used for a circle, ellipse, square, etc., Fig. 2-46.

When the comprehensive layout is prepared, all lines should first be drawn lightly in pencil. The lines may later be darkened or inked if desired.

Using the drafting techniques just described, the artist usually outlines all element areas of the comprehensive layout. The outlined areas must be measured and drawn carefully so that an accurate **prototype** is prepared. Headlines are sometimes carefully lettered in the proper location. The lettering should resemble the typeface that will be used. Other layout elements such as drawings, pictures and text material are keyed, by letter or number, to their location on the layout.

The comprehensive layout should contain all the necessary information that explains how the printing job is to be completed. Any necessary instructions should be placed in the marginal areas of the layout sheet, Fig. 2-47, and may indicate:

1. Size and kind of type
2. Size, color, and kind of paper
3. Color of ink to be used
4. Number of copies to be printed

COPYFITTING

Generally, printed text material must fit within a given area as drawn on the layout.

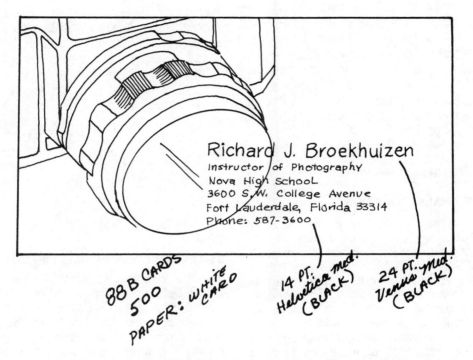

Richard J. Broekhuizen
Instructor of Photography
Nova High School
3600 S.W. College Avenue
Fort Lauderdale, Florida 33314
Phone: 587-3600

88 B CARDS
500
PAPER: WHITE CARD

14 PT.
Helvetica Med.
(BLACK)

24 PT. Med.
Venus Med.
(BLACK)

Fig. 2-47. A comprehensive layout has all the specifications

Copyfitting is the process of determining whether or not the copy, when set in type, will fit within the space available. Copyfitting will indicate the number of lines that must be set at the desired line length.

Most copy to be set in type is typewritten. **Pica** typewritten copy measures ten characters per inch, while **elite** measures twelve characters per inch, Fig. 2-48. Some typewriters use proportional spacing, and it is very difficult to copyfit the typed material because line lengths are unpredictable.

A designer or buyer may limit the finished printed piece to a certain number of pages as one, two, four, or eight. Therefore,

|← 1″ →|

Elite types 12 characters per inch

Pica types 10 characters per

Fig. 2-48. Elite and pica typewriter **character** sizes (1″ = 25.4 mm)

copyfitting is important to reduce production cost of an extra page that could be eliminated by a more precise layout.

An average character count per line may be obtained by drawing a vertical line through the typewritten copy at the average length of line. By multiplying the number of characters in one line on the left of the vertical line by the number of lines an average character count for the entire copy is obtained.

Fig. 2-49. Average character count

AVERAGE CHARACTER COUNT

An average character count per line may be obtained by drawing a vertical line through the typewritten copy at the average length of line, Fig. 2-49. The average length is determined by counting the character difference between the shortest and longest lines. One-half of the difference is the point at which the vertical line should be drawn. Multiply the number of characters in one line located left of the vertical line by the number of lines. In this way, an average character count for the entire copy is obtained. When the message is copyfitted, punctuation marks and spaces must be counted as characters.

ACTUAL CHARACTER COUNT

An actual character count can be obtained by drawing a vertical line through the typewritten copy on the right-hand side at the end of the shortest line, Fig. 2-50. The number of characters in each full line is multiplied by the number of lines in the type-written copy. The short line that may appear at the end of the copy is generally considered to be a full line. The number of characters that are on the right-hand side of the vertical line are added to this. Following this procedure results in an actual character count for the copy to be set in type.

An actual character count can be obtained by drawing a vertical line through the typewritten copy on the right hand side at the end of the shortest line. Multiply the number of characters in each full line by the number of lines in the typewritten copy. The short line that may appear at the end of the copy is generally considered to be a full line. Add to this the number of characters that are on the right hand side of the vertical line.

Fig. 2-50. Actual character count

DETERMINING THE NUMBER OF LINES

The size and face of the type must be known before the number of lines of type can be determined for the total amount of copy to be set. Also, the length of the line on which the copy will be set must be known in **picas.** The line length can be obtained by measuring the space allotted for the text on the layout.

Type specimen books give information on the number of characters that a line of type will contain in a particular size and face. If, for example, an 18 pica line of type were to be set using 10 point Century Schoolbook Italic type, each line would contain 49 characters. (This depends on the number of capital and lowercase letters in the line.) This was determined by comparing the desired line length for the copy to the printed type specimen book and counting the number of characters in that measure, Fig. 2-51. The total number of typewritten characters in the copy is divided by the number of characters per line of the face being used at the specified measure as obtained from copyfitting tables. If the total copy (according to the average or actual

| *Read the word or letter in this line that completes the desired measure, and the cha.* *cter count can then be found on the scale printed at the b*

| *READ THE WORD OR LETTER IN THIS LINE THAT COMPLETES THE DESIRED MEASURE, AND THE CHAR*

6 Point Century Schoolbook Italic — 420C (Monotype) 3.98 char per pica $1234567890&

| *Read the word or letter in this line that completes the desired measure, and the character count can then be four*

| *READ THE WORD OR LETTER IN THIS LINE THAT COMPLETES THE DESIRED MEA:*

8 Point Century Schoolbook Italic — 420C (Monotype) 3.14 char per pica $1234567890&

| *Read the word or letter in this line that completes the desired measure, and the character count can then*

| *READ THE WORD OR LETTER IN THIS LINE THAT COMPLETES THE DESIRED*

9 Point Century Schoolbook Italic — 420C (Monotype) 2.90 char per pica $1234567890&

| *Read the word or letter in this line that completes the desired measure, and the character count c*

| *READ THE WORD OR LETTER IN THIS LINE THAT COMPLETES THE DE:*

10 Point Century Schoolbook Italic — 420C (Monotype) 2.70 char per pica $1234567890&

| *Read the word or letter in this line that completes the desired measure, and the characte*

| *READ THE WORD OR LETTER IN THIS LINE THAT COMPLETES T:*

11 Point Century Schoolbook Italic — 420C (Monotype) 2.47 char per pica $1234567890&

| *Read the word or letter in this line that completes the desired measure, and the cha*

| *READ THE WORD OR LETTER IN THIS LINE THAT COMPLETE*

12 Point Century Schoolbook Italic — 420C (Monotype) 2.32 char per pica $1234567890&

CHARACTERS IN FONT

abcdefghijklmnopqrstuvwxyz

ABCDEFGHIJKLMNOPQRSTUVWXYZ

$1234567890.,:;'-""""!?&fiflffffiffl

```
  5    10   15   20   25   30   35   40   45   50   55   60   65   70   75   80   85   90   95   100  105  110
  |    |    |    |    |    |    |    |    |    |    |    |    |    |    |    |    |    |    |    |    |    |
Read the word or letter in this line that completes the desired measure, and the character count can then be found
```

TYPOGRAPHIC SALES, INCORPORATED • HOT-METAL • ST. LOUIS, MISSOURI

Fig. 2-51. The actual character count for an 18-pica line is determined by counting the actual characters in an 18-pica line of the size and face being used or by using the convenient scale at the bottom of a type specification sheet

Fourscore and seven years ago our fathers brought forth on this continent a new nation conceived in liberty and dedicated to the proposition that all men are created equal. Now we are engaged in a great civil war testing whether that nation, or any nation so conceived and so dedicated can long endure. We are met on a great battlefield of that war. We have come to dedicate a portion of that field as a final resting-place for those who here gave their lives that that nation might live. It is altogether fitting and proper that we should do this. But, in a larger sense, we cannot dedicate, we cannot consecrate, we cannot hallow this *ground. The brave men, living and dead, who*

A. Solid

Fourscore and seven years ago our fathers brought forth on this continent a new nation conceived in liberty and dedicated to the proposition that all men are created equal. Now we are engaged in a great civil war testing whether that nation, or any nation so conceived and so dedicated can long endure. We are met on a great battlefield of that war. We have come to dedicate a portion of that field as a final resting-place for those who here gave their lives that that nation might live. It is altogether fitting and proper that we should do this. But, in a larger sense, we cannot dedi*cate, we cannot consecrate, we cannot hallow this*

B. One-point lead

Fourscore and seven years ago our fathers brought forth on this continent a new nation conceived in liberty and dedicated to the proposition that all men are created equal. Now we are engaged in a great civil war testing whether that nation, or any nation so conceived and so dedicated can long endure. We are met on a great battlefield of that war. We have come to dedicate a portion of that field as a final resting-place for those who here gave their lives that that nation might live. It is altogether fitting and proper that we should do this. But, in a larger sense, we cannot dedi-

C. Two-point lead

Fig. 2-52. Vertical copyfitting is influenced by the point size of the type and the leading between lines

typewritten character count) contains 560 characters, then 11½ lines of type would have to be set if 10 point Century Schoolbook were used as the typeface (560 ÷ 49).

The amount of vertical space required for the copy is dependent upon (1) the point size of the type, (2) the amount of leading used between the lines, and (3) the number of lines that will be set, Fig. 2-52. If 10 point type is used and 2 point leads are placed between the lines, the actual vertical space required by each line is 12 points. The actual vertical space required by the copy set in type is determined by multiplying the total vertical space required by each line by the total number of lines to be set. A total of 12 lines of 10 point type with 2 point leading would require a vertical layout area of 144 points (or 12 picas). This answer was computed by multiplying 12 × 12 = 144.

Now that the total vertical space required by the copy when set in type is known, it is possible to determine whether or not the copy will fit within the allotted layout area. If it does not fit the space, (1) the type size or (2) the amount of leading between lines may have to be changed.

COMPUTING ENLARGEMENTS AND REDUCTIONS

Sometimes a layout needs artwork to communicate the message. Art such as pictures, drawings, and diagrams is prepared to fit the message. The art may be too small or too large for the layout space; therefore, it is enlarged or reduced so it will fit. This is done by comparing the "original size" of the art to the "size of the reproduction." The percentage of enlargement or reduction is computed with a **proportional scale.** The proportional scale is adjusted so that the width of the "original" dimension is directly under the desired width "reproduction" dimension on the outside scale. The percentage of enlargement or reduction will be indicated by the arrow in the window, Fig. 2-53. The percentage for both the (1) width and (2) height of the art should be computed following this procedure since different percentages will result for the reduction. In the following examples, the original art size must be reduced to fit the layout space. You will see in Fig. 2-53 how the proportional scale is used to determine percentages. Then compare the reproduction sizes with the size of the layout area. Which reduction percentage would you use?

1. Example using width reduction percentage
   Original art size = 8″ width × 10″ height
   (203 mm × 254 mm)
   Layout space   = 3″ width × 5″ height
   (76 mm × 127 mm)
   a. Reduce 8″ to fit into 3″.
      (Reduce 203 mm to fit into 76 mm)
   b. See top example of Fig. 2-53. Reduction is 37½%.
   c. Find 10″ on the original portion of the scale. Directly above it is the desired reproduction dimension — 3¾″.
   d. Compare this reproduction size with size of the layout space.
      Original size   8″ × 10″
                          (203 mm × 254 mm)
      Reproduction size 3″ × 3¾″
                          (76 mm × 95 mm)
      Layout space   3″ × 5″
                          (76 mm × 127 mm)
      The 37½% reduction **will** fit the layout space.

2. Example using height reduction percentage
   Original art size = 8″ width × 10″ height
   (203 mm × 254 mm)
   Layout space   = 3″ width × 5″ height
   (76 mm × 127 mm)

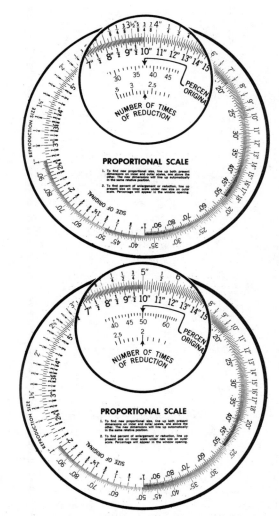

Fig. 2-53. Computing a typical picture reduction on a proportional scale. The enlarged view

WIDTH REDUCTION — 37%		
Size	**U. S. Customary (in.)**	**SI Metrics (mm)**
Original	8 x 10	203 x 254
Reproduction	3 x 3¾	76 x 95
Layout Space	3 x 5	76 x 127

Table 1 — Reproduction **fits** into layout space

HEIGHT REDUCTION — 50%		
Size	**U. S. Customary (in.)**	**SI Metrics (mm)**
Original	8 x 10	203 x 254
Reproduction	4 x 5	102 x 127
Layout Space	3 x 5	76 x 127

Table 2 — Reproduction **too large** to fit into layout space

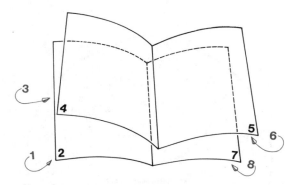

Fig. 2-54. An eight-page booklet

a. Reduce 10″ to fit into 5″.
(Reduce 254 mm to fit into 127 mm)
b. See bottom example of Fig. 2-53. Reduction is 50%.
c. Find 8″ on the original portion of the scale. Directly above it is the desired reproduction dimension — 4″.
d. Compare this reproduction size with the size of the layout space.

Original size   8″ × 10″
                    (203 mm × 254 mm)
Reproduction size 4″ × 5″
                    (102 mm × 127 mm)
Layout space   3″ × 5″
                    (76 mm × 127 mm)

The 50% reduction **will not** fit the layout space.

As you can see, it is necessary to **use the smaller percentage to fit the layout.** The percentage of enlargement or reduction is marked in the margin of the picture or on a tab attached to the picture.

MULTI-PAGE LAYOUT

A layout **and** folding dummy must be prepared when printing several pages. A **folding dummy** is folded sheets of paper that illustrate the size of the final product. The dummy should include both the front, interior, and back pages of the printing job. Each page of the folding dummy should be numbered so the layout sheets can be correlated accurately.

In the case of an eight-page booklet that is printed on two sheets to make the total book, one side of **one sheet** will be printed with pages 8 and 1, while the other side of the same sheet will have pages 2 and 7. The **second sheet** will be printed with pages 6 and 3 and pages 4 and 5, Fig. 2-54.

The individual page layouts are prepared and attached to the corresponding numbered dummy pages. All specifications for completing the job should be marked in the margin areas of each page of the comprehensive layout sheet.

MECHANICAL LAYOUT

Although the comprehensive layout is often considered the **prototype** for the printed product, it does not truly represent the final printed product. The comprehensive layout shows how to assemble the individual copy elements after they have been generated. The mechanical layout can only be prepared after all of the images have been generated for the product. It is often referred to as the **final paste-up.**

Once all the copy elements have been generated, they must be positioned on the mechanical layout sheet. A dull white finish paper is generally used as a paste-up sheet. A light blue non-reproducing pencil can be used to draw layout guidelines to indicate all copy areas. Only the copy that will be shot at the same percentage can be pasted-up into position. Copy that must be enlarged or reduced must be shot separately. If photographs are to be used in the printed product, the area should be indicated on the layout sheet. However, the photographs should not be pasted into position as they must be shot as halftone negatives rather than line negatives. (See Unit 31.) Instead, a black piece of paper may be pasted on the layout sheet. This area will be transparent on the negative and will indicate the halftone negative position. The negatives may be combined in the masking sheets during the stripping operation.

When drawing the guidelines and positioning the copy elements, a T-square, triangles, and rule should be used to assure accuracy. Rubber cement, wax, clear tape, or spray adhesive may be used to attach the copy elements to the layout sheet.

When the finished product will be printed in two or more colors, the copy elements for each color must be pasted-up on separate layout sheets. Registration marks in a triangular pattern are generally applied to each sheet to indicate copy positioning.

It is important that you understand the necessary steps of preparing for the production of the final "images." Therefore, review the following major steps:

1. First, you must determine the content and purpose of the message that is to be communicated. You also need to select the method of preparing and presenting the message. The graphic presentation for this book has been selected.

2. Second, you must analyze the message and select the elements of design to help you communicate to others. Do you need type, pictures, etc.?

3. Next, you need to plan all of the elements so they are appealing and legible and will help you communicate. The layout must be functional. Most of the major decisions are made in the planning stage to help control cost, design appearance, and the function of the printed product.

4. Next, you need to select the best typeface to help you communicate your message. You also need to copyfit or plan your message to fit the page size or number of pages you plan to produce.

5. Then, you prepare a comprehensive layout that explains exactly how to assemble and prepare the finished copy. This layout is the "master" plan to be followed by production personnel.

6. Now, you are ready to begin generating the images that you selected for your communication.

You are about to study various methods of image generation to finalize the copy that you designed or planned.

UNIT 3 — TERMS FOR   DISCUSSION AND REVIEW

layout	copyfitting	triangular	reductions
thumbnail sketches	pica	overlay	proportional scale
rough layout	elite	aligned	original size
comprehensive layout	average character	T-square	reproduction size
mechanical layout	count	horizontal lines	shooting
radius	actual character	vertical lines	percentage
diameter	count	angular lines	dummy
leading	line length	drafting triangles	final paste-up
multi-page layout	vertical space	compass	non-reproducing
registration marks	enlargements	arcs	pencil

Career Opportunities

Commercial Artist

Layout Artist

Photographer

IMAGE
GENERATION

At this point in the development of a printed communication, a comprehensive layout has been prepared. This layout specifies how to assemble the art and type. The image generation phase of graphic communication is concerned with the composition and preparation of the finished copy. Therefore, the personnel responsible for the generation of images will follow the comprehensive layout. The finished copy, when pasted up, becomes the **mechanical layout** which presents a true visualization of the printed product. The mechanical layout is a finished product that is further prepared for reproduction. The various products or processes you will study later in Section IV will explain how to prepare and produce many copies of the mechanical layout.

The method of image generation to be used for any printed communication is generally determined in the design stage. Keep in mind that all image generation methods may be used for any of the production processes. Some image generation methods, however, are best suited to a particular production process. The decision to use one method of image generation over another, as previously stated, can only be made after reaching a complete understanding of the graphic communications industry. The purpose of this book is to inform you of the many processes and alternatives that are available to designers, production personnel, and consumers in the graphic arts industry.

There are basically only two classifications into which all image generation methods fall:

1. Hot composition, and
2. Cold composition

The names of these two classifications represent a broad generalization of how the image is created.

All methods of image generation that use molten metal to create the image are considered hot composition methods. This classification can be subdivided into the image generation methods of hand-set foundry type and machine-set type.

Hand-set foundry type utilizes individually cast letters or symbols on type bodies. To generate images for printing, the individual type pieces must be assembled by hand to form words, sentences, and paragraphs, Fig. III-1. Machine-set type on the other hand, is automatically cast and assembled as the machine operator manipulates the keys on the keyboard, Fig. III-2.

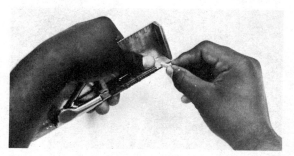

Fig. III-1. Image generation by hand-set foundry type

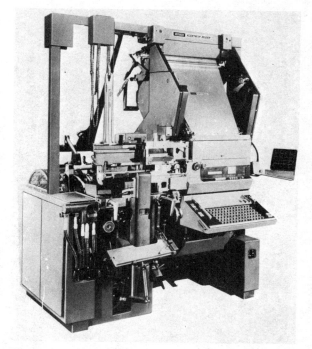

Fig. III-2. Typesetting machine

Some typesetting machines cast and assemble **individual** type characters (monotype), while others cast complete lines of type (linotype).

The cold composition methods of image generation include all methods that do not use molten metal, Fig. III-3. Cold composition encompasses a wide variety of image generation methods. The cold composition methods include linoleum block carving, technical illustrating, clip art and preprinted type, strike-on composition, photocomposition, and continuous tone photography.

To understand the similarities and differences, advantages and disadvantages of

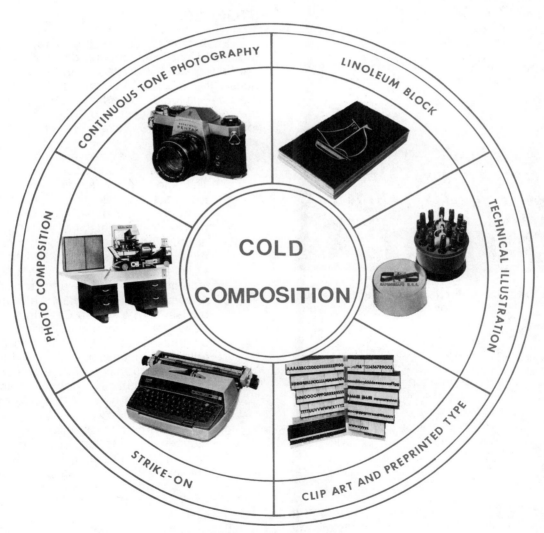

Fig. III-3. Methods of cold composition

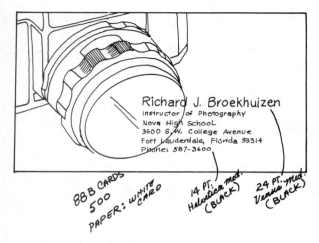

Fig. III-4. The comprehensive layout is the input stage for image generation

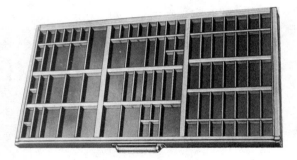

Fig. III-5. The California Job Case is the storage unit for hand-set foundry type

each image generation method, consider the four basic stages of:
1. input,
2. storage,
3. retrieval, and
4. output.

INPUT

The input is the "copy" or message to be prepared in finished form and detail. The comprehensive layout specifies typefaces, line lengths, horizontal and vertical spacing, the need for drawings, and all other particulars that are required to complete the preparation of the mechanical layout, Fig. III-4. Working from the comprehensive layout, compositors (typesetters) and artists alike must prepare the copy to meet the specifications. An artist may receive **inputs** in the form of ideas. Artistic skill and knowledge is applied to get the **output.**

STORAGE

Each method of image generation has a different and unique storage system. Storage refers to the system that is used to house the images until they are used by the compositor or the artist when preparing the mechanical layout copy, Fig. III-5. The following are a few examples of different storage systems:
1. Clip art is designed and preprinted on sheets for you to select and use. The **sheet** is the storage system.
2. An artist creates images that the customer describes. By drawing mechanically, sketching, painting, or airbrushing, the artist uses knowledge, experience, and manipulative skills (hands) to create the art. The storage system is the artist's **body.**
3. A compositor may select individual pieces of type from a California Job Case and arrange the letters in a composing stick. The compositor follows the manuscript copy and the specific instructions on the comprehensive layout. The **job case** that contains the type is the storage system.
4. A secretary or typist follow the employer's handwritten copy to assemble the message for a letter. The typewriter has a series of keys that are struck to recall the specific letter. The **typewriter** is the storage system.
5. A linotype operator has a machine

similar to the typewriter. When a key is struck, a metal form containing a specific character is assembled in a row with other characters until a "line of type" has been formed. The operator triggers the action where hot metal is pressed into the line of different casts which forms one line of type in lead. The **linotype machine** is the storage system.

There are other examples of storage systems for forming images. The purpose of these examples is to illustrate that machines are designed to function faster or more accurately than a human being. An artist could assemble all the different types of images by drawing and sketching by hand, but the machine is faster and more precise.

RETRIEVAL

The retrieval stage of image generation is concerned with the **assembly** of the symbols to make up the message, Fig. III-6. Like the storage stage, the process of retrieval is unique and different for each method of image generation. The process by which the images are retrieved and assembled is dependent upon the method that is employed for storage. The following are examples of different retrieval systems. These examples are related to the earlier examples used to explain the **input** and **storage** systems:

1. Clip art is stored on sheets of paper. After the specific piece of art has been selected, it is cut from the sheet and pasted on:
   a. a white background sheet ready for camera **or**
   b. the mechanical layout as a final assembly.
   Therefore, the retrieval system is the **cutting** and **pasting action** to make the assembly.
2. The artist's body is the storage system. The ideas and creative art **are** retrieved when the artist **applies images to paper.**

3. The California Job Case contains the different characters in various sections of the storage case. The compositor retrieves the characters from the storage case and assembles them in a composing stick. **The action of the compositor** is a manual retrieval method.
4. The typist uses the typewriter to retrieve the various characters from the machine to assemble a typed copy of the message. **The action of striking the keys** on the keyboard is the retrieval method.
5. The linotype operator uses the intertype (linotype) machine to retrieve the various characters from the machine to assemble a series of lines of type cast in lead as specified on the comprehensive layout. **The action of striking the keys** on the keyboard is the retrieval system.

OUTPUT

The output of image generation is the printing image that has been assembled or

Fig. III-6. Strike-on images are retrieved and assembled by pressing the typewriter keys

Examples of Input, Storage, Retrieval, and Output Systems for Image Generation

Image and Character Generation Method	Input System	Storage System	Retrieval System	Output System
1. Clip Art (Cold Composition)	Ideas of customer or designer on the comprehensive layout	Clip art sheet	Art is cut from the sheet and pasted on the mechanical layout	The mechanical layout or final assembly that will be used for reproduction
2. Artist (Cold Composition)	Ideas of customer or designer on the comprehensive layout	Hands and body of the artist	The artist applies design image on paper	The mechanical layout or final assembly that will be used for reproduction
3. Hand-Set Type (Hot Composition)	Copy or manu-script and the comprehensive layout	California Job Case	The compositor retrieves the characters by hand and assembles them in a composing stick	The type, ink, and paper that will be used for reproduction
4. Strike-On (Cold Composition)	Copy or manu-script and the comprehensive layout	Typewriter	The typist strikes the keys and the lever holding the character strikes the paper	The typed copy or the assembly of typed copy to other art on a mechanical layout
5. Machine-Set Type (Hot Composition)	Copy or manu-script and the comprehensive layout	Linotype machine	The operator strikes the keys which allow small metal forms to be posi-tioned in row to form line of casts; then hot metal is forced in mold to form a line of type	The type, ink, and paper that will be used for reproduction

Fig. III-7. The output of image generation is the printing image that has been assembled

prepared, Fig. III-7. All images that are generated by hand-set foundry type, machine-set type, and linoleum block carving are three-dimensional images. These images, because they are three-dimensional, are directly applicable to the relief printing process. The remaining methods of image generation result in a two-dimensional copy output, and they are more directly geared for use by the other production processes. The following are examples of different output systems. These examples are related to the earlier examples used to explain the input, storage, and retrieval systems:

1. After the clip art has been assembled on paper or on the final mechanical layout, it is used for making several copies by some production process. Sometimes the assembled images are photocopied, converted to negatives for platemaking, or photographed as continuous tone pictures. The **final mechanical layout** is the output and various production methods can be used for reproducing several copies.

2. The artist retrieves the images by putting them on paper or on the final mechanical layout. The final mechanical layout can be paper, a linoleum block carving, a piece of negative film, or some other form that contains images to be reproduced. **These various forms** represent the output of image generation.

3. The hand-set type is locked up (or tied together) in a chase for proofing, or reproduction. Ink is applied to the type surface, and pressure is applied so the ink is transferred to the surface of the paper. The proof is the output of this system.

4. The strike-on method of image generation is performed by a typewriter. The impact of a key hitting a carbon, or inked ribbon, transfers the image of the key to the paper. The paper with the images in position is a product of the output system. The finished typed page may be the final mechanical layout. The page of images may also be assembled on a mechanical layout with other types of artwork to represent the copy to be reproduced.

5. The output for machine-set type is the same as the output for hand-set type. The only difference in these two methods is the storage and retrieval methods of generating the images.

Fig. III-8. Many factors must be considered when planning the production of a graphic communication

SUMMARY

At this point in the study of the graphic communications industry, it should be evident that there is a great deal of complexity involved in the selection of the image generation method that is best suited for any particular production process. This complexity is compounded by such factors as the message design, quantity, quality, and the type of material that will receive the printed image, Fig. III-8.

Once again, any method of image generation may be used for any production process. Of course, there are certain design limitations that must be considered. For example, if the design calls for the use of a screen tint, it would be very difficult, if not impossible, to generate the screen tint image by carving a linoleum block.

An important factor to consider when selecting an image generation method is the number of intermediate steps that are required to advance the generated image to the production process. As already stated, hand-set foundry type results directly in a relief printing image. Images generated by photocomposition may also be used for relief printing; however, several intermediate steps are required. Is the equipment available that is necessary to convert photo-composition to a relief image? Is the cost of conversion prohibitive? What about the quality? Are there design limitations? These questions can only be answered when a complete understanding of the graphic communications industry has been obtained.

CHAPTER 3

HOT COMPOSITION

Hot composition, as previously stated, includes all methods of image generation that make use of **molten metal that is cast into relief printing type characters** (or symbols). The two methods of image generation in the classification of hot composition are (1) hand-set foundry type and (2) machine-set type.

Type characters are prepared by heating a metal alloy of lead, antimony, and tin to a molten state and casting it in prepared typeface molds. Each typeface mold has a symbol cavity in reverse of the printed symbol. After the metal alloy has been cast in the typeface mold, it is allowed to cool and harden in the shape and design of the mold. The cast symbol, when removed from the mold, has a raised "ink-carrying" surface that is supported by the body of the type, Fig. 3-1.

HAND-SET FOUNDRY TYPE

Hand-set foundry type characters (or symbols) are produced by **foundries** (a hot metal production plant) on individual type bodies. A complete **font** of type is stored in a **California Job Case** which is constructed with separate compartments for each character. To be usable as printing images, the individual type characters must be retrieved from the California Job Case by hand and then assembled in a **composing stick**, Fig. 3-2. This assembly operation is commonly referred to as **composition**. The type, after use, must be **distributed** (placed back into the California Job Case by hand) so that it

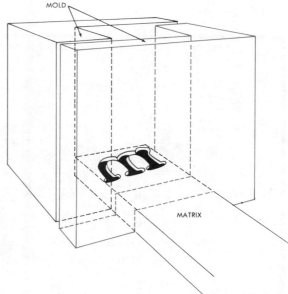

Fig. 3-1. Type is cast by pouring molten metal into a mold

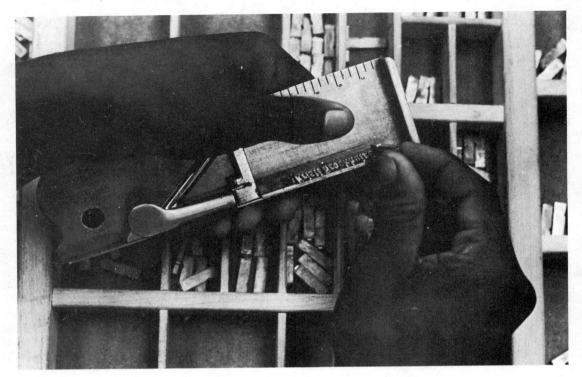

Fig. 3-2. Composition of hand-set foundry type

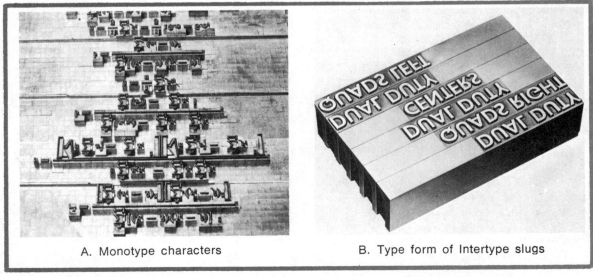

A. Monotype characters   B. Type form of Intertype slugs

Fig. 3-3. Machine-set type is cast in single characters or solid lines

may be reused for the generation of new usable printing images.

The following unit (Unit 4) provides more detailed information about image generation by the hand-set foundry type method. Unit 2 also is concerned with typography.

MACHINE-SET TYPE

Typesetting machines can be classified in two categories. Some typesetting machines cast (1) **individual** pieces of type, while others cast (2) complete **lines of type** at any given length, Fig. 3-3. The fundamentals of operation, however, are the same.

The basic difference between hand-set and machine-set type is in the storage and retrieval stages. Typesetting machines store the typeface molds rather than pieces of type, because the machine casts its own type. To retrieve molds, the operator depresses the key on the keyboard that corresponds to the mold desired, Fig. 3-4. This action causes the mold to be released from the storage magazine and placed in a posi-

tion for casting. Molten metal is then cast into the mold to form the typeface and body. The mold is then returned, automatically, to the proper storage **magazine** for reuse. Each magazine contains a specific typeface style and size.

Usually, the time required to compose a message by hand-set foundry type, as compared to machine-set type, is much longer. Hand-set type is first cast and then stored in California Job Cases. The composition of the individual pieces of type is accomplished by locating, picking up, and placing each individual piece in a composing stick by hand. The typesetting machine, on the other hand, automatically casts and assembles the message as the operator presses the keys on a keyboard similar to a keyboard of a typewriter. As a result, machine-set composition is generally considered to be faster than hand-set type because it takes longer to locate, pick up, and place a piece of hand-set foundry type in the composing stick. The operator of a typesetting machine can compose several letters or even words, while a hand composer assembles but a few letters. This is because the typesetting

Fig. 3-4. Keyboard of typesetting machine

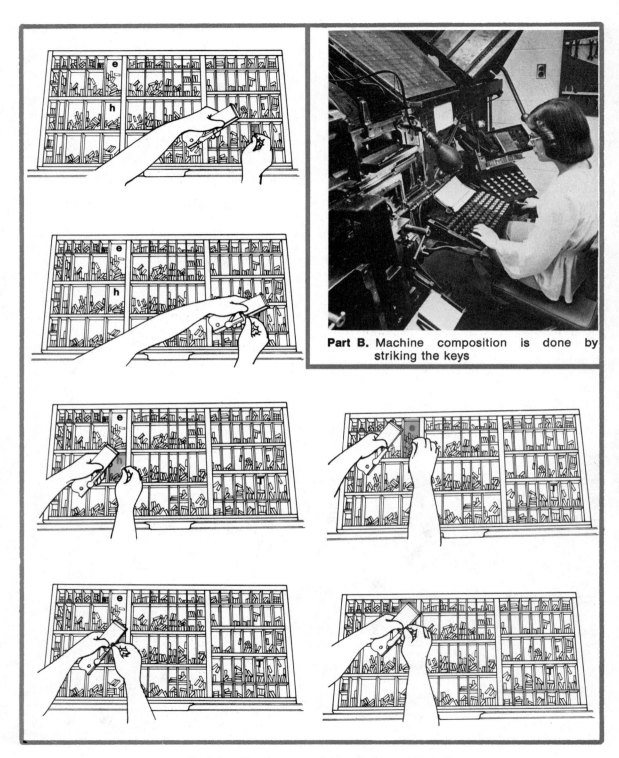

Part B. Machine composition is done by striking the keys

Part A. Hand composition of the word "the"

Fig. 3-5.

machine operator's hands move less distance, Fig. 3-5.

Not only does machine typesetting generally prove to be faster than handsetting, but it also provides new type for each message since machine-set type is remelted after use and recast for the generation of the next message. The advantage of handset type, however, is that it is more practical to use when only a small amount of type is set or when large display type is needed and it cannot be composed by machine.

For further details on image generation by machine-set type, refer to Unit 5.

UNIT 4

IMAGE GENERATION BY HAND-SET FOUNDRY TYPE

THE CALIFORNIA JOB CASE

The California Job Case, Fig. 3-6, is divided into three major sections for the storage of hand-set foundry type. Each type character is stored in a small compartment within the case. The location of the letters is referred to as the **lay of the case,** Fig. 3-7. The lay of the case is said to be **dirty** if the letters are in the wrong compartments. It is necessary to keep the case **clean** for accurate composition.

The right-hand one-third of the case holds the CAPITAL letters. The capital letters are arranged in alphabetical order with the exception of the *J* and *U* which follow the Z.

The lowercase letters are positioned in the left two-thirds of the case according to

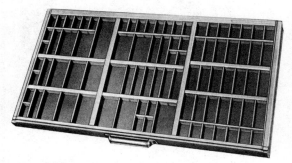

Fig. 3-6. California Job Case

Fig. 3-7. The lay of the California Job Case

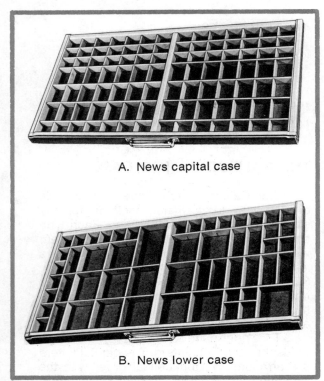

A. News capital case

B. News lower case

Fig. 3-8. News case

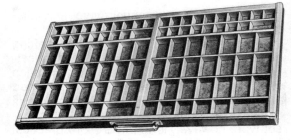

Fig. 3-9. Double-cap case

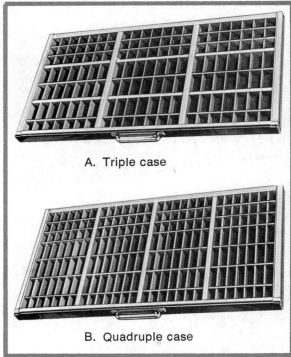

A. Triple case

B. Quadruple case

Fig. 3-10. Other type cases

their frequency of use. That is, the letters most used have a central location and generally have a larger compartment. Mixed in with the lowercase letters are the individual compartments for the numbers, punctuation marks, spaces, quads, and ligatures.

Typecases of varying styles such as the **news case** and the **double-cap case** are sometimes used. The news case is used in pairs, Fig. 3-8. The upper case holds the capital letters, while the lower case holds the lowercase letters. The double-cap case, Fig. 3-9, is used to store the type fonts that have no lowercase letters. Two fonts, each with capital letters only, may be stored in the same typecase. **Triple** and **quadruple cases,** Fig. 3-10, may also be encountered.

SPACES AND QUADS

When a line of type is composed by hand, metal spaces must be placed between the words. Spaces are pieces of type metal that are shorter than type and have no printing face. Even type will not make an impres-

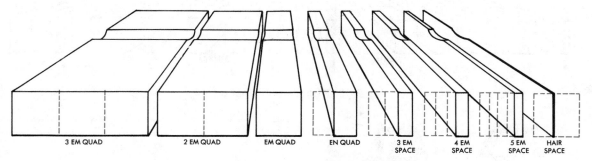

Fig. 3-11. Size relationship of the spaces and quads

sion when it is inked, so spaces will appear as white space on the printed copy.

These short, blank pieces of metal are called **spaces** and **quads.** Each California Job Case has a complete set of spaces and quads. How they relate in size is shown in Fig. 3-11.

The **em quad,** being square, serves as the basic unit for the rest of the spaces and quads. It is sometimes referred to as the "mutton quad." The **2 em quad** is twice as wide as the em quad while the **3 em quad** is three times as wide. The **en quad** is one-half the width of the em quad and is sometimes referred to as the "nut quad." The en quad is considered the ideal space to be placed between words set in all capital letters.

Quads are generally used for paragraph indention or for filling in blank space at the ends of lines. The first line of a paragraph that has a line length up to 18 picas should be indented with an em quad. The 2 em quad is used for indention of forms that have a line length of 19 to 25 picas. A line length between 26 and 35 picas should be indented with a 3 em quad, Fig. 3-12. The longer the line length, the greater the indention of the first line of the paragraph.

The **3 em space** is one-third the width of the em· quad and is commonly referred to as the **word space,** because it is considered the ideal space to be placed between words set in lowercase letters.

Em Quad Indention
■What are words? Of the many wonderful things in this world of ours, words must be one of the strangest. Indeed they might almost be said to belong to another world altogether — a world of ideas, a spiritual world where ideas are para-

2 Em Quad Indention
■ What are words? Of the many wonderful things in this world of ours, words must be one of the strangest. Indeed they might almost be said to belong to another world altogether — a world of ideas, a spiritual world where ideas are

3 Em Quad Indention
■ What are words? Of the many wonderful things in this world of ours, words must be one of the strangest. Indeed they might almost be said to belong to another world altogether — a world of ideas, a spiritual world where ideas are

Fig. 3-12. Paragraph indentions for various line lengths

The **4 em space** is one-fourth the width of the em quad, while the **5 em space** is one-fifth the width of the em quad. These spaces are used to **justify** lines of type, that is, regulate the space so the line of type will fill the desired line measure.

Hair spaces are also used for "spacing-out" and justifying lines of type. They are used, however, only when all other combinations of spaces and quads fail to make the line tight in the composing stick.

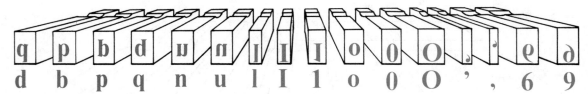

Fig. 3-13. The demon characters

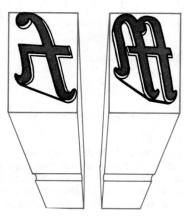

Fig. 3-14. Ligatures have two or more connected typefaces on one type body

DEMON CHARACTERS

As you look at a piece of type, you will notice that the typeface is cast in reverse. For this reason some characters appear to be a different letter than they really are. These are called the **demon characters**. The demon characters in Fig. 3-13 show how the typeface appears on the piece of type and how it will appear when printed. The type must be held with the nick up when reading the typeface.

LIGATURES

Two or more connected typefaces on one type body is called a **ligature**, Fig. 3-14. Typical examples of ligatures found in most California Job Cases are fi, ff, fl, ffi, and ffl. Ligatures are designed to prevent the breaking of the kern at the top of the "f" in some italic types, as the kern will come in contact with the dot of the "i" and the top of the

Fig. 3-15. Type bank with lead and slug rack

"l" and may break off if these characters were not set as ligatures.

TYPE COMPOSITION

The type bank, Fig. 3-15, serves as a storage unit for California Job Cases. Most type banks also provide a slanted work surface for the placement of the typecase while type is being set.

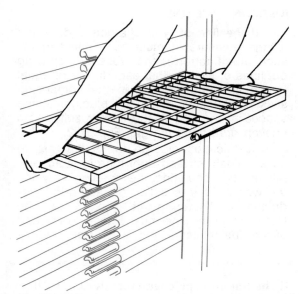

Fig. 3-16. Removing the California Job Case from the type bank

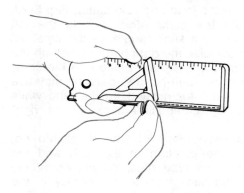

Fig. 3-18. Adjust the composing stick to the desired measure

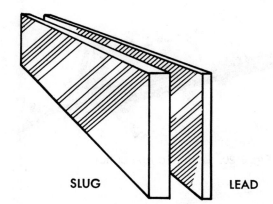

SLUG   LEAD

Fig. 3-19. Slugs are six points in thickness, while leads are two points in thickness

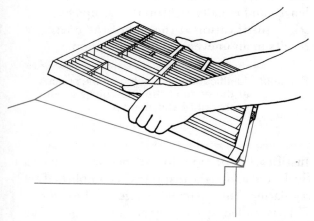

Fig. 3-17. Place the case on the slanted type bank surface

To begin type composition, locate the desired typecase and remove it from the type bank. Pull the case out far enough to get a firm hold on the case with both hands and carefully lift it from the type bank, Fig. 3-16. Place the case on the slanted surface of the bank, making sure it is supported by the rail and that it does not hang over the edge, Fig. 3-17.

Begin setting type by first adjusting the **composing stick** to the desired pica measure, Fig. 3-18. Select a slug that is the same length as the line to be set, and insert it in the composing stick. **Leads** and **slugs** are metal strips of spacing material that are placed between lines of type. **Slugs** are generally "six points" in thickness. **Leads** are "two points" in thickness, Fig. 3-19.

Leads and slugs may be cut to the desired length on the lead and rule cutter, Fig. 3-20.

Hold the composing stick in the left hand and at a slight angle so the type will not fall out. Use the right hand to pick up the type from the case and place it in the composing stick. (Left-handed persons may use the left hand for picking up the type while holding the composing stick in the right hand.)

As each piece of type is picked up, observe the position of the nick and the typeface. The type must be placed in the composing stick from left to right with the nick up and the typeface pointing out. The thumb catches and holds each piece of type as it is placed in the composing stick, Fig. 3-21.

JUSTIFYING THE LINE

If the line of type characters does not fill the measure, it must be justified in the stick. **Justification** is the process of spacing out lines of type so that each line is of equal length and equally tight in the composing stick. Justification made by placing all the spaces at the end of the lines results in an uneven right-hand margin, Fig. 3-22.

Justification of type forms that are to have a flush left and right margin is accomplished by regulating the spacing between the words. This is called "spacing-in" (reducing) or "spacing-out" (enlarging). The last word in the line must extend to the end of the line measure, Fig. 3-23. Some words

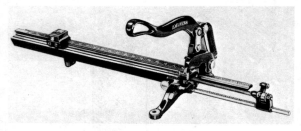

Fig. 3-20. Lead and rule cutter

If the line of type characters does not fill the measure it must be justified in the stick. Justification is the process of spacing-out lines of type so that each line is of equal length and equally tight in the composing stick. Justification at the end of the lines results in an uneven right-hand margin.

Fig. 3-22. Justification by placing all the spaces at the ends of the lines gives an uneven right-hand margin

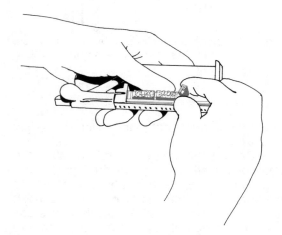

Fig. 3-21. Composition of hand-set foundry type

Justification of type forms that are to have a flush left and right margin is accomplished by regulating the spacing between the words. This is called spacing-in or spacing-out. The last word in the line must extend to the end of the line measure. Some words may have to be divided between syllables. A hyphen is placed after the syllable of the word at the end of the line and the remaining syllables of the word are then set in the next line.

Fig. 3-23. Flush left and right margins are accomplished by regulating the spacing between the words

may have to be divided between syllables. A hyphen is placed after the syllable of the word at the end of the line, and the remaining syllables of the word are then set in the next line.

If altering the spacing between words is necessary, consideration should be given to the shapes of the terminal letters of the words. The open letters such as c, r, t and j and the slanted letters such as v, w and y require less space when printed and therefore permit spacing-in (decreasing the space) between two words that end and begin with these letters. Periods and commas also permit spacing-in without causing the words to run together. Spacing-in is accomplished by carefully removing the 3 em space and inserting a smaller space such as the 4 em.

Spacing-out (adding space) between words is accomplished by placing additional spacing material, such as 4 em and 5 em spaces, between two words where one ends and the other begins with two ascending letters (such as b, d, l, t) or two descending letters (g, p, q, y). For example, spacing-out may be accomplished by placing additional spacing material after a word ending in **d** when the next word begins with **b** as in **red boat.** The en quad is sometimes used to replace the 3 em space when a line is justified if the addition of 4 em and 5 em spaces does not fill the measure.

It should be remembered when lines of type are justified that **insufficient spacing** between words causes them to run together and makes it difficult to read the sentence. Thislineoftypehasinsufficientspacingbetween words. Too much space between words, on the other hand, produces a large white space called a **lake.** If too much spacing between words continues for several lines, white streaks called **rivers** may appear, Fig. 3-24.

In addition to spacing-in or spacing-out, a line of type must sometimes be letter-spaced so that it will fill the measure and be justified. **Letter-spacing** is the process of placing spaces between the letters of words.

Too much space between words, on the other hand, produces a large white space called a **lake.** If too much spacing between words continues for several lines, white streaks called **rivers** may appear.

Fig. 3-24. Lakes and rivers produced by too much spacing between words

Unless there is a definite reason for letter-spacing, it should be avoided because it may cause the line to look stretched out or distorted. Letter-spacing, in addition to justification purposes, is also useful when letters or words are adapted to assume a particular shape or to create a desired typographical effect. NEVER letter space lowercase words.

When lines of type are letter-spaced, the spaces between words must also be increased. THIS LINE OF TYPE IS LETTER-SPACED WITH 1 POINT SPACES AND WITH 3 POINT SPACES ADDED BETWEEN THE WORDS. Without proportionately increasing the space between the words, the letters run together. Letter-spacing that is too wide causes the individual letters of a word to be separated from the other letters.

If the line of type is to be centered in the composing stick, an equal amount of spacing material must be placed on each side of the type. When justifying or centering type, keep the small spaces on the inside of the line or next to the type characters, Fig. 3-25.

Each line of type should be justified before the next line of type is started. Before

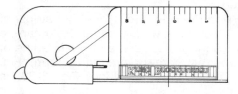

Fig. 3-25. A line of type that is centered in the composing stick

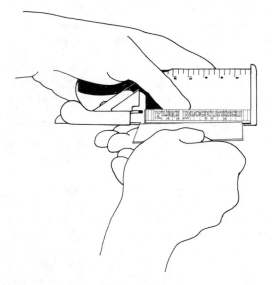

Fig. 3-26. Place a lead on top of the completed line before starting the next line

Fig. 3-28. Mitering machine

Fig. 3-29. A galley is used to store type forms

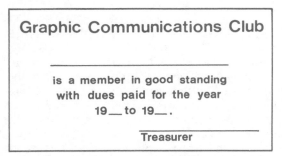

Graphic Communications Club

is a member in good standing with dues paid for the year 19__ to 19__ .

Treasurer

Fig. 3-27. Rule can be used to print lines and borders

starting the next line, place a lead in the composing stick that is equal in length to the measure being set, Fig. 3-26. If more than two points are desired between the lines of type, more than one lead may be inserted.

Printer's rule are type-high strips of metal which print on the paper. Rule can be set in type forms to print as lines in a line of type and as borders around a form, Fig. 3-27. The mitering machine, Fig. 3-28, is used to straight-shave or miter the rule at different angles. Rule that is used as a

border around a type form should be mitered at 45° angles on both ends.

For ease of handling, do not fill the composing stick more than three-quarters full of type. When the last line of type has been set and justified, place a slug in the composing stick. The **type form** is now removed from the composing stick and tied for proofing.

TYING A TYPE FORM

A **galley,** Fig. 3-29, is used for the storage and transporting of type forms. Place the galley on the slanted work surface of the type bank with the open end to one side.

Place the composing stick in the galley. Carefully slide the form from the composing stick onto the galley by pinching the lines of type between the thumbs and index fingers. The third fingers are used to hold the type from falling out the ends of the lines, Fig. 3-30. Slide the form into the lower corner

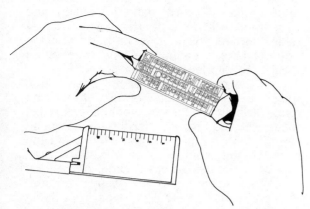

Fig. 3-30. Slide the type form from the composing stick onto the galley

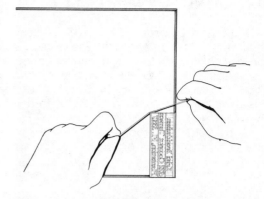

Fig. 3-32. Start the string in the exposed corner

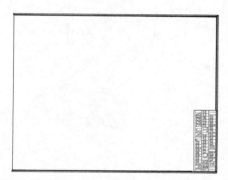

Fig. 3-31. Position the form in the corner of the galley

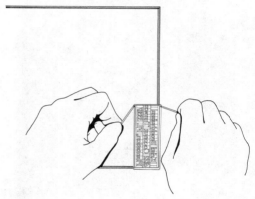

Fig. 3-33. Overlap the string end with the first winding

of the galley so that the leads and slugs run parallel to the bottom of the galley with the nicks toward the open end, Fig. 3-31.

Cut a piece of string that is long enough to go around the type form four or five times. Start the string in the exposed corner, and wind it clockwise around the form, Fig. 3-32. The first winding should overlap the beginning end, thereby binding the string in position, Fig. 3-33. Continue to wind the string around the type form. Tuck the end of the string under the windings in the open corner with a **makeup rule,** Fig. 3-34.

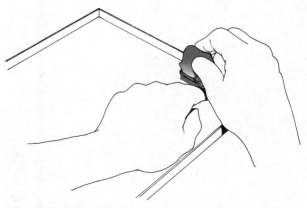

Fig. 3-34. Use the makeup rule to tuck the end of the string under the windings

PROOFING A TYPE FORM

The **proof press,** Fig. 3-35, is used to pull proofs of composed type forms. The proof is read so the form can be checked for errors in typesetting. The **brayer,** Fig. 3-36, is an ink roller on the proof press that inks the printing surface of relief forms for proofing.

To "pull" a proof, place the galley on the bed of the proof press at a slight angle.

The open end of the galley should be toward the cylinder. In this slanted position, the type form will be supported by two galley sides as the cylinder is passed over the form, thus preventing the type from being pushed off its feet.

If the proof press has not been inked, place a small quantity of ink on the ink plate. Distribute the ink evenly over the ink plate with the brayer. After the ink has been distributed, ink the type form by rolling the brayer lightly over the type, Fig. 3-37. Start the brayer at the exposed corner of the form and push toward the two galley-supported sides. This will prevent the type from being pushed off its feet. The feet of the brayer should be pointing up to prevent damaging

Fig. 3-35. The proof press is used to proof relief forms

Fig. 3-36. The brayer is used to ink relief forms for proofing

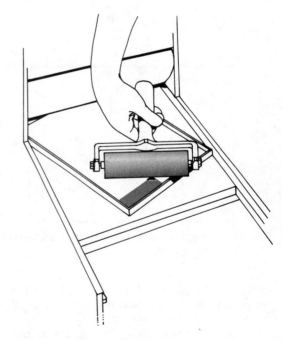

Fig. 3-37. Ink the type form to be proofed

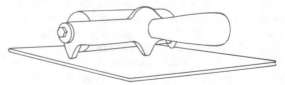

Fig. 3-38. Place the brayer on its feet

the type. Replace the brayer on the ink plate so that it rests on its feet, Fig. 3-38. This keeps the brayer roller from sticking to the ink plate and becoming flat.

After the form has been inked carefully, place one sheet of proof paper on the form, Fig. 3-39. Roll the cylinder over the form once to transfer the ink to the paper. Carefully lift the paper from the form and inspect the proof to be sure it is clear and legible. Before moving the galley from the proof press, clean the type with a cloth pad moistened with solvent to remove the ink.

Safety Note

Cloths that contain solvent and ink should be placed in metal safety cans.

Replace the galley on the slanted surface of the type bank. Carefully read the proof, checking it against the original copy. Errors are marked on the proof copy by using symbols called **proof marks**, Fig. 3-40. The proof marks are usually placed in the margin either on the right or left side of the error. A line may be drawn from the proof mark to the specific location of the error, Fig. 3-41.

Most corrections can be made with the type form in the galley. If a letter is to be

∧	Make indicated correction in margin
stet	Retain crossed out letter or word
√√√	Unevenly spaced
no ¶	No paragraph
¶	Make paragraph
tr	Transpose letters or words indicated
ᵭ	Delete
¢	Line through cap means lower case
9	Upside down, reverse
⊃	Close up, no space
#	Insert space here
⊏	Move to the left
⊐	Move to the right
sp	Spell out
w.f.	Wrong font
Qu?	Question, is this right?
l.c.	Put in lower case
s.c.	Put in small capitals
caps.	Put in capitals
ital.	Change to italic
≡	Beneath letter or word means caps
—	Beneath letter or word means italics
⌐	Insert comma
⊙	Insert period
bf	Bold face type

Fig. 3-40. Sample proof marks and their meanings

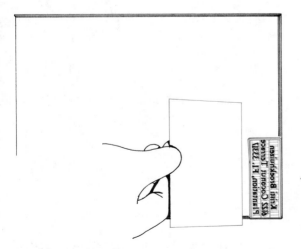

Fig. 3-39. Place one sheet of paper on the inked relief form

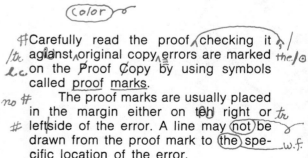

Fig. 3-41. Paragraph that has been marked with proof marks

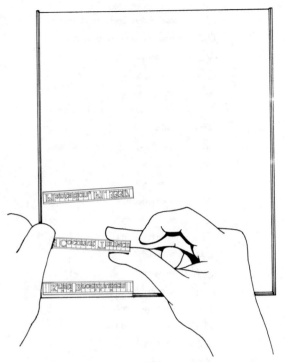

Fig. 3-42. Separate the line of type containing the error

replaced by a letter of equal width, carefully remove the letter and insert the correct letter. If a letter or space is to be replaced by a letter or space that is not the same width, the line of type should be returned to the composing stick.

Locate and separate the line of type containing the error from the rest of the form. Additional slugs must be inserted where the form is separated to hold the lines in place, Fig. 3-42. Return the line to be corrected to the composing stick with the nicks of the type pointing up, and make the necessary corrections, Fig. 3-43. The composing stick line length must be exactly the same as the length of the line that is being corrected.

After making the necessary corrections, return the line to the galley and place it in its proper position in the type form. Remove the additional slugs that were used when separating the form. This can easily be done by tipping up the slugs from the exposed end of the form, Fig. 3-44. Tie the form with

Fig. 3-44. Remove the slugs that were added when the line to be corrected was taken out of the type form

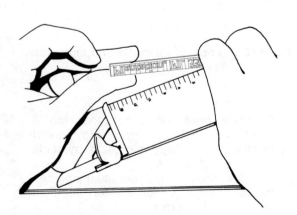

Fig. 3-43. Place the line of type to be corrected into the composing stick

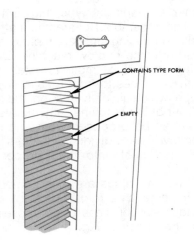

CONTAINS TYPE FORM

EMPTY

Fig. 3-45. Storage of galleys in the galley rack of the imposing table

string, and pull another proof. Check the second proof for errors.

If the type form is to be stored for future use, place the galley in the galley rack with the open end out. This indicates that there is a type form on the galley. When the galley is empty, it should be placed in the galley rack upside down with the open end inward, Fig. 3-45.

UNIT 4 — TERMS FOR DISCUSSION AND REVIEW

California Job Case	demon characters
lay of the case	ligature
symbol	composing stick
capital letters	leads
uppercase letters	slugs
lowercase letters	nick
alphabetical order	justification
frequency of use	spacing-in
dirty	spacing-out
clean	lakes
spaces	rivers
quads	letter-spacing
type fonts	type bank
news case	centering
double-cap case	printer's rule
triple case	galley
quadruple case	makeup rule
em quad	proof press
2 em quad	brayer
3 em quad	proof marks
en quad	
3 em space	
4 em space	
5 em space	
hair space	
nut quad	
mutton quad	

UNIT 5

IMAGE GENERATION BY MACHINE-SET TYPE

The composition and distribution of hand-set foundry type is a slow and expensive operation. Most volume producers of typesetting use machines. Without the use of machine-set type, many of our newspapers, magazines, and books could not be produced.

LUDLOW

The Ludlow machine is primarily used for producing display lines of type where large type sizes are needed. The composer, using the Ludlow system, assembles the character matrices (molds) into the desired form in a matrix composing stick, Fig. 3-46. The individual matrices are stored in matrix cabinets and are assembled in the same manner as hand-set type, Fig. 3-47.

The assembled character matrices and matrix composing stick are then inserted and locked into the Ludlow machine. During the casting operation, molten metal is forced into the matrices to form a solid line or **slug** of type which is delivered on the galley at the front of the machine. Any number of cast slugs may be produced from one matrices' assembly. The individual matrices are then distributed back into their proper storage cabinets.

The cast slugs are then composed into a completed type form. Leads or slugs are inserted between lines of composed type to form line spacing, Fig. 3-48.

Fig. 3-47. Ludlow matrix cabinets and casting machine

Fig. 3-46. Assembly of character matrices in a matrix composing stick

Fig. 3-48. Leading lines of Ludlow cast slugs

Fig. 3-49. Monomatic II keyboard unit

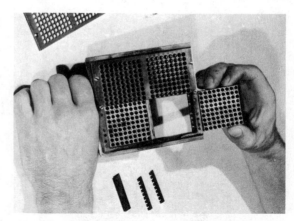

Fig. 3-51. Back view of matrix case showing changing of a font

Fig. 3-50. Monomatic II caster unit

MONOTYPE

The Monotype system of machine type-setting produces individual pieces of type. The Monotype system consists of a keyboard (Fig. 3-49) and a caster (Fig. 3-50).

The keyboard unit has 120 keys with an uppercase and a lowercase alphabet as well as numbers, punctuation marks, and symbols. Selected typefaces are placed in a matrix case and inserted into line position with the keyboard unit. The matrix case is divided into four quadrants, each quadrant containing one complete type font, Fig. 3-51. One or more of the four quadrants may be changed to combine the desired type fonts in the matrix case. By using the four shift keys on the keyboard, the operator can select characters from any one of the four quadrants in the matrix case. This makes it possible to mix typefaces without changing matrix cases.

As the keyboard operator types out the desired message and spacing, a perforated paper ribbon is produced. Small holes are perforated in the paper ribbon indicating the characters and spacing desired.

The paper ribbon is then placed on the caster unit which "reads" the perforated holes and casts the individual type characters. Complete lines of type, including spaces, are automatically produced. Spacing between lines of type is accomplished by inserting leads and slugs.

LINOTYPE AND INTERTYPE

The Linotype and Intertype machines both cast solid slugs of type matter. Because these machines operate in a similar manner,

Fig. 3-52. Linotype "Elektron Mixer" line-casting machine

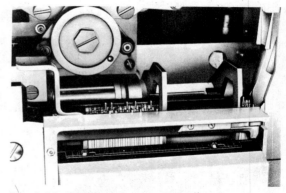

Fig. 3-53. The matrices are assembled into lines

Fig. 3-54. Assembled matrices and **spacebands**

the term **line-casting machine** will be used in the following explanation.

The line-casting machine, Fig. 3-52, uses a keyboard. As the keyboard operator depresses each key, a matrix, corresponding to the key character depressed, is released from the storage magazine at the top of the machine. As the matrix is released, it is picked up by a moving belt and then assembled into lines with the other keyed matrices, Fig. 3-53. The spaceband key is depressed to allow for spacing between words. This places a spaceband between the words, Fig. 3-54.

When the end of the composed line is reached, the line-casting machine automatically takes over. The composed line is automatically justified to the pre-set measure and is moved to the mold opening where molten metal is forced into the mold-assembled matrices to produce the cast slug. The slug is delivered to a galley on the front of the machine. After the casting is completed, the matrices are returned to and distributed into the storage magazines for additional use.

UNIT 5 — TERMS FOR DISCUSSION AND REVIEW

Ludlow	matrices
Linotype	casts
Intertype	quadrants
Monotype	font
keyboard unit	perforated paper ribbon
caster unit	spaceband
display lines	line-casting machine
slug	

Career Opportunities

Typesetter

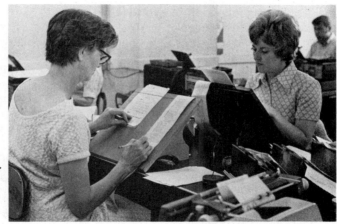

Proofreader

Editor

4 CHAPTER

COLD COMPOSITION

Cold composition is a classification of image generation methods. Only those image generation methods that do not use molten metal for casting the image can be classified as cold composition, Fig. 4-1.

The cold composition methods of image generation were developed for designers of printed communications who wanted.to present messages using images that could not be generated by hot composition. To present a message to a reader in a manner that results in some change in the reader's attitude, knowledge, personality, or actions requires complete freedom, flexibility, and use of creative expression in generating the images to be printed. Cold composition methods provided this freedom for the designer.

Each cold composition method of image generation has a unique system of storage and retrieval (previously described in Section III). The output of each method, as in all methods of image generation, is the **finished image** that has been prepared. Study Fig. 4-1 and try to identify the storage and retrieval systems employed by each of the cold composition methods of image generation.

The following descriptions of the various methods of cold composition for image generation are general in nature. Each method is presented in detail in Units 6 through 11.

LINOLEUM BLOCK

The linoleum block, like hand-set foundry type and machine-set type, is three-dimensional and was developed for the relief printing production process. Historically, the linoleum block was developed as designers found a need to present pictorial images that could not be cast by the hot composition methods.

Originally, wood blocks were carved and used. They were cut to the same height as the type characters (Fig. 4-2) so they could be used for printing. The design was drawn on the wood in reverse, and then those areas that were not to print were carved away, leaving the raised design surface. When completely carved, the **woodcut** was ready to be reproduced by relief printing.

Since wood was difficult to carve because of its hardness and grain structure, a thin layer of soft linoleum was adhered to a wood block and made type high. The soft linoleum permitted the carving of the design with much greater ease and efficiency.

TECHNICAL ILLUSTRATING

Sometimes a message is so specialized that the design (until created by an artist)

Fig. 4-1. Cold composition methods of image generation

does not exist. Before creating design images, artwork, or illustrations, the artist must have a complete understanding of the message. Only then can images be generated.

Technical illustrating permits the artist to express a great deal of creativity in communicating to the message receiver, Fig.

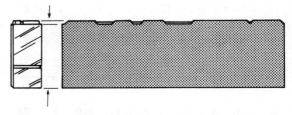

Fig. 4-2. Wood blocks and pieces of type are the same height

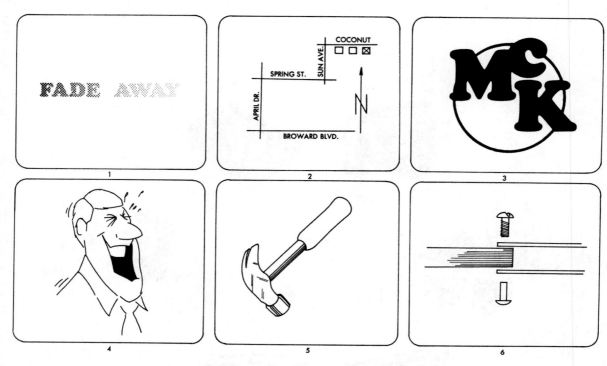

Fig. 4-3. Technical illustrating permits artistic creativity

4-3. As shown in this illustration, this type of image generation can be used to:
1. Create special lettering effects,
2. Describe the location of a city,
3. Identify or create a company's image,
4. Explain a situation or reaction,
5. Show the design of a manufactured product, or
6. Explain how to assemble components.

A variety of drawing instruments such as lettering guides, pencils, pens, charcoal sticks, water colors, and drafting tools is frequently used by the artist when generating images.

CLIP ART AND PREPRINTED TYPE

Clip art and preprinted type are designed and preprinted on sheets for the designer to select from and use. Then the design is cut out and pasted on the mechanical layout.

Clip art and preprinted type are prepared in a variety of designs that fit many different needs and situations, Fig. 4-4. They are attractive and easy to transfer to the mechanical layout. The wide variety available permits the less artistic person, who lacks the creative ability for better work, to prepare appealing layouts. Clip art and preprinted type may also be used as a substitute for creating original artwork when cost is a prohibitive factor.

STRIKE-ON

The cold composition method of strike-on makes use of a typewriter to generate the images. As each key is depressed on the keyboard, a corresponding lettered type bar is kicked up. The type bar in turn strikes a ribbon which is between the type bar and

Fig. 4-4. Clip-art encyclopedia

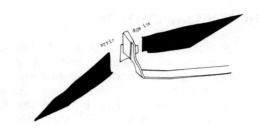
Fig. 4-5. Image generation by strike-on

the paper, Fig. 4-5. As the type bar strikes the ribbon, the ribbon is pressed against the paper, thus generating the character image on the paper.

Strike-on composition is commonly used for office work in the preparation of letters, stencils, memos, and other documents. Several copies may be generated at one typing by placing carbon paper between the sheets of paper that are placed in the typewriter.

Because typewriters are generally readily available and because the typing operation (to experienced typists) can be performed very rapidly, the cost of strike-on composition is very low. However, the variety of typefaces is usually limited, unless a typewriter such as the IBM "Selectric" is used. The IBM "Selectric" uses interchangeable type font elements, thus permitting the intermixing of typefaces, Fig. 4-6.

Strike-on composition is limited in the type and size of image that can be generated. Because of machine design, large display lines of type cannot be generated by strike-on composition. Most typewriters are also limited to generating only the standard alphabetical letters, numbers, punctuation marks, and a few special characters, such as #, $, %, ¼, and ( ). However, there are typewriters specially designed for generating images that are commonly used in math and science, Fig. 4-7. Strike-on composition machines have also been developed that employ the use of an electronic mem-

Fig. 4-6. IBM "Selectric" typewriter elements

Fig. 4-7. Keyboard of a math typewriter

ory system, Fig. 4-8. As the message is keyboarded, it can be stored for future use. Some machines can be programmed to automatically type the copy from the memory system in any typing configuration that is desired.

PHOTOCOMPOSITION

Photocomposition is a cold composition method of image generation that produces both display and text copy. Most phototypesetting machines use a film negative type font with transparent letters and characters, Fig. 4-9. To create images other than letters, film type fonts with special symbols, designs, patterns, screen tints, and screen patterns are also available.

The type font is positioned between the exposure lamp and the sensitized film or paper of the phototypesetting machine. As the operator selects and exposes each letter, the light passes through the transparent area and is projected onto the sensitized paper or film. Many phototypesetting machines permit the operator to enlarge or reduce the size of the letter as well as create other special effects. The exposed paper is then developed, fixed, washed, and dried and is ready to be positioned on the mechanical layout.

Phototypesetting machines range in complexity from those that require hand selection of each letter by positioning the font negative to those that are highly automated. The most sophisticated are operated by a typewriter keyboard, Fig. 4-10. In some cases, phototypesetting machines have the capability of setting type ranging from 5 point through 24 point in as many as 2000

Fig. 4-8. IBM "Selectric" Composer with memory

Fig. 4-10. AlphaComp Direct Input Phototypesetter

Fig. 4-9. Photocomposition negative type font

interchangeable type fonts. Some photo-typesetting machines permit several fonts to be loaded into the machines at the same time so that typefaces or sizes may be readily intermixed. The use of phototypesetting machines makes it possible to automatically set copy that is flush right, flush left, centered, or justified.

Recent statistics indicate that photo-composition is rapidly overtaking machine-setting as a method of generating images. One of the primary reasons for this is the industry's movement away from relief printing and toward offset printing.

CONTINUOUS TONE PHOTOGRAPHY

Continuous tone photography is the only image generation method that can produce images that are truly realistic. Continuous tone photography captures the likeness of the object or subject being photographed in terms of shape, size, color, and detail. This is accomplished by the produc-

Fig. 4-11. Continuous tone photography makes it possible to record image of event as it takes place

tion of an image on light-sensitive film. The light that is reflected from the object being photographed passes through the camera lens and registers the image likeness on the film. This produces (when the film has been developed) a **negative image.** When the negative is projected onto a light-sensitive paper, a **positive print** is produced.

Continuous tone photography will generate images of persons, buildings, actual events, or any other existing subject, Fig. 4-11. This method of image generation makes it possible to present photographic illustrations in printed messages.

IMAGE GENERATION BY LINOLEUM BLOCK

The design used for linoleum block printing should be limited to solid areas and heavy lines. Light lines are not suitable for reproduction by linoleum blocks because they break off easily under the pressure of printing. For each color in the design, a separate linoleum block must be carved. For example, when a three-color design is printed, three linoleum blocks must be carved, one for each color area.

TRANSFERRING DESIGN TO BLOCK

The design is placed on the linoleum block in reverse since it is a relief printing character. One method of transferring the design to the linoleum block is by using carbon paper. Place the carbon paper, carbon side down, on the block surface, and position the original artwork face down on top of the carbon paper. Tape the carbon paper and the original design to the block. Trace over the back of the original design to transfer the design in reverse onto the block, Fig. 4-12.

Another technique is to draw the design with a soft-lead pencil, and place it face down directly on the block surface. Rubbing the back of the original with a stylus will cause some of the lead to be transferred to the linoleum block surface, Fig. 4-13.

CARVING THE LINOLEUM BLOCK

The design may be carved either as a positive image or as a negative image, Fig. 4-14. The positive printing block is carved so the design area is left raised. In this case, the design will print, and there will be no background. The negative printing block allows the background to print and form the design area, Fig. 4-15.

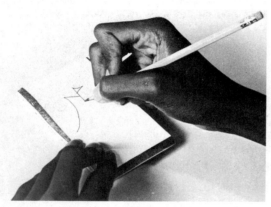

Fig. 4-12. Trace over the back of the design with carbon paper face down between the design and the block

Fig. 4-14. Linoleum blocks may be carved with a positive or a negative image

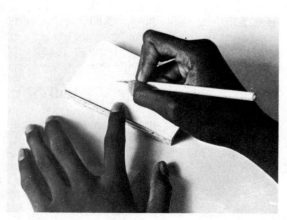

Fig. 4-13. Rub the back of the soft-lead pencil design with a stylus

Fig. 4-15. Positive and negative linoleum block prints

A set of linoleum block carving tools appears in Fig. 4-16. The blades can be interchanged in the same handle as needed. The assortment of cutting blades in Fig. 4-17 includes (1) a V-shaped veining tool, (2) a V-shaped gouge, (3) a large liner, (4) a U-shaped gouge, (5) a large gouge, and (6) a knife blade.

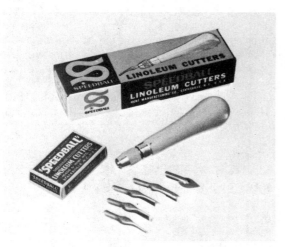

Fig. 4-16. Linoleum block carving tools

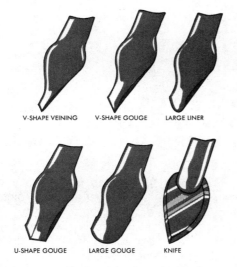

V-SHAPE VEINING   V-SHAPE GOUGE   LARGE LINER

U-SHAPE GOUGE   LARGE GOUGE   KNIFE

Fig. 4-17. Linoleum block carving blades with cutting edges

A bench hook is used to hold the block while the nonprinting areas are being carved away. Begin carving the block by outlining the printing design with the veining tool, Fig. 4-18. Whenever possible, push the cutting blade away from the printing image.

Safety Note

The cutting tool should always be pushed away from your hand.

The knife blade may also be used to outline the design area. Hold the knife blade at a slight angle to bevel the printing surface outward to the linoleum base, Fig. 4-19. This will give added support to the printing surface and reduce break-down of the printing edges during production.

After the entire design has been outlined, begin to remove the nonprinting areas with a larger cutting tool. The nonprinting areas should be removed to a depth of at least $\frac{1}{16}$" (1.6 mm).

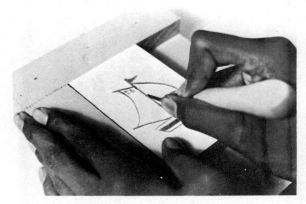

Fig. 4-18. Outline the design area with a veining tool

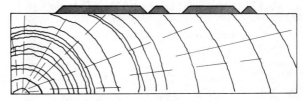

Fig. 4-19. Bevel the linoleum block from the printing surface to the base

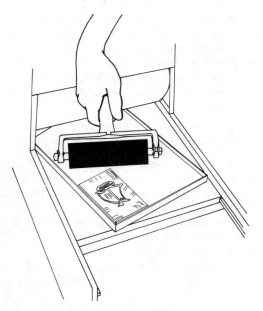

Fig. 4-20. Inking the linoleum block for proofing

Fig. 4-21. Unwanted printing areas must be carved away

PROOFING THE LINOLEUM BLOCK

When the carving has been completed, the block may be proofed by placing it on a galley and using the proof press. The block should be placed in the corner of the galley to give support to two sides. The galley, when placed on the bed of the proof press, should be at a slight angle, with the

open end toward the cylinder. Use the brayer to ink the block surface by rolling it gently over the carved design from the exposed corner toward the corner that is supported by the galley sides, Fig. 4-20. Be sure the feet of the brayer are up to prevent accidentally damaging the block surface. After inking the block, return the brayer to the ink plate so that it stands on its feet. This prevents the roller from sticking and becoming flat. Next place one sheet of paper on the inked surface, and pass the cylinder over the paper and block to transfer the image to the paper. Carefully remove the paper and inspect the print. Any unwanted areas that appear on the proof must be carved away with the cutting tools, Fig. 4-21. When a satisfactory proof is obtained, the linoleum block is ready for printing.

UNIT 6 — TERMS FOR DISCUSSION AND REVIEW

reverse
positive printing
background
design
negative printing
large liner

large gouge
V-shaped veining tool
knife blade
U-shaped gouge
V-shaped gouge
bench hook

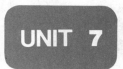

UNIT 7

IMAGE GENERATION BY TECHNICAL ILLUSTRATING

Technical illustrating is generally considered to be the generation of pictorial images using drawing and lettering techniques. Technical illustrating can be divided into the two areas of (1) **freehand** drawing and (2) **mechanical** drawing.

The generation of images by freehand drawing permits complete freedom in the preparation of the images. A certain amount of artistic skill, a sense of good line weight, proportion, balance, shape, harmony, and a creative imagination are necessary for drawing freehand. Mechanical drawing, on the other hand, is governed by the techniques of drafting and requires a working knowledge of orthographic projection, pictorial and schematic drawings, as well as the basic skills in using drafting tools and equipment.

Images generated by technical illustrating are generally used to supplement text material. The drawings attract the attention of the message reader, pictorially describe a situation, technical point, reaction, or expression, and clarify or emphasize the text material.

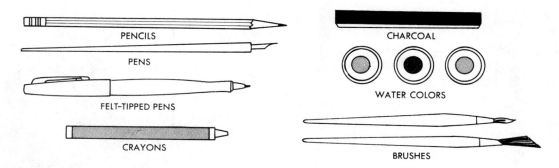

Fig. 4-22. Sampling of freehand drawing materials and tools

FREEHAND DRAWING

Freehand drawings may be prepared with a wide variety of materials and tools such as pencils, ink pens, felt-tip pens, crayons, charcoal sticks, and water or oil colors and brushes, Fig. 4-22. Many of the illustrations presented in this textbook were prepared by an artist using freehand drawing techniques.

The artist preparing freehand illustrations can only create an appropriate image after gaining a full understanding of the idea to be portrayed. In the case of this textbook, the author often prepared very rough sketches for the artist to refine, Fig. 4-23. In some instances, the author simply presented a verbal sketch and allowed the artist to apply creative, artistic skills. To fully understand the material to be illustrated, the artist usually read the manuscript so that an image appropriate to the text material could be prepared.

Several rough pencil sketches were then made by the artist to explore the possible ways of illustrating the text material, Fig. 4-24. When a particular sketch looked promising, it was redrawn in pencil, this time with more regard for shape detail, balance, line weight, proportion and impact. This drawing was viewed by the author for

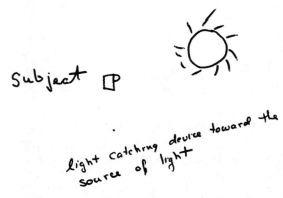

Fig. 4-23. Rough sketch prepared by author

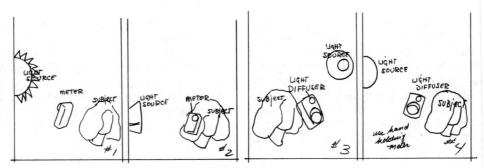

Fig. 4-24. Artist's exploratory sketches

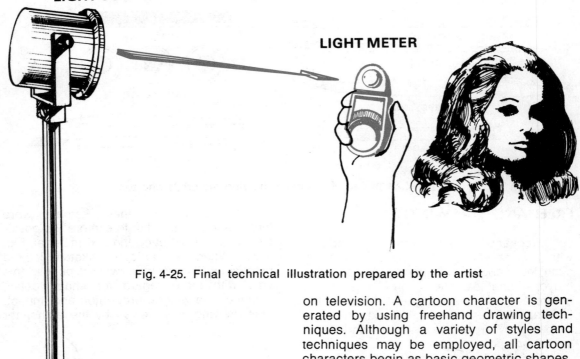

Fig. 4-25. Final technical illustration prepared by the artist

approval or any necessary changes. The final image was then prepared and inked by the artist, Fig. 4-25.

CREATING CARTOON CHARACTERS

Cartoons are often used in graphic communications to attract the readers' attention and to evoke a sense of amusement and comedy. They appear in newspapers, magazines, books, in movie theaters, and on television. A cartoon character is generated by using freehand drawing techniques. Although a variety of styles and techniques may be employed, all cartoon characters begin as basic geometric shapes.

A cartoon face is drawn by following four simple steps:

1. Begin by drawing any kind of semi-round enclosure, Fig. 4-26. The fact that the enclosure is crooked, lopsided or irregularly shaped does not matter.
2. Next, draw in a nose somewhere close to the proper area.
3. Draw the eyes as dots, slits, or angular lines, depending upon the type of character being created.

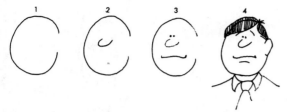

Fig. 4-26. Four steps in drawing a cartoon face

Fig. 4-28. Drawing a full-bodied cartoon character from a triangular shape

Fig. 4-27. Many cartoon faces may be created from the same basic geometric shape

Fig. 4-29. Several characters may be created from the same basic geometric shape

Add the mouth to complete the basic facial expression.

4. Add ears, hair, forehead wrinkles, shoulders, and a hat or tie to complete the cartoon face.

Working from the same basic, semi-round enclosure, you can create a variety of cartoon faces by simply changing the placement of the nose or the shape of the eyes, mouth, or ears, Fig. 4-27.

The full-bodied cartoon character also begins as a basic geometric shape such as a triangle, Fig. 4-28. With the addition of more triangles and perhaps an oval for the head, the cartoon figure develops into a man. A variety of characters may be created by working from the same basic geometric shape. In Fig. 4-29, several characters have been made by simply changing the type of clothing, the size and shape of the head, the

Fig. 4-30. The oval method of drawing a cartoon character

Fig. 4-31. Arrangement of the ovals produces different character positions

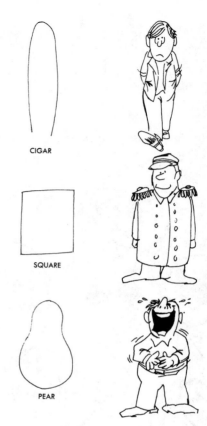

CIGAR

SQUARE

PEAR

Fig. 4-32. Any shape can be the basis for a cartoon character

Fig. 4-33. Separate drawings are prepared for each movement when creating animated cartoons

facial expressions, and the positions of the arms and legs.

Using the simple, oval method, the artist may show a cartoon character in many different positions. This method is generally prepared as an underdrawing which serves only as a skeleton.

Begin by drawing any kind of head oval. Draw a smaller oval for the neck, and then draw the body and arm ovals in their relative positions. Add the leg and foot ovals to complete the basic structure of the cartoon character, Fig. 4-30.

By simply changing the position and perhaps the shape of the ovals, the cartoon character can assume a variety of positions, Fig. 4-31. The addition of facial features and clothing creates many different cartoon characters.

The possibilities of preparing cartoon characters are endless. Almost any geometric shape may be turned into a cartoon character. What type of characters can you draw from a cigar shape, a square or pear shape, Fig. 4-32?

Animated cartoons (those that show movement) also begin as simple geometric shapes. After being created, the basic character may be "set in motion." For each movement, a separate drawing must be prepared, Fig. 4-33. The number of separate drawings depends on the speed of the desired movement. If the movement is to be very sharp and abrupt, only a few drawings may be required. If the movement is to be very slow and gradual, more separate drawings are necessary. By fanning (flipping) the upper right-hand corners page 97 to page 131, you will see an example of an animation prepared with separate, still drawings to show movement.*

When preparing a set of drawings for animation, the artist must use extreme care so that each image shows detail that is consistent with the images in other drawings of the sequence. The preparation of drawings for animation requires a great deal of artistic skill.

Once the drawings have been prepared, they are photographed on movie film. The resulting movie permits the individual drawings to be viewed in rapid succession, thereby bringing the character to life.

MECHANICAL DRAWING

Mechanical drawing is the phase of technical illustrating that is governed by drafting techniques. It is generally employed when special consideration must be given to size, shape, and detail.

The three basic types of mechanical drawings are (1) orthographic projection, (2) pictorial, and (3) schematic, Fig. 4-34.

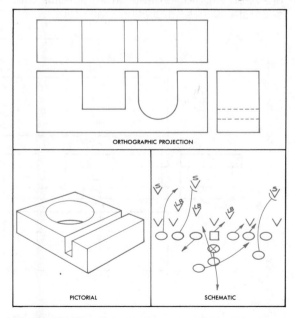

ORTHOGRAPHIC PROJECTION

PICTORIAL

SCHEMATIC

Fig. 4-34. The three basic types of mechanical drawings

---

*"Tony the Tiger" is a registered trademark of Kellogg Company. Animation is provided by Quartet Films, Inc. and Leo Burnett Company.

These three types of drawings may also be prepared by using freehand tools and techniques; however, the generated image may not be an accurate representation of the object being drawn.

To prepare any mechanical drawing, a basic understanding of the drafting tools and techniques is required. Because of this, a review of Unit 3 may be in order. All drawing should first be done very lightly in pencil. After the drawing has been completed and verified for correctness, the object lines may be darkened or inked if desired.

ORTHOGRAPHIC PROJECTIONS

Orthographic projection drawings are usually used when accurate details and dimensions must be shown. This type of drawing is generally prepared as a plan that is followed when objects are to be constructed. For this reason, orthographic projections are also referred to as **working drawings**.

Orthographic projection drawings are prepared in an orderly arrangement with separate views depicting the top, front,

bottom, left and right sides, and back of an object, Fig. 4-35. Only those views, however, that are required to pictorially present the object should be included in the drawing. Often two views (such as the top and bottom, or the front and back, or the right and left sides) are identical and therefore need not be drawn twice. On the other hand, some objects require that almost every view be drawn.

The front view should always be included in an orthographic projection drawing. Additional drawings needed are only those views that are necessary to clearly show the size and shape of the object. When selecting the views of an object, draw those views that will contain the least number of hidden lines. **Hidden lines** are lines that are present but not visible in a particular view and are represented on the drawing by a series of short dashes, Fig. 4-36.

— — — — — — — — — — — — — —

HIDDEN LINE

Fig. 4-36. Hidden lines are used to indicate lines that are not visible

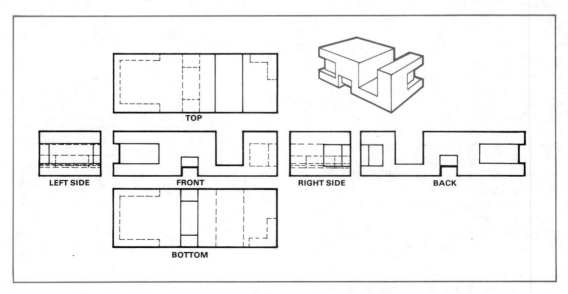

Fig. 4-35. Orthographic projections show each view of the object drawn separately

As an example, when an orthographic projection of the object shown in Fig. 4-37 is drawn, only two views are necessary. Additional views do not provide more detail in regard to shape and size. Although the left side and bottom views show thickness, as does the top view, they also contain hidden lines. Because of this, the top view is more appropriate for clearly depicting the object. The back and right side views are duplications of other views and therefore are unnecessary.

PICTORIAL DRAWINGS

Pictorial drawings generally show three adjacent faces of an object in one view. As the name implies, a pictorial drawing presents an object in a manner similar to a photograph. Pictorial drawings are commonly used in advertising literature such as product brochures, pamphlets, and the telephone book yellow pages. They are also used in repair and service manuals, parts catalogs, and textbooks. As shown in Fig. 4-38, the three most frequently prepared types of pictorial drawings are (1) **isometric,** (2) **perspective,** and (3) **oblique.**

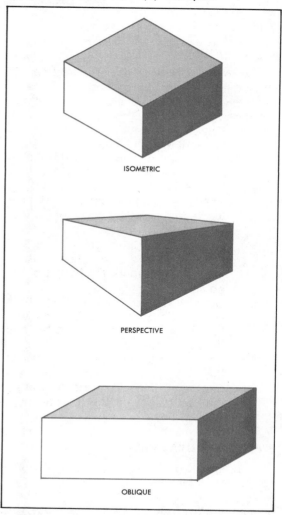

Fig. 4-38. The three most frequently prepared pictorial drawings

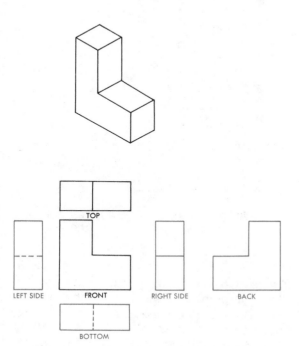

Fig. 4-37. Draw only those views that are necessary

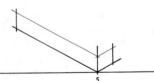
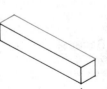

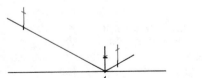

Fig. 4-39. How to prepare an isometric drawing

ISOMETRIC DRAWINGS

Isometric drawings are prepared on 30° angles to the horizon or horizontal plane. Refer to Fig. 4-39 for illustrations of the following six steps:

1. Establish the origin point on the horizontal plane line.
2. Draw the left and right isometric lines as well as the vertical axis line.
3. On the isometric axis lines and the vertical axis line, measure and mark the length, width, and height of the object being drawn.
4. Draw vertical lines on the left and right isometric axis lines. Also, measure and mark the height of the object.
5. Draw lines to connect the three vertical lines at the points marked, to show the length, width, and height of the object.
6. To complete the other two sides of the top of the object, draw the necessary lines from the previously marked height on the left and right vertical lines.

PERSPECTIVE DRAWINGS

Perspective drawings pictorially describe an object as it appears to the eye. That is, the most distant points appear smaller than those closest to the observer, although all points may actually be the same

Fig. 4-40. A perspective drawing describes the object as it is seen by the eye

dimension, Fig. 4-40. The two most commonly used types of perspective drawings are the **one-point** and the **two-point** drawings.

One-point perspective. The one-point perspective drawing is commonly used by architects to pictorially represent the interior of rooms. In the one-point perspective drawing, all lines that are parallel will converge at one point. For example, when looking straight down a railroad track or highway, you will notice that the rails and sides of the

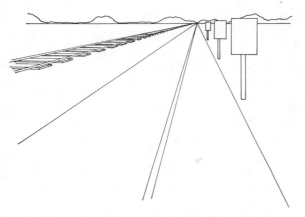

Fig. 4-41. All lines in a one-point perspective converge at one point

highway appear to come together as the distance becomes greater until they finally converge at one point, Fig. 4-41. To prepare a simple one-point perspective drawing, proceed as follows, using Fig. 4-42 as a guide:

1. Draw a light horizontal line. This line represents the **horizon line** (HL) or level of the eye when you view the object to be drawn.
2. Slightly below the horizon line, lightly draw the front view of the object.
3. Locate and mark the **center of vision** (CV) on the horizon line. The center-of-vision point may be posi-

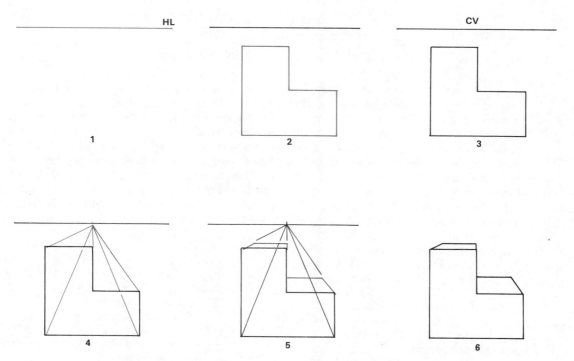

Fig. 4-42. How to draw a one-point perspective

102

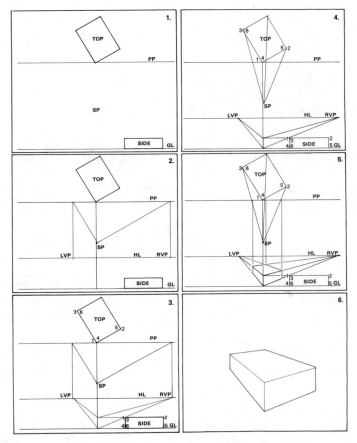

Fig. 4-43. How to draw a two-point perspective

tioned at any point on the horizon line. Its placement, however, will determine the outcome of the final drawing. If the object is being viewed straight on, the center-of-vision point should be centered behind the front view.

4. From all the corners of the front view, draw light lines extending to and converging at the center-of-vision point.

5. On the lines extending to the center of vision, locate the back of the object being drawn. Draw in the back object line(s) lightly. Be sure the line is drawn at the proper angle.

6. Darken the object lines after verifying the drawing for accuracy.

Two-point perspective. The two-point perspective drawing is used by architects to show how the elevations of buildings will appear when the structure is completed. It is called a "two-point perspective" because all lines that are drawn converge at two vanishing points. The preparation of a two-point perspective drawing is slightly more complicated than that for a one-point perspective drawing. To prepare a two-point perspective drawing, proceed as follows, using Fig. 4-43 as a guide:

1. On a sheet of paper, draw the top view of the object near the top and slightly to the left of center. This view may be drawn at any angle. A 30° angle is used in Fig. 4-43.

In the lower left or right corner of the sheet, draw the side view of the object. The side view will rest on the **ground line (GL)**.

Draw a light horizontal line to represent the **picture plane** (PP). The picture plane can be visualized as a plate glass window between you (the viewer) and the object. As you look at the object through the picture plane, you see the object as if it were drawn on the glass. For ease of construction, the picture plane line in these drawings is shown touching the corner of the top view of the object.

Locate, mark, and label the **station point** (SP). The station point is the point from which you wish to view the object. Draw a light vertical line downward from the corner of the top view that touches the picture plane line. The station point can be located at anyplace on the vertical line.

2. Draw the **horizon line** (HL). This line determines the elevation from which the object is viewed. A horizon line drawn above the side view will give you a view looking down on top of the object. This is the case in Fig. 4-43. If the horizon line is drawn through or below the side view, it will give a ground-level view or a view from underneath the object.

Locate the **right** and **left vanishing points** (RVP and LVP) by extending lines (that are parallel to the sides of the top view) from the station point until they touch the picture plane line. From the points where the extended lines touch the picture plane line, draw perpendicular lines down to the horizon line. The vanishing points represent the points where your line of sight would eventually converge.

3. At this time it would be helpful to label, by number, the corners of the object being drawn. The numbers that appear outside the top and side views represent the corners that are visible. The numbers that appear inside the top and side views represent those corners that are not visible.

4. Draw a light vertical line from corner 1,4 of the top view to intersect with the ground line. By drawing light horizontal lines from points 1 and 4 on the side view, the true height of the front perspective corner can be determined. Now extend light lines to both the left and right vanishing points from the top and bottom of this line.

From the station point, extend light lines, visual rays, to each of the four corners in the top view of the object.

5. From the point that the visual rays cross the picture plane, drop vertical lines down to the ground line. This will locate the corners of the object.

As you will notice, the lines extended from the true height to the vanishing points and the lines dropped from the junction of the visual rays and picture plane lines form the two sides of the object. The top of the object becomes visible when lines from the points 2 and 3 are extended to the opposite vanishing points.

6. After the drawing has been verified for completeness and accuracy, darken the object lines.

OBLIQUE DRAWINGS

The oblique drawing is prepared in a similar manner to that used for the preparation of an isometric drawing. The difference, however, is that the oblique drawing is prepared with one edge of the object on the horizontal plane line, Fig. 4-44. The view that represents the side of the object is drawn at an angle which may vary from 0° to 90°. The angle, however, is usually 30°, 45° or 60°. Once established, the angle must be maintained when drawing object lines that are parallel to one another.

Of the three types of pictorial drawings, the isometric is the most commonly prepared. It is easier to prepare than the perspective, and the results are more realistic when compared to an oblique drawing of the same object.

SCHEMATIC DRAWINGS

Schematic drawings, sometimes referred to as **network** or **system drawings**, are diagrams in which special symbols are used to describe electrical circuits, transportation systems, organizational structures, personnel movement, and flow patterns tracing the development of a product. Schematic drawings are not drawn to scale, but are prepared simply as a tool that permits the reader to understand the relationship of all components in the complete system or plan of action. Electrical schematics are prepared, for example, so that an entire circuit may be analyzed. The schematic not only serves as a plan, but for troubleshooting and repair reference as well.

Electrical schematics generally show electrical components within the circuit. These components are represented by standardized symbols, Fig. 4-45. When the

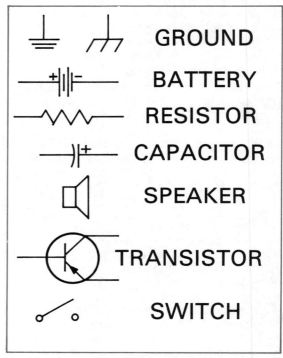

Fig. 4-45. Electrical components have standardized symbols

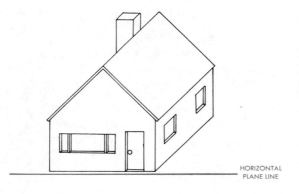

Fig. 4-44. The front view of an oblique drawing is on the horizontal plane line

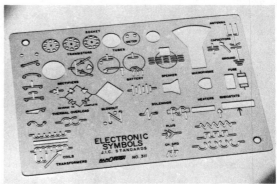

Fig. 4-46. Electronic symbol template

schematic is prepared, the artist often uses templates to trace the symbol on the drawing, Fig. 4-46. This eliminates the necessity of freehand drawing each electrical symbol that is required.

Schematic drawings are also used in planning and describing the relationships of

personnel movement for such activity as football plays, Fig. 4-47. Each member of the team, as well as those of the opposing team, is represented by a symbol. Arrows, lines, and arcs are employed to graphically illustrate the assignments of each player and the movement of the ball.

Organizational schematics are often used to show the structure of a club, school, business, or corporation. This type of schematic is generally prepared by drawing small rectangular areas to represent each of the positions of the organization. Within each rectangular area, the position title is lettered for ease of identification, Fig. 4-48. Connecting lines indicate the chain of command and seniority within the organization.

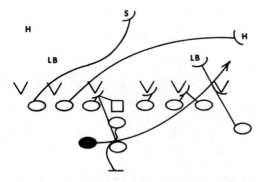

Fig. 4-47. A football play diagram is a type of schematic drawing

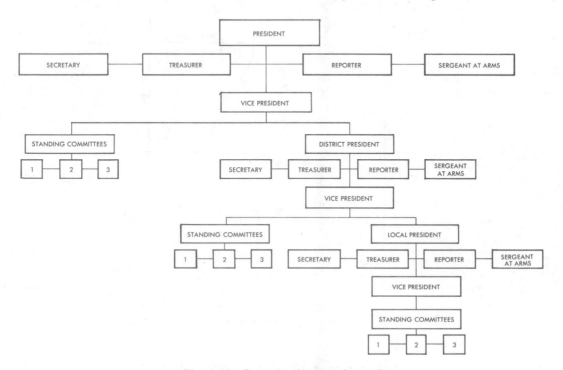

Fig. 4-48. Organizational schematic

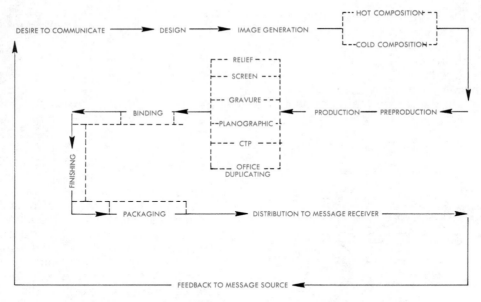

Fig. 4-49. Graphic communications manufacturing schematic (CTP refers to Continuous Tone Photography)

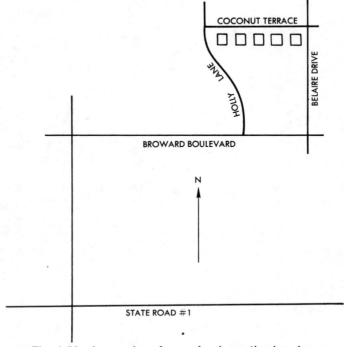

Fig. 4-50. A map is a form of schematic drawing

Schematic drawings can also graphically describe the flow of work through various developmental stages. This type of schematic is sometimes used as a **production plan**. Often, several alternative paths are available as in the case of the graphic communications industry, Fig. 4-49. The decision to follow one plan of action and not another is sometimes determined by special product features.

Maps that show possible routes of traffic flow are also a form of schematic drawing. Careful consideration must be given to the placement and direction of the streets, although they need not be drawn to scale, Fig. 4-50.

LETTERING

Lettering, as a phase of technical illustrating, can be accomplished by using freehand lettering techniques and mechanical lettering devices. Freehand lettering permits complete freedom in creating a lettering style and design and allows the artist to generate new lettering styles if needed. Lettering by freehand techniques is generally used to create a feeling of freedom, expression, and informality. This requires a certain amount of artistic skill.

Not only does the artist have complete design freedom, but he is also free to use a wide variety of hand lettering instruments, such as speedball pens, technical lettering pens, felt tipped pens, pencils, charcoal sticks, brushes, water colors, and oil paints, as well as crow quill pens and India ink, Fig. 4-51.

Lettering of mechanical drawings can be accomplished by free hand lettering techniques, but it requires accuracy and neatness. The appearance and usefulness of a carefully prepared mechanical drawing can be ruined by lettering that is carelessly prepared. Above all, the lettering must be legible and uniform.

Most lettering for mechanical drawings is done by the **single-stroke method**. This does not mean that the letters are made without lifting the pencil from the paper. Rather, the letters are made with several strokes. The width of the letters is uniform and equal in width to the pencil point. As a

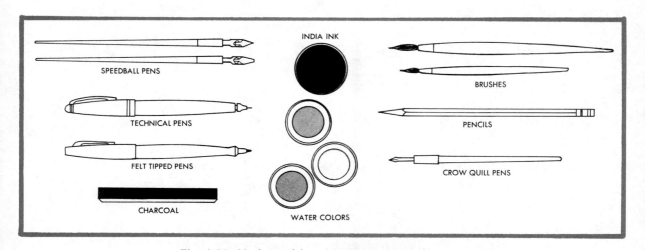

Fig. 4-51. Variety of hand lettering instruments

VERTICAL GOTHIC

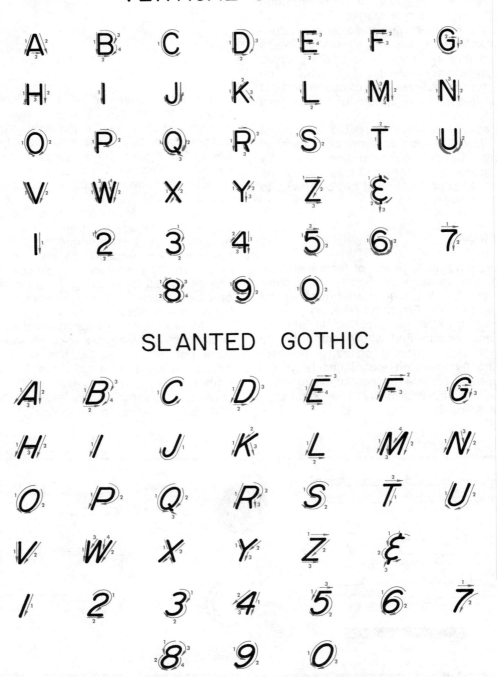

SLANTED GOTHIC

Fig. 4-52. Vertical and inclined lettering strokes for mechanical drawing

general rule, **vertical** or **inclined** lettering is used on mechanical drawings, Fig. 4-52.

Very light guidelines to form the top and bottom of the letters are drawn before the finished freehand lettering is done. Right-handed persons should begin lettering in the upper left-hand corner of the drawing. (Left-handed persons should begin in the upper right-hand corner.) This will prevent the drawing hand from resting on previously prepared lettering and will help eliminate letter-smudging. A clean sheet of paper may also be used to cover the drawing or lettering and thus eliminate smudges because of hand perspiration, Fig. 4-53.

Vertical, slanted, and curved strokes should be drawn with a steady, even finger movement, Fig. 4-54 (A). When horizontal lettering strokes are made, the whole hand is pivoted at the wrist while the fingers are also moved slightly to maintain the horizontal stroke, Fig. 4-54 (B). The pencil should be sharpened to a long conic point. The point is then rounded to prevent cutting the paper, Fig. 4-55. To maintain a good lettering point, it is recommended that the pencil

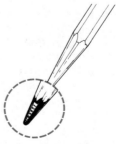

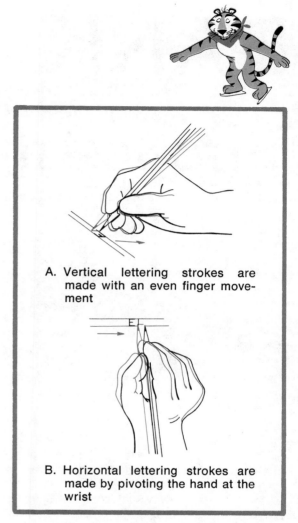

A. Vertical lettering strokes are made with an even finger movement

B. Horizontal lettering strokes are made by pivoting the hand at the wrist

Fig. 4-54. Lettering motion

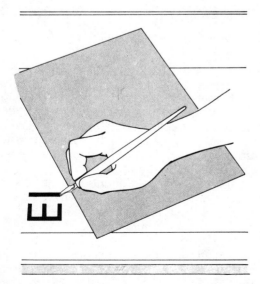

Fig. 4-53. Protect the drawing with a clean sheet of paper

Fig. 4-55. A rounded conical point is used for lettering

BANK VAULT

Fig. 4-56. The spacing between letters should appear equal

THEOWORLD

Fig. 4-57. The letter O is used as a word space

Fig. 4-58. Wrico lettering guide

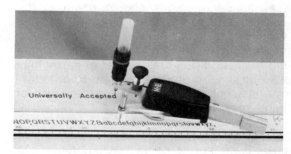

Fig. 4-59. Leroy lettering instrument

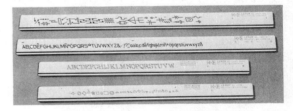

Fig. 4-60. Leroy lettering templates

be rotated frequently. Use a firm, uniform pressure to create freehand lettering.

The artist arranges the spacing between letters in a word by visual adjustment (eye appeal), since there is no prescribed rule for spacing. The space allowed, however, is determined by the shape of the letter. Letters that have straight sides, such as the N and K, must be spread apart to avoid tightness. On the other hand, letters such as the L and T are shaped so that they may actually overlap and still produce good spacing. However, the areas between letters in the word should **appear** approximately equal, Fig. 4-56.

The spacing between words should show a clear separation. As a rule of thumb, the width of the letter ''O'' is allowed between words, Fig. 4-57.

Mechanical devices such as lettering templates are also available to generate handlettered images. The template is placed firmly against the edge of the T-square, and a special pen is used to trace the letter shape, Fig. 4-58.

Another type of lettering device is a template, with a metal stylus that traces the images. As the artist uses the metal stylus to trace the template image, a pen generates the same image on the paper, Fig. 4-59. This type of lettering device usually allows the artist to change the lettering style from vertical to inclined by adjusting the relative position between the stylus and the pen. The same template, therefore, may be used to generate both types of lettering. Additional templates are also available that permit the generation of a variety of letterfaces and symbols, Fig. 4-60.

UNIT 7 — TERMS FOR DISCUSSION AND REVIEW

phase
technical illustrating
freehand drawing
mechanical drawing
governed
techniques
orthographic
   projections

origin point
horizontal plane line
perspective drawing
one-point perspective
two-point perspective
elevations
architects
center of vision

adjacent
pictorial drawings
schematic drawings
scale
cartoon characters
geometric shapes
animated
working drawing
visible
hidden
isometric drawing
vertical axis line

vanishing points
ground line
picture plane
station point
oblique drawing
network drawing
electrical circuits
symbolic description
single-stroke method
vertical gothic
slanted gothic

Career Opportunities

Camera Operator

Film Stripper

Press Operator

UNIT 8

IMAGE GENERATION BY CLIP ART AND PREPRINTED TYPE

CLIP ART

Pictures, sketches, decorations, words, slogans, borders, and symbols are available from clip-art sheets and books. Clip-art books generally contain black and white illustrations, although multi-color artwork is also available, Fig. 4-61. Some clip-art books supply illustrations in a variety of sizes. This generally eliminates the necessity of enlarging or reducing the illustration size

before it can be applied to the mechanical layout. To use clip art, the artist simply cuts out the desired artwork and pastes it into position on the mechanical layout sheet.

When a commercially prepared clip-art book is purchased, the price includes the permission to reproduce the illustrations. As a general rule, literary, musical, or artistic work that is copyrighted cannot be legally copied without the written permission of the copyright owner. The copyright owner has the exclusive right to copy, sell, and distribute the work. Copyright notice is usually given on the page that follows the title page of a book or other work. The copyright generally consists of (1) the word, **copyright**; or its abbreviation, **copr.**; or the symbol, ©, (2) the copyright owner's name, and (3) the publication date.

PREPRINTED TYPE

Preprinted type is available in sheets of (1) transfer type, (2) individual letters on tabs, and (3) pressure-sensitive letters, words, symbols, decorations, and borders in sheets or rolls. Preprinted type can be easily applied directly to the mechanical layout and for this reason is often used when preparing copy for electrical schematic drawings, house floor plans, and in other instances where existing preprinted type symbols are needed. Using preprinted type often eliminates having to draw many symbols and patterns and is thus a labor- and time-saving device.

TRANSFER TYPE

Transfer type is prepared on a transparent plastic sheet in a wide variety of

Fig. 4-61. Clip art samples

Fig. 4-62. Samples of transfer type lettering styles

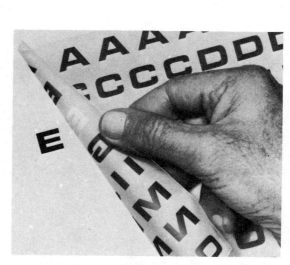

Fig. 4-64. The letter sticks to the layout when the transfer sheet is lifted

Fig. 4-65. Fototype tab type

Fig. 4-63. Rub the surface of the letter with a burnishing tool

letter styles and sizes, borders, illustrations, symbols, and designs, Fig. 4-62.

To use transfer type, draw guidelines to indicate character placement. Then place the sheet of transfer type over the guidelines so that the desired character is in position. Use a burnishing tool (or the smooth end of a ball point pen or pencil top) to rub over the surface of the sheet, Fig. 4-63. The downward pressure causes the ink on the back of the character to be transferred to the

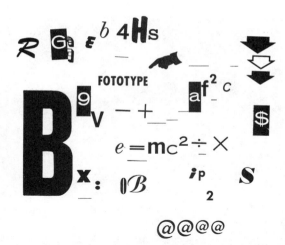

Fig. 4-66. Samples of Fototype letter styles and sizes

Fig. 4-67. Placing the letter tabs in the composing stick

desired position, Fig. 4-64. Carefully lift the sheet and position the next transfer.

TAB TYPE

Display lines of type may be composed by using Fototype.* Fototype is supplied on tabs of paper pads, Fig. 4-65, and offers a wide variety of type styles and sizes as well as borders, symbols, reverse lettering, and screen patterns, Fig. 4-66.

As you remove each letter from the pad, snap it into position in the composing stick with the blue side up. Start at the left side of the stick and push each successive letter tab snugly to the left against the one before it, Fig. 4-67. To space between words, insert a blank tab.

After all the desired characters have been positioned in the stick and proofread, tape is applied. Cut a piece of tape a little longer than the type line, and lay it over the letters, Fig. 4-68. Press down on the tape to be sure each character and space tab is in good contact with the tape. Remove the line

*A product of Fototype, Inc.

Fig. 4-68. Place tape over the letters in the composing stick

Fig. 4-69. Trim the composed line of tab type

Fig. 4-70. Lift the desired letter from the backing sheet

Fig. 4-71. Position the letter on the mechanical layout

from the stick, turn it over so the black side is up, and trim the composed line. Leave a margin of about ⅛" (3 mm) on the top and bottom of the composed line, Fig. 4-69.

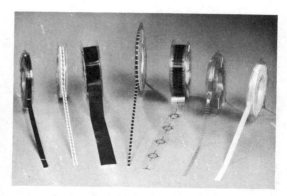

Fig. 4-72. Samples of adhesive tape borders, symbols, and patterns

Fig. 4-73. Applying adhesive tape border to a mechanical layout

Position the trimmed display line on the mechanical layout with rubber cement. Use a T-square and triangle to align the composed line.

PRESSURE-SENSITIVE TYPE

Pressure-sensitive (self-adhesive) letters can be applied directly to the mechanical. This is done by cutting around the desired letter and lifting it from the backing sheet, Fig. 4-70. The guideline under each letter should also be lifted with the letter. The letter is then placed in the desired position by aligning the drawn guideline with the letter guideline, Fig. 4-71. The letters (but not the guidelines) are burnished down and then the guidelines are cut away.

Adhesive tape, another pressure-sensitive device, is available in a wide variety of border patterns, sizes, and symbols, Fig. 4-72. Adhesive tapes are used by simply pressing them into position on the mechanical layout. The self-adhesive backing holds them in position, Fig. 4-73.

UNIT 8 — TERMS FOR DISCUSSION AND REVIEW

clip art
multi-color
illustrations
enlarging
reducing
mechanical layout
reproduce
copyright
preprinted type
transfer type
pressure-sensitive
    letters

transparent
burnishing tool
Fototype
tab type
composing stick
blank tab
margin
T-square
triangle
align

UNIT 9

IMAGE GENERATION BY STRIKE-ON

Strike-on composition is accomplished with the use of a typewriter. Typewriters are available in a wide variety of styles including both manually-operated and electric machines. As each key is depressed on the keyboard, the corresponding type bar is kicked up, causing the desired relief character to strike a ribbon which is between the paper and the character. As the character strikes the ribbon, the image of the character is transferred to the paper.

Copy that is being typed for reproduction purposes should be prepared on smooth, dull-white paper. The relief characters should be cleaned and a ribbon used that produces a sharp, dense, black image for reproduction copy. For best results, a one-time carbon ribbon, which is not available for all typewriters, should be used.

SCM CORPORATION SECRETARIAL C-13

The SCM Corporation Secretarial C-13, Fig. 4-74, is a standard electric typewriter which features a 44-key, 88-character keyboard. This machine uses either a reusable fabric ribbon or a one-time carbon film ribbon which is most suitable for typing copy that is to be printed, copied, or duplicated. The ribbons are housed in cartridges. This makes it easy to insert and remove the ribbon. Correction tape is also available in cartridge form. When an incorrect character is typed, the typist can quickly remove the typing ribbon and insert the correction tape

Fig. 4-74. SCM Corporation Secretarial C-13

Fig. 4-77. IBM Correcting "Selectric" Typewriter

Fig. 4-75. Pica and elite typewritten character
sizes (1″ = 25.4 mm)

Fig. 4-78. IBM "Selectric" typewriter elements

Fig. 4-76. Justification of strike-on composition
on a typewriter which has equal
letter widths

cartridge. It is then necessary to back space to the incorrect character. The incorrect character is struck a second time. The typist then removes the correction tape cartridge and inserts the ribbon cartridge before continuing to type. The fabric ribbons are available in a variety of colors. This makes it possible to intermix colors when typing copy.

The SCM Corporation Secretarial is available in both pica and elite pitch sizes in a variety of typefaces. **Pica** type produces 10 characters per inch while **elite** type is slightly smaller and gives 12 characters per inch, Fig. 4-75.

Each character and space on most standard typewriters have the same width. As a result, most copy prepared on a standard typewriter does not have a flush right-hand margin. However, it is possible to manually **justify** copy on a standard typewriter.

To manually justify the right-hand margin, the same copy must be typed twice. The first copy is marked at the end of each line with the number of units needed to jussify to the desired line length. In this copy,

Courier 72 Code 015   10 Pitch

IBM COURIER 72 Type is a square-serif design
in the Pica family of type styles.

Pica 72 Code 008   10 Pitch

IBM PICA 72 Type is similar to the Pica type
styles offered with the IBM Model C Typewriter.

Delegate Code 070   10 Pitch

IBM DELEGATE Type is a weighted type conveying
the feeling of printed material.

Scribe Code 001   12 Pitch

IBM SCRIBE Type is a modern square-serif design in the
Elite family of type styles. It is ideally suited for
the preparation of routine correspondence and reports.

Letter Gothic Code 005   12 Pitch

IBM LETTER GOTHIC Type is one of the Artisan family of
type styles. It is well suited to a variety of typing

Elite 72 Code 007   12 Pitch

IBM ELITE 72 Type is similar to the Elite type styles
offered with the IBM Model C Typewriter..

Light Italic Code 014   12 Pitch

*IBM LIGHT ITALIC Type is a "fine-line" style that may
be used alone or in combination with Pica or Elite type*

Manifold 72 Code 010   10 Pitch

IBM MANIFOLD 72 TYPE IS A SANS-SERIF TYPE STYLE
DESIGNED FOR BILLING AND FORMS PREPARATION.

Orator Code 059*   10 Pitch

IBM ORATOR TYPE IS A LARGE, SANS-SERIF TYPE
STYLE RECOMMENDED ESPECIALLY FOR SPEECHES AND

1403 Alphameric Code 022   10 Pitch

IBM 1403 ALPHAMERIC TYPE PROVIDES MACHINE-
READABLE, OPTICAL SCANNING COPY AS SIMPLY

12L2/12F2 Alphameric Code 023   10 Pitch

IBM 12L2/12F2 ALPHAMERIC TYPE PROVIDES MACHINE-
READABLE, OPTICAL SCANNING COPY AS SIMPLY AS

Symbol 10 Code 061   10 Pitch

The Following Symbols are Available on the IBM Symbol 10 Typing Element:

French-English Code 057   12 Pitch

IBM FRENCH-ENGLISH Type is designed for use on domestic
IBM "Selectric" Typewriters for French applications.

Script Code 090   12 Pitch

*IBM SCRIPT Type is a special-purpose type style that
simulates handwriting.*

Symbol 12 Code 004   12 Pitch

The Following Symbols are Available on the IBM Symbol 12 Typing Element:

**Fig. 4-79. Sample variety of type styles and
pitch sizes. Actual typefaces are
larger than shown in this illustration**

**Fig. 4-80. IBM Correcting "Selectric" Type-
writer with the lid up**

IBM CORRECTING "SELECTRIC" TYPEWRITER

The IBM Correcting "Selectric" Type-writer, Fig. 4-77, has the unique features of a stationary carriage and a spherical typing element which replaces the type bars. Each typing element, which is about the size of a golf ball, contains all the necessary letters, numbers, and symbols, Fig. 4-78. Each of the available typing element styles is coded to indicate the size and style of type. The elements are available in 10 pitch and 12 pitch sizes, Fig. 4-79.

When a key is depressed, the element spins, and the character of the depressed key strikes the ribbon in front of the paper. The element then returns to its original position and advances one space. The typing element and ribbon move across the paper in the stationary carriage, Fig. 4-80.

The Correcting "Selectric" Typewriter is equipped with an IBM Correctable Film Ribbon and Lift-Off Tape. If an error is made in typing, the typist depresses the correcting key to back space to the correct character. The correcting key activates the Lift-Off Tape which removes the error when the incorrect character key is struck again. The typist then types in the correct letter, number, or punctuation mark and continues typing.

the type never exceeds the length of the desired line. A vertical line drawn on the paper indicates the maximum line length. During the second typing, the units necessary for justification are added between words in the form of spaces, Fig. 4-76.

The typing elements may be interchanged at any time, making it possible to mix typefaces. When a type element is changed, the machine must be turned off and be in the lowercase typing position. Lift the typewriter cover. You will observe the arrow on the type element points toward the platen (away from the typist), when the element is in the lowercase position. Carefully lift the element lock lever and remove it from the element post, Fig. 4-81.

To replace an element, the typewriter must also be turned off and be in the lowercase typing position. Lift the element lock lever and place the element on the post with the arrow pointing toward the platen. Gently press down on the element lock lever until the element clicks into position.

IBM "SELECTIC" COMPOSER

The IBM "Selectric" composer, Fig. 4-82, is similar to the "Selectric" typewriter in that it features a stationary carriage and removable type elements. Typing elements are available in 6, 7, 8, 9, 10, 11, and 12 points. In addition, it uses a one-time carbon ribbon and will accommodate many different typefaces. The composer also features proportional spacing. With proportional spacing, the individual characters have varying widths. A choice of line spacing is also available from 5 to 20 points.

Justification of the right-hand margin of typed copy is semiautomatic on the IBM "Selectric" composer. The operator first types a rough draft, stopping before the right-hand margin is reached. The required spacing needed to justify the typed line is indicated by color and number on the justification tube which is directly above the keyboard. Before typing the finished, justified copy, the operator sets the justification control to the setting that was indicated on the justification tube. The justification control is located to the right-hand side of the keyboard. During the second typing, the ma-

Fig. 4-81. Removing the typing element

Fig. 4-82. IBM "Selectric" composer

chine automatically justifies the copy by adding space between words, Fig. 4-83 and 4-84.

The IBM Electronic "Selectric" Composer is similar in operation. However, this machine only requires one typist keyboard-

Justification of the right hand margin of typed copy is semi-automatic on the IBM "Selectric" Composer. The operator first types a rough draft, stopping before the right hand margin is reached. The required spacing needed to justify the typed line is indicated by color and number on the justification tube which is directly above the keyboard. Before typing the finished justified copy the operator sets the justification control to the setting that was indicated on the justification tube. The justification control is located to the right hand side of the keyboard. During the second typing the machine automatically justifies the copy by adding space between letters and words.

Fig. 4-83. IBM "Selectric" composer rough copy

Justification of the right hand margin of typed copy is semi-automatic on the IBM "Selectric" Composer. The operator first types a rough draft, stopping before the right hand margin is reached. The required spacing needed to justify the typed line is indicated by color and number on the justification tube which is directly above the keyboard. Before typing the finished justified copy the operator sets the justification control to the setting that was indicated on the justification tube. The justification control is located to the right hand side of the keyboard. During the second typing the machine automatically justifies the copy by adding space between letters and words.

Fig. 4-84. IBM "Selectric" composer justified copy

ing operation. During the first typing, the copy is stored in an 8000 character electronic memory. The operator then programs the machine to justify, set flush right, or any other typing configuration that is desired. The machine then automatically types finished copy based upon the programming instructions at a speed of 150 characters per minute.

There are 125 typing elements in 11 different type styles available for the IBM Electronic "Selectric" Composer. The point sizes range from 6 to 12 and are available in 13 languages.

VARITYPER

The VariTyper®, Fig. 4-85, features proportional spacing and uses a one-time carbon ribbon and interchangeable type fonts. The VariTyper will semiautomatically produce justified typed copy.

Each type font contains all the necessary letters, numbers, and symbols, Fig. 4-86. At any one time, two different type fonts may be placed in position. This makes it possible to mix, for example, a bold and an italic typeface without replacing type fonts. Hundreds of type font styles and sizes are available.

To justify the copy, it must be typed twice. The rough draft copy is typed to the desired column width on the left side of the paper. The margin dial pointer and the justifier dial pointer are used to guide the typist in beginning and ending each typed line. The same copy is then typed again on the right-hand side of the paper. The VariTyper automatically inserts the required spacing and produces clean, sharp, justified copy.

Fig. 4-85. VariTyper Model 1010

FRIDEN "JUSTOWRITER" COMPOSER

The Friden "Justowriter"® composer is a tape-operated strike-on composition machine, consisting of a recorder unit and a reproducer unit, Fig. 4-87. Justified copy is automatically produced with one keyboarding or typing operation. It is first typed on the recorder unit. A panel light signals when the justification zone has been reached, indicating that the line must be ended. As the operator types on the recorder unit, a visual proof copy and a punched tape are produced. If an error is made in typing, the line is cancelled and retyped.

The punched tape is then fed into the reproducer. The reproducer unit reads the combinations of punched holes and automatically types justified copy at a rate of 100 words per minute.

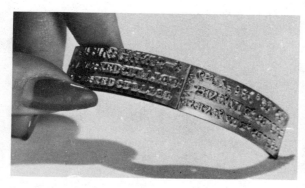

Fig 4-86. Varityper type font

Fig. 4-87. Friden "Justowriter" Recorder (left) and Reproducer (right)

UNIT 9 — TERMS FOR DISCUSSION AND REVIEW

strike-on
composition
accomplished
typewriter
copy
reproduction
carbon ribbon
pitch

pica
elite
flush right margin
justify
unique
stationary
spherical
proportional spacing

IMAGE GENERATION BY PHOTOCOMPOSITION

Photocomposition is a cold composition process of image generation that makes use of (1) type font negatives, (2) in most cases, light-sensitive paper or film, and (3) light. The type font negatives have transparent letters and symbols. When positioned between the light-sensitive paper (or film) and the exposure light, the negative fonts permit the generation of an image. The light, during exposure, passes through the transparent areas, strikes the light-sensitive paper (or film), and produces a **latent** or hidden image. After exposure, the paper (or film) is developed, fixed, and washed. The developer causes the **latent** image to appear, while the fixing bath stabilizes the image after it has been developed. The wash removes all traces of previously used chemicals. The paper (or film), when dried, can then be pasted into position on the mechanical layout.

Fig. 4-88. StripPrinter phototypesetting machine

STRIP PRINTER

The StripPrinter, Fig. 4-88, is a photo-typesetting machine that sets display lines of type. Type sizes ranging from 6 points to 96 points may be set in a wide variety of styles. Fonts are also available for setting reverses and patterns, Fig. 4-89.

The StripPrinter uses a **filmstrip font.** Each font contains one size and style of type. The StripPrinter is operated by threading the desired film type font through the exposure unit. This positions the font between the lamp and the sensitized paper which has been loaded inside the machine.

Each font has a left and right registration mark for each character. The distance between the marks is slightly greater than the width of the character, Fig. 4-90. This permits uniform spacing between characters.

The left registration mark of the character to be composed is aligned with the zero registration mark on the registration scale, Fig. 4-91. When they are aligned, the upper transport block is grasped, and the transport lever is locked to assure accurate positioning, Fig. 4-92. Once the transport is locked, the font and the paper are moved into position for exposure by carefully moving the transport block to the left and aligning the right-hand registration mark with the zero registration mark on the scale, Fig. 4-93. When they are properly positioned, the exposure is made by simply pressing the exposure button. The same process is then repeated for each successive letter that is composed. After all the exposures have been made, the paper is removed from the machine, developed, fixed, washed, and dried.

Fig. 4-90. StripPrinter type font with registration marks for each letter

Fig. 4-89. Sample photocomposition with the StripPrinter

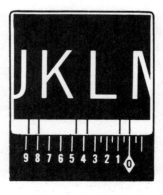

Fig. 4-91. Align left registration mark of a letter with the zero registration point

Fig. 4-92. Lock the transport when the letter is accurately positioned

Fig. 4-93. Advance the transport to align the right-hand letter registration mark with zero

PHOTO-TYPOSITOR

The Photo-Typositor, Fig. 4-94, can compose both single and multiple lines of display type. The projection lens system permits enlarging to 200% and reducing to 25%.

Multiple film fonts can be stored on the font reels at one time, permitting intermixing of type styles. With minor machine adjust-

Fig. 4-94. Photo-Typositor®

ments, it is possible to backslant, stagger, curve, distort, overlap, and condense the type. Typefaces may also be composed in perspective, circles, italics, and with shadow effects, Fig. 4-95. The desired letters are positioned between the lamp and the sensitized paper or film by turning the handwheels on the machine.

Immediately after each exposure, the letter is automatically developed while still in the machine. The developed composition, when removed from the machine, must be fixed, washed, and dried.

HEADLINER

The Headliner®, Fig. 4-96, composes lines of type ranging from 10 points to 84 points and is available in several models. It uses both photosensitive paper (for producing black lettering on white) and photosensitive film (for producing black lettering on a transparent backing).

125

A clear plastic disc called a Type-master® contains the type font. Film negatives of the type characters are laminated to the disc, Fig. 4-97. Hundreds of type styles and sizes are available on Typemasters, each of which usually contains a complete type font of one size and style.

The Typemaster is positioned on the Headliner between the exposure light and the photographic paper or film. To begin composition, the selector knob is turned in either direction until the desired character appears in the indexing window. The print space lever is then moved to the print position. This automatically centers the desired character in the indexing window, advances the paper (or film), and makes the exposure. The same procedure is followed for each character that is to be composed.

When composition has been completed, the paper (or film) is cut and automatically fed into the three-compartment developing tank where the developing, fixing, and washing are automatically timed. When the paper (or film) emerges from the Headliner, it is ready to be pasted into position on the mechanical layout.

COMP/SET PHOTOTYPESETTER

The Comp/Set Phototypesetter, Fig. 4-98, can produce camera-ready photocomposition in as many as 150 different typefaces. The machine consists of three major units: (1) keyboard, (2) screen, and (3) typesetter.

The **keyboard** unit makes it possible to program the Comp/Set to produce type in a variety of sizes, styles, and line lengths. After programming is completed, the operator types the copy to be set photographically.

The **screen** displays (1) the function field, (2) the line being typeset, and (3) the line being keyboarded. The function field section of the screen displays the programmed instructions as to line length, type size, and type style. As the operator keyboards copy, it is displayed in the bottom section of the screen. This permits visual inspection for proofreading purposes. Once approved, the operator enters a return code and the bottom line moves to the center of the screen.

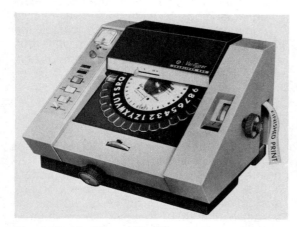

Fig. 4-95. Sample composition with the Photo-Typositor

Fig. 4-96. VariTyper Headliner Model 820

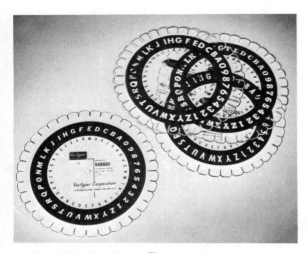

Fig. 4-97. Headliner Typemaster

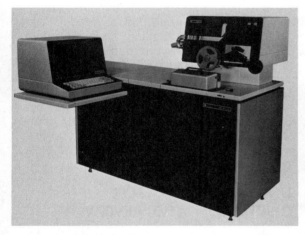

Fig. 4-98. Comp/Set Phototypesetter

The paper or film, which is stored in cassette rolls, is automatically fed through the photographic unit during typesetting. At the end of the typesetting operation, the paper or film is cut and the exposed portion is removed for processing.

The Comp/Set is also available with either a perforated tape or a magnetic diskette unit. These units make it possible to store the copy for future playback of the keyboarded copy.

COMPUGRAPHIC DISPLAY PHOTOTYPESETTER

The Compugraphic Display Phototypesetter has a standard keyboard, Fig. 4-99.

Fig. 4-99. Compugraphic Phototypesetter

The line of type is now in position for the **typesetter.** It will be automatically phototypeset according to the programmed instructions. The operator can keyboard the next line of type while the previous line is being phototypeset. Each type disc used by the Comp/Set contains four different type styles. In addition, the automatic lens mechanism makes it possible to set up to 70 different sizes of type up to 74 points.

The actual copy is produced photographically on light-sensitive paper or film.

127

As the keys are depressed, the characters can be viewed on the visual display unit. The operator should proofread the visual display. After checking the line length and copy for errors, the operator can expose photographic film or paper. The film or paper is then transferred to a lightproof cassette for processing. The processed copy can be pasted into position on a mechanical layout.

Type fonts are available in a wide variety of styles. Each filmstrip type font contains two styles. Two filmstrips can be placed in the machine at the same time. The operator may select any of the four different styles while composing type.

The size of the typeface is selected by regulating the lens selection dial. Eight different type sizes are possible for each font. The lens can also be adjusted to produce type up to 120 points in size.

QUADRITEK 1200 PHOTOTYPESETTER

The Quadritek 1200 Phototypesetter has a keyboard similar to a standard electric typewriter, Fig. 4-100. It has the capability of setting text or display type ranging from 5½ to 36 points. It can set a variety of interchangeable typefaces. The operator has access to four different typefaces at a time. The operator can program the machine to center, justify, or set the copy flush right or left.

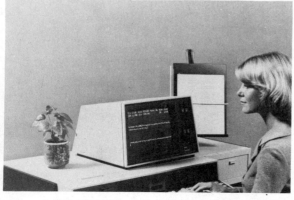

Fig. 4-100. The Quadritek 1200 Phototypesetter

The visual display screen permits the operator to proofread and edit the copy before it is typeset. The copy specifications such as line length, type font being used, point size, and line space available are always visible at the top of the display screen. As copy is keyboarded, it appears in the lower half of the screen. After proofreading the displayed copy, the operator activates the phototypesetting unit to set the type on either film or paper. The photosensitive film or paper is supplied in rolls. The exposed paper or film is automatically fed into a lightproof cartridge for processing.

As many as four lines of type can be keyboarded before it is typeset. Once the operator activates the phototypesetting unit, the displayed copy moves from the lower half of the screen to the upper half. While the unit is setting the first four lines, additional keyboard entries can be made.

In addition to setting type on either paper or film, the keyboarded message can be recorded on magnetic tape. The taped message can be used repeatedly to generate new phototypeset copy. The recorded message is displayed on the display screen before it is phototypeset. This permits the operator to edit and update the recorded message without retyping the complete message.

UNIT 10 — TERMS FOR DISCUSSION AND REVIEW

photocomposition	reductions
cold composition	backslant
image generation	stagger
type font negative	distort
light-sensitive paper or film	condense
developer	compose
latent	single and multiple lines
phototypesetting machine	film negatives
display lines	type characters
fonts	laminated
reverse	camera-ready
filmstrip font	perforated tape
enlargements	magnetic diskette
	keyboarded copy

UNIT 11

IMAGE GENERATION BY CONTINUOUS TONE PHOTOGRAPHY

Continuous tone photography, as a means of image generation, uses reflected light from a subject to expose a light-sensitive material known as **film.** Because light areas of the subject being photographed reflect more light than dark areas, the film is exposed to more light in the light areas. Black areas, on the other hand, reflect little light, and therefore the film emulsion is only slightly affected in these areas.

All shades of gray, from white to black, reflect different amounts of light and therefore register as continuous tones on the film. The amount of light that strikes the film emulsion determines the degree to which the emulsion is hardened.

TYPES OF CAMERAS

The simplest camera consists of a light-tight box with a film holder, lens, and shutter.

The film holder holds the film in the camera, while the lens directs the light to strike the film when the shutter is opened, Fig. 4-101.

There are a variety of cameras available today which range from the very simple to the very complex. The **box camera,** for example, is one of the simplest cameras, Fig. 4-102. This type of camera generally does

Fig. 4-102. Box camera

Fig. 4-101. Cameras are light-tight boxes with a film holder, lens, and shutter

Fig. 4-103. Folding camera

Fig. 4-104. Crown Graphic press camera

Fig. 4-105. Polaroid folding camera

not have any means of controlling the size of the lens opening, called an **f-stop.** Also, it usually has no control on focusing the image being photographed. The **shutter speed,** which is the time the light is allowed to pass through the lens, is generally fixed at 1/25 of a second. The box camera is simple to operate, inexpensive, and will produce excellent results under favorable conditions. Modern box cameras may be equipped with flash for taking indoor pictures.

The **folding camera** is essentially a box camera with an accordion-like device known as a bellows, Fig. 4-103. The bellows allows the camera to be folded together when not in use. This makes it more compact. Some folding cameras have simple f-stop adjustments and a means of adjusting the distance between the lens and the film. Then pictures can be taken closer to the subject than with the box camera.

The **press camera** is a type of folding camera, Fig. 4-104. As the name implies, this camera is used by press photographers. It generally uses a large film, such as 4″ x 5″ (101.6 mm x 127 mm), for achieving maximum detail. The Polaroid is another type of folding camera, Fig. 4-105.

The **reflex cameras** are classified as either **single lens** or **twin lens**. The single lens reflex camera allows the camera operator to see directly through the lens to the subject being photographed, Fig. 4-106. Twin lens reflex cameras have two lenses.

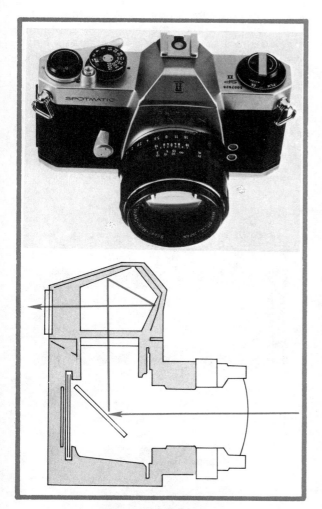

Fig. 4-106. Single lens reflex camera

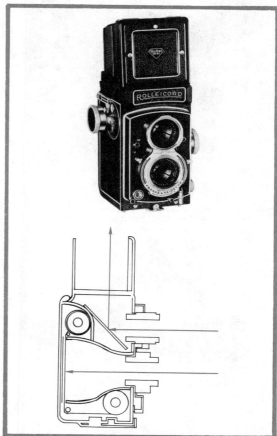

Fig. 4-107. Twin lens reflex camera

The top lens is for viewing the subject being photographed while the bottom lens is for actually taking the picture, Fig. 4-107.

The **view** camera is generally used by studio photographers. The subject being photographed is located and focused on a ground glass in the back of the camera. Because of this procedure, the view camera is not suitable for photographing moving subjects. This camera is large and heavy and is generally mounted on a tripod for use, Fig. 4-108.

FUNCTION OF CAMERA PARTS

Most makes of cameras vary slightly in regard to operating features and their location on the camera. The function of each of the parts, however, is basically the same. As you read the remainder of this unit, refer to Fig. 4-109 to identify each camera part described.

Fig. 4-108. View camera

The **camera body** provides the light-tight box that holds the film. When a 35mm film camera is loaded, the unexposed film, which is a **cassette,** is placed on the left-hand side of the camera (as the camera is viewed from the back). The film leader is then pulled across the camera focal plane and attached to the take-up spool, Fig. 4-110. After the film perforations on both sides of the film are securely engaged in the sprockets, the camera back is closed.

Fig. 4-110. Attach the film leader to the take-up spool

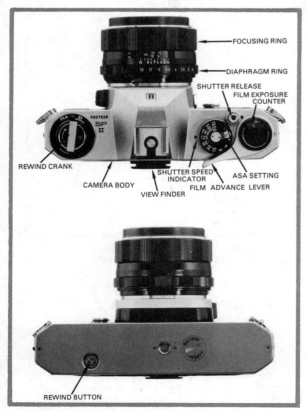

Fig. 4-109. Camera parts

Fig. 4-111. Completely remove the seal after the film has been placed in the camera

Cameras that use such film sizes as 120 and 620 have the supply sprocket at the bottom of the camera and the take-up sprocket at the top. These films have a paper backing which the 35mm films do not have. Remove the empty spool from the bottom sprocket and place it in position in the top sprocket. Place the film in the bottom sprocket before breaking the seal to prevent accidental exposure if the film is dropped during the loading process. Once the film is securely in place, break and completely remove the seal, Fig. 4-111. Attach the paper backing leader to the take-up spool, being sure that it is securely in place, and close the camera back, Fig. 4-112.

Fig. 4-112. Attach the paper leader to the take-up spool

Fig. 4-113. Clip-on reflected light exposure meter

Before the first picture is taken, the **film advance lever** is used to advance the film a number of frames. (Refer to the camera manufacturer's recommendations.)

FILM EXPOSURE

Before any exposures are made, the **ASA rating** of the film being used must be set on the exposure meter. The ASA rating is the film sensitivity rating that was set by the American Standard Association. The higher the ASA rating, the more sensitive the film is to light.

Two types of exposure metering devices are in common use today: (1) the **reflected light meter** and (2) the **incident light meter**. The reflected light meter reads the amount of light that is reflected from the subject being photographed. This type of light meter is available in models that clip onto the camera (Fig. 4-113) or are held in the hand, Fig. 4-114. Cameras that employ a through-the-lens metering system that reads reflected light may be known as **spot metering cameras.**

Incident light meters read the amount of light that falls upon the subject being photographed. When an incident light meter is used, it should be held near the subject being photographed with the light-gathering device pointed directly toward the main source of light, Fig. 4-115.

Fig. 4-114. Hand-held light meter

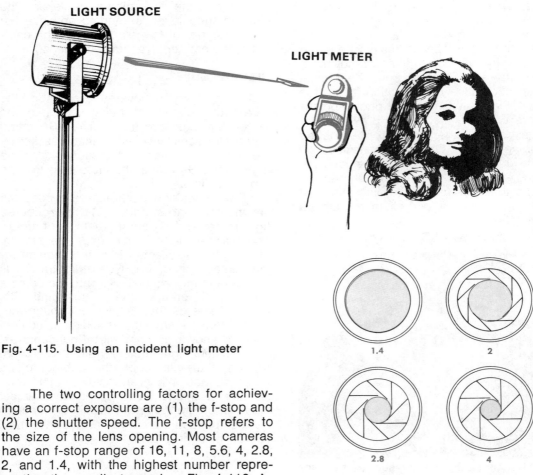

Fig. 4-115. Using an incident light meter

The two controlling factors for achieving a correct exposure are (1) the f-stop and (2) the shutter speed. The f-stop refers to the size of the lens opening. Most cameras have an f-stop range of 16, 11, 8, 5.6, 4, 2.8, 2, and 1.4, with the highest number representing the smallest opening, Fig. 4-116. As the numbers decrease, the lens opening doubles in size for each f-stop setting. Thus, f/8 is one-half the size opening of f/5.6.

The shutter speed is the amount of time that the light reflected from the subject being photographed is allowed to pass through the lens and strike the film emulsion. The shutter speed range on many cameras is 1/1000, 1/500, 1/250, 1/125, 1/60, 1/30, 1/15, 1/8, 1/4, 1/2 of a second, and 1 second.

The combination of f-stop and shutter speed that will be used when a subject is photographed depends on the amount of light that is reflected from the subject. This combination also depends on the ASA rating of the film being used.

Fig. 4-116. Size relationship of camera f-stops

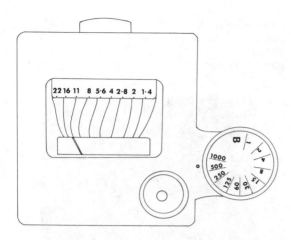

Fig. 4-117. Exposure reading of f/11 at 1/500

Fig. 4-119. Depth of field

Fig. 4-120. Set the camera f-stop and shutter speed

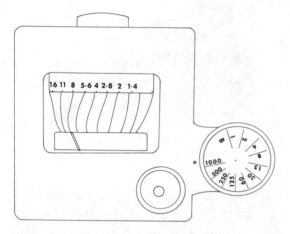

Fig. 4-118. Exposure reading of f/8 at 1/1000

With the ASA rating of the film properly set, a light meter reading may indicate that a combination of f/11 at 1/500 of a second will produce a correct exposure, Fig. 4-117. The same correct exposure may also be made at f/8 at 1/1000 of a second, Fig. 4-118. This is possible because when the f-stop is opened up by one full stop, the shutter speed is cut in half. The main advantage of using a small f-stop is that of increasing the depth of field.

Depth of field is the distance between the closest subject to the camera and the farthest subject from the camera which appears in sharp focus, Fig. 4-119. A slow shutter speed, however, may cause image distortion because (1) the camera or (2) the subject moved. The f-stop setting is adjusted by turning the **diaphragm ring** on the lens barrel. The **shutter speed** must also be set, Fig. 4-120.

PICTURE COMPOSITION

The picture can be composed by studying the subject through the **view finder** of the camera. Although there are no set rules regarding photocomposition, the key is simplicity. Background clutter should be avoided as it tends to distract from the main subject in the photograph, Fig. 4-121. A few steps to either side, toward or away from the subject, often eliminates background clutter, Fig. 4-122.

When photographing scenes such as sunsets, avoid placing the horizon in the center of the picture. The horizon should generally run straight across the picture, but

Fig. 4-121. Avoid objects that distract from the subject being photographed

Fig. 4-123. Placement of horizon line in top one-third of the picture

Fig. 4-122. Slight movement of the camera or subject position will eliminate distracting objects

Fig. 4-124. Placement of horizon line in bottom one-third of the picture

slightly above or below the center. The rule of "thirds" is usually employed when such scenes are photographed. The placement of the horizon in the top one-third or the bottom one-third of the picture should depend on where the interest lies. If the foreground is the most interesting, photograph the scene with the horizon in the top one-third of the picture, Fig. 4-123. If the sky is most interesting because of cloud formations, place the horizon in the bottom one-third of the picture, Fig. 4-124.

The picture being composed through the view finder should be balanced. When subjects of equal size and weight are photographed, each subject should appear equal distance from the center pivot point to achieve formal balance, Fig. 4-125. When two different-size subjects are photographed,

informal balance is achieved by composing the picture with the largest subject nearest the pivot point of the picture, Fig. 4-126.

CAMERA FOCUS

Focus the subject being photographed by turning the **focusing ring** on the lens barrel as you look through the view finder.

There are three basic types of view finders, also called "range finders":

1. The **split image** range finder splits the image in half. When the focusing ring is turned, the top and the bottom halves may be moved into alignment or focus, Fig. 4-127.

2. The **coincidental** range finder uses a superimposed image. When the subject is out of focus, the same image appears twice. When the subject is in focus, only one image appears.

3. Reflex cameras use a **ground glass screen** range finder. This type of range finder employs a pattern of concentric rings, Fig. 4-128. When

Fig. 4-125. Formal photocomposition balance

Fig. 4-126. Informal photocomposition balance

Fig. 4-127. Split image range finder

Fig. 4-128. Microprism ground glass range finder

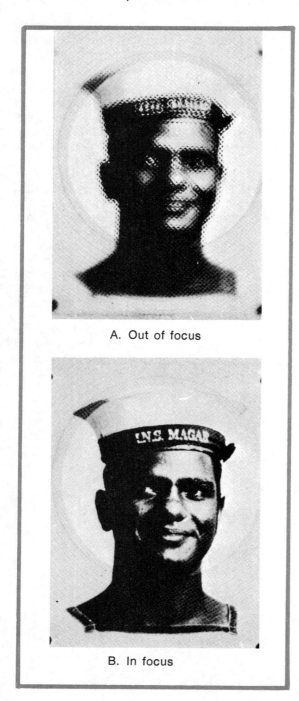

A. Out of focus

B. In focus

Fig. 4-129. Microprism focusing

the subject is out of focus, it will appear as many small dots in the microprism center area. When the subject is in focus, it will appear sharp and clear in the microprism, Fig. 4-129.

FINAL PROCEDURES

With all settings properly adjusted, the picture is ready for exposure. Hold the camera steady and gently, but firmly, press the **shutter release.** When the shutter release is pressed, the shutter opens and closes at the speed set on the shutter speed dial. The reflected light from the subject is allowed to pass through the lens and open shutter, producing a **latent** or hidden image on the film. The image will not be visible until after the film has been developed.

Before the next picture is taken, the film must be advanced. The **film exposure counter** will indicate the number of exposures that have been taken. Before making the next exposure, use the exposure meter to determine the best f-stop and shutter speed settings to be used for the picture, because different lighting conditions require different exposure controls. The subject must also be focused for each exposure.

When all the exposures have been made on the 35mm films, the film must be rewound before the camera is opened. This is accomplished by depressing the **film rewind release button** and turning the **rewind crank,** Fig. 4-130.

Fig. 4-130. Press the rewind release button and turn the rewind crank

Cameras that use 120 and 620 films require the film to be advanced before the camera back is opened. Continue to advance the film until it is free of the supply spool. Open the camera back and remove the exposed film from the take-up spool. The paper wrapping on the exposed film should be held taut and sealed to prevent light from striking the film, Fig. 4-131. The exposed film is now ready for the developing operation.

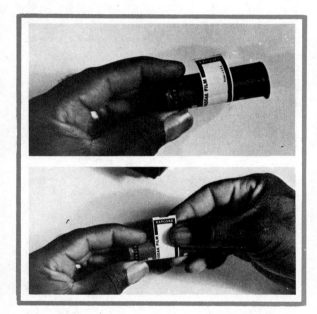

Fig. 4-131. Seal the exposed film when it is removed from the camera

UNIT 11 — TERMS FOR DISCUSSION AND REVIEW

continuous tone photography	reflected light meter
image generation	incident light meter
reflected light	through-the-lens metering system
light-sensitive film	spot metering cameras
emulsion	shutter speed indicator
lens	depth of field
box camera	diaphragm ring
f/stop	lens barrel
focus	view finder
shutter speed	rule of "thirds"
folding camera	pivot point
bellows	formal balance
press camera	informal balance
single lens reflex camera	focusing ring
twin lens reflex camera	split image
view camera	concentric
ground glass	microprism
tripod	shutter release
camera body	latent
film advance lever	film exposure counter
ASA rating	film rewind release button
ASA setting	rewind crank
exposure meter	

IV SECTION

PREPRODUCTION
AND
PRODUCTION

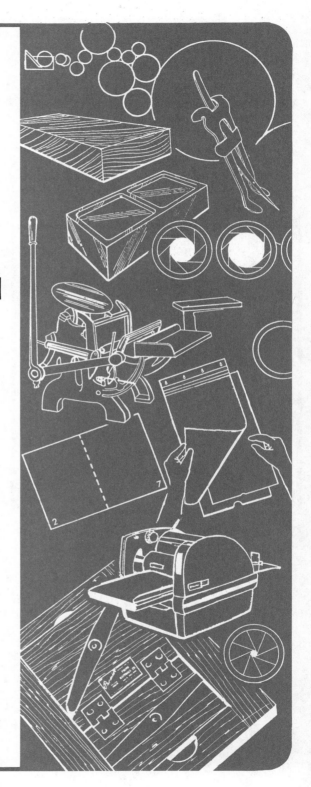

Once the images have been generated, they must be made ready for the production operation. This is known as the **preproduction stage** of graphic communications. The preproduction stage includes all preparation steps required to convert or prepare the generated images so that they will carry ink to the receiving surface (usually paper).

Each of the major printing production processes requires particular preproduction operations to prepare the **ink carrier.** The method of image generation that was employed often determines the number and type of preproduction operations that are required. The following review of each of the production processes will indicate the type of ink carrier that must be prepared for each process.

RELIEF PRINTING

The relief printing production process requires a three-dimensional ink carrier. The ink-carrying surface is raised above a supporting body, Fig. IV-1. Images generated by hand-set foundry type, machine-set type, and linoleum-block carving are directly applicable to relief printing because they are three-dimensional. Two-dimensional images generated by any of the cold composition methods may also be used, but they must be converted into three-dimensional letterpress plates.

During the production phase of relief printing, the **raised surface carries the ink to the receiving surface.** The ink is transferred to the receiving surface as the paper and the raised surface of the generated image are pressed together.

SCREEN PROCESS PRINTING

Screen process printing employs a stencil which is adhered to an open-weave material that is tightly stretched across a printing frame, Fig. IV-2. During the production operation, ink is forced through the open areas of the stencil onto the receiving surface.

The preparation of the stencil can be considered the preproduction phase of screen process printing. The type of stencil used is often determined by such factors as design complexity, design detail, number of impressions to be printed, and the desired quality of the message being printed. Stencils may be prepared by hand-cutting paper and film, by freehand application of tusche, and by photographic processing.

GRAVURE (OR INTAGLIO) PRINTING

The ink carrier for the gravure printing production process is one that has the printing areas cut into or below the surface of

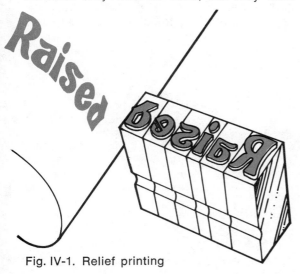

Fig. IV-1. Relief printing

Fig. IV-2. Screen process printing

the plate. During production, the entire surface of the plate is covered with ink. The surface ink is then removed, leaving ink in the image recesses of the plate. When the plate and the paper are pressed together, the ink is transferred to the paper, Fig. IV-3.

The preparation of industrial gravure plates is a highly sophisticated and complex procedure. As most schools do not have the necessary equipment required to produce gravure plates, two methods of making facsimile gravure plates are presented here. These are (1) the drypoint engraving and (2) the metal etching. The **drypoint engraving** is made by scratching lines in clear plastic. The plastic plate is then inked, wiped clean, and pressed against paper to reveal the image. The **metal etching,** which more truly represents industrial practices, is prepared by coating the entire metal plate with an acid resist. The image is then scratched in the resist to expose bare metal. The plate is then placed in an acid bath which dissolves the bare metal in the image areas, thus creating the printing depressions or ink wells. The metal etching is printed by pressing the plate against paper after the etching has been inked and the surface wiped.

PLANOGRAPHIC (LITHOGRAPHIC) PRINTING

Planographic printing is the method of graphic communications production that employs a **flat ink carrier,** Fig. IV-4. The fact that grease (ink) and water do not readily mix is the basis of operation.

The flat planographic ink carrier is prepared by placing the image on metal, plastic, or paper plates by photographic processing. The ink carrier can also be prepared by writing, drawing, or typing directly on the flat surface of special plates with pens, pencils, and typewriter ribbons designed for that purpose.

During the production phase of planographic printing, water is first applied to the plate which is secured to the plate cylinder. Because the plate image has a grease base, the water is repelled by the image areas. The non-image areas, however, accept a thin coating of water. When ink is applied, it is repelled by the moisture-coated, non-image areas but sticks to the grease-base plate image. The inked plate image is then offset to a rubber blanket. As the paper passes between the blanket and the plate cylinders, the ink is transferred to the paper.

Fig. IV-3. Gravure (or intaglio) printing

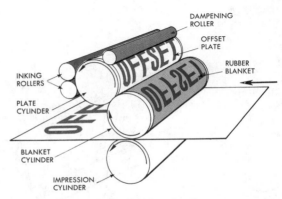

Fig. IV-4. Planographic (lithographic) printing

CONTINUOUS TONE PHOTOGRAPHY

Images generated by continuous tone photography are registered as latent images on light-sensitive material known as **film**. In the preproduction phase of continuous tone photography, the film is developed to reveal the generated images. The development procedure requires the use of processing chemicals which cause changes in the film, and thus bring the images into view in negative form.

The developed negatives can then be used to produce photographic prints or enlargements, Fig. IV-5. The enlarging procedure is either a preproduction process or a production process, depending on the product desired. If the product is to be a photographic enlargement, the enlarging process can be considered a production process. On the other hand, the photographic enlargement can be considered a preproduction process when it is produced for use in any other production process.

OFFICE COPYING AND OFFICE DUPLICATING

Office copying and **office duplicating** methods of production are often used in situations where only a few copies of original documents are required. The equipment used is easy to operate and generally does not require a highly skilled dedicated operator. Also, the equipment is less expensive to rent or purchase and operate than high-quality printing equipment.

Office copying methods do not require an intermediate image carrier, Fig. IV-6. The original copy is usually generated by cold composition methods of strike-on and technical illustration. Photocomposition, clip art and preprinted type, and continuous tone photography prints may also be used to create paste-up original copy. Images generated by linoleum block, hand-set and machine-set type can be reproduced by office copying production methods.

Office duplicating methods of production require the use of an intermediate image carrier such as a stencil. The stencil may be made by using strike-on and technical illustration methods directly on the stencil surface. The other image generation methods may be used to generate paste-up copy. The completed paste-up copy is then used to make the stencil by electronic scanning.

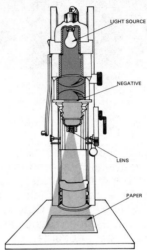

Fig. IV-5. Producing photographic enlargements

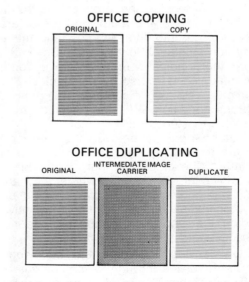

Fig. IV-6. Office copying - office duplicating

5 CHAPTER

PAPER MANUFACTURING

Paper and paper products are the most widely used materials for producing printed messages. Paper can be classified as **fine** and **coarse.** Fine paper is also known as printing or writing paper. Coarse papers, such as wrapping paper, bags, and corrugated board, are considered industrial papers.

Paper and paper products are produced by a complex manufacturing process, Fig. 5-1. Generally, the process begins in the forest where the pulpwood trees are harvested, cut into short lengths, and made ready for shipment to the paper mill. Although the principal source of pulp is wood, pulp may also be made by mechanically or chemically reducing old paper and rags to a fibrous condition. All paper is made from pulp which is the basic raw material.

After the bark is removed, the pulpwood logs are reduced to chips about the size of a quarter. The chips are then screened as they move into a **digester** where they are mixed with chemicals for pulping. The action of the chemicals softens the lignin adhesive bonding the wood fibers together and reduces them to pulp.

On leaving the digester, the wood pulp is processed through several stages of washing, screening, and cleaning. If necessary, the pulp passes through the bleaching stage to obtain the required brightness. After additional refining, the pulp is combined with other ingredients such as pigments, dyes, sizings, and resins. The addition of the other ingredients to the pulp depends on the type of paper or paper product being produced. At this point, the paper is known as the furnish. The furnish consists of approximately 99% water and 1% fiber and other solid materials.

The highly diluted furnish now flows onto a moving wire screen at the **wet end** of the Fourdrinier paper machine. With much of the water drawn through the screen, the fibers mat together, forming a continuous sheet of paper. The paper, still laden with water, is passed through a series of heavy rollers which press out most of the remaining water. The drying process is completed as the paper proceeds over steam-heated rollers where the remaining moisture is driven off by evaporation. When completely dry, the paper is wound onto rolls or cut into sheets, ready for shipment.

The preceding description briefly outlines how paper and paper products are manufactured. With slight variations in the basic manufacturing process, thousands of varieties of paper may be produced to meet the many special printing requirements.

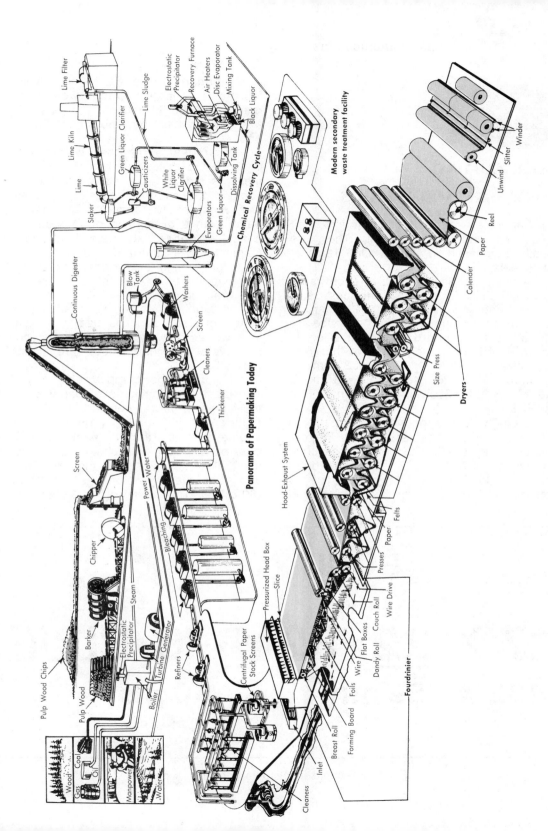

Fig. 5-1. The manufacture of paper

PAPER CUTTING

PAPER SIZES AND WEIGHTS

Papers are ordered according to their base size and basis weight. They are usually purchased in reams. One ream is 500 sheets.

A **base size** is assigned to each paper classification. For example, the base size of bond paper is 17″ × 22″ (432 mm × 559 mm). Sizes other than the base size are referred to as **standard** or regular sizes. In the case of bond paper, some of the standard sizes are 17″ × 28″ (432 mm × 711 mm), 19″ × 28″ (483 mm × 610 mm), and 22″ × 34″ (559 mm × 864 mm). See Fig. 5-3.

Basis weight is the weight of one ream of a paper in the base size sheet. For example, using U. S. Customary measures, 500 sheets of 17″ × 22″ 20-pound bond paper would have a total weight of 20 pounds. If the sheet size were increased to a **standard** size of 34″ × 44″, which is four times as large, the **total weight** of one ream would be 80 pounds. The paper, however, would still be known as 20-pound paper.

In SI Metrics, the basis weight is given in grams per square meter (g/m²). This measure may be referred to as grammage. Look at the same example using metrics. One ream of 432 mm × 559 mm bond paper with a grammage of 75 would have a **total weight** of 9 kg. If the sheet size were increased to a **standard** size of 864 mm × 1118 mm, which is four times as large, the **total weight** of one ream would be 36 kg. The grammage, however, would still be 75.

In addition to being available in a variety of sizes, paper is also manufactured in a variety of weights. Bond paper comes in several weights. These are listed in Fig. 5-3.

Refer to the sample label Fig. 5-2. The label on a package of paper contains the following information: Bond, 17″ × 22″ (432 mm × 559 mm) 32/M ● 16 (60 g/m²) ● Blue. It means that the package contains blue bond paper with sheet size measurement of 17″ × 22″ (432 mm × 559 mm) and the basis weight is 16 pounds (60 g/m²). The weight of 1000 sheets is in-

BOND

17 X 22 • 32M • 16 • BLUE
432 X 559 mm   60g/m²

Fig. 5-2. Sample label for a package of paper

CLASSIFICATION	SIZE (in.)	(mm)	WEIGHT (pounds)	(g/m²)
Bond	**17 x 22** 17 x 28 19 x 28 22 x 34 24 x 38 28 x 34 34 x 44	**432 x 559** 432 x 711 483 x 610 559 x 864 610 x 965 711 x 864 864 x 1118	9, 13, 16, 20, 24	34, 49, 60, 75, 90
Book	20 x 26 22-1/2 x 35 24 x 36 **25 x 38** 28 x 42 28 x 44 32 x 44 35 x 45 36 x 48 38 x 50 41 x 54	508 x 660 572 x 889 610 x 914 **635 x 965** 711 x 1067 711 x 1118 813 x 1118 889 x 1143 914 x 1219 965 x 1270 1041 x 1372	**Uncoated** 35, 40, 45, 50, 60, 70, 80, 100 **Coated one side** 50, 60, 70, 80 **Coated two sides** 50, 60, 70, 80, 90, 100, 120	**Uncoated** 52, 59, 67, 74, 89, 104, 118, 148 **Coated one side** 74, 89, 104, 118 **Coated two sides** 74, 89, 104, 118, 133, 148, 178
Offset	17-1/2 x 22-1/2 19 x 25 22-1/2 x 35 **25 x 38** 28 x 42 28 x 44 32 x 44 35 x 45 36 x 48 38 x 50 38 x 52 41 x 54 44 x 64	445 x 572 483 x 635 572 x 889 **635 x 965** 711 x 1067 711 x 1118 813 x 1118 889 x 1143 914 x 1219 965 x 1270 965 x 1321 1041 x 1372 1118 x 1626	50, 60, 70, 80, 100, 120, 150	74, 89, 104, 118, 148, 178, 222
Text	23 x 29 23 x 35 **25 x 38** 26 x 40 35 x 45 38 x 50	584 x 737 584 x 889 **635 x 965** 660 x 1016 889 x 1143 965 x 1270	60, 70, 80	89, 104, 118
Cover	**20 x 26** 23 x 29 23 x 35 26 x 40 35 x 46	**508 x 660** 584 x 737 584 x 889 660 x 1016 889 x 1168	40, 50, 60, 65, 85 10, 16, 20 **point**	108, 135, 162, 176, 230
Duplicator	**17 x 22** 17 x 28 19 x 24 22 x 34 24 x 38 28 x 34	**432 x 559** 432 x 711 483 x 610 559 x 864 610 x 965 711 x 864	16, 20, 24, 28	60, 75, 90, 105
Ledger	**17 x 22** 17 x 28 19 x 24 22 x 34 24 x 38 28 x 34 22-1/2 x 22-1/2 22-1/2 x 34-1/2 24-1/2 x 24-1/2	**432 x 559** 432 x 711 483 x 610 559 x 864 610 x 965 711 x 864 572 x 572 572 x 876 622 x 622	24, 28, 32, 36	90, 105, 120, 135

Fig. 5-3. Some common paper classifications, sizes, and weights (Bold type indicates base sheet size)

Use this formula to convert from basis weight in pounds to grams per square meter:

$$\text{g/m}^2 = \frac{(\text{Basis Weight} \times 1406.5)}{\text{Square Inches in Base Sheet}}$$

147

dicated by the 32/M. Since 500 sheets weigh 16 pounds, 1000 sheets weigh 32 pounds. M stands for 1000.

The **grain** direction of the paper may be indicated by underlining one of the dimensions on the label such as 17" x 22" (432 mm x 559 mm). The grain direction may also be printed on the label as *grain short* or *grain long*. **Grain** refers to the fiber direction or structure of the paper. Grain direction is a primary consideration if the paper is to be folded. Paper folded with the grain, which is generally stiffer, makes a smoother and longer lasting fold. Folding against the grain will crack the paper, Fig. 5-4.

With the variety of standard sizes and weights available, the printer has the opportunity to select the size and weight of paper to fulfill printing needs. In addition, the printer has basic classifications of paper from which to choose.

PAPER CLASSIFICATIONS

Each of the basic paper classifications contains many different varieties of paper which all have the same general uses and characteristics. The chart in Fig. 5-3 lists

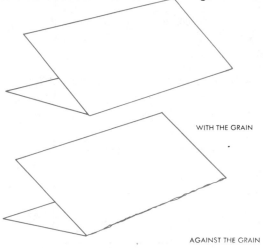

WITH THE GRAIN

AGAINST THE GRAIN

Fig. 5-4. Paper folds uniformly with the grain and ragged against the grain

some of the basic paper classifications, their available sizes, and their available weights. The dimensions printed in bold type indicate the base size for each classification.

Papers are classified in terms of their use. The most common paper classifications are (1) bond, (2) book, (3) offset, (4) text, (5) cover, (6) duplicator, and (7) ledger.

BOND PAPER

There are two types of bond paper. One type has a cotton or rag content. The second is manufactured from chemical wood pulp. The rag content bond is more expensive. It is made in four grades of 25%, 50%, 75%, and 100% rag content. Chemical wood pulp composes the remainder of the ingredients in the first three grades.

Bond paper is a quality paper characterized by strength, good appearance, and a surface which readily accepts ink. It is lint free and displays good erasing qualities. Bond paper is recommended for use when printing letterheads, business forms, stationery, announcements, and direct mail advertising brochures or flyers. It is also commonly used for typing paper, ruling paper, and pen and ink drawing paper. The highest quality bond paper is watermarked. A **watermark** is a design, name, or trademark which is impressed on the paper during manufacturing. The watermark can easily be seen by holding the paper up to light. When using paper that has a watermark, the printed copy and the watermark should be readable at the same time.

BOOK PAPER

Book paper is available either uncoated, coated on one side, or coated on both sides. Coated book paper is made when a mixture of clay and other ingredients is applied to the surface of the paper during manufacturing. This gives it a smooth finish. Coated book paper is often used when it is necessary to print fine screen halftones.

Book paper is widely used for printing brochures, pamphlets, catalogs, and mailing advertisements. It is generally less expensive than text paper, but has similar strength, appearance, and opacity qualities.

OFFSET PAPER

Offset paper is a type of book paper that is available in both uncoated and coated surfaces. The basic principle of offset printing is the fact that grease (ink) and water do not readily mix. Therefore, offset paper must be manufactured with the proper moisture content. It must also be acid free.

Offset paper is commonly used when single and multiple-color form letters, brochures, pamphlets, magazines, and manuals are printed. Coated offset paper is more suitable than uncoated when halftones and colors are to be printed. Lint and fuzz are eliminated during manufacturing.

TEXT PAPER

Text paper is frequently used for printing books, booklets, brochures, pamphlets, programs, announcements, catalogs, manuals, and menus. It is attractive in appearance and is available in a variety of colors and textures. Text paper is strong and opaque. Thus, when printed on both sides, there is little **show-through.** The copy printed on one side will not be seen through the paper when reading the second side. It also permits a sharp, crisp fold to be made.

COVER PAPER

Cover paper is primarily used for covers of catalogs, brochures, manuals, books, and booklets. The 85-pound weight is most commonly used. Some cover paper is pasted together into double thickness and is sold in weight by points.

Cover paper is strong and durable. Its primary function is to serve as a protective covering for the printed product. It is available in a variety of colors. Textured surface finishes, such as linen, fabric, ripple, and corduroy are also available.

DUPLICATOR PAPER

Duplicator paper is manufactured to be used with spirit duplicating, mimeograph duplicating, and other office duplication systems. This combination of processes and material provides an inexpensive method of reproducing such items as form letters, bulletins, schedules, and other office related material. Duplicator paper is not recommended for use on offset duplicators or presses.

LEDGER PAPER

Ledger paper is sometimes referred to as record paper. It is primarily used for bookkeeping and accounting record cards, business ledgers, and statements. It is a strong, durable paper with a smooth, nonglare finish. Ledger paper readily receives pen writing and is resistant to erasures.

FIGURING PAPER CUTS

Consider this problem: If 550 copies of a letterhead are to be printed on 8½" x 11" (216 mm x 279 mm) bond paper, how many base size sheets are required? The base size of bond paper is 17" x 22" (432 mm x 559 mm).

First, it is necessary to determine the number of desired size sheets that can be cut from one base size sheet. To do this, write the base size sheet dimension over the desired size sheet dimension and divide. To obtain an accurate figure showing the least amount of waste, it is necessary to divide both straight up and diagonally, Fig. 5-5.

As you can see, it is possible to obtain either two or four desired size sheets from one base size sheet, depending on the cutting technique. The first method of cutting,

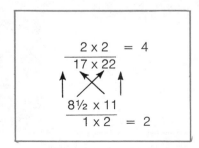

Fig. 5-5. Divide **straight up and diagonally**

shown in Fig. 5-6, results in the least amount of waste, and it is, therefore, most economical.

Since four (4) desired size sheets can be cut from one base size sheet and 550 sheets are required, divide 550 by 4 to determine the number of base size sheets required, Fig. 5-7. When paper cuts are figured, it is necessary to add a full sheet if a fraction appears in the final answer. In this case, it would require 138 base size sheets to cut 550 sheets that are the desired size.

The mathematical method of computing paper cuts does not always indicate the maximum number of desired size sheets that can be cut from one base size sheet. The mathematical method indicates that 10 sheets measuring 5″ x 7″ (127 mm x 178 mm) may be obtained from one 19″ x 25″

$$\begin{array}{r} 137.5 = 138 \\ 4\overline{)550} \\ 4 \\ \overline{15} \\ 12 \\ \overline{30} \\ 28 \\ \overline{20} \end{array}$$

Fig. 5-7. Divide the number obtained from one sheet into the total number desired

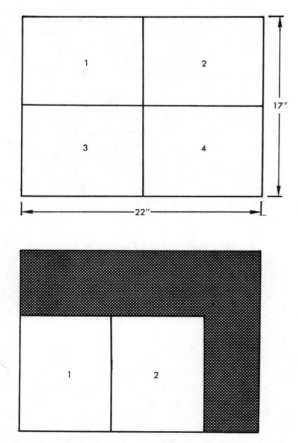

Fig. 5-6. Cut the paper with the least amount of waste

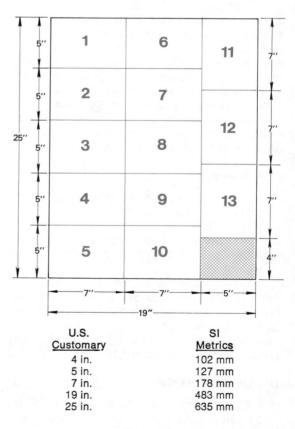

U.S. Customary	SI Metrics
4 in.	102 mm
5 in.	127 mm
7 in.	178 mm
19 in.	483 mm
25 in.	635 mm

Fig. 5-8. Diagram method of figuring paper cuts

(483 mm x 635 mm) sheet of offset paper. However, the diagram method indicates that 13 sheets of the same size may be cut from one base size sheet, Fig. 5-8. Therefore, it is wise to consider the size of the waste when using the mathematical method of computing. More desired size sheets may actually be obtained from one base size sheet than calculated.

PAPER CUTTERS

The paper cutter is designed to accurately cut large sheets of paper into the desired size sheets. Paper cutters range from the small hand-lever cutter (Fig. 5-9) to the large hydraulic power-driven cutter (Fig. 5-10).

The depth of the cut is set by turning the **hand wheel** on the front of the paper cutter. This regulates the distance between the **blade** and the **back fence**. This distance is indicated by a **measuring tape** which is generally in view just below the hand wheel. When the desired cutting dimension is set, the thumbscrew on the hand wheel should be tightened to maintain an accurate setting.

The cutting sequence should be planned so that the least number of cutter settings are used. A cutting chart makes it possible to plan the cutting sequence. It will also help to prevent cutting the paper incorrectly, Fig. 5-11. Once a cutter setting has been made, **all** cuts at that setting should be made before changing to the other dimension. Whenever possible, the paper should be back trimmed to assure consistent paper sizes and to eliminate paper dust. **Back trimming** is the operation of making the final cut on all sides of the paper with the back or flat side of the blade. This is accomplished by always placing the paper in the cutter so the desired dimension is between the back fence and the blade.

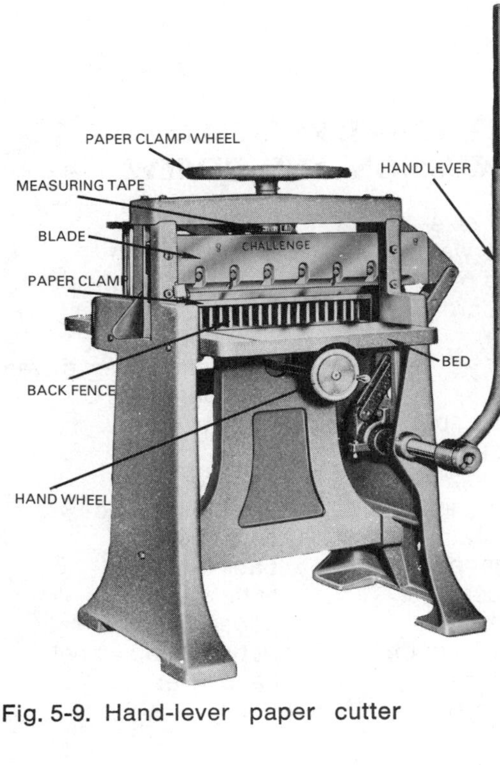

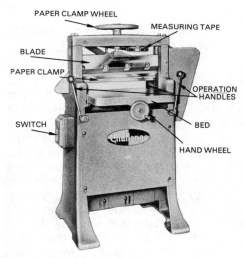

Fig. 5-10. Hydraulic paper cutter

Safety Note

Only one person should operate the paper cutter at a time.

The paper to be cut is placed on the **cutter bed** and jogged to the back fence and the left side, Fig. 5-12. A piece of chipboard or thin cardboard should be placed

Fig. 5-9. Hand-lever paper cutter

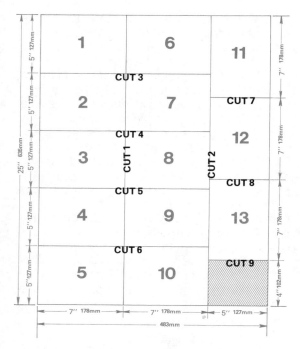

Fig.5-11. A cutting chart should be made before cutting the paper

Fig. 5-12. Jog the paper to the left side and back fence

on top of the paper and under the paper clamp. This prevents the paper from receiving clamp marks.

Lower the paper clamp by turning the **paper clamp wheel** on top of the cutter to hold the paper securely in position while it is being cut. Lower the blade in one continuous motion to obtain a smooth, even cut. Most paper cutters are equipped with a built-in safety device that requires the operator to use both hands. After the cut has been made, raise the paper clamp and remove the paper. Before leaving the paper cutter, lower the paper clamp to the bed and remove all scraps. Be sure the power is OFF if you are using an electrically powered cutter.

Safety Note

Do not leave any machine running while it is unattended.

UNIT 12 — TERMS FOR DISCUSSION AND REVIEW

base size
basis weight
bond paper
standard size
ream
M
grain
book paper
offset paper
text paper
cover paper
duplicator paper
ledger paper
rag content
chemical
   wood pulp
watermark
uncoated

coated
show-through
desired size sheets
hand-lever paper
   cutter
hydraulic power-driven
   paper cutter
hand wheel
blade
back fence
measuring tape
cutting chart
back trimming
cutter bed
paper clamp
paper clamp wheel
hand lever

6 CHAPTER

RELIEF PRINTING

Relief printing (often referred to as **letterpress**) is printing from a **raised surface.** The actual printing surface, which is cast in **reverse,** extends above a supporting body, Fig. 6-1. Images that have been generated by hand-set foundry type, machine-set type, and linoleum-block carving are three-dimensional and can be directly used in the relief printing production process. That is, there are no intermediate image conversion steps required. Images generated by the other methods may also be used by the relief printing production process.

However, several intermediate steps are required to convert the two-dimensional images into three-dimensional letterpress plates.

Fig. 6-2. Locked-up relief printing form

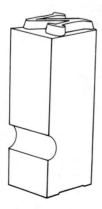

Fig. 6-1. The relief printing surface is raised above the supporting body

Kristi Broekhuizen
6122 Coconut Terrace
Plantation, Florida 33313

Fig. 6-3. The ink on the raised surface is transferred to the paper

Relief printing images must be locked-up so they can be positioned in the platen press. **Lockup** refers to the preproduction operation of clamping the relief form in a **chase**, Fig. 6-2.

After the press has been inked and the necessary "makeready" completed, **production begins.** During production, ink rollers pass over the relief surface, depositing a supply of ink on the raised printing area. When the relief form is pressed against the paper, the ink is **transferred** to the paper and prints a right (correct) reading image, Fig. 6-3.

UNIT 13

LOCKUP

Lockup, as previously stated, refers to the preproduction operation of clamping a relief form in a chase so that it can be placed in position in the press.

TOOLS AND EQUIPMENT

Seven basic tools and pieces of equipment are used in the lockup operation.

Fig. 6-4. A chase is used for locking up type forms

Fig. 6-5. Rubber stamp chase

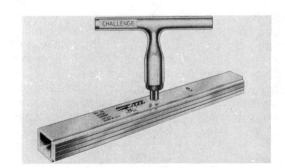

Fig. 6-6. Hi-speed quoin and quoin key

1. The **chase** (Fig. 6-4) is a rectangular metal frame used for locking up a relief form. The chase size varies according to the press size being used. The rubber stamp chase (Fig. 6-5) has a handle that provides a gripping surface for inserting and removing the chase from the hot rubber stamp press.
2. **Quoins** (Fig. 6-6) are expandable locking devices used to exert pres-

Fig. 6-7. Planing block

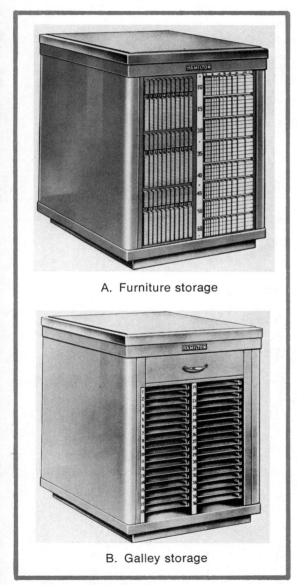

A. Furniture storage

B. Galley storage

Fig. 6-8. Imposing table

sure and secure a relief form in the chase.

3. The **quoin key** is used to expand the quoin.

4. The **planing block** (Fig. 6-7) is a wooden block that is placed on top of the relief form during lockup and gently tapped. This levels the relief surface so that all the characters are at the same height.

5. The **imposing table** (Fig. 6-8) is a smooth flat-top table that is used as a lockup surface. One side of the imposing table provides a storage place for furniture and reglets. Type forms on galleys can be stored in the galley rack on the opposite side of the imposing table. (A quick review of Unit 4 may help you recall such terms as type form and galley.)

6. **Furniture** (Fig. 6-9) is made of both wood and metal. The wooden furniture is used for locking up press relief forms. The metal furniture is primarily used for locking up rubber stamp forms where heat is a factor. Furniture is measured in length and width by picas. The length is stamped on the ends of the furniture and is shown in five-pica multiples from 10 to 60. The width of furniture is 2 picas, 3 picas, 4 picas, 5 picas, 6 picas, 8 picas, and 10 picas.

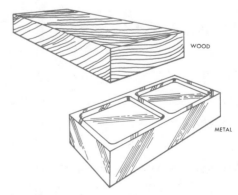

WOOD

METAL

Fig. 6-9. Furniture is made of either wood or metal

7. Reglets (Fig. 6-10) are measured in length by picas and come in 6 and 12 point thicknesses. Reglets are used in lockup to fill spaces which are too small for wooden furniture.

Fig. 6-10. Reglets are 6 and 12 points in thickness

METHODS OF LOCKUP

The two most commonly used methods of lockup are the **chaser** method and the **furniture-within-furniture** method, Fig. 6-11. The furniture-within-furniture method can only be used when the line length of the relief form is in multiples of five picas. If the line length is not in five-pica multiples, the chaser method must be used.

Slide the type form from the galley and onto the surface of the imposing table. Measure the length of the form to determine the method of lockup to be used, Fig. 6-12. Place a chase around the form. Position the form in approximately the center of the chase, Fig. 6-13.

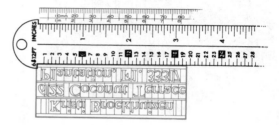

Fig. 6-12. Measure the length of the form to determine the method of lockup to be used

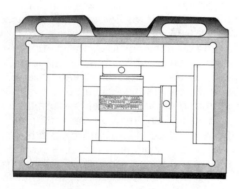

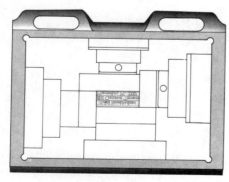

Fig. 6-11. Two methods of lockup for relief printing

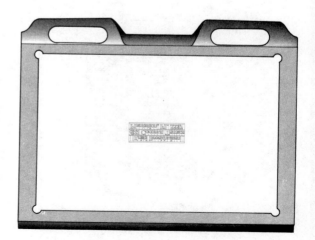

Fig. 6-13. Position the type form in the center of the chase

Depending upon the shape of the form, the heading should be to the left or the bottom of the chase. Generally, the form should be positioned so that the long dimension of the paper to be printed runs parallel to the long dimension of the chase.

CHASER METHOD

Select two pieces of furniture that are slightly longer than the form, and place them on the top and bottom, Fig. 6-14. Two pieces of furniture that are slightly longer than the width should also be placed on the left and right sides of the form. Each piece of furniture will overlap or **chase** the next piece around the form, Fig. 6-15.

Slide the four pieces of furniture away from the form, and carefully remove the string that holds the type form. After removing the string, slide the furniture back into position.

Position the quoins to the top and right of the form, Fig. 6-16. The space to the bottom and left must now be filled with furniture. Pyramid the furniture to the edge of the chase by placing longer pieces to the out-

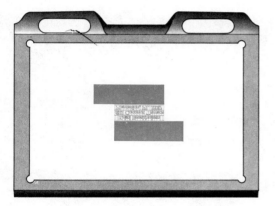

Fig. 6-14. Position furniture to the top and bottom of the form

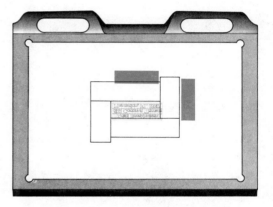

Fig. 6-16. Position the quoins to the top and right of the type form

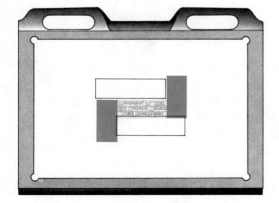

Fig. 6-15. Position the two side pieces of furniture

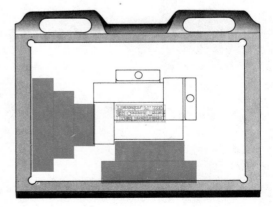

Fig. 6-17. Fill in the bottom and left side with furniture

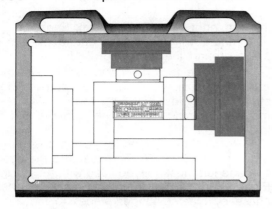

Fig. 6-18. Fill in the top and right side with furniture

side, Fig. 6-17. When positioning the furniture, always start near the form and build out toward the chase. The pyramid structure will distribute the pressure exerted by the quoins over a wider area. Fill in the remaining space to the top and right of the form. **Reglets** are used where the space is too small for the placement of furniture, Fig. 6-18.

Tighten the quoins slightly. Place the planing block on top of the form and tap it gently with a quoin key, Fig. 6-19. Tighten the quoins alternately, first one then the other. Repeat this procedure until the form is tight in the chase. Pressure exerted by the thumb and first finger usually applies adequate pressure to hold the form, Fig. 6-20.

Test the lockup for lift by carefully raising one corner of the chase only far enough to slide a quoin key under the corner. Press the surface of the form with

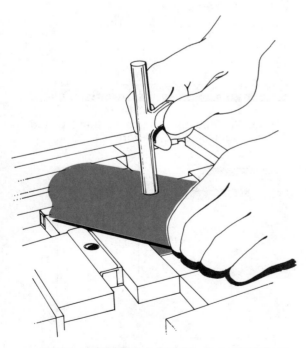

Fig. 6-19. Plane the type form by gently tapping the planing block with a quoin key

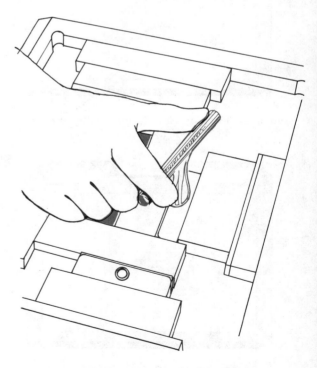

Fig. 6-20. Tighten the quoins alternately

the fingers, Fig. 6-21. If the characters of the form do not push down or drop out, the form is said **to lift** and is ready to be placed in the press. If the characters of the form push down easily, either the lockup furniture is binding or the lines are not justified. Loosen the quoins and make the necessary adjustments.

FURNITURE-WITHIN-FURNITURE METHOD

The furniture-within-furniture method of lockup differs from the chaser method only in the placement of the first four pieces of furniture. The two pieces of furniture that run parallel to the lines must be exactly the same length as the lines. The other two pieces of furniture must be long enough to enclose the form and the first two pieces of furniture, Fig. 6-22.

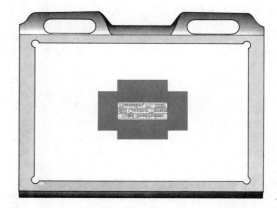

Fig. 6-22. The furniture-within-furniture method of lockup differs from the chaser method only in the placement of the first four pieces of furniture

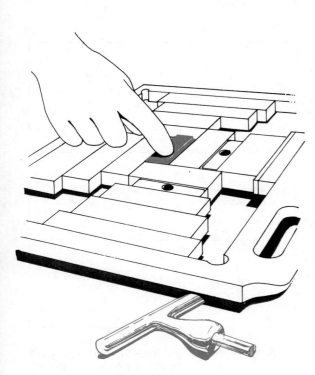

Fig. 6-21. Test the lockup for lift

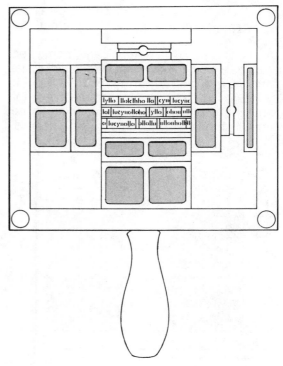

Fig. 6-23. Rubber stamp lockup using metal furniture

RUBBER STAMP LOCKUP

In the lockup for making a rubber stamp, either the chaser or the furniture-within-furniture method is used. Metal furniture must be used, as the heat from the rubber stamp press will cause the wooden furniture to shrink. Type-high furniture called **bearer strips** about 12 points thick should be placed on the top and bottom of the type form to bear the pressure and hold the form in place. The bearer strips must be of an equal line measure as the lines of type. Perform the lockup operation with the limit stops on the chase in the **up** position, Fig. 6-23.

MULTI-PAGE LOCKUP

Many times it is desirable to print more than one relief form at a time. For example, all four pages of a four-page pamphlet may be printed at one time on one large sheet of paper. After printing, the sheet is cut and folded.

In the case of a four-page pamphlet, it is necessary to lockup the four individual forms in a **work-and-turn** lockup, Fig. 6-24. By doing so, one lockup can be used for printing both sides of the sheet which in the end will be cut to become two pamphlets.

After printing on one side, the paper is then turned over and printed on the other side using the same lockup. In the second run, page 1 is printed on the back of page 2, page 4 on the back of page 3, page 2 on the back of page 1, and page 3 on the back of page 4, Fig. 6-25.

Because the same form is printed on both sides of the sheet, and each sheet is printed with the images for two complete pamphlets, it is only necessary to print half the number of sheets for the required number of finished pamphlets. For example, if 1000 pamphlets were required, it would only be necessary to print 500 sheets.

When a multi-page form is locked up, furniture must be placed between the individual page forms to provide the necessary

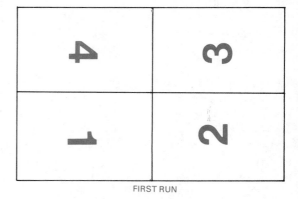

FIRST RUN

SECOND RUN

Fig. 6-25. With a work-and-turn lockup, both sides of the same sheet are printed

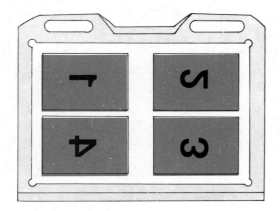

Fig. 6-24. Work-and-turn lockup

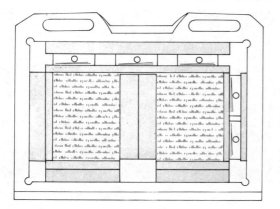

Fig. 6-26. Multi-page lockup

margins. It is also necessary to use additional quoins, Fig. 6-26.

UNIT 13 — TERMS FOR DISCUSSION AND REVIEW

lockup	points
chase	chaser method
quoins	furniture-within-
quoin key	furniture method
planing block	test for lift
imposing table	work-and-turn
furniture	parallel
pica	pyramid
reglets	rubber stamp chase

LETTERPRESS PLATES

Relief or letterpress printing may also be done by using plates on cylinder and rotary presses. Cylinder presses use a flat plate. The paper is carried by the cylinder and **receives an ink impression as it rolls over the flat letterpress plate**, Fig. 6-27.

Curved letterpress plates are used on the rotary press. The plate is held in position on one cylinder while the paper is carried by a second cylinder, Fig. 6-28. As the two cylinders make contact, the impression is transferred to the paper. Letterpress plates are classified as either (1) **electrotypes** or (2) **stereotypes**. These plates are capable of producing (1) line copy or (2) halftone copy.

PHOTOENGRAVING

Original drawings and photographs may be printed by the relief process. First, however, they must be converted to a relief printing surface called a **photoengraving,** a process in which the original copy is photographed to produce a line negative or a halftone negative.

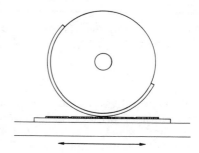

Fig. 6-27. Cylinder letterpress

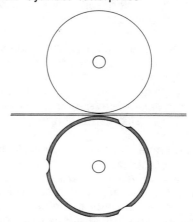

Fig. 6-28. Rotary letterpresses use curved letterpress plates

nova HIGH SCHOOL
land of **TITANS**

parking permit no. _____

nova HIGH SCHOOL
land of **TITANS**

parking permit no. _____

Fig. 6-29. A line negative is produced from original line copy

A. A halftone negative produced with a 150 line screen.

B. A halftone negative produced with a 65 line screen.

Fig. 6-30. A halftone negative is made from continuous tone copy

A **line negative** would be produced when the original artwork is composed of solid lines and areas, Fig. 6-29. A **halftone negative** would be produced when the continuous tone quality of the original must be retained. A photograph, for example, is continuous tone copy because it contains all shades of gray from white to black. The continuous tone quality is retained by placing a halftone screen between the original and the film when the negative is prepared. By doing so, the negative that is produced consists of a series of small dots which vary in size and shape, depending on the screen used, Fig 6-30. Those areas of the negative that will reproduce as light areas are composed of large dots that are close together. When the dots are small and spread apart, the negative areas will reproduce a dark area. Refer to Unit 31 for further information and illustrations of halftone screens.

The negative is then placed **face down** on a sensitized zinc or copper plate. The negative must be positioned face down because a relief surface is a mirrored or reverse image. The zinc or copper plate (with the negative in position) is then exposed by a strong carbon arc lamp. The light passes through the transparent areas of the negative and affects the sensitized plate coating. The development process fixes the image areas that were affected by the exposure light and washes away the coating from the unexposed areas. After development, the plate is placed in an acid

Fig. 6-31. Photoengraved relief printing plate

Fig. 6-32. Mounted engraving may be locked in a chase for printing

bath which etches or eats away the unexposed plate areas. Those areas that were exposed, however, are untouched by the acid and remain as a raised or relief surface. The plate engraving is then mounted to type-high on a wooden block and is ready to be printed by the relief production process, Fig. 6-31. The mounted engraving may be locked up in a chase for relief printing, Fig. 6-32.

DUPLICATE PLATES

Many printing establishments, however, do not use the original engravings and type forms for printing. Duplicate letterpress plates, called **stereotypes** or **electrotypes,** are made. Using duplicate plates protects the more expensive original type forms and engravings from possible damage while on the press.

ELECTROTYPES

Electrotypes are commonly used for the long-run production of magazines. The original type forms and engravings are placed in the proper order and locked in a chase. A mold is then made by placing either a wax-coated sheet, a plastic compound sheet, or a lead sheet on top of the locked-up form and applying pressure. The mold is then sprayed with silver or coated with graphite so that it will conduct electricity. Next it is placed in an electrolytic bath. While the mold is in the electrolytic bath, a copper, nickel, iron, or chromium shell is deposited on the mold by the electroplating process.

The shell (when removed from the mold) is an exact duplicate of the original type forms and engravings. A molten electrotyping metal is then applied to the back of the shell to give added thickness and support.

The electrotype, if it will remain flat for use on a cylinder press, is mounted on a wooden base to make it type-high. For use on a rotary letterpress, the electrotype must be curved so that it will fit the letterpress plate cylinder.

STEREOTYPES

Stereotypes do not lend themselves to the reproduction of fine work. Because of this, halftones that are to be reproduced by stereotypes must be made with a **coarse screen.** Stereotypes are, however, suitable for newspaper production.

Stereotypes are produced by making a paper matrix of the original type forms and engravings that have been locked in a chase. The paper matrix is then placed in a casting box into which molten metal is poured. Upon hardening, the metal becomes a duplicate of the original type forms and engravings. A flat stereotype cast must be mounted to type-high for use on cylinder presses. Stereotypes may also be curve-cast for use on rotary letterpresses.

UNIT 14 — TERMS FOR DISCUSSION AND REVIEW

cylinder press
rotary press

halftone negative
continuous tone copy

electrotypes
stereotypes
line copy
halftone copy
photoengraving

electrolytic bath
electroplating process
paper matrix
casting box

PLATEN PRESS ORIENTATION

In relief printing, the **platen press** is used for the production phase. There are three varieties of platen presses: (1) the hand-lever, (2) the power-driven, and (3) the automatic.

The **hand-lever** platen press, Fig. 6-33, is designed to print limited numbers of small items such as business cards. The hand-lever press is hand-fed and hand-operated.

The **power-driven** platen press, Fig. 6-34, is also hand-fed, but it is power-driven. This press is also used on a limited basis for printing small quantities of small items.

The **automatic** platen press, Fig. 6-35, is not only power-driven but is mechanically fed. Because of this, the automatic platen press is often used for printing large numbers of copies from relief forms.

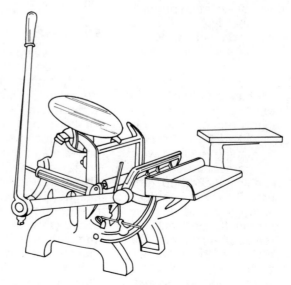

Fig. 6-33. Hand-lever platen press

Fig. 6-34. Power-driven platen press

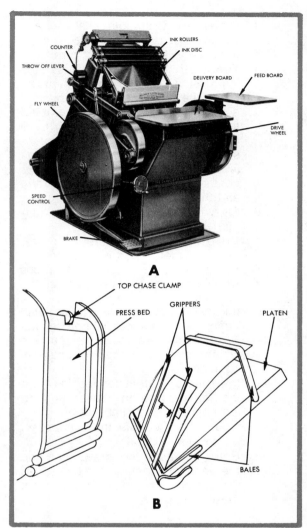

Fig. 6-36. Parts of the power-driven platen press (part B shows details of press-board)

Fig. 6-35. Automatic platen press

Fig. 6-36 identifies the main operating parts of the platen press. The following briefly describes the purpose of each part.

1. **Feed board** — holds the paper stock that is to be printed.

2. **Delivery board** — provides a surface for piling the printed paper after it has been removed from the press.

3. **Grippers** — hold the paper to the platen after the impression is made to prevent it from sticking to the face of the relief form.

4. **Platen** — a smooth, flat surface which holds the paper to receive the impression from the relief form.
5. **Throw-off lever** — regulates the impression of the platen press. When the throw-off lever is pushed away from the operator, the relief form and the paper do not make contact and, therefore, no impression is made. When the throw-off lever is pulled toward the operator, contact is made between the form and the paper.
6. **Fly wheel** — keeps the press running smoothly and evenly.
7. **Drive wheel** — transfers the power from the motor to drive the press.
8. **Brake** — slows or stops the press when pressure is applied with the left foot.
9. **Ink disc** — supplies the rollers with fresh ink before each impression.
10. **Press bed** — smooth, flat surface which holds the locked-up chase in position.
11. **Ink rollers** — transfer the ink from the ink disc to the relief printing form before each impression.
12. **Counter** — counts the number of printed impressions.
13. **Bales** — hold the drawsheet and the packing sheets to the surface of the platen. (Unit 16 explains what these sheets are.)

14. **Speed control** — regulates the operating speed of the press.
15. **Top chase clamp** — holds the chase to the bed of the press.

The platen press requires lubrication to run smoothly and to reduce bearing wear. Turn the press over by hand until the rollers rest on the ink disc. Begin oiling at the feed board and work around the press, oiling each bearing. Check with your instructor to determine the need for lubricating the press.

Safety Note

Under no circumstances should the press be oiled or adjusted while it is running.

UNIT 15 — TERMS FOR DISCUSSION AND REVIEW

relief printing	fly wheel
platen press	drive wheel
hand-lever press	brake
power-driven press	ink disc
automatic press	press bed
feed board	ink rollers
delivery board	counter
grippers	bales
platen	speed control
throw-off lever	top chase clamp

UNIT 16

PLATEN PRESS PREPARATION

Dressing the press is the operation of positioning the drawsheet and the packing on the surface of the platen. The **drawsheet** is made of a tough, oily, manila-colored paper called **tympan paper.** The **packing** generally consists of (1) one piece of pressboard and (2) a specified number of book paper sheets called **hanger sheets,** Fig. 6-37. The amount of packing, however, varies according to the adjustment of the platen. Check with your instructor for the proper amount of packing to be used.

The drawsheet should be cut to a size that is 4″ to 5″ (102 mm to 127 mm) wider than the sheet to be printed and long enough to extend under both bales. The hanger sheets should be cut to a size large enough to cover the platen but not to extend under the bales. Raise the top and bottom bales. Place the drawsheet under the lower bale, and lock it in position. Now place the pressboard and hanger sheets under the draw-

sheet. Stretch the drawsheet tightly over the platen by placing both hands on the drawsheet. Press down and pull up toward the top bale. Lock the top bale in the same motion using the heel of the hand, Fig. 6-38. Tear off any excess paper that extends beyond the bales.

The press should be inked before the locked-up chase is placed in the press. With the press **off** and the rollers at their lowest point of travel, place a small amount of ink on the left side of the ink disc, Fig. 6-39.

Fig. 6-38. Stretch the drawsheet, and lock it under the top bale with the heel of the hand

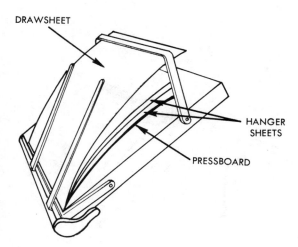

DRAWSHEET

HANGER SHEETS

PRESSBOARD

Fig. 6-37. Dressing the platen

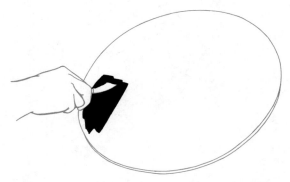

Fig. 6-39. Place the ink on the left side of the ink disc

Use an ink spatula to scrape the ink from the surface. Do not dig holes in the ink as this will cause the ink to dry out.

Before the press is turned on, shirt sleeves should be rolled up and shirt tails should be tucked in. Jewelry such as rings and watches should be removed.

Start the press on a slow speed, and allow the rollers to distribute the ink evenly over the surface of the ink disc. Stop the press with the rollers at their lowest point of travel. With the rollers in this position, the bed is fully exposed.

Place the locked-up chase in the bed of the press, with the quoins to the top and the right. Rest the bottom of the chase against the lugs, and lift the top chase clamp. Push the chase back against the press bed, and lower the top chase clamp until it firmly engages the top of the chase, Fig. 6-40.

Check the gripper position. If the grippers are in front of the relief form, they will crush the type. The grippers may be moved by loosening the bolt and sliding them along the gripper bar, Fig. 6-41. Move the grippers away from the form and tighten the bolt. Stand in front of the press and double-check the gripper position in relation to the form.

Turn the press on and let it run slowly with the throw-off lever in the **off** position. After the press has turned over several times, pull the throw-off lever to the **on** position. Allow the relief form to come in contact with the drawsheet only once.

After the single impression on the drawsheet is made, push the throw-off lever to the **off** position, and stop the press with the rollers at the lowest point of travel. In this position the platen is fully opened for inspection of the print on the drawsheet.

The **kiss impression** on the drawsheet should be clear enough to show the outline of the relief form, Fig. 6-42. If no impression appears on the drawsheet, there is not sufficient packing. Add another sheet of book paper and repeat the process of pulling the kiss impression. It is important to add only

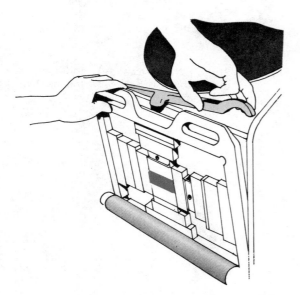

Fig. 6-40. Place the locked-up chase in the press bed

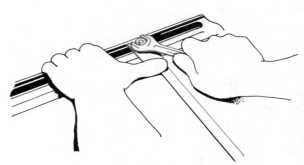

Fig. 6-41. Loosening the bolt on the gripper

one sheet of book paper at a time. If the impression is dark and heavy, there is too much packing which may damage the type. Remove some of the book paper hanger sheets.

Guides, called **gauge pins** (Fig. 6-43), are placed in the drawsheet to hold the paper in the correct position during the impression. Three gauge pins are generally used — two at the bottom of the platen and one on the left-hand side.

To center the image on the paper, place the edge of the sheet to be printed on the edge of the impression on the drawsheet. Mark on the sheet of paper the length of the longest line of type, Fig. 6-44.

The remaining amount must be divided in half to determine the side margins. Fold the edge of the paper over to the mark on the paper and crease, Fig. 6-45. Now place

Fig. 6-42. The kiss impression should show the type outline

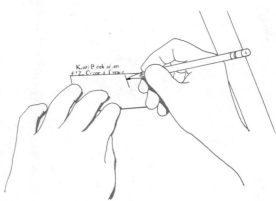

Fig. 6-44. On the paper, mark the length of the longest line

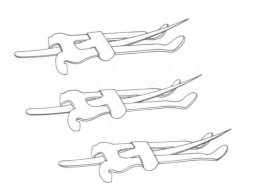

Fig. 6-43. Gauge pins are used to hold the paper during impression

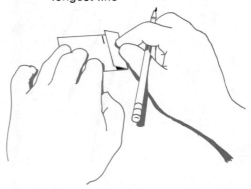

Fig. 6-45. Fold the paper to the mark and make a crease

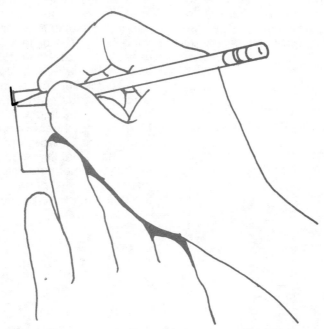

Fig. 6-46. Scribe a line along the edge of the paper

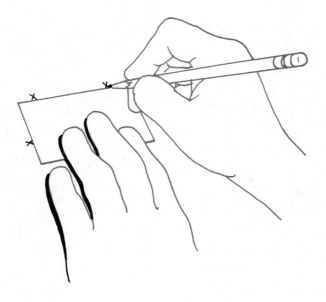

Fig. 6-47. Mark the position of the gauge pins

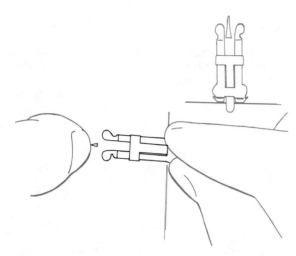

Fig. 6-48. Bring the point of the gauge pins back through the surface of the drawsheet

the fold crease on the right side, or end of the longest line, of the impression on the drawsheet. The edge of the sheet should run parallel with the impression on the drawsheet. Using the paper as a straightedge, scribe a pencil line along the edge of the paper, Fig. 6-46. Repeat this process for determining the placement of the two bottom gauge pins. Use the widest part of the impression on the drawsheet when marking the paper.

If the impression is not to be centered on the sheet, the margins can be determined by measuring and then marking the drawsheet. Mark on the drawsheet the actual position of the gauge pins by placing a piece of paper on the scribed lines. The two bottom pins should be located approximately one-fourth the length of the sheet in from each side. Place an "X" at these points. The position of the gauge pin on the left side should be marked with an "X" approximately one-fourth the distance up from the bottom of the sheet, Fig. 6-47.

Start the point of the gauge pin through the drawsheet about 1/4" (6 mm) away from the scribed line at the point marked with the "X". Push the gauge pin down about 1/2" (13 mm). To keep the gauge pin from mov-

ing during production, the point must be brought back through the surface of the drawsheet. Push the drawsheet down with your thumb in front of the gauge pin and bring the point back through the surface, Fig. 6-48. Continue to push the pin down until the small feet on the bottom of the gauge pin are on the scribed line. Check the position of the tongue of the gauge pin to make sure it will not touch the type during impression. Repeat this process for positioning each of the three gauge pins.

To prevent offset of ink on the back of the printed sheets, the wet ink on the drawsheet must be removed. Use a cloth with solvent to remove the ink and then dust with talcum powder.

UNIT 16 — TERMS FOR DISCUSSION AND REVIEW

dressing
drawsheet
tympan paper
hanger sheets
chase

kiss impression
packing
gauge pins
offset of ink

PLATEN PRESS MAKEREADY AND PRODUCTION

MAKEREADY

Before production is started, final adjustments must be made. **Makeready** for platen press operation is the procedure in which the amount of packing is adjusted to compensate for high and low areas in the impression.

Place a sheet of paper to be printed against the gauge pins on the platen. With the throw-off lever in the **off** position, start the press on a slow speed. After several revolutions, pull the throw-off lever to the on position and allow the relief form to contact the paper once.

After a single impression is made, return the throw-off lever to the off position and stop the press. The rollers should always be at the lowest point of travel when the press is stopped. Remove the paper from the gauge pins and inspect (1) the impression location, (2) amount of impression, and (3) ink coverage.

The location of the impression on the paper can be checked by measuring with a line gauge. The impression should be located on the printing stock as it was planned in the mechanical layout. Adjust the gauge pins to correct the location of the impression. Remember that you move and readjust the paper, and that the form remains stationary.

The impression on the paper should print clearly. Too little packing behind the drawsheet will result in an impression that is too light and spotty, Fig. 6-49. Increase the thickness of the packing under the drawsheet to improve the evenness of the impression. Generally, one sheet of tissue paper will provide the needed additional packing. Under no circumstances should

more than one sheet of book paper be added.

Too much packing will result in an embossed image (deep impression) on the back of the paper and may damage the relief form. Run your finger over the back of the paper. If you can feel the impression, the thickness of the packing sheets must be reduced.

If the ink is too thick on the press, the impression will smudge very easily during the finger test, Fig. 6-50. Rub your finger over the printed image. If the ink smudges easily, some of the ink must be removed from the ink disc. Little or no ink smudge indicates there is not enough ink on the press, and a small amount should be added.

Another sheet should now be printed to check your location, packing, or ink adjustments. Check the impression for the same three points just described. Repeat this procedure until a satisfactory impression is obtained on the paper.

During press production, the paper often sticks to the surface of the relief form after the impression. This causes the paper to be pulled from the gauge pins as the platen opens. To prevent this, position a gripper over the margin of the sheet being printed. A gripper finger may be used if there is not sufficient margin for the gripper,

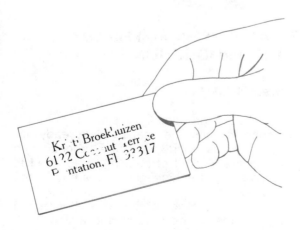

Fig. 6-49. A light spotty print usually indicates the need for more packing

Fig. 6-50. An easily smudged print indicates that there is too much ink

Fig. 6-51. Care must be taken when positioning the gripper to eliminate crushing the relief form or the gauge pins during impression.

Double-check the location of the printed impression on the paper. If the location is satisfactory, the gauge pins must be firmly **set** in the drawsheet to prevent them from slipping during production. This is accomplished by gently tapping the gauge pins with a quoin key to imbed the two small points on each pin into the drawsheet, Fig. 6-52.

PRODUCTION

Set the **impression counter** at zero, and place the paper to be printed on the **feed board.** All other tools and materials should be removed from the press.

Start the press at a slow speed with the throw-off lever in the **off** position. With the right hand, pick up one piece of paper from the feed board. This should be done with the thumb under the paper and the

fingers on top, Fig. 6-53. As the platen opens, place the paper first against the bottom pins and then slide it over to the left-

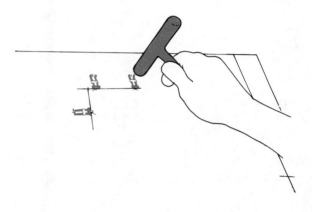

Fig. 6-52. Set the pins by gently tapping them with a quoin key

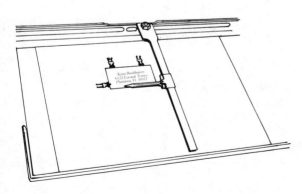

Fig. 6-51. Position a gripper and gripper finger to prevent the paper from sticking to the type face

Fig. 6-53. Pick up the sheet to be printed with the right hand

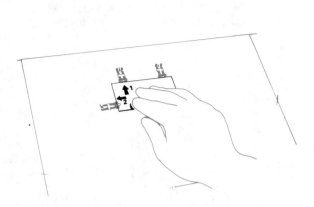

Fig. 6-54. Place the sheet against the bottom pins, and then slide it over to the side pin

Fig. 6-56. A sandpaper finger will prevent ink smudging when removing the printed sheet

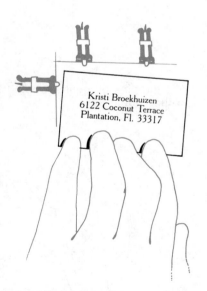

Fig. 6-55. Remove the printed sheet from the pins with the left hand

side pin, Fig. 6-54. Withdraw your hand as the platen begins to close.

Pull the throw-off lever to the **on** position. The printed sheet is removed with the fingers of the left hand (Fig. 6-55) as the

platen opens after the impression has been made; the sheet then is placed on the delivery board. **If at any time a sheet is not properly positioned in the gauge pins,** the throw-off lever should be pushed to the **off** position to prevent printing on the drawsheet.

If the fingers used to slide the printed sheet from the gauge pins touch the printed area after the impression, the ink may be smudged. To prevent this, use a sandpaper finger, Fig. 6-56.

When operating the press, stand erect and squarely on both feet at the delivery board.

Only one person should operate the press at one time. If at any time you must leave the press, push the throw-off lever to the **off** position and **stop** the press. **Always** stop the press before making any adjustments.

Speed is not important to the beginning press operator. Take your time and concentrate on feeding and delivering the paper smoothly and evenly. Speed and skill will develop with the experience of press operation.

UNIT 17 — TERMS FOR DISCUSSION AND REVIEW

makeready	gripper finger
spotty print	setting the pins
embossed image	sandpaper finger

CLEANING THE PLATEN PRESS

At the completion of the production run, the press must be cleaned.

All cleaning must be done with the press power to the **off** position.

Begin cleaning by removing the chase from the bed of the press. Place the chase on the imposing table, and remove the ink from the surface of the relief form.

Remove the gauge pins. Lift the bales and remove the drawsheet and packing. Be sure to lock the bales back in position on the platen.

Moisten a clean cloth with solvent and clean the ink from the ink disc, Fig. 6-57. The cloth should be folded neatly into a pad. Turn the fly wheel with your hand to bring the rollers up to a position just below the

Fig. 6-57. Clean the ink disc with a cloth dampened with solvent

ink disc where they can be cleaned. Clean the ink from the first roller, Fig. 6-58. Continue to turn the fly wheel by hand and clean the remaining rollers. Make sure that the ends of the rollers are also cleaned. It may be necessary to repeat this process several times before all the ink is removed from the press. Clean the ink spatula and cover the ink that was used, if this has not already been done.

Cloths that contain solvent and ink should be placed in metal safety cans.

Leave the press with the throw-off lever in the **off** position and with the rollers at their lowest point of travel. *Do not leave the rollers on the ink disc* because they will become flat at the point of contact over a period of time.

TYPE DISTRIBUTION

Distribution is the process of returning the type to the compartments of the California Job Case.

With the chase on the imposing table, loosen the quoins. Return all quoins, reglets, furniture, and the chase to their respective storage places.

Slide the form into the corner of a galley with the nicks toward the open end, and place the galley on the slanted surface of the type bank, Fig. 6-59.

Remove the proper typecase from the type bank, and place it on the slanted sur-

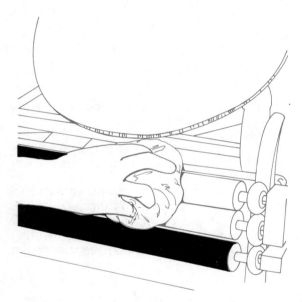

Fig. 6-58. Clean the rollers of the platen press

Fig. 6-59. Place the form in the corner of the galley

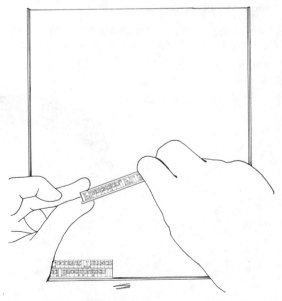

Fig. 6-60. Separate the line to be distributed from the form

face next to the galley. Compare the size, face, and nick position of the type in the form with the type in the case before distributing the type.

Select the first one (or two) lines of the type form and carefully move it away from the remaining portion of the form. A lead or slug must be on the top and bottom of the selected line, Fig. 6-60. Pinch the line together by exerting pressure on all four sides. This makes it possible to lift the line without the pieces of type dropping out.

Transfer the type to the left hand if you are right-handed (or to the right hand if you are left-handed). The type should be held between the thumb and second finger with the index finger under the line for support, Fig. 6-61.

Type should be distributed starting from the right-hand side (or left-hand side for the left-handed person). Pick up a word or syllable one at a time between the thumb and index finger. Separate the individual pieces of type by rocking the fingers back and forth, Fig. 6-62. Read each letter, space,

or quad and then drop it in the proper compartment of the California Job Case. A clean case (one in which all the characters are in their proper compartments) will be maintained if you carefully distribute the type.

After all the type has been distributed, store the leads and slugs, and place the typecase in the type bank.

UNIT 18 — TERMS FOR DISCUSSION AND REVIEW

production run	distribution
chase	quoins
bed	reglets
imposing table	furniture
relief form	galley
gauge pins	type bank
bales	typecase
drawsheet	size
packing	face
solvent	nick position
ink disc	lead
fly wheel	slug
rollers	California Job Case
ink spatula	clean case
metal safety cans	

Fig. 6-61. Holding the line of type for distribution

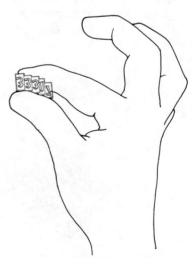

Fig. 6-62. Rock the type between the fingers

RUBBER STAMPMAKING

A rubber stamp is a relief printing image that is cast or molded in rubber. To use a rubber stamp, gently press it on an ink pad to cover the raised surface with ink. Then press the rubber stamp against the surface receiving the image, Fig. 6-63.

In rubber stampmaking, the image is generally prepared by hand-set foundry type or machine-set type. The composed type is used to make a matrix or mold which has the recessed impression of the type. In turn, the matrix is used to prepare the rubber stamp relief surface.

PREPARING THE MATRIX

To make a rubber stamp, proceed first to prepare a matrix of the locked-up relief form.

1. Slide the chase into the rubber stamp press and preheat the type form to 300° F (149° C) for two minutes.
2. Remove the preheated form from the press and place a piece of Bakelite® molding material, red side down, against the type. The Bakelite should be slightly larger on all four sides than the type form. Cover the Bakelite with a piece of paper to prevent it from sticking to the platen of the press, Fig. 6-64.

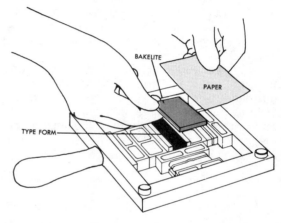

Fig. 6-64. Place the bakelite on top of the type form, and cover it with a piece of paper

Fig. 6-63. A rubber stamp is pressed on an ink pad before it is pressed against the paper

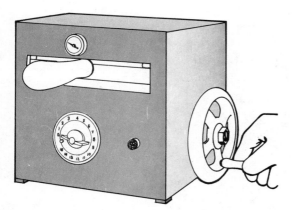

Fig. 6-65. Turn the hand wheel until the first resistance is felt

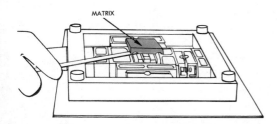

Fig. 6-66. Pry the matrix from the form

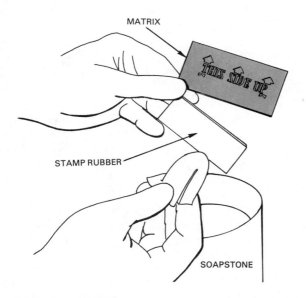

Fig. 6-67. Dust the rubber and the matrix with soapstone

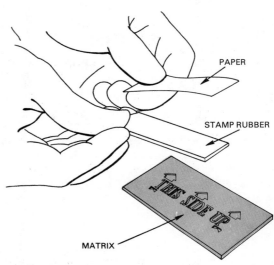

Fig. 6-68. Place the stamp rubber on top of the matrix and cover it with a piece of paper

3. Insert (a) the locked-up form, (b) Bakelite molding material, and (c) paper cover into the rubber stamp press. Turn the hand wheel in a clockwise direction to raise the bed until the first resistance is felt. Allow the Bakelite to heat for one minute. As the Bakelite is heated, it will become soft, allowing the bed to be raised to the height permitted by the limit stops on the chase, Fig. 6-65.

4. After the mold has baked for 10 minutes, lower the bed of the press, and remove the chase and mold. Place the hot chase on a metal surface and carefully pry the matrix from the type form, Fig. 6-66. Allow the matrix to cool.

Safety Note

Exercise caution when removing the matrix from the form because the chase, type, and form are extremely hot and could cause severe burns.

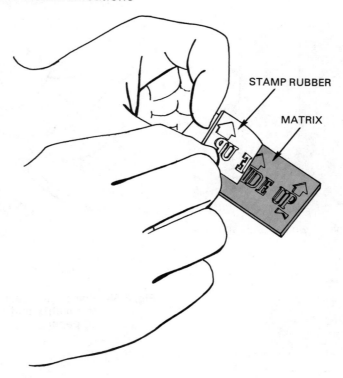

STAMP RUBBER

MATRIX

Fig. 6-69. Strip the stamp rubber from the matrix

PREPARING THE RUBBER RELIEF SURFACE

Cut a piece of stamp rubber that is slightly larger (on all sides) than the type area of the matrix. To prevent the rubber from sticking to the matrix, dust both surfaces with soapstone, Fig. 6-67. Remove all the excess soapstone powder from the matrix cavities.

Place the matrix face up on the vulcanizing tray. Then place the stamp rubber face down over the cavities in the matrix. Cover the back of the stamp rubber with a piece of paper (Fig. 6-68), and place the vulcanizing tray in the rubber stamp press. Raise the bed of the press by turning the hand wheel to the full extent allowed by the limit bars of the vulcanizing tray.

Fig. 6-70. Trim off the excess rubber

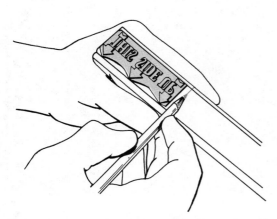

Fig. 6-71. Mark and cut the handle to length

Allow the stamp rubber to bake for 6 minutes. During this time the rubber will become soft and will be forced into the cavities of the matrix to form the rubber stamp.

Turn the hand wheel counterclockwise to lower the bed, and remove the vulcanizing tray. Allow the matrix and rubber to cool before stripping off the vulcanized rubber, Fig. 6-69.

Inspect the vulcanized rubber to be sure all the letters are clear and sharp. Trim off the excess rubber by tapering away from the raised printing surface. Trim as close to the printing surface as possible, Fig. 6-70.

MOUNTING THE RUBBER

Cut a piece of rubber stamp mounting handle that is slightly longer than the rubber. The handle should be just wide enough to mount the rubber, Fig. 6-71. The ends of the mounting handle may be sanded and stained if desired.

Using rubber cement, attach the trimmed rubber to the rubber pad of the mounting handle. Make a trial impression of the rubber stamp and inspect the print. Trim the impression so that it will slide under the plastic on the mounting handle. This will identify the printing matter of the rubber stamp.

UNIT 19 — TERMS FOR DISCUSSION AND REVIEW

rubber stamp	vulcanizing tray
matrix	cavities
rubber stamp press	vulcanized rubber
Bakelite®	mounting handle
stamp rubber	rubber cement
soapstone	

7 CHAPTER

SCREEN PROCESS PRINTING

Screen process printing is accomplished by forcing ink through a prepared stencil which has been adhered to a piece of tightly stretched, open-weave material, Fig. 7-1. The stencils used for screen printing may be made by a variety of processes using many types of material.

PAPER STENCIL METHOD

The paper stencil method of screen printing is the least expensive and the simplest to prepare. The stencil can be easily cut from paper and attached to the screen, Fig. 7-2. Paper used for making stencils must be tough (but not too fibrous) to prevent tearing and rough edges. If water-base ink will be used for printing, the paper

stencil should be made of waterproof paper.

The paper stencil method is primarily used for short runs of less than 100 impressions. It is commonly used for simple designs, generally of one color. This method is not recommended for designs that have loose centers such as the letters "o," "p," "b," and "d." Multicolor printing can be done by preparing a separate stencil for each color.

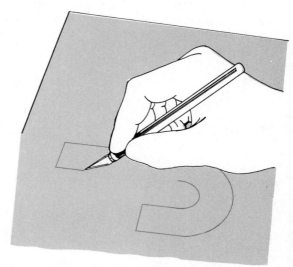

Fig. 7-2. Paper stencil method of screen process printing

Fig. 7-1. Screen process printing

The paper stencil is quick and easy to attach and remove from the screen. Because the paper stencil is prepared to a size that is equal to the size of the frame, the block-out operation is not necessary.

TUSCHE STENCIL METHOD

Tusche stencils are most practical and adaptable for fine art printing. The design is drawn directly on the screen, thus permitting the creation of the design and the preparation of the stencil in a single operation, Fig. 7-3. Stencils may also be prepared by placing the original artwork design under the screen and tracing the design onto the silk. The type of detail that can be reproduced is governed only by the instruments used to apply the tusche and the skill of the person preparing the stencil.

HAND-CUT FILM METHOD

The hand-cut film method of screen printing reproduces designs of sharp, clean-cut lines and infinite, precision detail as well as large solid areas.

Hand-cut stencil film is flexible and very durable. Up to 10,000 impressions can be made from a single stencil. The stencil film is easily cut and peeled, Fig. 7-4. It also is easily adhered to and removed from the screen fabric.

Multicolor designs may be printed with excellent registration. A separate stencil must be cut for each color. A great deal of care and dexterity are required for accuracy in cutting film stencils.

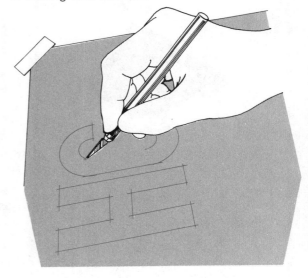

Fig. 7-4. Hand-cut film stencil method

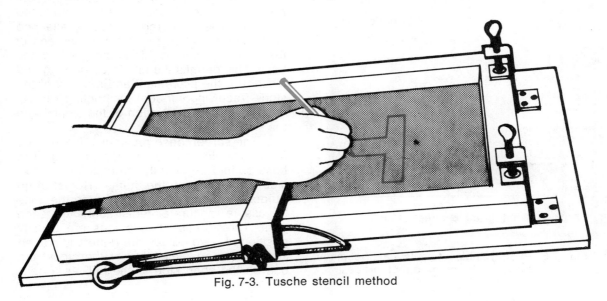

Fig. 7-3. Tusche stencil method

PHOTOGRAPHIC STENCIL METHOD

Photographic stencilmaking can be accomplished by using either the photographic **indirect** or the photographic **direct** method, Fig. 7-5. The photographic indirect method

A. Photographic indirect stencil

B. Photographic direct stencil

Fig. 7-5. Photographic stencils can be made by an indirect or direct process

(sometimes referred to as the **transfer method**) uses a special photographic film. Photographic film for the indirect method is first processed and then transferred to the screen fabric. However, the **photographic direct method allows the stencil to be exposed on a sensitized screen.**

Photographic stencils reproduce very fine detail such as needed to print color halftones. Separate stencils are required for each printing color.

UNIT 20

PRINTING EQUIPMENT

Printing equipment for all hand screen-process printing methods consists of (1) a screen frame, (2) a screen board or base, (3) registration guides, (4) a side kick, and (5) a squeegee, Fig. 7-6. The **screen frame** holds the screen fabric in a tightly stretched position. The prepared stencil is attached to the screen fabric for printing. One end of the screen frame is hinge-clamped to the base. This permits the unit to be opened and closed for the placement and removal of the stock (receiving surface) for printing without destroying the registration of the stencil and the stock.

The **screen base** provides a flat surface for positioning the stock for printing. The base should be slightly larger than the outside dimension of the frame. **Registration guides** are generally positioned on the base to assure accurate registration for each print. Three registration guides are usually positioned. Two guides are generally placed along the long dimension of the stock and one on the short side to the left. As a general rule, the long dimension of the receiving surface should run parallel to the long dimension of the screen frame. The two long-dimension registration guides should be located approximately one-fourth the length of the receiving surface in from each edge. The location of the third registration guide should be about one-fourth the distance up from the corner of the receiving surface. The registration guides may be held in position with tape.

The **side kick** is clamped on either side of the screen frame. It holds the printing unit open when stock is positioned for printing and when the printed stock is to be removed.

The **squeegee** is used to force ink through the open areas of the stencil. The squeegee is a rubber blade with a wooden or metal handle. The resting device on the handle of the squeegee prevents it from falling into the ink.

The shape of the squeegee blade varies with the type of printing that is being done, Fig. 7-7. A square-edged blade is used for

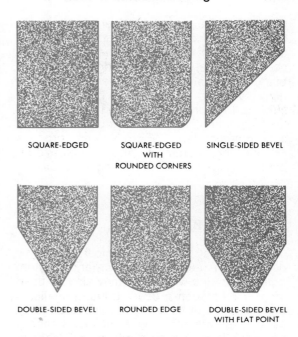

SQUARE-EDGED SQUARE-EDGED WITH ROUNDED CORNERS SINGLE-SIDED BEVEL

DOUBLE-SIDED BEVEL ROUNDED EDGE DOUBLE-SIDED BEVEL WITH FLAT POINT

Fig. 7-7. Select the squeegee recommended for the printing job

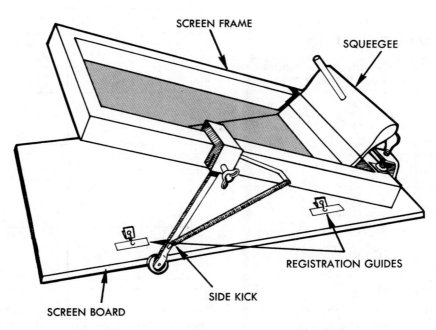

SCREEN FRAME

SQUEEGEE

REGISTRATION GUIDES

SIDE KICK

SCREEN BOARD

Fig. 7-6. Equipment for screen process printing

printing on flat surfaces. Where extra heavy deposits of ink are required, a square-edged squeegee with rounded corners should be used. A single-sided bevel-edged squeegee blade is generally used when printing on glass, while a double-sided bevel edge is suitable for printing on uneven surfaces. For textile printing, a rounded-edged squeegee is recommended. When screen process printing on ceramics, the double-sided, bevel-edged, flat-point squeegee is used.

SCREEN FABRICS

The most popular and most commonly used screen fabric is silk. Organdy, nylon, cotton, and fine wire mesh may also be used for special screen-process printing qualities.

The size of the mesh or weave opening of silk is indicated by number. Standard bolting silk ranges in number from 0000 to 25. Silk with a mesh count from 6 to 18 is

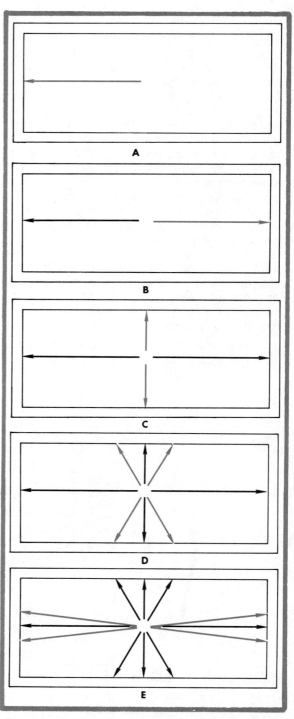

Fig. 7-9. Stretching silk by the staple method

DOMESTIC SILK		
NUMBER	OPENINGS PER SQUARE INCH	PERCENT OF OPEN AREA
6XX	74	47
8XX	86	45
10XX	108	41
12XX	124	33
14XX	138	31
16XX	152	29
17XX	164	28

Fig. 7-8. Mesh count of silk
(1 sq. inch = 645 sq. mm)

generally used. The mesh count indicates the number of openings per lineal inch (25.4 mm) of fabric with the higher numbers representing the smaller-size mesh openings, Fig. 7-8. For example, a number 6 silk is a very open-weave material and is considered a coarse fabric, while number 18 is a fine-weave material.

The quality or strength of silk is indicated by an "X" after the number. The more "X's" that appear, the stronger the silk. For example, a number 12XX silk is stronger than a number 12X silk.

The most commonly used all-purpose silk is number 12XX. This silk combines a medium mesh count with a medium strength. For printing extremely fine detail, a finer mesh silk such as 18XX is recommended. If the mesh is too fine, however, it will become clogged very easily and will be more difficult for the ink to pass. A coarse silk, such as 6XX, is often used when an extra heavy deposit of ink is required.

STRETCHING THE SCREEN FABRIC

Two commonly used methods of stretching silk on a screen printing frame are (1) the **staple** method and (2) the **tite-stretch** or cord method. Each method accomplishes the same result; however, the tite-stretch method is longer lasting. Also, the tite-stretch method can only be used when the screen frame has grooves cut along all four sides.

Before attempting to stretch the silk, inspect the frame. All burrs or rough edges must be removed to prevent **runs** in the silk. Cut the silk to a size that is slightly larger than the outside dimensions of the frame. Wash the silk in warm water to remove any starch in the fabric.

STAPLE METHOD

1. Place the silk, while it is still wet, over the screen frame. Begin stapling the silk to the frame by placing one staple in the center of one end,

Fig. 7-9A. The staples should be inserted at about a 45° angle to the side of the frame and approximately 1″ (25.4 mm) apart. (See Fig. 7-10.) This provides for maximum holding strength. A staple gun with heavy-duty staples should be used.

2. Pull the silk to the opposite end of the frame, and place one staple in the center of the end, Fig. 7-9B. Do not pull too hard as the silk may rip.

3. Staple the silk to the sides of the frame by placing one staple in the center of each side, Fig. 7-9C. Stretch the silk before inserting the staple.

4. Working from the center to the ends, begin stapling the silk to the frame along the long sides, Fig. 7-9D. Pull the silk tight before inserting each staple. **Do not staple the corners.**

5. Stretch and staple the silk on the ends, working from the center to the corners of the frame, Fig. 7-9E. The last staples that are inserted in the frame are in the four corners.

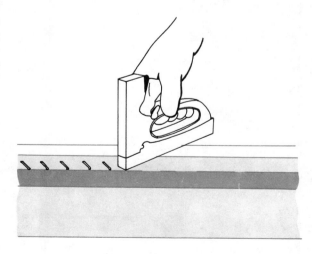

Fig. 7-10. Insert the staples at 45° angles about 1″ (25.4 mm) apart

TITE-STRETCH METHOD

1. Place the silk, while it is still wet, over the screen frame. Cut four pieces of tite-stretch cord, one for each side, Fig. 7-11A. The cord should be the same length as the grooves in the frame.

2. Press the cord and the silk into the groove along one side of the frame with finger pressure, Fig. 7-11B Pull the silk lightly to the opposite side of the frame, and press in the tite-stretch cord. Repeat this process for the remaining two opposite sides.

3. Inspect the silk for position and to be sure it is free of wrinkles. If there are no wrinkles, gently tap the cord with a mallet, forcing it into the groove so that it is flush with the frame, Fig. 7-11C.

4. Using a **tite-stretch tool** or a thin piece of wood, drive the cord deeper into the grooves, Fig. 7-11D. In order to stretch the silk evenly, work around the frame several times, driving the cord down into the grooves only a small amount each time.

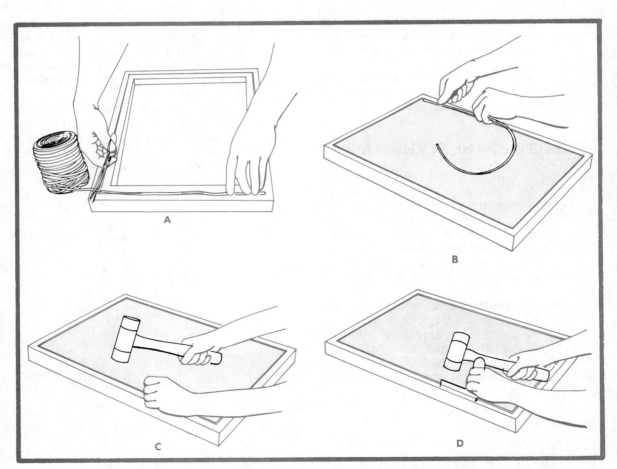

Fig. 7-11. Stretching silk by the tite-stretch method

FINISHING PROCEDURE

After the silk has been stretched by either method, trim off the excess silk that hangs over the edge of the frame. Cover the staples or the tite-stretch cord with gummed tape. Turn the frame over and mask the four inside edges with gummed tape. The tape should be folded in half lengthwise and applied so that it contacts both the silk and the inside of the frame, Fig. 7-12. This will prevent ink from seeping under the frame during production and thus aids in the cleanup operation. A coat of lacquer or shellac should be painted on the gummed tape to make it waterproof.

BASE COVER

Cut a piece of kraft paper that is the same length as, but wider than, the base. Place the paper on top of the base. Fold the long ends under and tape them to the back of the base.

During the production operation, it may be necessary to build up the base by sliding packing sheets under the base cover. A small gap, however, should remain between the silk and the surface receiving the ink, Fig. 7-13. The gap permits the printed product to drop free of the screen and also prevents the ink from smearing. The action of the squeegee over the silk will force the silk and stencil into direct contact with the receiving surface.

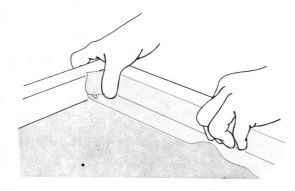

Fig. 7-12. Tape the four inside edges of the screen frame

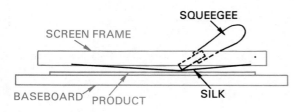

Fig. 7-13. A small gap should be left between the silk and the receiving surface

UNIT 20 — TERMS FOR DISCUSSION AND REVIEW

screen process printing
screen frame
screen board or base
registration guides
side kick
squeegee
screen fabric
stencil
hinge-clamped
stock
parallel
square-edged blade
square-edged squeegee with rounded corners
single-sided bevel-edge squeegee
double-sided bevel edge
textile printing
rounded-edge squeegee
ceramics
double-sided bevel-edge flat point squeegee
organdy
nylon
cotton
wire mesh
mesh opening
mesh count
12XX silk
staple method
tite-stretch or cord method
runs
tite-stretch tool
gummed tape
lacquer or shellac
kraft paper

UNIT 21

PAPER STENCIL METHOD

The original design should be prepared on paper that is the same size as the paper to be used for reproduction. The design should be drawn to actual size and in the desired location on the sheet. If more than one color will be printed, the different color areas should be indicated. This is done by simply labeling the color areas or by using colored pencils. A separate stencil must be prepared for each color.

Kraft wrapping may be used for making the paper stencil. A waterproof paper or oil-treated paper is recommended for the stencil paper when water-base ink is used for printing.

Cut a piece of stencil paper that is the same size as the outside dimension of the screen frame. Trace the original design in approximately the center of the stencil

paper. Remember, only one color per stencil. Using a sharp stencil knife, cut out the design, Fig. 7-14. All cutting should be done on a smooth, hard surface.

After the stencil has been completely cut, assemble the screen frame, the printing base, and the side kick. Place the original design in the center of the base and position the registration guides; then tape the registration guides in position.

Place the prepared stencil in register on top of the original design, Fig. 7-15. Carefully lower the screen frame. Do not allow the stencil and original design to move from the registered position against the registration guides.

Apply several spots of glue on the silk around the design area, Fig. 7-16. The glue,

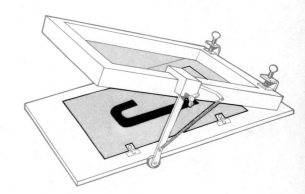

Fig. 7-15. Register the stencil on top of the original design

Fig. 7-14. Cut out the design with a sharp stencil knife

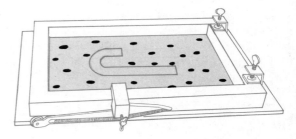

Fig. 7-16. Apply spots of glue around the design area

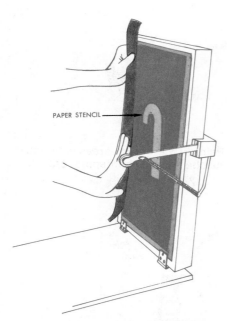

PAPER STENCIL →

**Fig. 7-17. Tape the paper stencil to the under-
side of the frame along all four
edges**

when dry, will hold the stencil in position on
the screen. The glue serves only as a temporary adhesive.

After the glue has dried, raise the
frame. Do not remove the screen frame from
the base as this will move the stencil and
original design out of registration. Tape all
four sides of the paper stencil to the frame,
Fig. 7-17. Gummed tape or masking tape
may be used. The stencil is now ready for
production.

Paper stencils may also be prepared from
standard mimeograph stencils. They may be
used to generate stencil images that are too
difficult to hand-cut from kraft paper. They
can be made by typing the message with a
standard typewriter, drawing by hand, or
lettering with a stylus. For complete instructions on preparing a mimeograph
stencil refer to Unit 51. A mimeograph stencil for screen process printing may be adhered in the same manner as a kraft paper

stencil. When used in screen process printing, a mimeograph stencil will yield about
100 good copies before starting to print
weak images.

UNIT 21 — TERMS FOR DISCUSSION AND REVIEW

original design
reproduction
waterproof paper
stencil paper
stencil knife
stencil
screen frame

printing base
side kick
registration guides
adhesive
gummed tape
mimeograph stencil

UNIT 22

TUSCHE STENCIL METHOD

The original design should be prepared
on paper that is the same size as the paper
to be used for reproduction. The design
should be drawn to actual size and in the
desired location on the sheet. If more than
one color is to be printed, label the different color areas or use colored pencils.
A separate stencil must be prepared for
each color.

Assemble the printing frame and the
base, and attach the side kick. Raise the
screen frame and place the original design
in approximately the center of the base.
Position the registration guides, and secure
them to the base with tape, Fig. 7-18.

Lower the screen frame, being careful
not to allow the original design to move
from position against the registration
guides. With the screen lowered, the design
will be visible through the silk. Trace the
design outline on the silk, Fig. 7-19. Trace
only the areas for one color at a time.

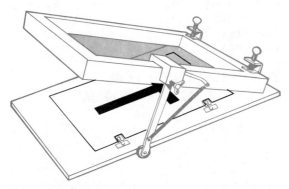

Fig. 7-18. Position the registration guides with the original design in place

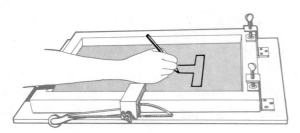

Fig. 7-19. Trace the design on the silk

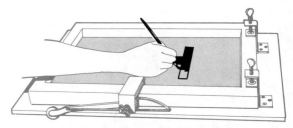

Fig. 7-20. Paint in the design areas with liquid tusche or a lithographic crayon

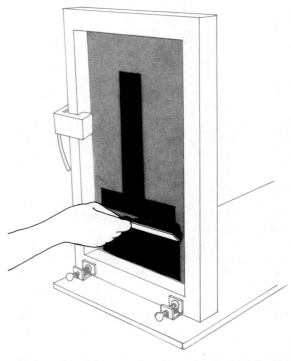

Fig. 7-21. Coat the entire surface of the screen with glue

Once the design has been traced on the silk, the original design may be removed from the printing base. The printing (design) areas must now be painted-in with liquid tusche or a lithographic crayon, Fig. 7-20. If the printing design consists of letters, transfer type may be used as a replacement for the tusche or lithographic crayon. Transfer type is opaque and black and can be applied directly to the screen fabric. (See Unit 8.)

While the tusche is wet, it may be washed out with water. After it has dried, use benzine or lacquer thinner. The tusche should be opaque and black when it is dry. About one-half hour should be allowed for drying. Inspect the tusche coating by holding it to a strong light. If there are areas

that permit light to pass, a second tusche coating should be applied.

When the tusche is completely dry, the screen is coated with glue. This seals the open weave and prevents the flow of ink through the non-printing areas. The glue will not seal the silk weave in the design

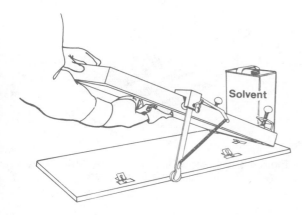

Solvent

Fig. 7-22. Wash away the tusche design by rubbing with a cloth and solvent

areas because it has been coated with either the tusche or lithographic crayon, or the transfer type has been applied.

Raise the screen frame, allowing the side kick to keep it up. Pour a small quantity of water-soluble glue on the silk. Using a stiff piece of cardboard, spread a thin coat of glue evenly over the surface of the silk, including the design area, Fig. 7-21. Apply a second coat after the first coat has dried completely.

After the glue has thoroughly dried, the design is washed from the screen. The same procedure may be used for tusche, lithographic crayon, and transfer type. Using

a cloth pad dampened with benzine or lacquer thinner, begin rubbing the design area. Concentrate on the underside of the screen as the top of the design is coated with glue, Fig. 7-22. This will dissolve the tusche, lithographic crayon, or transfer type and create open areas in the shape of the design to allow the passage of ink. As the tusche, lithographic crayon, or transfer type dissolves, the glue coating over the design areas will begin to flake off.

Safety Note

Cloths that have been used with solvent to remove the tusche should be placed in metal safety cans.

The stencil is now ready for production. Water-base screen inks may not be used with this type of stencil because the ink will dissolve the glue.

UNIT 22 — TERMS FOR DISCUSSION AND REVIEW

original design	lithographic crayon
reproduction	transfer type
printing frame	opaque
base	benzine
side kick	lacquer thinner
registration guides	open weave
printing areas	non-printing areas
liquid tusche	water soluble glue

HAND-CUT FILM STENCIL METHOD

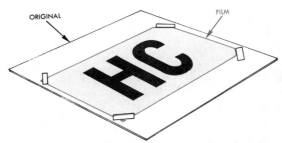

Fig. 7-23. Tape the film to the original design with the gelatin side up

TYPES OF FILM

Hand-cut film is a thin layer of gelatin material with a plastic, wax paper, or mylar backing. There are two types of hand-cut film for screen process printing: (1) lacquer film and (2) aqua film. As the name implies, laquer film is soluble in lacquer thinner and, therefore, must be used with a water-soluble ink. Aqua film requires the use of a lacquer-base ink because the film is water-soluble.

STENCIL PREPARATION

The original design must be prepared to actual size on paper the same size as that to be used for production. If the original design contains two or more colors, each color area should be clearly marked by labeling each area or using colored pencils. A separate stencil must be cut for each color.

Cut the stencil film to a size that is about 2″ (51 mm) larger on all sides than the original design. Place the film on top of the design with the gelatin side up. The gelatin side is usually the shiny side, and it is always the side which is easily cut and peeled away. Tape the film to the original copy, with the design positioned approximately in the center of the film. The design is visible through the stencil film, Fig. 7-23.

When cutting the stencil film, work on a hard, smooth surface such as the glass surface of a light table. Use a sharp-pointed stencil knife. Light pressure on the stencil knife is required since you only need to cut through the gelatin coating. Intersecting

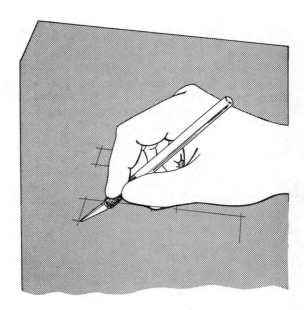

Fig. 7-24. Overcut the intersecting lines

lines should be slightly overcut, thus assuring sharp, even corners, Fig. 7-24. The overcuts will close up when the stencil is adhered to the screen fabric. Too much pressure will emboss the backing and make it difficult to adhere the stencil to the silk. Use one piece of stencil film to cut only those areas that will print in the same color.

After the design area has been completely cut, lift the gelatin from the backing with the point of the stencil knife, Fig. 7-25. Peel the gelatin from the backing very slowly and carefully, checking to be sure that no part of the design area has been overlooked during the cutting. Only remove the gelatin from the printing areas of the film. When the gelatin has been peeled away, remove the tape and original design from the back of the stencil film.

To position the registration guides, place the original design in the approximate center of the screen base. When the registration guides have been secured in position, place the prepared stencil in register on top of the original design, Fig. 7-26. Lower the screen frame carefully, making sure that the original design and the stencil do not move away from the registration guides.

Direct contact between the screen and the stencil is necessary for good adhesion. It may be necessary to build up the stencil by placing several layers of newspaper (smaller than the screen frame) under the base cover.

ADHERING THE STENCIL

Adhering the stencil bonds the screen fabric to the stencil. When lacquer film is used, lacquer thinner is the adhering liquid. Aqua film is adhered with water. Moisten a cotton pad with a small amount of the proper adhering liquid. Too much adhering liquid will completely dissolve the gelatin. Press the cotton pad to the stencil, Fig. 7-27. **Do not rub,** as this will burn the stencil.

The adhering liquid softens the gelatin, and the downward pressure forces the silk into the softened gelatin. The stencil will darken in color when properly adhered to the screen. Light spots indicate poor adhesion.

Fig. 7-25. Peel the gelatin from the cut design areas

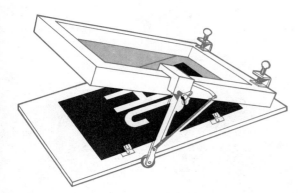

Fig. 7-26. Position the registration guides with the original design in place

Fig. 7-27. Press a cotton pad (dampened with adhering liquid) to the stencil

Allow the adhered stencil to dry. A fan may be used to accelerate the drying time which is normally between 15 and 20 minutes.

After the drying period, remove the stencil backing. Pick up one corner and peel the entire backing from the stencil, Fig. 7-28. This should be done slowly and carefully, checking to be sure the gelatin is not disturbed.

BLOCK-OUT

Nonprinting areas of the screen must be blocked out (masked out) to prevent the flow of ink. The two most commonly used methods of block-out are (1) the paper mask method and (2) the lacquer mask or water mask method.

PAPER MASK METHOD

The paper mask is prepared by cutting a piece of kraft paper that is slightly smaller than the inside dimension of the screen frame. Place the paper mask on top of the adhered stencil, and outline those areas that must be removed to allow the printing of the design, Fig. 7-29. The cutouts should be about 2″ (51 mm) away from the design on all edges.

Using gummed tape, secure the paper mask in position. The final masking should not interfere with the passage of the squeegee over the stencil, Fig. 7-30. If the squeegee does not make direct contact with the silk, the prints may be fuzzy.

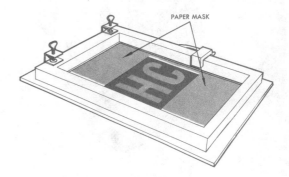

Fig. 7-29. Outline the paper mask

Fig. 7-28. Peel off the stencil backing

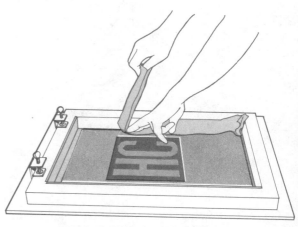

Fig. 7-30. Tape the paper mask to the screen

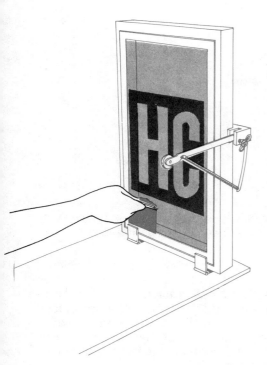

Fig. 7-31. Coating the non-image areas of a screen with water mask or lacquer mask

UNIT 23 — TERMS FOR DISCUSSION AND REVIEW

hand-cut film	emboss
gelatin	printing areas
mylar backing	registration guides
screen process	screen frame
printing	base cover
lacquer film	lacquer thinner
aqua film	adhering liquid
water-soluble ink	nonprinting areas
lacquer-base ink	block-out
original design	paper mask
stencil film	lacquer mask
stencil knife	water mask
intersecting lines	kraft paper
overcut	gummed tape
adhere	

UNIT 24

PHOTOGRAPHIC INDIRECT STENCIL METHOD

PREPARING THE POSITIVE

Use a positive image design to prepare a photographic indirect stencil for screen process printing, Fig. 7-32. The printing areas must be opaque, while the nonprinting areas are transparent. A negative image design cannot be used because the area desired for printing is transparent, Fig. 7-33. Separate positives and separate stencils must be made for printing each color. The positive may be prepared by making the original design on a transparent material

WATER MASK AND LACQUER MASK METHODS

Water mask and lacquer mask are also available for blocking out or masking out unwanted printing areas. Water mask is not recommended ·for use with water-base ink. The ink will dissolve the water mask during the production operation. Lacquer mask should not be used when printing will be done with lacquer-base ink.

Water mask and lacquer mask can be applied by brushing or. by spreading with a stiff piece of cardboard, Fig. 7-31. The masking may be applied to either side of the screen fabric. Allow the first coat to dry before applying a second coat. The second coat usually assures a leakproof coverage. When the block-out mask is completely dry, the stencil is ready for the production operation.

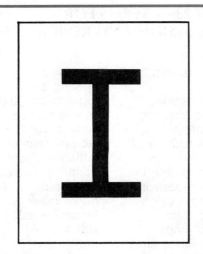

Fig. 7-32. A photographic positive has opaque image areas

Fig. 7-33. A photographic negative has transparent image areas

A photographic positive must be used to prepare a photographic indirect stencil for screen process printing.

such as clear glass, tracing paper, or clear plastic. If the design is prepared by drawing, black india ink should be used. Transfer type may also be used to generate the positive image. (See Unit 8.)

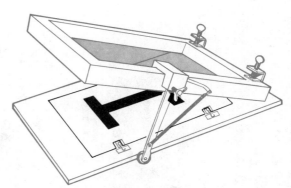

Fig. 7-34. Position the registration guides with the original design in place

The positive may also be prepared photographically. Because of this, any of the image generation methods may be used to create the original image. If a continuous tone photograph is to be reproduced, a halftone positive must be prepared. See Unit 31 for information on making photographic positives.

PREPARING THE STENCIL

Before making the stencil, prepare the printing unit by assembling the screen frame, the screen base, and the side kick. Place the original design on the base, and position the registration guides. The design should be placed in the approximate center of the base. Secure the registration guides to the base with tape, Fig. 7-34. To assure direct contact between the silk and the stencil when adhering the stencil, it is advisable to build up the base by inserting several layers of newspapers under the base cover. The newspapers should measure less than the inside dimension of the frame.

The photographic indirect stencil film described here consists of a presensitized emulsion on a vinyl-supported backing. Because the stencil film is presensitized, all film handling operations should be done in subdued light.

Fig. 7-35. Cut the stencil film larger than the design area

Cut a piece of stencil film about 2″ (51 mm) larger on all sides than the original design, Fig. 7-35. The contact printing frame may be used to hold the stencil film and the positive in tight contact during exposure, Fig. 7-36. Open the back of the contact printing frame and clean the glass if necessary. Place the positive, face up, on the glass in the frame. Position the stencil film on top of the positive with the emulsion side up, and then replace the contact frame back, Fig. 7-37. The emulsion side of the stencil film is the shiny side. In this position the exposure light passes through the glass, the transparent areas of the positive, the stencil film backing, and finally strikes the emulsion.

For best results, use a carbon arc light source for the exposure. The exposure time will vary with the light source and the distance between the light source and the film. It may be necessary to make a series of exposures to determine the best exposure time. A three-minute exposure with a 35amp carbon arc at a distance of 30″ (762 mm) will produce a suitable exposure.

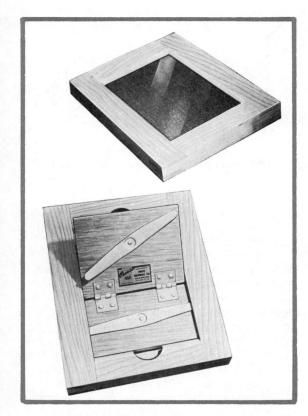

Fig. 7-36. Contact printing frame

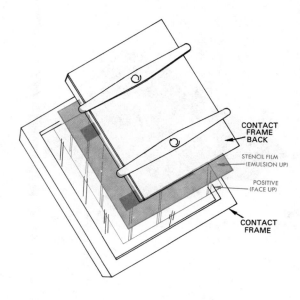

CONTACT FRAME BACK

STENCIL FILM (EMULSION UP)

POSITIVE (FACE UP)

CONTACT FRAME

Fig. 7-37. Loading the contact printing frame for exposure

Safety Note

Do not look directly at the exposure light as the bright light may cause eye damage.

As the exposure light strikes the emulsion, it causes it to harden. In the areas of the image or the areas that are opaque, the light does not strike the emulsion and it remains soft. After exposure, the stencil film is placed in a tray containing prepared developer. The developer should be mixed and used according to the manufacturer's recommendations.

At the end of the development time, the film is washed on the emulsion side in water at the temperature recommended by the manufacturer. Wash by holding the film under running water, Fig. 7-38. During the washing operation, the image areas that were not exposed to light will wash away. Continue to wash the film until all the image area is clear and free of emulsion.

Immediately after washing, place the wet film, emulsion side up, in register on top of the design which is against the registration

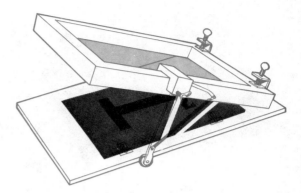

Fig. 7-39. Place the washed film in register over the original artwork design

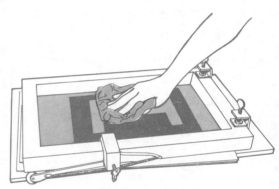

Fig. 7-40. Blot the excess water from the stencil

guides on the screen base, Fig. 7-39. Lower the screen so that the silk makes direct contact with the film.

Spread several layers of absorbent paper on the silk and press down, using your hands or a roller, Fig. 7-40. The paper will absorb the moisture from the film. Repeat this procedure until all the moisture has been absorbed. Raise the screen frame so that it is supported by the side kick. An electric fan may be used for drying the adhered film stencil, Fig. 7-41. The drying time will be approximately 30 minutes.

After drying, remove the backing. Starting at one corner, carefully peel the backing sheet from the stencil, Fig. 7-42. This should

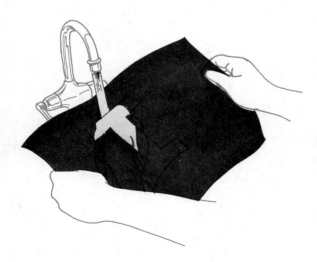

Fig. 7-38. Wash the exposed film in running water

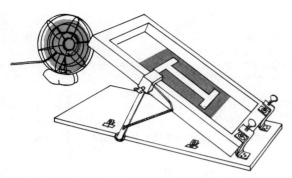

Fig. 7-41. A fan may be used to dry the stencil

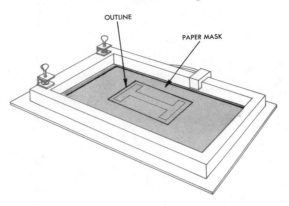

Fig. 7-43. Outline the paper mask

The two most commonly used methods of block-out are (1) the paper mask method and (2) the lacquer mask or water mask method.

PAPER MASK METHOD

The paper mask is prepared by cutting a piece of kraft paper that is slightly smaller than the inside dimension of the screen frame. Place the paper mask on top of the adhered stencil, and outline those areas that must be removed to allow the printing of the design, Fig. 7-43. The cutouts should be about 2″ (51 mm) away from the design on all sides.

Using gummed tape, secure the paper mask in position, Fig. 7-44. The final masking should not interfere with the passage of the squeegee over the stencil. If the squeegee rides over the masking, it will not make direct contact with the silk and the prints may be fuzzy.

WATER MASK AND LACQUER MASK METHODS

Water mask and lacquer mask are also available for blocking out or masking out unwanted printing areas. Water mask is not recommended for use with water-base ink. The ink will dissolve the water mask during the printing operation. Lacquer mask should not be used when printing will be done with lacquer-base ink.

Fig. 7-42. Peel off the stencil backing

be done slowly and carefully, checking to be sure the emulsion is not disturbed.

BLOCK-OUT

Nonprinting areas of the screen must be blocked out to prevent the flow of ink.

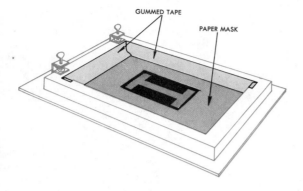

GUMMED TAPE

PAPER MASK

Fig. 7-44. Tape the paper mask in position

Water mask and lacquer mask can be applied by brushing or by spreading with a stiff piece of cardboard, Fig. 7-45. Either side of the screen may be coated. Allow the first coat to dry before a second coat is applied. The second coat usually assures a leakproof coverage. When the masking has completely dried, the photographic indirect stencil is ready for the production operation.

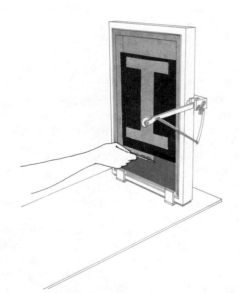

Fig. 7-45. Coating the non-image areas of a screen with water mask or lacquer mask

UNIT 24 — TERMS FOR DISCUSSION AND REVIEW

photographic indirect stencil	adhering
	base cover
screen process printing	presensitized emulsion
positive image	contact printing frame
opaque	
nonprinting areas	emulsion side
transparent	carbon arc
stencil	light source
original design	developer
india ink	block-out
transfer type	paper mask
continuous tone photography	lacquer mask
	water mask
halftone positive	gummed tape
screen frame	squeegee
screen base	water-base ink
side kick	lacquer-base ink
registration guides	

PHOTOGRAPHIC DIRECT STENCIL METHOD

PREPARING THE POSITIVE

Use a positive image design to prepare a photographic direct stencil for screen process printing, Fig. 7-46. The printing areas must be opaque, while the nonprinting areas are transparent. A negative image design cannot be used because the area desired for printing is transparent, Fig. 7-47. Separate positives and separate stencils must be made for printing each color. The positive may be prepared by making the original design on a transparent material, such as clear glass, tracing paper, or clear plastic. If the design is prepared by drawing, black india ink should be used. Transfer type may also be used to generate the positive image. (See Unit 8.)

The positive may also be prepared photographically. Because of this, any of the image generation methods may be used to create the original image. If a continuous tone photograph is to be reproduced, a halftone positive must be prepared. See Unit 31 for information on making photographic positives.

PREPARING THE EMULSION AND SENSITIZER

The emulsion used for coating a screen must be sensitized when a photographic direct stencil is made. If you use commercially prepared emulsions and sensitizers, follow the manufacturer's recommendations for mixing. Prepare only enough sensitized

Fig. 7-46. A photographic positive has opaque image areas

Fig. 7-47. A photographic negative has transparent image areas

A photographic positive must be used to prepare a photographic direct stencil for screen process printing.

emulsion for the screen being coated. Use only glass or plastic containers and mixing tools.

COATING THE SCREEN

The sensitized emulsion is applied directly on the screen in liquid form. The emulsion is then spread over the screen fabric, generally on the underside, in a smooth, even coating. Safe light conditions vary with manufacturers.

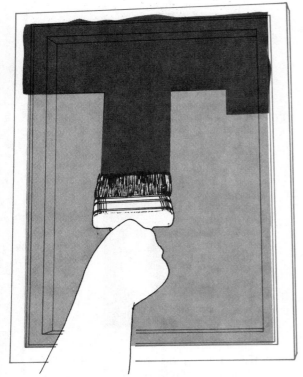

Fig. 7-48. Brushing photographic direct emulsion on the screen

The emulsion may be applied to the screen by brushing or by using a squeegee device. By coating the entire screen surface, later block-out can be avoided. If you **brush** on the emulsion, use a camel's-hair brush. Brush in one direction only, Fig. 7-48. Do not go over the surface a second time because some of the emulsion already applied may be picked up.

If you **spread** on the emulsion, use a stiff piece of cardboard or binder's board

as a squeegee, Fig. 7-49. Hold the screen at a slant, and pour a small quantity of sensitized emulsion directly on the underside of the screen fabric. Spread the emulsion over the screen in a thin, even coating. Follow the manufacturer's recommendations for drying the screen.

PREPARING A PERFECT CONTACT

The sensitized screen and positive must be held in perfect contact during exposure. Perfect contact can be achieved by using either (1) the cementing method or (2) the contact unit method.

THE CEMENTING METHOD

The cementing method is a simple technique for preparing the sensitized screen and positive for exposure. Place the positive, right-reading-side up, on a flat surface. Coat the entire surface of the positive with rubber cement that has been thinned on a one-to-one ratio with solvent, Fig. 7-50. Also coat the underside of the screen with rubber cement, and allow both surfaces to dry completely.

As soon as both surfaces are dry, place the screen on top of the positive. Lay several thicknesses of newspaper on the inside of the screen frame, and apply downward pres-

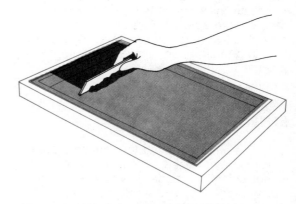

Fig. 7-49. Spreading photographic direct emulsion with a stiff piece of cardboard

sure by rubbing over the newspaper with a cloth. A roller may also be used. This pressure will assure direct contact between the screen and the positive. After the exposure, the positive is peeled from the screen. A cloth dampened with solvent can be used to remove spots of rubber cement that remain on the screen.

CONTACT UNIT METHOD

The sensitized screen and the positive may also be held in perfect contact by using a contact unit. Place the positive, face up, on the plate glass of the contact frame. Position the coated screen on top of the positive, and place the contact frame back inside the screen frame, Fig. 7-51. Tighten the locking bars to exert pressure for holding the screen and the positive in direct contact.

EXPOSURE

The exposure time varies with the type of sensitized emulsion being used, the light source, and the distance between the screen and the light source. Photoflood lights, carbon arc lamps, or direct sunlight may be used for exposure. Follow the manufacturer's recommendations for exposure time.

Correct exposure time may also be determined by making a series of test exposures. Cover all but a small strip, 1″ (25.4 mm) for example, of the screen area with a piece of black paper. Expose the screen for a short time, 15 seconds for example. Move the black paper to expose another strip of the screen area and repeat the exposure, this time for 15 seconds. The first strip now has been exposed for 30 seconds and the second strip for 15 seconds. Repeat this procedure for the entire screen, recording each exposure time. When the screen is developed, the correct time can be determined by the exposure showing the best results. If this procedure is used, another screen will need to be coated with sensitized emulsion and this new screen used for exposing the final stencil.

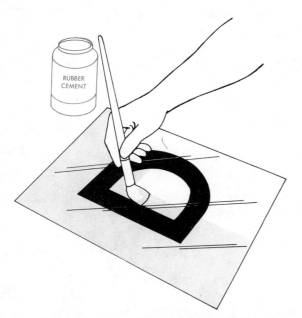

Fig. 7-50. Coat the surface of the positive with rubber cement

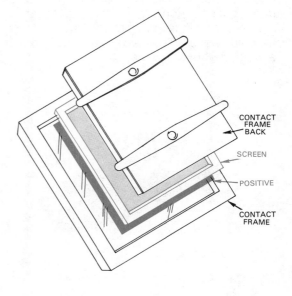

Fig. 7-51. Preparing the photographic direct screen for exposure

DEVELOPING

During the exposure, light passes through the transparent areas of the positive and strikes the sensitized emulsion on the screen. The light causes the emulsion to harden, while the unexposed emulsion (in the design areas) remains soft.

Working in the darkroom, develop the exposed screen by placing the whole screen in a tray of water or by gently spraying the water on the screen, Fig. 7-52. Consult the manufacturer's recommendations for the correct water temperature and method of application.

The water should be applied to both sides of the screen. Usually, hot water is used to develop the exposed screen. Cold water, however, is used for developing some commercially prepared emulsions. If hot water is used, it should be between 110° and 115° F (43° and 46° C). Water above 115° (46° C) should not be used because it may melt away some of the detail in the design. Once the screen is completely wet, normal room lighting may be used because the hot water has removed the sensitizer from the emulsion. When the design areas are free of emulsion, the screen is bathed in cold water. This stops the developing action of the hot water.

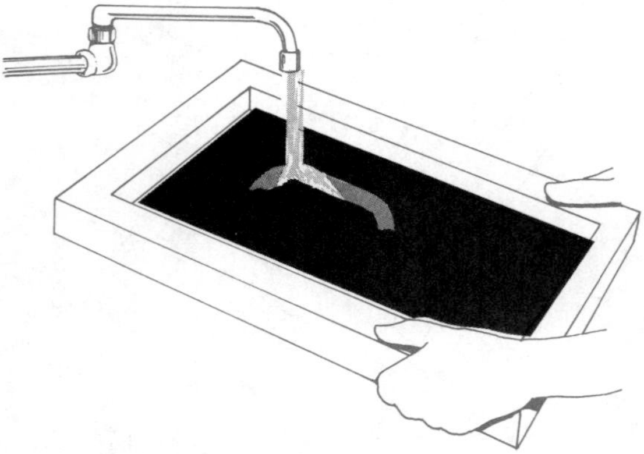

Excess water may be blotted from the screen by placing the underside of the screen against several layers of newspaper or a soft, smooth cloth, Fig. 7-53. Blot the inside of the screen with a cloth. For final drying, the screen may be placed in a vertical position and a fan directed at it.

Inspect the screen and block out any unwanted printing areas. These areas, known as pinholes, can be easily seen when the screen is held up to a strong light. If **water-base** ink will be used, a lacquer mask can

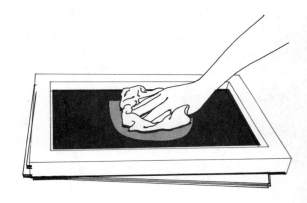

Fig. 7-53. Blotting the excess water from the screen

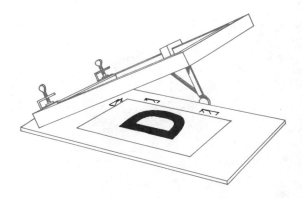

Fig. 7-52. Develop the photographic direct stencil by holding it under running water

Fig. 7-54. When the registration guides have been positioned, the stencil is ready for production

be brushed over the pinholes. Water mask may be applied when **lacquer-base** ink will be used in the production of the design. Gummed tape can be used on the inside corners of the screen to prevent leaks and make it easier to clean the screen after production.

After the photographic direct stencil has been prepared, assemble the screen frame, the screen printing base, and the side kick. To position the registration guides, place the original design on the base. Lower the screen frame and adjust the position of the original design until the stencil and design are perfectly aligned. Place the registration guides in position and secure them to the base with tape, Fig. 7-54. Double-check the position of the guides to be sure that the stencil and the original design are in alignment. With the registration guides secured, the photographic direct stencil is ready for production.

UNIT 25 — TERMS FOR DISCUSSION AND REVIEW

photographic direct stencil	block-out
screen process printing	cementing method
positive image	rubber cement
opaque	ratio
nonprinting areas	contact unit
transparent	exposure
stencil	photoflood lights
original design	carbon arc lamps
india ink	test exposure
transfer type	pinholes
continuous tone photograph	water-base ink
halftone positive	lacquer-base ink
emulsion	lacquer mask
sensitized	water mask
safe lights	gummed tape
squeegee	screen frame
	printing base
	side kick
	registration guides

UNIT 26

DECALCOMANIA PRINTING

Having prepared the stencil for **screen process printing** by one of the five methods just presented, you are ready for production printing (as detailed in Unit 28). Screen process printing is adaptable to a great variety of applications, many of which are quite unusual. Unit 27 gives an overview of these applications; however, this unit (Unit 26) deals with a very specialized and unique use of screen process printing — that of decalcomania printing.

A decalcomania is a design, picture, or type matter that has been printed on specially prepared paper. It is commonly referred to as a **decal** or a **transfer.** The printed design can be transferred from the decal paper to another surface.

Decal printing can be done by lithography, letterpress, gravure, or by screen process printing. The advantage of screen process printing is that a heavier deposit of ink can be applied to the decal paper.

DECAL PAPER

The most commonly used decal papers are (1) simplex paper and (2) duplex paper. **Simplex** (or single) paper is coated with a decal solution on which the decal design is printed. Simplex paper is most generally used for slide-off decals.

Duplex (or double) paper has a semi-permanent tissue paper attached to a heavy backing paper. The decal solution, which receives the printing, is coated on the tissue paper. Duplex paper is generally used for large, outdoor decals. Decals made on duplex paper are classified as duplex decals and are applied to the receiving surface with varnish or cement.

A third, less commonly used, paper for decals is called **body stock.** One side of the body stock is coated with a tacky adhesive which is protected by a release or backing paper. Body stock is used for printing pressure-sensitive decals. It is available with both a permanent and an easily removable adhesive, allowing for removal of the decal if necessary.

DECAL COATINGS AND INK

The colored inks of a decal are generally printed between two clear lacquer coatings. The **first clear lacquer coat** is applied directly to the surface of the decal paper in a solid area that is the same general shape as the finished decal. The clear lacquer coating should be between $\frac{1}{16}''$ and $\frac{1}{8}''$ (2 mm and 3 mm) larger, on all sides, than the design area.

After the design colors are printed, the **second clear lacquer coating** is applied over the colors. The same stencil can be used for printing both the first and the second coatings of clear lacquer. The lacquer

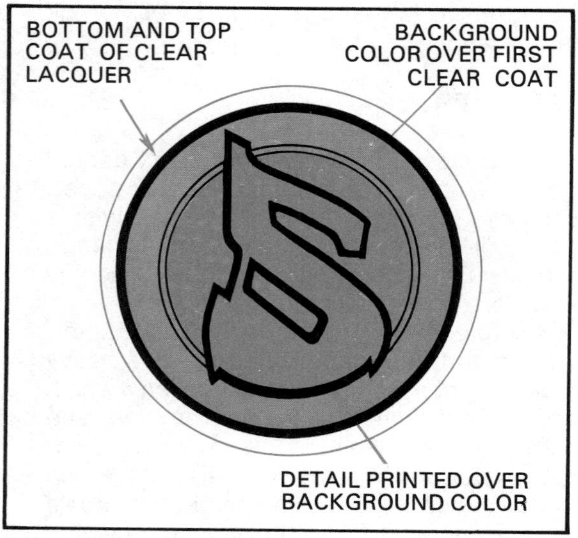

Fig. 7-55. Slide-off decal for opaque surface

coatings tie in the details of the design and also protect the decal if it is directly exposed to weather conditions.

The most commonly used ink for printing decals is decal lacquer. Decal lacquer is soluble in lacquer thinner and will cause lacquer film stencils to dissolve. For this reason, lacquer film stencils are not recommended for use when decal lacquer is to be printed.

TYPES OF DECALS

The three most commonly used decals are the (1) slide-off, (2) duplex, and (3) pressure-sensitive. The slide-off decal can be adhered to either an opaque surface or a transparent surface.

SLIDE-OFF DECAL FOR OPAQUE SURFACE

The slide-off decal, Fig. 7-55, is printed by first applying the clear lacquer coating on the decal paper (generally simplex). The colors are then printed, with the background printed first and the rest of the colors printed over it in their correct order. The final clear lacquer coat is applied over the printed colors. **Each coat of lacquer or ink must be perfectly dry before the next coat is applied.**

Slide-off decals are transferred to opaque surfaces by first soaking the decals in water for a short period of time. The transfer is then slid or pulled over the edge of the decal paper and placed in position by gently withdrawing the paper. The area receiving the transfer must be clean.

SLIDE-OFF DECAL FOR TRANSPARENT SURFACE

Slide-off decals can be applied to the inside or back of transparent surfaces by either of two methods: (1) decal adhesive or (2) printing the decal in reverse.

Decal Adhesive. This method requires the application of decal adhesive over the entire design area. Most decal adhesives are water-soluble and should not be used with water-soluble screening stencils.

To apply the slide-off decal, first clean the surface to receive the decal. Soak the decal in water. When loose, slide the decal only slightly over the edge of the backing paper before it is positioned in the desired location. Once positioned, completely remove the backing paper. A soft cloth or paper towel may be used to blot the excess water from the applied decal.

Printing in Reverse. This type of decal is known as a **face-down** decal. It does not require the application of an adhesive. Both the design and the color order are printed in reverse directly on the decal paper, Fig. 7-56. For example, consider the printing of a two-color decal consisting of a background color and a detail color. The first clear lacquer coat is applied. Then the detail color would be printed, in reverse, on top of the clear lacquer. The background color would be printed next, in reverse, on top of the detail color. The second clear lacquer coat would then be applied over the background color. The decal is then transferred in the same manner as for an opaque surface.

DUPLEX DECALS

Duplex decals are also known as **varnish-on** decals. The duplex decal is commonly used on the sides of trucks, on airplane fuselages, and on car doors. This is a permanent decal.

Duplex decals are usually printed face-down on duplex paper. The first clear lacquer coat is applied directly to the tissue paper. The design images and colors are then printed in reverse and in reverse order. A second coat of clear lacquer is then applied, Fig. 7-57.

To apply the duplex decal to the desired surface, separate the backing paper and the tissue slightly at one corner or along one edge. This will make the removal of the backing paper easier once the decal has been adhered.

Using a brush, apply a thin coat of adhering varnish or cement to the back of the decal, that is, on top of the last clear lacquer coat (or the varnish may be applied to the receiving surface rather than to the decal).

Apply the decal, varnish-side down, to the desired clean area. Smooth the backing paper with a roller or squeegee to prevent wrinkles and air bubbles.

Once the decal has been adhered, remove the backing paper. Be careful not to disturb the transfer. A mineral cleaner may be used to remove the excess adhering varnish without damaging the decal. Remove the tissue paper by soaking it with water.

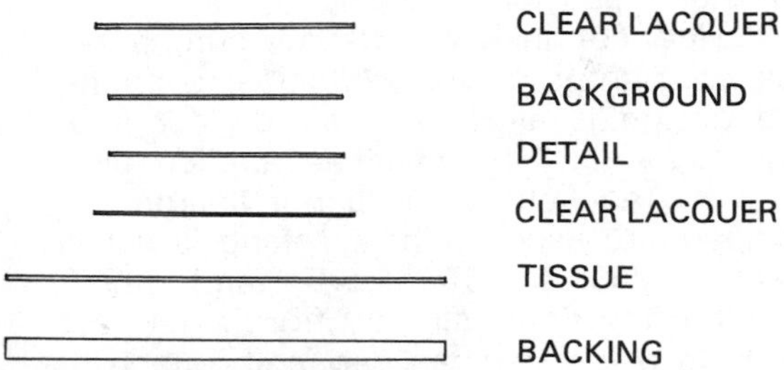

CLEAR LACQUER

BACKGROUND

DETAIL

CLEAR LACQUER

TISSUE

BACKING

Fig. 7-56. Face-down decal

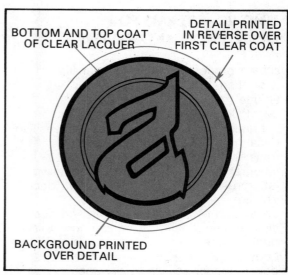

Fig. 7-57. Varnish-on (duplex) decal

PRESSURE-SENSITIVE DECALS

Pressure-sensitive decals are sometimes referred to as "pressure-sensitive labels," "dry decals," or "dry-release decals." The paper used for printing pressure-sensitive decals is body stock.

The printed design is screened on the surface of the body stock in a face-up position. In the case of a two-color decal, the background color is printed first, and then the detail color is applied. A protective clear lacquer coat can be screened over the entire decal area, Fig. 7-58.

A pressure-sensitive decal is applied by removing the release backing paper and then pressing the decal into position, adhesive-side down. The receiving surface should be cleaned before application of the decal.

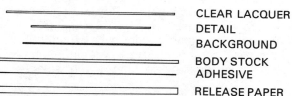

	CLEAR LACQUER
	DETAIL
	BACKGROUND
	BODY STOCK
	ADHESIVE
	RELEASE PAPER

Fig. 7-58. Build-up of a two-color pressure-sensitive decal

UNIT 26 — TERMS FOR DISCUSSION AND REVIEW

screen process printing
unique
decalcomania printing
decal
transfer
lithography
letterpress
gravure
decal paper
simplex paper
duplex paper
body stock
decal lacquer
lacquer thinner

lacquer film stencil
slide-off
deplex
pressure-sensitive
opaque
transparent
decal adhesive
face-down decal
reverse
varnish-on decals
adhering varnish
pressure sensitive labels
dry decals
dry-release decals

UNIT 27

APPLICATIONS OF SCREEN PROCESS PRINTING

Screen process printing is the most versatile of all printing processes. It can be done on almost any material, such as paper, wood, plastics, ceramics, and metal. Screen process printing can also be done on concave, convex, and irregularly shaped surfaces as well as on flat surfaces.

TEXTILE PRINTING

Textile printing is the process of applying designs to cloth materials. Small items such as T-shirts, towels, scarves, felt banners, and cloth napkins can easily be printed with the simplest equipment.

The stencil used for textile printing may be made by any of the stencil preparation methods. However, since **textile ink** is used in this process, the proper stencil material must be carefully chosen. Also, the blockout medium to be used must be considered.

As just mentioned, textile printing requires the use of textile ink. The most commonly used textile inks are (1) air-set inks and (2) heat-set inks. As the name implies, **air-set inks** dry at room temperature, without the use of heat. They are not meant to withstand constant washing.

Heat-set inks are used where a permanent print is desired. After being printed, the design is allowed to air dry for about one-half hour. Then heat is applied either by infra-red light or by a hot flatiron. The temperature used for heat setting is usually between 250° and 375° F (121° and 191° C). The heating time will vary from a few seconds to a few minutes depending upon the heat source used, the type of ink, and the

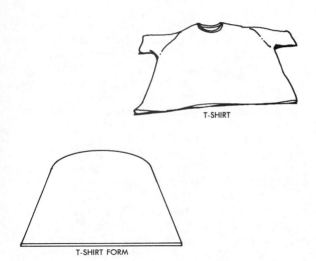

Fig. 7-59. A cardboard form should be used when printing on T-shirts

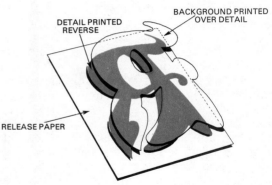

Fig. 7-60. Printing build-up of a heat transfer

thickness of the textile material. Manufacturer's recommendations should be followed for specific heating and time requirements.

In textile printing, the color or position registration for items such as handkerchiefs, scarves, and napkins can be achieved by using registration guides on the screen printing base. When T-shirts are to be printed, it may be necessary to make a cardboard form to stretch and hold the T-shirt in position, Fig. 7-59. Then registration guides can be used for positioning the T-shirt.

HEAT TRANSFERS

Heat transfers are sometimes referred to as **iron-on decals**. The design is printed on a **release paper**. To apply a heat transfer to a receiving surface, heat and pressure are used causing the transfer.

Heat transfers are printed with a classification of inks known as plastisols. **Plastisol** inks are designed for printing where opacity, flexibility, and washability are required. Plastisol inks are not air dry inks and must be heat-cured. Once they are heat-cured, they will remain flexible and will stretch with

an open-weave fabric. The heat-curing process makes an inseparable bond between the ink and the fabric. Plastisol inks are thermoplastic and will soften with the application of heat. Therefore, fabrics which are printed with plastisol inks should not be washed in hot water or dry-cleaned.

Plastisol inks are lacquer-base. They must be printed with any lacquer-proof stencil, such as aqua film, or with a wash-soluble photographic stencil. A coarse screen fabric, such as 2XX to 8XX, is recommended for printing these inks.

When printing heat transfers, the design is first printed in reverse onto a release paper. The release paper is only a temporary receiving surface. The color order of multicolor designs must also be reversed, Fig. 7-60.

After printing the design on the release paper, the ink must be heat-cured to relieve the tack or stickiness of the ink. A lower temperature and a shorter time is used for heat-curing on the release paper than on a fabric. Final heat-curing will be accomplished when the heat transfer is applied to the receiving fabric. A temperature of 225° to 250° F (107° to 121° C) for one minute is recommended for heat-curing on the release paper.

When printing multi-color designs on release paper, the first printed color must be heat-cured before the next color is printed. To check the effectiveness of the heat-cure, peel the ink from the paper. If the design breaks apart, more heat is needed for curing. If the design stretches, the heat-cure is good.

Although a heat transfer press is recommended, heat transfers may also be applied to fabric using a household pressing iron. During application, the fabric must lie flat on a firm, smooth surface. If an ironing board is used, it should be covered with a smooth board or piece of heavy cardboard to provide firmness. If the receiving surface is a T-shirt, the smooth board or heavy piece of cardboard should be placed inside the shirt, Fig. 7-61. This will prevent the transfer from affecting the bottom layer of fabric.

Set the temperature of the iron between 375° and 400° F (191° and 204° C). Follow the ironing and pressing instructions for the fabric receiving the transfer. Be sure the fabric can withstand the heat before attempting application. (Too much heat causes some synthetic fabrics to deteriorate.) Then iron out all the wrinkles in the fabric. Place the transfer, ink-side down, in the exact position that is desired. A firm downward pressure with the iron will transfer the ink design from the release paper to the fabric. A slight circular motion with the iron may be used. Too much movement, however, may cause the transfer to move. The iron should be left in contact with the release paper

until an even scorch mark over the entire surface is visible. Permit the transfer to cool before peeling off the release paper. If the design fails to transfer completely, replace the paper and apply more heat and pressure.

Heat transfers may also be printed by the offset process. (See Chapter 9.) The offset plate must be made with a reverse image — one that is "wrong-reading." This image will produce a wrong-reading image when printed on the paper. However, when the image from the paper is transferred to the receiving fabric, a right-reading image will be produced.

When the offset plate is printed, a dye-based ink must be used. Although specially manufactured transfer paper is available, an uncoated 70 lb. offset paper with a smooth finish produces good results.

To transfer the printed image to the receiving fabric, a transfer press, dry mounting press, or household electric iron may be used. The heat and pressure cause the image to transfer through a process known as **sublimation**. Sublimation is the process of changing the dye-based ink from solid to gas and back again without the ink entering the liquid state. This process causes the design to actually become part of the fabric. This differs from screen printing plastisol inks where a rubbery layer is formed on top of the fabric.

PRINTED CIRCUITS

Screen process printing is also used for printing systems of wires on electrical printed circuit boards. Printed circuit board material generally consists of a nonconductive backing material that is coated with a thin layer of copper.

The stencil is made to actual size and utilizes a material that will be unaffected by the lacquer ink. An acid-resistant ink is used to print the design on the metal coating of the circuit board. When the ink is dry, the board is lowered into an acid bath to be etched. The areas of exposed metal are

Fig. 7-61. Ironing on a heat transfer

Fig. 7-62. Printed circuit boards are often screen printed

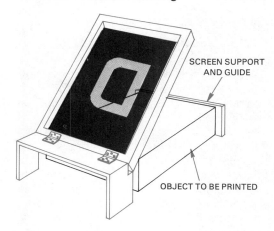

Fig. 7-63. Printing unit for large objects or thick stock

removed by the acid, while the metal protected by the acid-resistant ink is left unetched.

After the etching process, the ink is removed from the board, leaving the desired bare copper circuit. The board is then drilled, and the electrical components are soldered to the printed circuit board, Fig. 7-62.

IRREGULARLY SHAPED OBJECTS

Screen printing on thick objects or large objects requires adjustments in the printing unit. The printing unit shown in Fig. 7-63 can be used for printing on large objects.

Screen printing units that are easily adjustable for different thicknesses of objects can be made by placing springs between the screen frame and the base, Fig. 7-64. The front part of the screen can be supported with pieces of wood that are the same thickness as the object on which the printing is being done.

Round objects can be screen printed by machines, as shown in Fig. 7-65. Most machines of this type hold the squeegee in

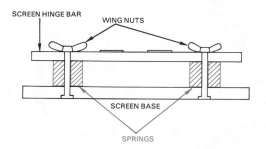

Fig. 7-64. Adjustable printing unit

Fig. 7-65. Screen process printing machine used for round objects

a stationary position. The cylinder supporting the round object rotates either by friction with the moving screen or by mechanical means.

UNIT 27 — TERMS FOR DISCUSSION AND REVIEW

screen process
  printing
versatile
concave
convex
irregularly shaped
textile printing
block-out
  medium
textile ink
air-set ink
heat-set ink
registration
registration guides
printing base
heat transfers
iron-on decals
release paper
plastisol
heat-cured
thermoplastic
lacquer-base

lacquer-proof
  stencil
aqua film
reverse
heat transfer
  press
synthetic fabrics
deteriorate
offset process
offset plate
wrong-reading
right-reading
dye-based ink
dry mounting
  press
sublimation
solid
liquid
printed circuit
  boards
acid-resistant
  ink

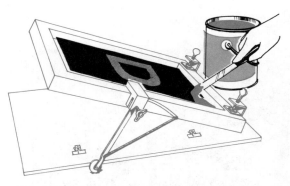

Fig. 7-66. Place a small quantity of ink on the inside of the screen frame

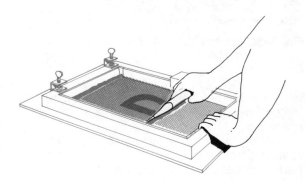

Fig. 7-67. Hold the squeegee at a 30° angle

UNIT 28

SCREEN PROCESS PRINTING PRODUCTION

The printing procedures for the various types of stencils are the same. The kind of ink used must not dissolve either the stencil material or the block-out medium that is used.

PRODUCTION PROCESS

Using an ink spatula, place a quantity of ink on the inside of the screen frame, Fig. 7-66. Apply enough ink so that when it is rolled in front of the squeegee, it will cover the design completely.

Select a squeegee that is slightly wider than the design area. Take a sheet of paper to be printed, and place it against the registration guides. Lower the screen frame. Hold the squeegee at approximately a 30° angle and so that the rubber blade is in contact with the screen fabric. Apply downward pressure as you pull the squeegee across the open areas of the stencil, Fig. 7-67. For best results, go over the stencil only once for each print.

Rest the squeegee against the side of the frame. Raise the screen frame so that it is supported by the side kick in the open position, Fig. 7-68. Remove the printed copy

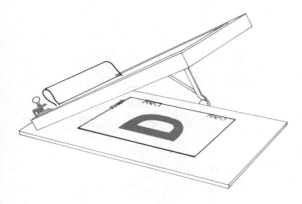

Fig. 7-68. Open the printing unit to remove the printed sheet

Fig. 7-70. Print the impression on the transparent flap

Fig. 7-69. Dry rack for screen process printing

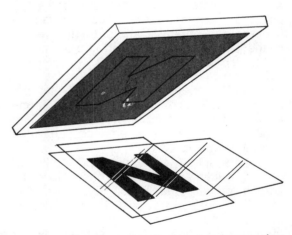

Fig. 7-71. Register the first color impression under the transparent flap

and place it in the dry rack, beginning at the bottom shelf, Fig. 7-69. As one shelf fills up, another may be lowered.

Place another piece of paper against the registration guides and repeat the printing operation. Additional ink must be added from time to time.

MULTICOLOR PRODUCTION

In multicolor production, a stencil is cut for each color. Registration for printing

Fig. 7-72. Fold the flap back and print the second color

Fig. 7-73. Manual four-color textile printer

multicolor screen prints is made easier by using a transparent flap. Tape or tack a sheet of transparent plastic or tracing vellum to the printing base. Print an impression on the transparent flap, Fig. 7-70. Register the stock, which has been printed in the previous color, under the flap, Fig. 7-71. Fold the flap back and lower the screen frame to print the second color of the design, Fig. 7-72. This procedure is repeated each time a print is made.

High speed production of multicolor screen printing designs is often done by screen printing machines, Fig. 7-73. The receiving surface is held in a stationary position. Four screen frames are on a movable screen head. Each screen has a stencil which has been prepared for printing one color of the design. After printing the first color, the entire screen head is rotated to the next position. The next color can then be printed in register with the previously printed color. This operation is repeated for each color that is to be printed.

CLEANUP

At the completion of the printing operation, all ink must be removed from the ink spatula, squeegee, and the screen fabric. The excess ink remaining on the screen may

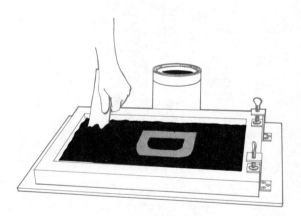

Fig. 7-74. Remove the excess ink with a piece of cardboard

be scraped up with a piece of cardboard and returned to the can, Fig. 7-74. Do not use the ink spatula for this purpose as it may puncture the screen fabric. The excess ink on the squeegee may also be returned to the can. Replace the cover and seal the can.

Remove the gummed corner tape from the screen, Fig. 7-75. (If a paper stencil

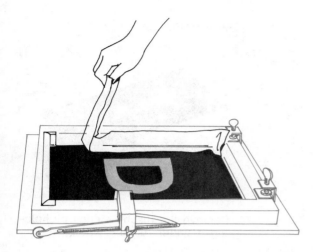

Fig. 7-75. Remove the tape from the inside corners of the frame

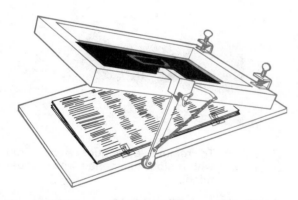

Fig. 7-76. Place newspapers on the printing base

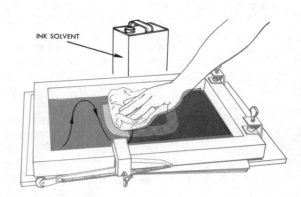

Fig. 7-77. Clean the silk screen

was used for printing, it must also be removed and discarded. Other type stencils, if not to be reused, can be removed after the ink has been cleaned from the screen.)

Raise the screen frame and place several layers of newspaper on the printing base, Fig. 7-76. Lower the screen frame and pour (directly on the screen) a small quantity of the recommended solvent for the ink used, Fig. 7-77. Using a cloth or paper towels, begin wiping the screen. Much of the ink and the solvent will be absorbed by the newspaper. Therefore, it may be necessary to change the newspaper several times.

Continue to wipe the screen with solvent until all ink has been removed from both sides of the screen fabric. The ink spatula and the squeegee must also be cleaned with the solvent and a cloth. Remove the registration guides and the kraft paper cover sheet from the printing base.

The screen fabric may be checked for ink removal by holding it up to a strong light. Although the fabric may be stained or discolored from the ink used, there should be no clogged mesh areas.

At this point the stencil may be saved on the screen for reuse, or it may be removed to make the screen ready for a new stencil.

REMOVING THE STENCIL

After the ink is removed, the block-out medium and stencil can be removed from the screen. The block-out medium can be removed with the appropriate solvent in a manner similar to that used for removing the ink. Water mask may be removed under running water in a sink.

Tusche stencils can be removed from the screen with water. To dissolve the stencil, place the screen in a sink and apply water generously to both sides of the screen fabric, Fig. 7-78. A screen brush may be used, if necessary.

Aqua film stencils may be removed from the screen fabric under warm water. Place the screen in a sink and allow warm water to run over the stencil. If necessary, a screen brush may be used.

Lacquer film stencils must be removed by using lacquer thinner. Place the screen on several layers of newspaper. Pour a small quantity of lacquer thinner on the screen, and begin rubbing with a cloth, Fig. 7-79. As the lacquer film dissolves, it will stick to the newspaper. Therefore, it will be necessary to periodically change the layers of newspaper under the screen. Repeat this process until all traces of the stencil have been removed from the screen fabric.

Photographic indirect stencils may be removed under hot running water. A screen brush may be used to scrub the screen and aid in stencil removal.

Most **photographic direct stencils** require a commercial solvent for removal from the screen. Consult the manufacturer's recommendations for the proper type of solvent. Some photographic direct stencil emulsions may be removed by rubbing on a solution consisting of one teaspoon of lye in a glass of water. Because **this solution may be injurious to the hands,** it is advisable to wear rubber gloves. A coarse piece of silk dipped in a good laundry soap and hot water may also be rubbed over the stencil to remove the emulsion.

As before, the cleanliness of the screen fabric may be checked by holding the screen up to a strong light. The screen may be slightly discolored from use, but there should be no clogged areas in the mesh. A properly cleaned screen may be used many times.

Safety Note

All cloths that have been used with ink and solvent must be placed in metal safety cans.

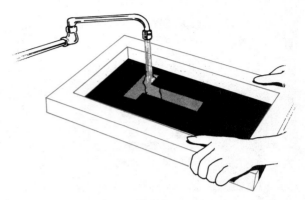

Fig. 7-78. Remove the tusche stencil by holding it under running water

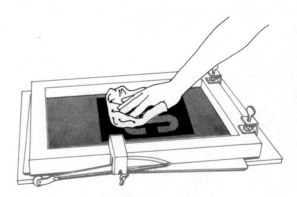

Fig. 7-79. To remove a lacquer stencil, rub with a cloth dampened with lacquer thinner

UNIT 28 — TERMS FOR DISCUSSION AND REVIEW

stencil	water mask
block-out	tusche stencil
ink spatula	aqua film stencil
squeegee	lacquer film
registration guides	stencil
screen frame	lacquer thinner
side kick	photographic
dry rack	indirect stencil
multicolor	photographic
transparent flap	direct stencil
printing base	lye
solvent	

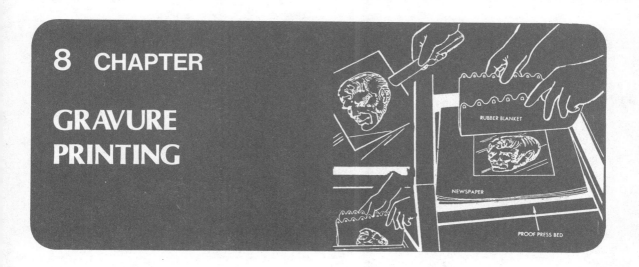

Gravure printing is defined as printing from cells or depressions that are below the surface of the printing plate, Fig. 8-1. Gravure plates used in industry may be made from zinc, steel, or copper. If etched gravure cylinders are used, the process is called **rotogravure.** Gravure is also known as intaglio (in-tal-yo) printing.

GRAVURE PLATES

Gravure plates may be made by engraving or by etching the metal surface. In some instances, a combination of engraving and etching is used. **Engraved plates** result directly in a gravure printing surface with varying line depths. Engraved plates are cut by an engraver who uses hand tools that are harder than the plate to cut the depressions into the plate surface.

The **etching** method of making gravure plates requires that the metal plate surface first be coated with an acid resist. The design area is then scratched through the acid resist to expose the bare metal. Next, the plate is placed in an etching (acid) bath which attacks and dissolves the bare metal in the design area to produce the desired depressions in the plate surface. The areas left untouched by the etching bath will not print, but will appear as white areas on the printed copy. The nonprinting areas are referred to as **lands.**

Fig. 8-1. Gravure (or intaglio) printing

GRAVURE CYLINDERS

The first step in making a gravure plate is to coat the cylinder with a thin layer of copper. The plated cylinder is then ground and polished smooth. A photographic positive of the copy is exposed on sensitized carbon tissue through a gravure screen. All copy, even type, is screened for gravure plates. Carbon tissue consists of a gelatin layer on a paper base. The gelatin becomes sensitive to light when chemically treated and receives the image during exposure.

The gelatin coating of the exposed carbon tissue is then placed in direct contact with the copper-plated cylinder, Fig. 8-2. Hot water is used to develop the tissue. During development, the hot water melts and washes away the unhardened gelatin areas. Those areas that were exposed to light remain on the cylinder and act as an acid resist. The paper backing is then removed, and the gelatin is allowed to dry and harden before the cylinder is put in the etching solution.

The cylinder is placed in an etching tray where it rotates through the etching

Fig. 8-2. Attaching the carbon tissue to the gravure cylinder

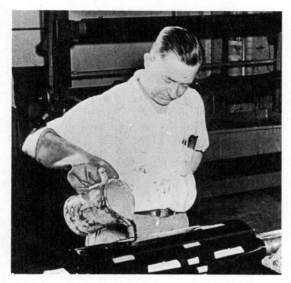

Fig. 8-3. Etching the gravure cylinder

solution, Fig. 8-3. The etching solution attacks and dissolves those areas of bare copper to form the printing image. The etching solution has no effect on the copper that is protected by the gelatin acid resist. The depth of the image is determined by the length of time the cylinder is etched.

After etching, the cylinder is washed with water to remove all traces of the etching solution. The resist is then removed, and the cylinder is made ready for printing, Fig. 8-4.

GRAVURE PRESSES

Gravure presses are classified as rotary presses and have two cylinders. One cylinder (the **plate cylinder**) holds the gravure plate, while the other, the **impression cylin-**

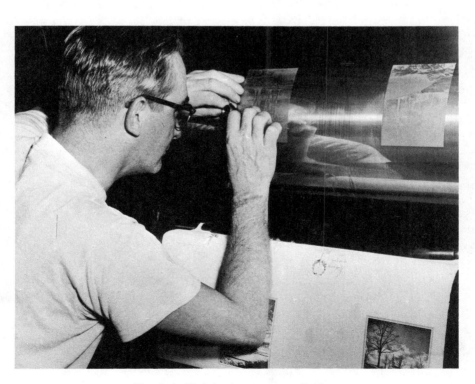

Fig. 8-4. Finished gravure cylinder

der, brings the paper into contact with the plate. The plate cylinder revolves through a fountain of ink, thus filling the depressions of the plate. The ink that is deposited on the nonprinting areas of the plate must be removed before contact is made with the paper. This is done by the **doctor blade** which is a dull, knifelike blade that makes contact with the lands of the plate. The doctor blade scrapes away the surface ink, but leaves the ink in the depressions of the plate, Fig. 8-5.

After doctoring or wiping, the plate and paper are pressed together. The pressure exerted between the two cylinders causes the ink in the depressions of the plate to be transferred to the paper. Before the next impression, the plate is inked and doctored.

Gravure printing presses are also classified as either (1) sheet-fed or (2) web-fed.

Sheet-fed press. As the name implies, sheet-fed presses are fed with individual sheets of paper. These presses are primarily used for the production of fine cut reproductions, greeting cards, and advertising materials. Sheet-fed gravure presses are available for printing single-color, two-color, three-color, and four-color materials with one press run. Each color requires a separate plate and doctor blade. As each color must be completely dry before the next color can be printed, most sheet-fed presses are equipped with driers.

Web-fed press. Rotogravure presses are all roll or web fed. A **web** is one large, continuous roll of paper. Rotogravure is primarily used for long-run printing of newspaper color supplements, magazines, and catalogs. Many rotogravure presses are equipped to print four or more colors on both sides of the paper in one press run. Each plate has its own inking unit and doctor blade.

As the web paper passes between the printing plate and the impression cylinder, the image is transferred to the paper. After receiving the image, the paper is cut (and

sometimes folded and stitched) before it is stacked at the delivery end of the press.

Since the preparation of industrial gravure plates is such a highly sophisticated and complex procedure, most schools do not have the necessary equipment required to produce them. Therefore, two methods of making **facsimile gravure plates** are presented in Unit 29. Also, since few schools could invest in a gravure printing press, Unit 30 describes production using a proof press.

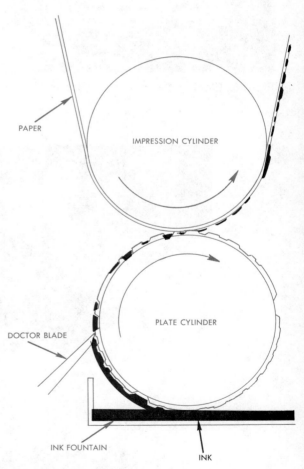

Fig. 8-5. The doctor blade removes the surface ink

UNIT 29

GRAVURE PLATES

DRYPOINT ENGRAVING

A drypoint engraving is a gravure plate that is prepared by scratching a design into the surface of a sheet of clear plastic. The design used for preparing a drypoint engraving plate must lend itself to line reproduction; that is, the design must be composed of a series of definite lines rather than one that is made up of solid tonal areas, Fig. 8-6.

Prepare the design on paper to actual size. If the printing is to be done directly on the paper, the design must be prepared in reverse on the plate to achieve a right-reading image. On the other hand, if the design is to first be transferred to a rubber blanket (as can be done on the proof press) and then to the paper, the design should be prepared as a right-reading image.

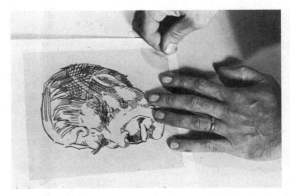

Fig. 8-7. Attach the design to the plastic plate with tape

Fig. 8-6. The design for a drypoint engraving should be composed of lines

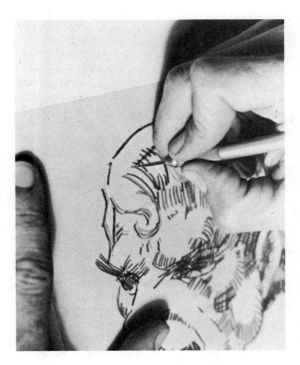

Fig. 8-8. Engrave the plastic with a sharp, pointed instrument

Attach the design to a piece of clear plastic that is about 1″ (25.4 mm) larger, on all sides, than the design area, Fig. 8-7. Polished Vinylite®, about .015 inch (.4 mm) in thickness, is recommended for making the plate.

Using a sharp, pointed instrument, engrave the design into the surface of the plastic plate, Fig. 8-8. Generally, the deeper the incised line, the darker it will reproduce. Lines that are engraved close together will reproduce as dark areas.

Shaded areas can be produced by engraving crosshatched lines. The closeness of the crosshatched lines will determine the darkness of the reproduced shaded area.

To check the design as it is being engraved into the plastic plate, slide a piece of dark-colored paper between the original drawing and the plate, Fig. 8-9.

METAL ETCHINGS

Metal gravure printing plates can be made by coating a thin sheet of copper, zinc, or aluminum with an acid resistant material. The design is then scratched through the acid resist with a sharp, pointed instrument to expose the bare metal, Fig. 8-10. Next the metal plate is placed into an etching solution bath, Fig. 8-11. The etching

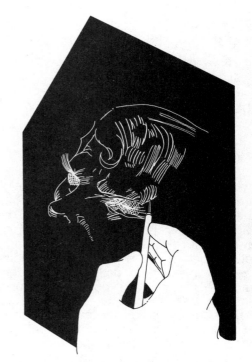

Fig. 8-10. Remove the acid resist in the design areas

Fig. 8-11. Place the plate in the etching solution

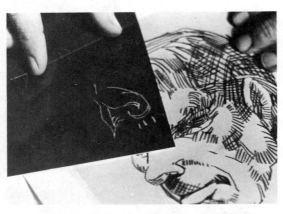

Fig. 8-9. Check the engraving by sliding a piece of dark paper between the design and the plastic

solution may be made by mixing acid and water. The strength of the acid in the solution determines the etching time. The stronger the etching solution, the faster the etching process.

Safety Note

When mixing the etching solution, **always add the acid to the water** and never water to acid. **Tongs** should be used for placing the plate in the etching solution, removing the plate, and washing the plate.

The etching solution eats away those areas of bare metal, causing wells or depressions to appear. Those areas that are coated with the acid resistant material will be unaffected by the etching bath. The length of time the plate is left in the etching bath will determine the depth of the depressions. The longer the etching time, the deeper the depressions.

The plate is removed from the etching bath and washed immediately in water to remove all traces of the etching solution. The acid resist is then removed. Weak spots in the plate may be touched up with engraving tools.

UNIT 29 — TERMS FOR DISCUSSION AND REVIEW

drypoint
  engraving
gravure plate
line
  reproduction
solid tonal
  areas
reverse
right-reading
  image

rubber blanket
incised lines
crosshatched lines
reproduction
acid resistant
  material
wells or
  depressions
etching
  solution bath

UNIT 30

GRAVURE PRODUCTION

INKING THE PLATE

The printing procedure for both the drypoint engraving and the metal etching is the same. Printer's ink and oil that have been mixed to a 1:3 ratio is recommended. The ink and oil are mixed together on a sheet of glass with the index finger, Fig. 8-12.

When the ink has been thoroughly mixed, begin inking the plate. Using your index finger, rub the ink and oil mixture into the recessed lines, Fig. 8-13. Work the ink into every depression of the plate.

To remove the excess surface ink, use a cloth pad or a folded paper towel. Wipe the surface of the entire plate, Fig. 8-14. To prevent the removal of the ink from the depressions, wipe at right angles to the engraved lines whenever possible.

Multicolor prints may be made from one gravure plate. However, care must be exercised in inking and wiping the plate when more than one color is used.

PRINTING THE PLATE

Printing may be done directly on the paper or the design may first be transferred to a rubber blanket and then to the paper. Printing the design directly on paper would reverse the image; therefore, the design would have to be prepared in reverse on the plate to achieve a right reading image.

An ordinary proof press may be used for printing the gravure plate. Build up the bed of the proof press so that the total height including the rubber blanket is about .925″ (23.5 mm). Place the inked plate face up on the built-up material. Place an offset rubber blanket face down on top of the plate, Fig. 8-15.

Roll the cylinder over the printing unit in a **single** smooth movement. (More than one impression may cause a blurred transfer of the design.) The pressure exerted by the cylinder will cause the ink in the depression of the plate to be transferred to the rubber blanket.

After the impression has been made, carefully lift the rubber blanket. Remove the plate and place in its place a sheet of paper

Fig. 8-14. Remove the surface ink

Fig. 8-12. Mix the ink and oil on a sheet of glass

Fig. 8-13. Rub the ink and oil mixture into the recessed lines

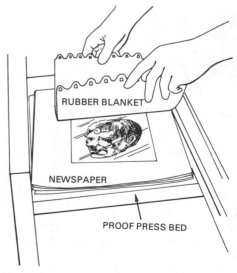

RUBBER BLANKET

NEWSPAPER

PROOF PRESS BED

Fig. 8-15. Place the blanket on top of the gravure plate

Fig. 8-16. Remove the plate and position a sheet of paper

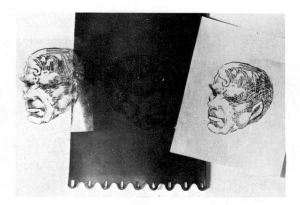

Fig. 8-17. A drypoint engraving print

that is to be printed, Fig. 8-16. Replace the blanket face-down on top of the paper. Once again, roll the cylinder over in one smooth movement to transfer the image from the blanket to the paper. Remove the blanket and inspect the print, Fig. 8-17.

If the print is light and not clear, it generally indicates that there was too little ink in the depressions of the plate. Either the ink was too thick or too much ink was removed from the depressions during the wiping operation. Too little pressure may also cause a light and unclear print.

Insufficient wiping will not remove all the surface ink and will result in the print having undesirable printed areas. Inspecting the print may also reveal areas that must be touched up. The plate must be re-inked for each impression.

CLEANING THE PLATE

The gravure plate may be cleaned with a cloth pad dampened with solvent. Remove all the ink from the depressions. Also remove the ink from the rubber blanket and the piece of glass used for mixing the ink and oil.

Safety Note

All cloths that have been used with solvent and ink must be placed in metal safety cans.

UNIT 30 — TERMS FOR DISCUSSION AND REVIEW

drypoint engraving	reverse
metal etching	right-reading
recessed lines	image
depressions	proof press
right angle	gravure plate
multicolor	insufficient
rubber blanket	solvent

CHAPTER 9

PLANOGRAPHIC PRINTING

Planographic printing is a production process that uses a flat surface printing plate. This process is also referred to as **lithography, photolithography, photo-offset lithography** and **offset lithography.** The most commonly used term is simply **offset** which describes the transfer of the image from the plate to the paper. The plate is held in position on the plate cylinder. During the duplicating operation, the image is transferred or offset to the rubber blanket on the blanket cylinder. As the paper passes between the blanket cylinder and the impression cylinder, the image is transferred to the paper. The paper never makes actual contact with the plate, Fig. 9-1.

The basic principle of offset operation is the fundamental fact that grease and water do not readily mix. The ink carriers (plates) are flat, having both the image areas and the non-image areas at the same level. The image areas have a grease surface, while the non-image areas do not. When water is applied to the surface of the plate, it is repelled by the grease image but will form a thin layer of moisture over the non-image areas. When ink is applied, it will stick to the grease image areas but will be repelled by the moisture layer over the non-image areas. The water must be applied to the plate surface first because if there is no

moisture present to repel the ink, the entire plate surface will accept the ink.

Offset plates may be made of metal, plastic, or paper. Most often the image is placed on these plates by photographic processing. However, special plates can be prepared by writing, drawing, or typing directly on the flat surface with pens, pencils, and typewriter ribbons designed for that purpose. The preparation of the offset plate is the **pre**production phase of offset printing and is described in Units 31-34.

Production printing on the offset duplicator is detailed in Units 35-42.

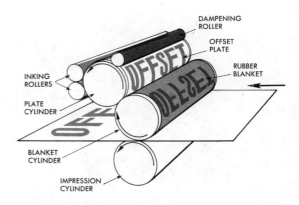

Fig. 9-1. Offset printing

UNIT 31

PROCESS PHOTOGRAPHY

Process photography is a means of producing negatives and positives. Process photography negatives are classified as either (1) **line** negatives or (2) **halftone** negatives. (Do not confuse process photography with continuous tone photography. The latter production process is explained in Chapter 10 and Units 43 through 49.)

Line negatives are produced by shooting line copy (copy that is black and white with no intermediate tones or gradations of tone). The line negative is black or opaque in the non-image areas and transparent in the image areas. Lines of type, photo-composition, hand lettering, clip art and pre-printed type, and typewritten copy are all examples of line copy artwork.

Halftone negatives are produced by exposing sensitized film, through a halftone

A. Photograph

B. Halftone negative

Fig. 9-2. Photographs are continuous tone copy

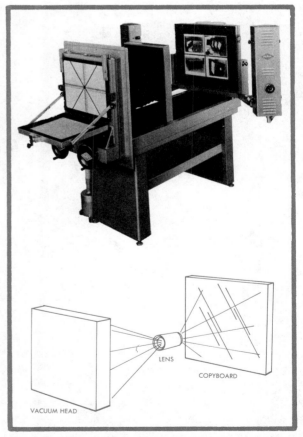

Fig. 9-3. NuArc Supersonic Horizontal Camera Model SST1418

screen, to reflected light from continuous tone copy. Continuous tone copy has gradations of tone from white to black. Photographs are examples of continuous tone copy. The halftone negative registers the gradations in tone by a **series of dots.** A close examination of a halftone negative will show large dots in the light areas of the continuous tone photograph and small dots in the dark areas. Remember, this is a negative, Fig. 9-2.

Process cameras are classified as being either (1) horizontal or (2) vertical. The **horizontal process camera** has the copyboard, lens, and vacuum head in a horizontal line, Fig. 9-3. The **vertical process camera** has the copyboard, lens, and vacuum head positioned in a vertical line, Fig. 9-4. Most process cameras have basically the same operating points. As you study the remainder of this unit, refer to Fig. 9-5 for location of camera parts discussed.

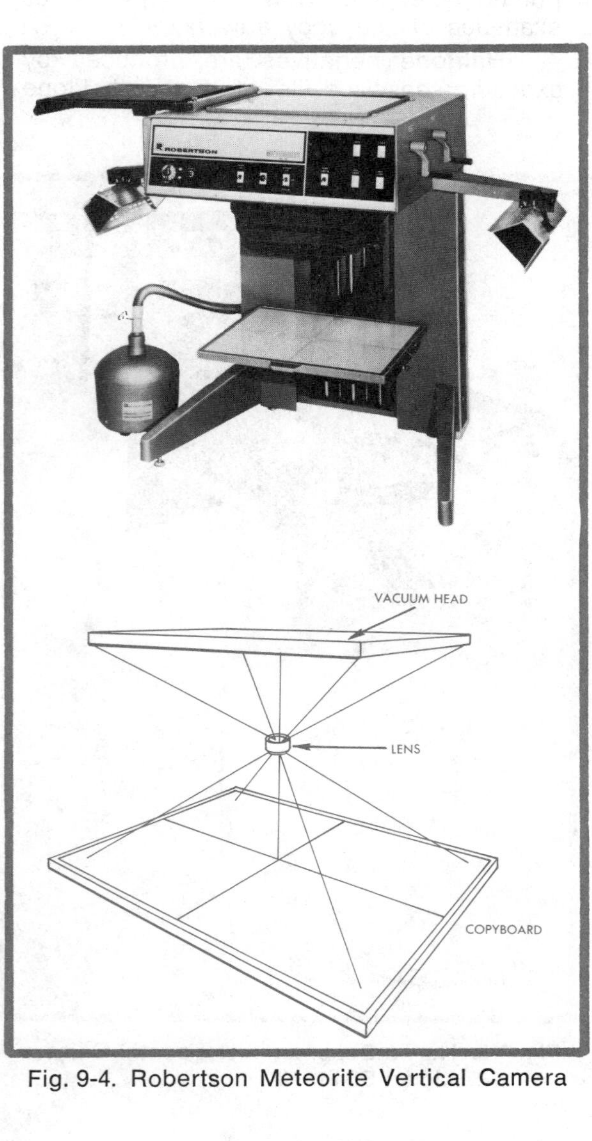

CHEMICAL PREPARATION

Before any copy is photographed (shot), the processing chemicals should be prepared. The processing chemicals should be placed in order from left to right. Four individual trays are generally used, and they contain (1) developer, (2) stop bath, (3) fixer, and (4) running water, Fig. 9-6.

Fig. 9-4. Robertson Meteorite Vertical Camera

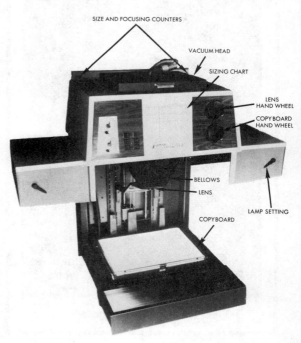

SIZE AND FOCUSING COUNTERS

VACUUM HEAD

SIZING CHART

LENS HAND WHEEL

COPYBOARD HAND WHEEL

BELLOWS

LENS

LAMP SETTING

COPYBOARD

Fig. 9-5. Operating points of the process camera

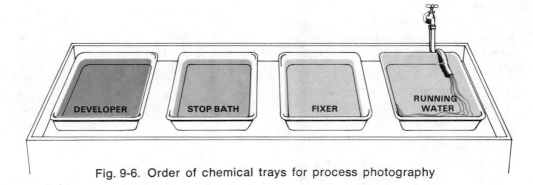

Fig. 9-6. Order of chemical trays for process photography

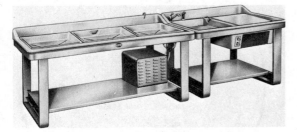

Fig. 9-7. Temperature control film processing sink

To maintain accuracy in processing, the chemicals should be maintained at a constant temperature of 68° F (20° C). A temperature control sink, Fig. 9-7, allows the trays to float in water, while a refrigeration unit keeps the chemicals in the trays at the desired temperature.

1. The first tray holds the **developer.** Generally, it is sold in a concentrated liquid or powder form. Developer usually consists of Part A and Part B which are prepared separately in containers marked **A** and **B**, according to the manufacturer's instructions. Equal amounts of **A** and **B** are combined into one solution for use as a working solution in the developing tray, Fig. 9-8. A ¾″ (19 mm) depth of developer in the tray is recommended.

2. The **stop bath** tray is prepared by mixing 8 ounces (236.6 ml) of liquid 28% acetic acid with one gallon (3.8 liters) of water, Fig. 9-9.

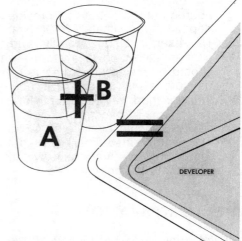

Fig. 9-8. Preparing the developer

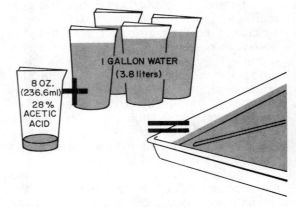

Fig. 9-9. Preparing the stop bath

Safety Note

When preparing the stop bath, **always add the acid to the water.** Prepared stop bath should be stored in a clearly labeled container.

As an alternative, commercially prepared stop bath, called Indicator Stop Bath, may be used. It is in a concentrated form and must be mixed with water to prepare a working solution. Indicator Stop Bath is straw yellow in color but turns purple when exhausted, at which time it must be discarded.

Sufficient stop bath should be poured into the tray to provide a depth of approximately ¾″ (19 mm).

3. The **fixer** is also generally sold in concentrated powder form and should be mixed according to manufacturer's instructions. It is poured into the third tray to a depth of ¾″ 19 mm). The container for this solution should be labeled "Fixer."

4. The **water rinse** is set up in the fourth tray so that fresh water is continually being supplied.

CAMERA PREPARATION

If the copy is to be shot at 100% or 1:1, the size and focus counters must be set at 100% or 1:1. However, if the copy is to be enlarged or reduced, the **shooting percentage** must be determined. This is done by comparing the maximum copy size to the maximum desired size (as indicated on the layout). The shooting percentage is computed with a **proportional scale.** The proportional scale is adjusted so that the copy dimension is directly under the desired reproduction dimension on the outside scale. The percentage of enlargement or reduction is indicated by the arrow in the window of the scale, Fig. 9-10.

The percentage of both the length and the width must be computed because most reproduction copy must fit the copy space

allowed on the layout. In the following examples, the original art size must be reduced to fit the layout space. You will see in Fig. 9-10 how the proportional scale is used to determine percentages. Then compare the reproduction sizes with the size of the layout area. Which reduction percentage would you use?

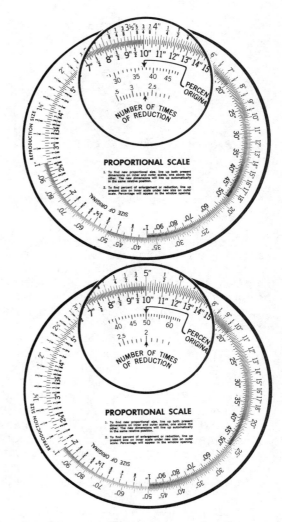

Fig. 9-10. Computing shooting percentage with the proportional scale. The enlarged view

WIDTH REDUCTION — 37%

Size	U. S. Customary (in.)	SI Metrics (mm)
Original	8 x 10	203 x 254
Reproduction	3 x 3¾	76 x 95
Layout Space	3 x 5	76 x 127

Table 1 — Reproduction fits into layout space

HEIGHT REDUCTION — 50%

Size	U. S. Customary (in.)	SI Metrics (mm)
Original	8 x 10	203 x 254
Reproduction	4 x 5	102 x 127
Layout Space	3 x 5	76 x 127

Table 2 — Reproduction too large to fit into layout space

1. Example using width reduction percentage
   Original art size = 8″ width × 10″ height
   (203 mm × 254 mm)
   Layout space = 3″ width × 5″ height
   (76 mm × 127 mm)
   a. Reduce 8″ to fit into 3″.
      (Reduce 203 mm to fit into 76 mm)
   b. See top example of Fig. 9-10. Reduction is 37½%.
   c. Find 10″ on the original portion of the scale. Directly above it is the desired reproduction dimension — 3¾″.
   d. Compare this reproduction size with size of the layout space.
      Original size   8″ × 10″
                          (203 mm × 254 mm)
      Reproduction size 3″ × 3¾″
                          (76 mm × 95 mm)
      Layout space   3″ × 5″
                          (76 mm × 127 mm)
   The 37½% reduction will fit the layout space.

2. Example using height reduction percentage
   Original art size = 8″ width × 10″ height
   (203 mm × 254 mm)
   Layout space = 3″ width × 5″ height
   (76 mm × 127 mm)
   a. Reduce 10″ to fit into 5″.
      (Reduce 254 mm to fit into 127 mm)
   b. See bottom example of Fig. 9-10. Reduction is 50%.
   c. Find 8″ on the original portion of the scale. Directly above it is the desired reproduction dimension — 4″.
   d. Compare this reproduction size with the size of the layout space.
      Original size 8″ × 10″
      (203 mm × 254 mm)
      Reproduction size 4″ × 5″
      (102 mm × 127 mm)
      Layout space 3″ × 5″
      (76 mm × 127 mm)
   The 50% reduction will not fit the layout space.

As you can see, it is necessary to **use the smaller percentage to fit the layout.**

After the shooting percentage has been determined, refer to the **sizing chart.** Opposite the percentage are indicated both the lens and copyboard size and focus counter setting numbers. Set the lens and copy counters by turning the corresponding control hand wheels.

Before positioning the copy, clean both the inside and outside surfaces of the copyboard glass. Glass cleaner and a soft cloth pad, such as cotton, may be used to remove settled dust and fingerprints.

Position the copy in the center of the copyboard, using the size markings as guidelines. A **sensitivity guide,** also known as a gray scale, should be positioned on the copyboard for each exposure. For the most accurate or consistent results, the sensitivity guide should be placed, when possible, near the center of the copy, Fig. 9-11. The sensitivity guide will serve as a guide in development but will later be blocked out. Lower the copyboard glass and latch the spring lock.

Set the lens f-stop by turning the diaphragm ring to the best setting for the ex-

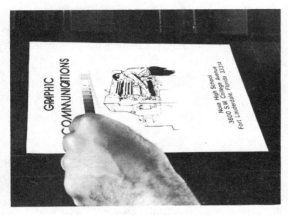

Fig. 9-11. Position the sensitivity guide near the center of the copy

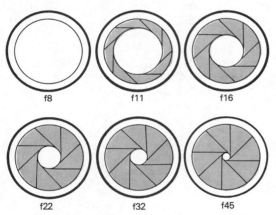

Fig. 9-12. Size relationships of f-stop openings

posure. The f-stop setting may vary with exposure time, type of film being used, the shooting percentage, and the copy being shot. The f-stop refers to the size of the lens opening or aperture, Fig. 9-12. The higher the f-stop number, the smaller the opening.

Remove the lens cap and clean the lens if necessary. Use only lens tissue moistened with lens cleaning liquid. Do not touch the lens glass with your fingers as the surface may be etched by the perspiration.

Set the timer for the desired exposure time, Fig. 9-13. This may also vary with the f-stop being used, type of film being used,

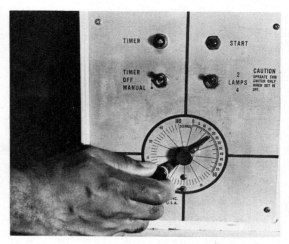

Fig. 9-13. Set the timer to the desired exposure time

the shooting percentage, and the copy being shot.

ADJUSTING EXPOSURE TIME AND f-STOP

When enlargements or reductions are necessary, the **exposure time** and/or f-stop must be changed accordingly. To compute the change, use an exposure guide. It shows the basic exposure time at a given f-stop for shooting a line negative at 100%.

For example, assume that the basic exposure time of 20 seconds at f/22 is used for shooting a 100% line negative. If the copy is to be enlarged to 150%, the exposure factor (as found on the exposure guide) is 1.42. The exposure factor is then multiplied by the basic exposure for shooting at 100% to determine the new exposure time.

Exposure factor	1.42
Basic exposure at 100%	×20
New exposure time	28.40 or 28 seconds

Exposures may also be varied by changing the lens f-stop. By opening the lens one f-stop without changing the timer, the film is exposed with twice the amount of light. By closing the lens one f-stop without changing the timer, the film is exposed with one-half the amount of light. A 30-second exposure at f/22 allows the same amount of light to expose the film as a 15-second exposure at f/16. Remember, the higher the f-stop number, the smaller the lens opening.

As a general rule, original artwork is prepared with a black image area on a white background. This combination permits the exposure and development of high contrast line negatives. In some cases, the copy to be shot may be a printed sheet and not original artwork. If the copy to be shot

is black ink on yellow paper, the negative contrast may be less than desirable. Not as much light will be reflected from the yellow paper to expose the film.

To improve negative contrast when shooting a line negative of copy with various colors, use filtration to **hold** or **drop out** the color, Fig. 9-14. Place the filter in front of the lens so the light will pass through it before striking the film. The filter will absorb some of the exposure light making necessary an increase in the total exposure time. The required exposure time can be computed by multiplying the filter factor of the filter being used by the basic exposure time used when shooting original copy prepared in black on white. For example, the filter factor of a deep yellow filter (G or #15) is 3.4. If the basic exposure time is 20 seconds, the new exposure time with the filter would be 3.4 x 20 or 68 seconds.

EXPOSING A LINE NEGATIVE

After all camera adjustments have been made, the chemicals prepared for processing the film, and the copy positioned, the next step is to expose the negative. Select the desired exposure lighting and turn the **on-off** switch to the timer position.

Under the recommended safelight conditions, cut a sheet of film to size. (Safelight conditions may vary with the film being used. However, most film used for process photography is Orthochromatic film which is

FILTER GUIDE		
TO PHOTOGRAPH:	FILTER	NUMBER
BLUE AS BLACK	K2 or G	8 or 15
GREEN AS BLACK	47B	—
YELLOW AS BLACK	47B	—
ORANGE AS BLACK	47B or none	—
RED AS BLACK	47b or none	—
BLUE AS WHITE	47B	—
GREEN AS WHITE	B or K2	58 or 8
YELLOW AS WHITE	K2 or G	8 or 15

FILTER FACTORS							
	No. 6 Light Yellow K-1	No. 8 Yellow K-2	No. 15 Deep Yellow G	No. 30 Rose	No. 47-B Blue	No. 58 Green B	Lateral Reversal Factor
PULSED XENON (6000 watts)	1.5	1.8	4.2	6.7	13.3	3.7	1.8
QUARTZ- IODINE	1.3	1.5	3.4	12.0	21.0	2.5	1.9
CARBON ARC (3000 watts)	2.0	3.3	8.7	5.0	16.8	5.0	1.5

Fig. 9-14. Filter and filter factor guide

Fig. 9-15. Place the film in the center of the vacuum head

A. Printed halltone

B. Enlarged portion of a printed halftone

Fig. 9-16. The size and density of the dots maintain the continuous tone qualities

A. 65-line screen

B. 150-line screen

Fig. 9-17. Halftone screens are designated by the number of dots per linear inch (25.4 mm)

not sensitive to red light. A Kodak Safelight Filter, Wratten Series 1A may be used.) The film size should be slightly larger than the image area size. Return the extra film to the light-tight container. Handle the film by the edges only.

Position the film, emulsion side facing out, in the center of the vacuum head, Fig. 9-15. The emulsion side of the film is the lighter of the two sides. If the film is notched,

the emulsion side is facing out when the notch is in the upper right-hand corner. Turn on the vacuum pump.

Close the vacuum head and press the exposure button to make the exposure. During exposure, the light reflected from the white areas of the copy passes through the lens and bellows and produces a latent image on the film. At the end of the exposure time, open the vacuum head, turn off the vacuum pump, and remove the film which is now ready for processing. If no other negatives are to be made, turn the camera off and cap the lens. The vacuum head should also be closed when the camera is not in use to prevent dust from settling in the bellows.

FILM PROCESSING

Safelights are on in the darkroom. The exposed film is immersed in the developer with the emulsion side up. Be sure the entire sheet of film is under the surface of the developer. Gently rock the tray during development by raising and lowering one edge. The agitation will keep the chemicals moving, continually supplying new developer to the surface of the film.

During development, the latent image begins to appear. The negative may be checked periodically by holding it up to a safelight. The non-image areas will appear as black, opaque areas, while the image develops as clear, transparent areas. A properly exposed Kodalith Ortho Type negative should develop a solid step 4 on the sensitivity guide in 2¾ minutes using Kodalith developer at 68° F (20° C). Step 5 will appear as light gray before solid 4 has been reached.

When satisfactory development has been achieved, lift the negative from the developer. Allow it to drain a few seconds before immersing it in the stop bath. The stop bath neutralizes or stops the action of the developer. The negative should be agitated in the stop bath for ten seconds, and then allowed to drain.

The negative is then placed in the fixing bath. The fixing solution removes the unexposed silver particles from the film and the milky white appearance of the image area. The negative should remain in the fixer for two to four minutes with agitation. The normal room lights may now be turned on.

Remove the negative from the fixer, and immerse it in a running water rinse for about ten minutes to remove all trace of chemicals. Negatives that are not rinsed long enough may discolor when dried.

To dry, remove the negative from the water rinse and allow it to drain for a few seconds. Hang the negative in a dust-free area. Be sure the negative is not touching another negative when drying as they will stick together. Handle the film by the edges since the negative emulsion is soft and will show scratches and fingerprints.

EXPOSING A HALFTONE NEGATIVE

As stated earlier, halftone negatives make it possible to reproduce what appear to be gradations of tone from white to black. Close inspection of the halftone print, however, reveals that there is no actual gradation of tone. The relative size and density of the halftone dots create an optical illusion. When the halftone dots are large or close together, the area appears dark. In the light areas of the print, the dots are small and sometimes do not exist, Fig. 9-16.

Halftone negatives are made by exposing continuous tone copy on film through a halftone screen. Halftone screens are classified by the number of dots that appear per linear inch (25.4 mm). A halftone print made with a 65-line screen is composed of dots that are coarse and easily seen. There is loss of detail when compared to a halftone print made from a 133-line screen. The more dots per linear inch, the finer the screen and the less noticeable is the dot pattern, Fig. 9-17.

Special effect screen tints are sometimes used instead of the traditional halftone screens to create special or unique patterns, Fig. 9-18.

When making a high quality halftone negative from a continuous tone original, three exposures may be necessary. These are (1) a **flash exposure** for the dark **shadow** areas, (2) a **detail exposure** for the **middletones** and (3) a **bump exposure** to accent the white or **highlight** areas of the original. The bump exposure is not always used.

The flash exposure is made to create the shadow detail of the original copy. The

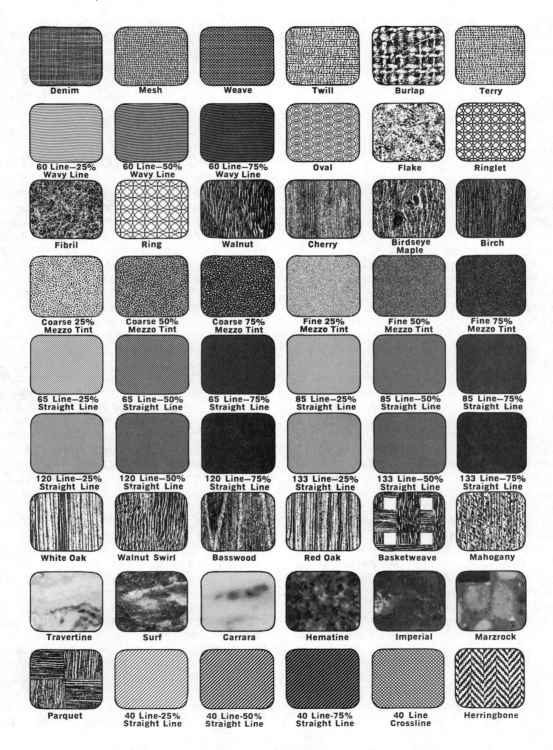

Fig. 9-18. Special effect screen patterns

shadow of the original is the darkest areas and will be represented by the smallest black dots on the negative.

The highlight areas of the original are the white or lightest areas of the original. The highlight areas will be represented by the smallest white dots on the negative.

The middletones of the original are the gradations that fall between the shadow and highlight areas. The middletone dot size on the negative will vary from the smallest black dot to the smallest white dot.

To produce high quality halftone negatives, it is first necessary to establish **base exposures** for the equipment and supplies that you are using. After the base exposures are calculated, the same conditions should be maintained. Halftone exposures are determined by the screen density, film speed, and developer strength. If the brand of film being used is changed or the type of contact screen being used is changed, it may be necessary to calculate new base exposures. Mixing standards for chemicals should also be strictly maintained. A fresh developer solution should be used for each piece of film processed. The developer should always be used at the same temperature for consistent results.

CALCULATING THE DETAIL EXPOSURE

The detail exposure (also called the **middletone** or **main exposure**) should be established **first**. Select a continuous tone original that has good highlight and shadow areas as well as a wide range of middletones. Place the selected original and a Kenro Developing Scale on the copyboard of the camera. Position the lights and adjust the percentage setting for 100% for a same size negative.

The exposure time necessary for making a halftone negative will vary depending upon the brand of film, type of halftone screen and type of lighting system being used. Consult the manufacturer's recommendations for a suggested exposure time and f/number setting.

To calculate the detail exposure time, three exposures should be made. All three pieces of film will be exposed for the same time and of the same copy. The f/number setting should be changed for each negative. To make each piece of film easy to identify after processing, cut one corner from the first piece of film, two corners from the second piece, and three corners from the third.

Place the first piece of film on the vacuum head of the camera. A halftone screen about 2″ (50 mm) wider than the film on all sides should be **rolled** over the film, Fig. 9-19. Be sure the **emulsion side of the screen** (dull side) and the **emulsion side of the film** are in direct contact (no air bubbles between them).

Close the vacuum head and make the first exposure for the manufacturer's suggested time at a given f/stop, for example, f/11. At the end of the exposure, remove the screen and film. A second piece of film should then be exposed for the same time but at a different f/stop — f/16. Repeat the procedure for the third piece of film at f/22.

Develop the three pieces of film at the same time in the same developing solution for 2½ minutes. At the end of the development time, place the three negatives in the stop bath, fixer, and water using the same techniques as used for processing a line negative. Dry the negatives.

Fig. 9-19. Place the halftone screen over the film on the vacuum head

Place the three negatives on a light table and examine the developing scales. The black dots in the step #4 should be large but not connected, Fig. 9-20. The black dots in the #3 step should be larger and connected. This step should have 45% clear area and 55% black connected dots. Select the negative that meets these requirements and record the exposure time and f/number that was used during the exposure. This becomes your detail or middletone base exposure.

Examine step #5 of the selected negative. If a small black dot appears, a flash exposure will not be necessary. If no dot pattern appears, it will be necessary to flash expose the film to extend the screened tones into the clear areas of the negative.

DETERMINING THE FLASH EXPOSURE

Set up the flash unit (light source) directly in line with the vacuum head at a distance of 6 feet (1.8 meters), Fig. 9-21. Set the time for 5 seconds.

Place a sheet of film on the vacuum head with the emulsion side out. Position the halftone screen over the film. To make the test exposure, cover ¾ of the film with a piece of black cardboard and make a 5-second exposure. Move the cardboard to uncover an additional ¼ of the film and repeat the exposure of 5 seconds. The first section of film has now been exposed for 10 seconds and the second section for 5 seconds. Move the cardboard to uncover ¾ of the film and repeat the exposure.

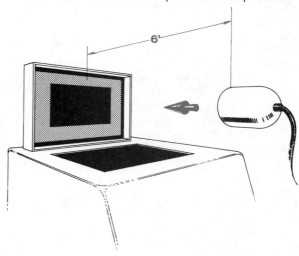

Fig. 9-21. Flash exposure diagram

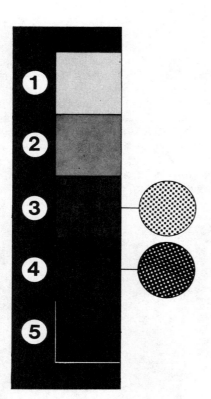

Fig. 9-20. Evaluate steps 3 and 4 on the developing scale for the middletone test negative

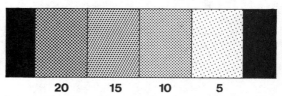

Fig. 9-22. The test flash exposure negative reveals four different dot patterns

Finally, remove the cardboard to uncover the entire sheet of film and make the last 5-second exposure. The film now has 4 exposures of 20, 15, 10 and 5 seconds.

Remove the screen and film. Process the film in fresh developer for 2½ minutes at the same temperature as was used for the middletone test negatives. Stop, fix, wash, and dry the negative.

Examine the flash negative on the light table. Four different size dot patterns should be visible, Fig. 9-22. The largest and darkest dot will appear in the 20-second exposure strip. Determine which strip has the smallest solid black dot. The exposure time used for that strip will be the **base flash exposure time** to use when shooting halftone negatives.

COMBINING THE FLASH AND MIDDLETONE EXPOSURES

Now that the base flash and base middletone exposures have been calculated, another test negative should be made combining the two exposures.

Position the copy and developing scale on the copy board. Place the film and screen on the vacuum head and make the calculated flash exposure. Then make the calculated middletone exposure and process the film under the same conditions and using the same techniques as before.

Examine the development scale of this negative. Step #1 should have a clean, clear, round pinpoint window, Fig. 9-23. Step #3 should match your middletone test negative. Step #5 should have a small, round, black pinpoint dot. If step #1 develops as a solid black, reduce the middletone exposure time by 10% for the next negative exposed.

THE BUMP EXPOSURE

The purpose of the **bump exposure** is to increase the white or highlight areas. The bump is the third exposure and is made

without a screen. It is a line shot. After the flash and middletone exposures have been made, the halftone screen is removed without moving the film. The vacuum head is then closed and the bump exposure is made at f/45 for 20% of the middletone exposure time. As a result, the clear pinpoints in step #1 should be reduced in size. This makes the white areas print much whiter.

When shooting halftones that require enlargement or reduction, it will be necessary to increase or decrease the middletone exposure time. Consult the enlargement and reduction factor numbers chart from the camera manufacturer.

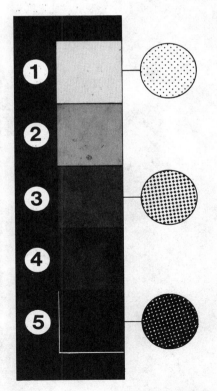

Fig. 9-23. Evaluate the development **scale** of the combined flash and middletone exposures

Fig. 9-24. A duotone

AUTOSCREEN ORTHO FILM

Autoscreen film has a 133-line halftone screen pattern built into the light sensitive emulsion. It can be used for making halftones of both black and white and color originals. Because of the **built-in screen**, it is not necessary to use a contact halftone screen over the film on the vacuum head.

When using autoscreen film, two exposures are made. These are (1) the detail exposure and (2) the flash exposure. The detail exposure is made first. The exposure time and f/stop used for this exposure will vary with the type of lighting system used. A series of test exposures may be required to determine the most satisfactory exposure.

The flash exposure is made after the detail exposure. Any low-level, tungsten light source may be used. A typical flash exposure would be 30 seconds at a distance of 4 feet (1.2 meter) using a 15-watt bulb in a Kodak Adjustable Safelight Lamp with a OA Safelight filter. A series of test flash exposures should be made to determine the best results.

DUOTONES

Two halftone negatives of the same original copy are used to create a duotone illustration, Fig. 9-24. One negative is used for producing the principal image color area. The principal color is generally a "dark" color. The second negative is used to produce the "lighter" color area.

Black is commonly used as the principal color in combination with any other color for the lighter area. Complimentary color combinations may also be used to produce duotones, or two primary colors may be used. The selection of the colors is often determined by the illustration and the effect desired.

The halftone negative for the principal color image area should be exposed and processed for less than normal contrast. It should favor detail **outside** highlight areas. The second negative must be exposed at a 30° angle to the first. For example, if a 45°

screen angle were used for the first negative, a 15° or a 75° screen angle must be used for the second negative. The second negative should be exposed and processed to register detail **in** the highlight areas. It may have more contrast than the first negative.

MAKING A POSITIVE

A film positive is used for burning (exposing) an offset plate so that a reverse image may be printed. A printed **reverse image** is one in which the actual printed area is the background. The letter or de-

Fig. 9-25. A positive is the reverse of a negative

picted image is not printed and appears as the color of the paper. Film positives **are** also used for making photographic silk screen stencils.

CONTACT PROCEDURE

Original copy that is to be printed as **a reverse** must first be shot as a film negative. After processing, the film negative can be contact printed onto another sheet of film to make the positive. When the positive is made, the film negative clear areas become opaque while the opaque areas become clear, Fig. 9-25.

To make a positive from a negative, **a** contact printing frame can be used, Fig. 9-26. Open the back and place the negative against the glass **face up** if the film being made will be used to burn an offset plate,

Fig. 9-27. If the film will be used to burn a photographic silk screen stencil, however, place it **face down**. The relationship of the negative emulsion to the unexposed film emulsion makes a difference in later stages of processing.

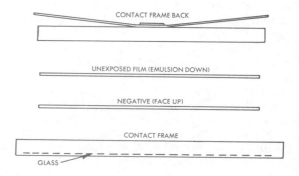

CONTACT FRAME BACK

UNEXPOSED FILM (EMULSION DOWN)

NEGATIVE (FACE UP)

CONTACT FRAME

GLASS

Fig. 9-27. Loading the contact printing frame to produce a positive

After the negative and unexposed film are properly positioned, replace the back of the contact printing frame. Turn the contact printing frame over and place it under a point light source for exposure, Fig. 9-28. The exposure time will vary depending upon the brightness of the light source and its distance from the film. A series of test exposures may have to be made to determine the correct exposure time. The exposed film is processed in the same manner as the original negative.

ETCH-BLEACH REVERSAL PROCESS

The etch-bleach reversal process produces a positive image of original art work copy. The main advantage of this process is that only one piece of film must be used. The original art work copy is first shot on negative film. A 10 to 15 percent increase in exposure time is allowed as a slightly darker than normal negative is required.

1. The exposed film is processed on Kodalith developer for 2¾ minutes. To achieve best results using the etch-bleach reversal process, stop agitating

Fig. 9-26. Contact printing frame

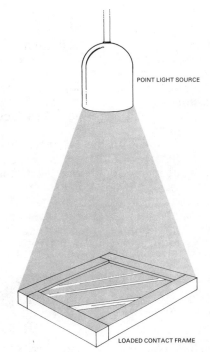

POINT LIGHT SOURCE

LOADED CONTACT FRAME

Fig. 9-28. Make the exposure with the point light source

the developer as soon as the image begins to appear.

2. At the end of the development time, place the film in Kodak Stop Bath SB-1a. The film should be agitated for at least 15 seconds.

3. As soon as the film is placed in Kodak Etch-Bleach Bath EB-3 or EB-4, the room lights may be turned on. Agitate the film until the silver image is completely bleached through to the back. Only the developed silver will be bleached. The silver that was not developed will remain on the film.

4. Wash the film at least 15 seconds in running water to remove the softened gelatin. If traces of gelatin remain on the film, it may be removed by gently wiping the film surface with a wet cotton swab.

5. The undeveloped silver is now re-exposed and registers a positive image. The re-exposure can be accomplished by normal handling of the film while washing under the room lights. Both sides of the film must be re-exposed. If

the normal room lights are weak, a 100-watt light may be used for a few seconds. Excessive re-exposure will do no harm.

6. A second development period using Kodalith developer is required. The film should be left in the developer until the image is completely black. Kodak Dektol developer may also be used. It will shorten the second development time.

7. Rinse the film in Kodak Stop Bath SB-1a.

8. The film should be placed in Kodak Hardener F-5a for 30 seconds to harden the image.

9. Wash the film for 5 minutes in running water before drying.

UNIT 31 — TERMS FOR DISCUSSION AND REVIEW

process
  photography
negative
positive
line negative
halftone
  negative
gradations of
  tone
halftone screen
continuous
  tone copy
horizontal
  camera
vertical camera
sizing and focus
  counters
vacuum head
sizing chart
lens hand wheel
copyboard
  hand wheel
bellows
lens
lamp setting
copyboard
developer
stop bath
fixer
shooting percentage

proportion scale
reduction
enlargement
sensitivity guide
f/stop
filtration
hold or
  drop out
filter factor
safelight
emulsion side
film latent
  image
agitation
non-image
  areas
opaque areas
flash exposure
shadow areas
detail exposure
middletones
highlight areas
Autoscreen film
duotone
reverse image
contact printing
  frame
etch-bleach
  reversal process

UNIT 32

STRIPPING

Stripping is the operation of arranging and mounting process negatives on goldenrod paper to produce a **flat**. The flat holds the negatives in position for "burning" (exposing) the offset plate. The goldenrod paper used is generally an 80-pound double-coated paper that is ruled in ¼″ (6.4 mm) graduations. The person who makes up the flat is called a stripper.

The stripping operation is begun by placing a sheet of goldenrod paper (sometimes referred to as a **masking sheet**) on the glass-top surface of the light table so that the end marked **gripper margin** is to the stripper's left-hand side. In this position, the gripper margin corresponds to the head or leading edge of the plate and of the paper as it is fed into the press.

Line up the lower edge of the masking sheet with the upper edge of a T-square. Be sure the T-square is held tightly to the edge of the light table. Use tape to fasten the two corners of the gripper end of the masking sheet to the light table surface, Fig. 9-29.

Locate and mark on the masking sheet the outside dimensions of the paper size that will be used for printing. Within this area, locate and mark the exact location of the image area that will be printed, Fig. 9-30. The printing image area should not extend into the gripper margin because this area is gripped by the press grippers

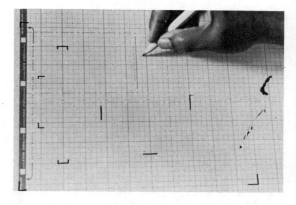

Fig. 9-30. Mark the location of the image area on the masking sheet

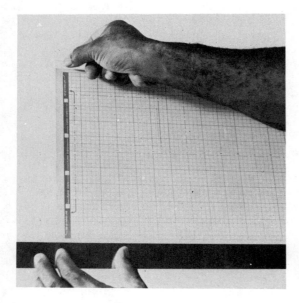

Fig. 9-29. Tape the masking sheet to the surface of the light table

Fig. 9-31. The emulsion is removed when scratched with a razor blade

to feed and deliver the paper. The gripper margin area will not receive a printed impression.

Slide the negative, readable side up, under the masking sheet. The emulsion side is down. In some cases, negatives may not have a readable side. The emulsion side may then be determined by scratching the negative (in a nonprinting area) with a sharp pointed object. The emulsion, when scratched, will scrape away, Fig. 9-31. The emulsion side is generally the duller of the two sides of the negative. The heading of the negative should be positioned to the gripper margin end or to the top of the masking sheet as it is positioned on the light table, Fig. 9-32.

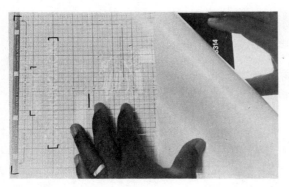

Fig. 9-32. Slide the negative under the masking sheet in the marked position

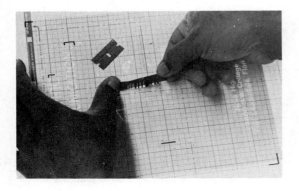

Fig. 9-33. Tape the masking sheet to the negative by placing a piece of tape over the oval cut-out

Position the image (transparent areas) of the negative in the designated image area on the masking sheet. To assure correct positioning, a T-square and triangle may be used. The image may also be aligned by using the graduation lines printed on the masking sheet.

When the masking sheet and negative have been properly positioned, apply downward pressure with one hand. This will hold the masking sheet and negative in position.

With the other hand, cut a small oval shape in the masking sheet with a single edge razor blade or stencil knife. This opening should be cut near the center of the image area. Apply pressure to cut through the masking sheet only. **Do not** cut through the negative.

With the downward pressure still exerted, remove the oval-shaped cut-out and place a piece of red lithographer's tape over the opening, Fig. 9-33. The tape should contact both the masking sheet and the negative.

Turn the masking sheet over so that the negative is now on top. Tape the four corners of the negative to the back of the masking sheet using transparent tape.

After the four corners of the negative are taped to the back of the masking sheet, the flat may be turned over so that the masking sheet is once again on top. Check the position of the masking sheet in relation to the position of the negative to be sure that they are still properly aligned.

Using a sharp razor blade or stencil knife, cut a **window** in the masking sheet. The window should be between $1/8''$ and $1/4''$ (3 mm and 6 mm) larger than the image area on all sides. Use very light pressure so that the negative is not cut. Remove the window from the masking sheet and inspect the negative, Fig. 9-34. Be sure all the desired image area is exposed by the removal of the window.

A step gray scale (sensitivity guide) may be stripped into the gripper margin of the flat to serve as an exposure and development guide. Although this image will be burned on the plate, it will not appear on the printed copy.

Fig. 9-34. Cut out and remove the windows

Fig. 9-35. Opaque any pinholes

OPAQUING THE FLAT

The only transparent areas in the negative should be the words or pictures that are to print. However, you will usually find some unwanted transparent areas in the negative. These are referred to as **pinholes** and are usually caused by careless negative handling or are the result of small dust particles that were not cleaned off the camera lens or copyboard glass. If these pinholes are not blocked out, they will appear as a printing image on the plate.

Working on the light table makes locating pinholes easier. Opaquing should be done on the readable or nonemulsion side of the negative. Use a small brush and photographic opaquing solution to block out the pinholes, Fig. 9-35. If the opaque becomes too thick, it may be thinned with a small amount of water. If an error is made

and the opaque covers a portion of the desired image area, a damp cloth may be used to wipe off the opaque.

To prevent smearing the wet opaque, start at the top of the negative and work toward the bottom. The opaque requires from three to five minutes to dry.

Check the negative carefully to be sure that all of the unwanted transparent areas have been opaqued. Wash the brush with water and close the opaquing solution tightly.

SCREEN TINTS

The layout may call for the image area of the negative to be printed as a screen tint. (Screen tints, as you may recall, were

Fig. 9-36. All or any part of the image may be screen tinted

Listen to
the cold

Fig. 9-37. Lettering superimposed over a halftone

discussed in Unit 1.) If a screen tint is to be used, the screen tint sheet may be taped to the back of the flat. In this position, the screen tint sheet will be between the negative and the plate (the emulsion side of the sheet against the plate) when the plate is burned. If only a portion of the negative is to be printed as a screen tint, it is necessary to attach the screen tint sheet to only that portion of the flat, Fig. 9-36. To achieve interest and variety, several different screen tint sheets may be taped to the back of the same flat.

COMPLEMENTARY FLATS

Sometimes in the production of a printed message, lettering must be superimposed over a halftone illustration or screen tint, Fig. 9-37. This requires the stripping of two flats, called **complementary flats,** for burning one offset plate image.

To assure accurate alignment, the two masking sheets are positioned in exact register on top of one another. Both masking sheets are then punched in at least two corners (preferably the two gripper margin

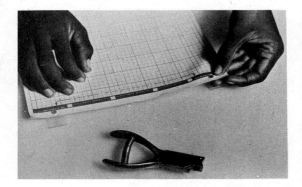

Fig. 9-38. Inserting the register pins in the masking sheets

Fig. 9-39. A sheet of paper printed two up

corners), and register pins are inserted to hold the masking sheets in position for stripping, Fig. 9-38.

The halftone illustration is stripped into the desired position on the bottom masking sheet. The line negative is then stripped into position, in exact register, on the top masking sheet.

STEP-AND-REPEAT

The step-and-repeat process of stripping allows for the use of one negative for producing an offset plate which contains more than one image. This process is often used when the size of the finished product is considerably smaller than the basic sheet size, as would be the case in printing cards, labels, letterheads, etc. For example, it is possible by using the step-and-repeat process to print 5½″ x 8½″ (139.7 mm x 215.9 mm) finished sheets two up on 8½″ x 11″ (215.9 mm x 279.4 mm) paper, Fig. 9-39. After being printed, the paper is cut to the desired finished size. The step-and-repeat process is economical both in cost of materials and in production time.

Begin the step-and-repeat stripping operation by locating and marking on the masking sheet the outside dimensions of the stock that will be run through the press. After this has been done, locate and mark the exact dimensions of the sheets for the

Fig. 9-40. Cut the step-and-repeat notches in the margin of the masking sheet

finished product. A small notch can be cut in the margin of the masking sheet to register the steps, Fig. 9-40.

Place the negative under the masking sheet, emulsion side down, and position the image area in the desired location. The negative should be stripped in the marked finished size area that is nearest the gripper margin on the masking sheet. Secure the negative to the back of the masking sheet, cut the windows, and opaque if necessary, Fig. 9-41. This masking sheet is now ready to be exposed in a number of locations to cover the entire plate.

Fig. 9-41. A completed step-and-repeat flat

COLOR STRIPPING

Each color that is to be printed on a multicolor printed message requires the preparation of individual color flats. The flats, one for each color, are then used to burn the plates, one for each color.

Place the required number of golden-rod masking sheets in perfect register on top of one another. To assure proper registration, all the masking sheets should be punched at the same time. A minimum of two punches in the corners of the gripper margin end of the masking sheet should be made. Registration pins are then inserted

to hold the masking sheets in position for stripping the negative.

Begin stripping by placing one negative under the bottom masking sheet. (The other masking sheets may be rolled back out of the way.) Locate and strip the first negative into position. Cut the necessary windows.

Fold down the next to the last masking sheet, and strip the second negative into position. Be sure to align registration marks on the negatives. Repeat this procedure for each negative. Each flat must be labeled to indicate the negative image color.

UNIT 32 — TERMS FOR DISCUSSION AND REVIEW

stripping
process negative
goldenrod paper
flat
burning
offset plate
stripper
masking sheet
light table
gripper margin
head or
   leading edge
T-square
image area
printed
   impression
negative
emulsion side
transparent
   areas

triangle
oval cut
red lithographers
   tape
window
step gray scale
pinholes
opaquing
nonemulsion
layout
screen tint
superimposed
halftone
complementary
   flats
register pins
punch
alignment
line negative
step-and-repeat

UNIT 33

PLATEMAKING

After the flat has been prepared, a metal offset plate may be made. Metal offset plates are generally presensitized; some on both sides. (Other types of offset plates are described in Unit 34.)

The platemaker, Fig. 9-42, is used for burning the plate. Open the vacuum frame and clean both sides of the glass to remove any dust or fingerprints. Place the metal plate in the vacuum frame with the presensitized side up.

Safety Note

Because metal plates are thin, they are also sharp and, therefore, should be handled carefully.

Fig. 9-43. Position the flat on top of the plate in the vacuum frame

The flat is positioned face up or in a readable position on top of the plate. Align the gripper margin end of the masking sheet with one end of the plate. The edge of the masking sheet nearest the operator should also be aligned with the corresponding edge of the plate, Fig. 9-43. You will notice that the plate is slightly smaller than the flat.

Carefully close the vacuum frame, checking to see that the flat does not slip from position. Turn on the vacuum pump and double-check the position of the flat to the plate. Flip the vacuum frame over so that the flat is now between the plate and the light source. Set the timer and expose the plate for the desired length of time.

Safety Note

Do not look directly at the exposure light as it may result in damage to the eyes.

The exposure time may vary in accordance with (1) the type of plate being used, (2) the type of light source, and (3) the distance between the light source and the plate.

During the exposure time, the light passes through the transparent areas of the negative and hardens the presensitized plate coating. Where the plate is not struck by the exposure light (in the opaque negative areas), the plate coating remains soft.

The second side of the plate, if it is presensitized, may be exposed in the same

Fig. 9-42. NuArc Platemaker

Fig. 9-44. Pour a small puddle of **process** gum onto the surface of the plate

Fig. 9-45. Wipe the developer over the plate with a soft sponge

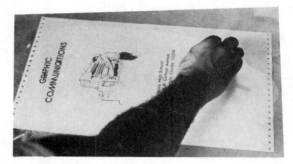

Fig. 9-46. Wipe the plate with a cotton pad while rinsing

manner using a second flat. If only one flat is to be burned, the same image may be exposed on both sides of the plate.

After exposure, the plate is **rubbed up** or developed to bring the image into view. Turn off the vacuum and remove the plate, placing it on a flat work surface.

Pour a small puddle of process gum in the center of the plate, Fig. 9-44. Using a clean, soft sponge, wipe the process gum over the entire plate surface. The process gum removes the unhardened plate coating.

While the process gum is still wet, pour a small puddle of developer on the plate. A second clean, soft sponge should be used to spread the developer over the entire plate surface. For best results, use very light pressure and long, even wiping strokes, Fig. 9-45. The image will begin to appear as the plate is rubbed with the developer. A solid step 6 on the sensitivity guide in the gripper margin usually indicates that the plate has been properly exposed and developed. Repeat the rub-up procedure for the second side of the plate. Apply running water to both sides of the plate to remove all traces of the developer. A cotton pad may be used to lightly wipe the plate surface during the rinsing operation, Fig. 9-46.

Allow the plate to dry. The plate is now ready to be placed on the offset duplicator. If it is to be stored, gum arabic is used to coat the surface of the plate to prevent oxidation of the non-image areas. Gum arabic may be applied with a cotton pad to the entire plate surface, Fig. 9-47.

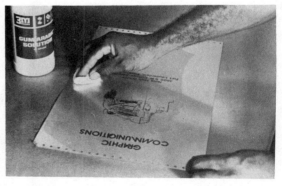

Fig. 9-47. Coat the plate with gum arabic

COMPLEMENTARY FLATS

When complementary flats are burned, extreme care and accuracy must be exercised in positioning the flats on top of the

Fig. 9-48. Trace the step-and-repeat notches onto the plate

Fig. 9-49. Cover the first step before burning the second step

plate. Position the first flat on the plate and make the exposure. At the end of the exposure, turn off the vacuum, remove the first flat but **do not turn the plate over**. Position the second flat and make the second exposure, thus burning the same side of the plate with the second image.

STEP-AND-REPEAT

Place the step-and-repeat flat in position on top of the plate in the vacuum frame. Using a pencil, trace the registration marks (that were cut in the edge of the masking sheet) onto the plate, Fig. 9-48. Close the vacuum frame and make the first exposure.

After the first exposure, the flat must be **stepped down** (the negative moved to the next position). Align the registration marks cut in the masking sheet with those traced on the plate. In stepping down the flat, a portion of the plate will be uncovered. To prevent exposure of this portion, use a masking sheet to block out the exposure light, Fig. 9-49. Repeat this procedure for each step-down when burning the plate.

COLOR

Once again extreme care and accuracy must be exercised in positioning the flat on the plate when color plates are to be burned. Only one color may be burned on any one side of a plate. Each plate (or each plate side) should be marked to indicate its printing color.

UNIT 33 — TERMS FOR DISCUSSION AND REVIEW

flat
offset plate
presensitized
platemaker
burning
vacuum frame
align
gripper margin
masking sheet
vacuum pump
light source
timer
expose
transparent areas
negative

rubbed up
developed
process gum
developer
sensitivity guide
offset duplicator
gum arabic
oxidation
non-image areas
complementary
    flats
step-and-repeat
registration marks
stepped down

UNIT 34

OTHER TYPES OF OFFSET PLATES

In Unit 33, the procedure for making only one type of offset plate was discussed. To meet the demands of the graphic communications industry, a variety of plate materials and processes are available. This unit will present some of the additional plate-making procedures.

DIRECT IMAGE PLATES

Direct image plates are sometimes referred to as **direct image masters** or **paper plates.** Direct image plates do not have a photosensitive coating. These plates are generally a paper base material. They have a special surface coating which provides a smooth water receptive surface. Direct image plates are used frequently. They are inexpensive and easy to prepare. **Short run** direct image plates are capable of printing approximately 50 copies, while **medium run** plates are designed for runs of 1000 copies. As many as 5000 copies can be run with the **long run** direct image plates. The main advantages of this type of plate are (1) they are inexpensive when compared to metal plates, (2) no negative is required, therefore there is no stripping operation, and (3) the printing image is prepared directly on the plate surface.

Direct image plates are generally manufactured with guide markings showing the center line, gripper margin, image area, and typewriter line scale. These guide markings make it possible to regulate the image location when it is prepared on the plate surface.

Much of the copy that must be run is line copy generated by strike-on composition (typewritten). If direct image plates are used, the copy can be prepared directly on the plate using a special typewriter ribbon. Lithographic typewriter ribbons are recommended. They produce a greasy ink image on the plate which repels the water and accepts the offset ink. These ribbons may be used eight to ten times before the ink supply is exhausted. Carbon ribbons may also be used for typing copy on direct image plates. They generally produce a much better image than lithographic ribbons, but may be used only once.

Direct image plates may also be prepared by hand lettering, writing, or drawing with special pencils or pens. A nonreproducing pencil can be used to lightly draw guidelines or preliminary sketches. The surface of the plate should not be disturbed. These lines can be removed with fountain solution before printing. A reproducing pencil is then used to create the desired printing image on the plate surface. If errors are made when creating the image, a soft, nonabrasive eraser may be used to make the correction.

Lithographic crayons, special ball-point pens, and drawing fluid are also available for preparing direct image plates. The lithographic crayons are generally used for making large image areas on the plate. The ball-point pens can be used for lettering and drawing. The drawing fluid can be used in ruling pens, as well as lettering devices. This makes it possible to prepare detailed mechanical drawings directly on the plate surface.

PHOTO DIRECT PLATES

Photo direct plates are generally referred to as masters. Photo direct plates can be made quickly and economically. No darkroom is needed. Photo direct platemakers consist of both a camera and processor in one unit.

The Itek Platemaster Unit 15-18, Fig. 9-50, uses a film-base plate material. Up to 10,000 impressions can be made from one plate. This unit uses master material that is roll fed. Some manufacturers use master material that is pre-cut into sheets.

In the photo direct process, a negative is not required. The original copy is placed on the copy board. During exposure, light is reflected from the white areas of the copy. It passes through the lens and strikes the presensitized master material. The exposed master is then automatically processed and delivered ready for use on the offset duplicator.

The Itek Platemaster 15-18 has the capability of reducing original copy to 50% or enlarging to 150%. Line, as well as halftone, printing images may be produced. The speed and low cost of producing plates make the photo direct plate making procedure popular for printing newsletters, announcements, reports, minutes of meetings, and other short run items.

SILVER DIFFUSION TRANSFER PLATES

In the silver diffusion transfer plate process, the original copy is placed in contact with a negative paper material. The original copy can also be projected onto the negative paper using a camera. This is done to enlarge or reduce the image. The exposure, either by contact or projection, produces an invisible (latent) image on the negative paper.

The exposed negative paper is then placed in contact with a specially prepared aluminum plate, Fig. 9-51. The plate and paper are processed by passing them through a developing solution. There the latent image on the paper is developed. The exposed silver salts of the negative paper emulsion turn to black metallic silver. The roller pressure of the processor causes the black metallic silver positive image to be transferred to the plate surface. As the plate and paper leave the processing unit, the two are stuck together. When peeled apart, the positive silver image remains on the plate, Fig. 9-52. The plate must be treated with fixer and lacquer to give it the required

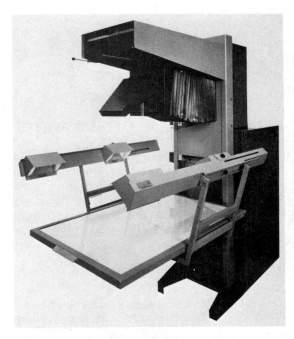

Fig. 9-50. Itek 15-18 Platemaster Unit

Fig. 9-51. The plate is placed in contact with the negative paper

offset properties. The image areas must repel water and accept ink. The non-image areas must accept water and repel ink.

The plate is now ready to be run on the offset duplicator. If the plate is to be stored for future use, a coating of plate conditioner should be applied to the surface as a preservative.

Fig. 9-52. The negative paper is stripped from the plate

XEROGRAPHIC PLATES

Xerography is a term which means "dry writing." The xerographic process is a dry electrostatic process which permits the making of both metal and paper offset plates from typewritten, drawn, printed, or photographic original copy. The nature of the process does not permit the original image to be enlarged or reduced. The plate image is the same size as the original image. Three pieces of equipment are necessary for making xerographic plates: (1) the camera, (2) the processor, and (3) the heat fuser, Fig. 9-53.

The xerographic process is illustrated in Fig. 9-54. The xerographic plate is first charged electrically in the processor. The positively charged plate is then placed in the camera where it receives the projected

Fig. 9-53. Xerography camera, processor, and heat fuser

OFFICE COPYING

OFFICE DUPLICATING

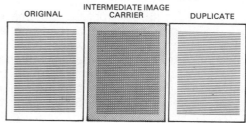

Fig. 9-54. Electrostatic printing (Courtesy of Xerox Business Products Group)

image from the original copy. The exposed plate is then developed by cascading negatively charged powder over the surface, causing the image to become visible. A paper (or metal) offset plate is then placed in contact with the xerographic plate and placed in the processor. In the processor, the image is transferred to the offset plate. After processing, the offset plate is inserted into the heat fuser which makes the plate image permanent.

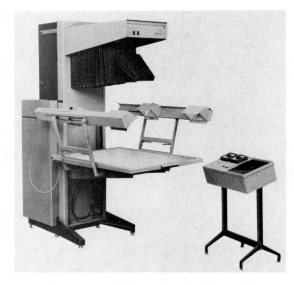

Fig. 9-55. Itek 175 Electrostatic Platemaker

Fig. 9-56. A. B. Dick 675 Master Maker

ELECTROSTATIC PLATES

The Itek 175 Electrostatic Platemaker, Fig. 9-55, produces press-ready offset plates from typewritten copy, drawings, printed material and prescreened halftones. The original copy is held in place on the copy board. Enlargements and reductions ranging from 45% to 150% can be produced.

When the exposure button is depressed, a preselected length of plate material is advanced and cut from the continuous roll. The length of plate material to be exposed can be adjusted from 10″ to 18″ (254 mm to 457.2 mm). The plate image is created by a liquid toner system. The plates can be placed directly on an offset duplicator as they emerge from the platemaker.

The electrostatic platemaking process is one that has become more and more popular as inexpensive, quality plates can be prepared in a minimum amount of time. Electrostatic plates permit rapid duplication of announcements, bulletins, reports, and other materials on a "quick copy basis".

The A. B. Dick 675 Master Maker, Fig. 9-56, is an electrostatic offset master maker which uses a liquid toner. An optional Jet Toner System is available which assures maximum coverage of solid areas and uniform copy density. The Model 675 is fed from a 350-foot (8890 mm) roll of master material in 9″ and 10″ (228.6 mm and 254 mm) widths. The maximum master length which can be produced is 15″ (381 mm).

When coupled with the Model 167 Master Conversion and Drying Unit plus the Transport Kit, Fig. 9-57, the unit automatically produces dry, converted, press-ready offset masters. The Model 167 makes it possible to go from original copy to press-ready masters in one step. It eliminates the necessity of manual conversion of wet masters. This also reduces press down time.

Fig. 9-57. A. B. Dick Model 167 Master Conversion and Drying Unit with Transport Kit

UNIT 34 — TERMS FOR DISCUSSION AND REVIEW

offset plate
direct image plate
direct image
  master
paper plate
photosensitive
  coating
water receptive
  surface
negative
stripping
  operation
guide markings
gripper margin
image area
line copy
strike-on
  composition
lithographic
  typewriter ribbon
repels
exhausted
carbon ribbon
nonreproducing
  pencil
fountain solution
non-abrasive
lithographic
  crayons
drawing fluid
ruling pens
photo direct plate
masters
camera
processor
original copy
copyboard
reflected light
offset duplicator
reducing
enlarging
halftone
  printing image
silver diffusion
  transfer plate
negative paper

projected
contact
latent image
aluminum plate
developing
  solution
exposed
  silver salts
emulsion
black metallic
  silver
fixer
lacquer
plate conditioner
xerography
dry writing
dry electrostatic
  process
liquid toner
  system

OFFSET DUPLICATOR ORIENTATION

Offset duplicators are available in a large variety of kinds and sizes to meet every printing requirement. The fundamental fact that grease and water do not readily mix is the basic operating principle of all offset duplicators.

The A. B. Dick Model 360 duplicator, Fig. 9-58, is capable of printing sheet sizes ranging from 3″ x 5″ to 11¾″ x 17″ (76 mm x 127 mm to 299 mm x 432 mm). The maximum image area that can be printed is 10½″ x 16½″ (267 mm x 419 mm). The Model 360 is a single-color duplicator which has a maximum output of 9000 copies per hour.

Fig. 9-58. A. B. Dick Model 360 CMC Offset Duplicator

Fig. 9-59. A. B. Dick 1600 Copy Printer

Fig. 9-60. Multilith Offset Model 1275

The A. B. Dick 1600 Copy Printer, Fig. 9-59, is a complete copy center. It can be programmed to make offset masters and produce the desired number of copies automatically. The 1600 Copy Printer consists of a master station and a duplicating station which are connected by a master transport unit. The two units can also be used independently.

Once the master has been processed, it is transported to the duplicating station. Programming starts the duplicating unit. The master is inserted and etched automatically and the desired number of copies is produced. At the end of the production run, the master is ejected and the blanket is cleaned. The next master is then inserted and the procedure is repeated. Masters can be made at a rate of 7 per minute. They can be stacked at the duplicating station for continuous automatic duplication at speeds ranging from 5000 to 9000 copies per hour.

With the Multilith Model 1275, Fig. 9-60, a single sheet of paper may be printed on both sides in the same or different colors or one side of the paper may be printed in two colors.

The Heidelberg Offset-Letterset, Fig. 9-61, is a single-color press. It is unique in that it can be used as either an offset or a letterset. This is made possible by interchanging the removable plate cylinder segments.

Fig. 9-61. Original Heidelberg Offset-Letterset

Some offset duplicators are fed from a continuous roll of paper known as a **web**. One example is the Apollo offset duplicator, Fig. 9-62. It is capable of printing one or two colors on one side of the paper, or one color on both sides of the paper. After being printed, the web paper is sheared into flat sheets. These are stacked at the delivery end of the machine.

The ATF Solna 425, Fig. 9-63, is capable of printing four colors on a sheet of paper in a single press run. Each color requires the use of a separate plate, a separate set of dampening rollers, and a separate set of inking rollers.

The variety of offset duplicators is almost endless. The Multilith 1250 is used in this text for describing the procedure of preparing and operating an offset duplicator. Although the names and locations of the operating controls may vary with different machines, the procedure used to prepare and operate any offset duplicator is basically the same.

The offset duplicator can be divided into six systems which are all necessary for operation, Fig. 9-64.

1. The **dampening system** is made up of a series of rollers that apply the moisture to the non-image areas of the plate.
2. A series of rollers also makes up the **inking system** which applies ink to the image areas of the plate.
3. The **feeding system,** which is usually vacuum-operated, feeds individual sheets of paper to the register board system.
4. In the **register board system,** the paper is jogged into position on the board before it is fed to the printing system.

Fig. 9-62. Didde-Glaser Apollo Web Offset Duplicator

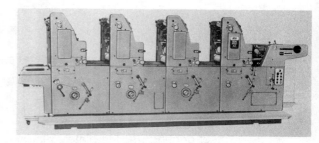

Fig. 9-63. ATF Solna 425

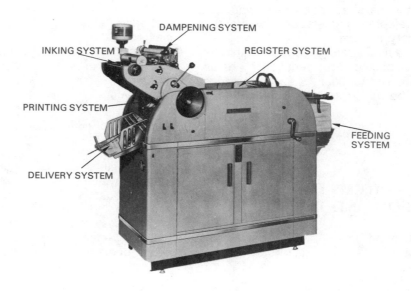

Fig. 9-64. Six offset duplicator systems

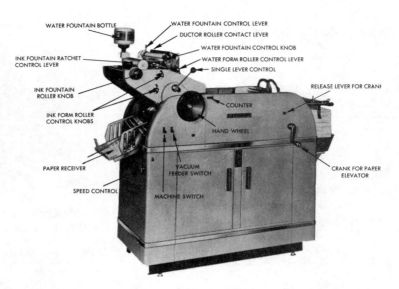

WATER FOUNTAIN BOTTLE

WATER FOUNTAIN CONTROL LEVER

DUCTOR ROLLER CONTACT LEVER

WATER FOUNTAIN CONTROL KNOB

WATER FORM ROLLER CONTROL LEVER

SINGLE LEVER CONTROL

INK FOUNTAIN RATCHET
CONTROL LEVER

INK FOUNTAIN
ROLLER KNOB

INK FORM ROLLER
CONTROL KNOBS

RELEASE LEVER FOR CRANK

COUNTER

HAND WHEEL

PAPER RECEIVER

VACUUM
FEEDER SWITCH

CRANK FOR PAPER
ELEVATOR

SPEED CONTROL

MACHINE SWITCH

Fig. 9-65. The major operating points of an offset duplicator

5. The **printing system** is composed of the three cylinders necessary for offset printing: (a) the plate cylinder, (b) the blanket cylinder, and (c) the impression cylinder.
6. After the sheet has been printed, it is ejected and stacked by the **delivery system.**

The main operating control points of the offset duplicator are identified by name in Fig. 9-65. The function of each operating point will be discussed in the units that follow.

UNIT 35 — TERMS FOR DISCUSSION AND REVIEW

offset duplication
image area
copy center
ink fountain ratchet
    control lever
ink fountain

offset masters
master station
duplicating station
master transport
    unit
master
etched
ejected
blanket
single-color press
letterset
plate cylinder
web
dampening rollers
inking rollers
dampening system
inking system
feeding system
register board
    system
printing system
delivery system
water fountain bottle

roller knob
ink form roller
    control knobs
paper receiver
speed control
machine switch
vacuum feeder
    switch
hand wheel
counter
crank for
    paper elevator
release lever
    for crank
single-lever
    control
water form roller
    control lever
water fountain
    control knob
ductor roller
    contact lever
water fountain
    control lever

UNIT 36

DAMPENING AND INKING SYSTEMS

DAMPENING SYSTEMS

Two types of dampening and inking systems are generally employed on offset duplicators: (1) the molleton system and (2) the aquamatic system.

MOLLETON SYSTEM

The **molleton** system uses separate inking and dampening rollers, Fig. 9-66. The water rollers and the water fountain make up the dampening system. The **fountain roller** has a rough, knurled surface and

is partly immersed in the solution in the **fountain.** The fountain roller transfers the fountain solution to the **ductor roller** which is covered by a molleton sleeve. The **oscillating roller** is a smooth-surfaced roller that moves from end to end as it is revolving. This action tends to distribute the supply of fountain solution evenly over the roller length, thereby preventing streaking. The **form roller** receives the fountain solution from the oscillating roller and coats the non-image areas of the plate with a thin layer of moisture. In the molleton system, the form roller is also covered with a molleton sleeve. In this unit, procedure given for the dampening and inking systems is that used for the molleton system.

AQUAMATIC SYSTEM

The aquamatic system uses one set of rollers for applying both fountain solution and ink to the offset plate, Fig. 9-67. All of

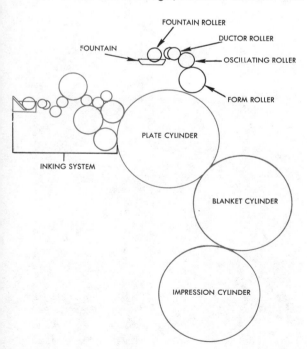

Fig. 9-66. The molleton system has separate dampening and inking rollers

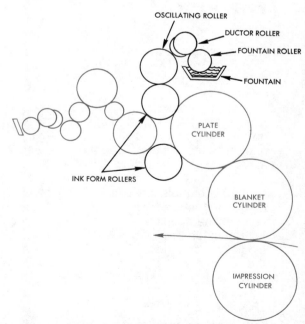

Fig. 9-67. The aquamatic system uses one set of rollers for dampening and inking

the rollers are covered with ink, including the **fountain roller** which has a smooth surface. The fountain solution is transferred to the **ductor roller,** the **oscillating roller,** and finally to the **ink form rollers** which apply both ink and fountain solution to the plate surface.

FOUNTAIN SOLUTIONS

The fountain solution bottle usually has a mixture ratio scale printed on the side. The ratio of fountain solution concentrate to distilled water often varies with the type of ink and plates being used. Check the manufacturer's instructions for the proper mixture ratio.

Tighten the cap onto the fountain solution bottle, and insert the bottle in its bracket in the fountain. The fountain solution will drain from the bottle and automatically stop when the solution in the fountain has reached the proper level.

DAMPENING SYSTEM PREPARATION

Turn the water form roller control knob and the single-lever control to the **off** position, Fig. 9-68. This prevents the water form roller from making contact with the plate cylinder.

Move the water fountain control lever to the **number 2** or **3** notch, which is the normal operating position, Fig. 9-69. The ductor roller contact lever should also be moved to the **on** position, Fig. 9-70.

Start the duplicator and allow it to run so that the molleton-covered rollers of the dampening system are moistened. To speed up the dampening process, the fountain control knob may be turned by hand in a clockwise direction. This should be done at the time the ductor roller makes contact with the fountain roller, Fig. 9-71.

INKING SYSTEM

A schematic drawing of the inking system is shown in Fig. 9-72. The **ink fountain** serves as a reservoir from which the **ink**

Fig. 9-68. Move the single-lever control to **off**

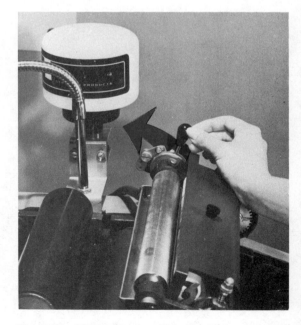

Fig. 9-69. Move the **water fountain control** lever to the **second** or **third notch**

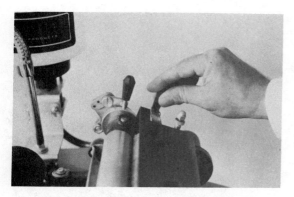

Fig. 9-70. Move the ductor roller contact lever to **on**

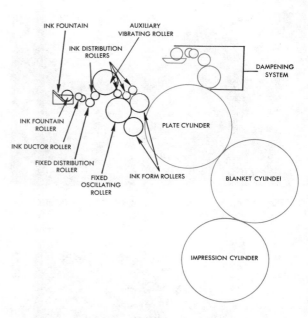

Fig. 9-72. Inking system rollers

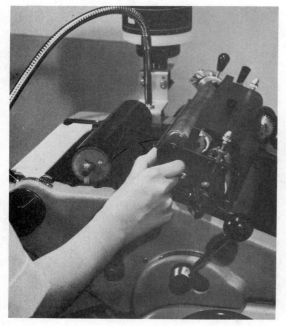

Fig. 9-71. Turn the water fountain control knob in a clockwise direction

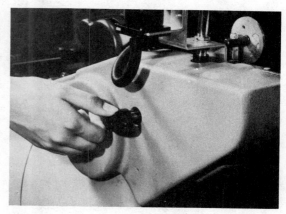

Fig. 9-73. Turn the night latch to the **off** position

fountain roller supplies ink to the ink rollers. The **ink ductor roller** makes and breaks contact with the fountain roller and carries ink to the **fixed distribution roller**. As the ink passes through the **distribution rollers**, the **auxiliary vibrator roller**, and the **fixed oscillating roller**, it is distributed evenly and uniformly. The ink is finally transferred

to the **ink form rollers** which apply ink to the image areas of the plate.

INKING SYSTEM PREPARATION

Remove the night latch by turning the disengaging lever on the nonoperating side of the duplicator to the **off** or **horizontal** position, Fig. 9-73. (When this lever is in

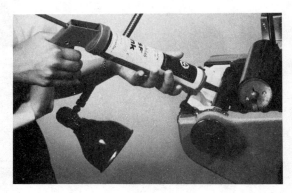

Fig. 9-74. Squeeze the ink on the ink fountain roller

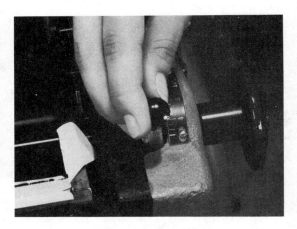

Fig. 9-77. Move the ink fountain ratchet control lever to number 4

Fig. 9-75. Adjust the ink fountain screws

Fig. 9-76. Turn the ink fountain roller knob to pull the ink from the ink knife

the **on** position, the ink form rollers are not in contact with the rest of the ink rollers. This prevents flat spots from developing on the form rollers when the duplicator is not in use.) In the **off** position, the form rollers are in the operating position, making contact with the rest of the ink rollers. The ink form roller control knobs and the single-lever control should also be moved to the **off** position. Refer again to Fig. 9-68.

With the duplicator stopped, turn the hand wheel until the ductor roller is **out** of contact with the fountain roller. If fountain liners are used, they should be installed before the fountain is placed in position.

If **tube ink** is used, start at one end and squeeze a bead of ink the entire length of the fountain roller, Fig. 9-74. Turn the fountain roller knob by hand in a counterclockwise direction and adjust the fountain screws, Fig. 9-75. The fountain screws regulate the flow of ink to the fountain roller. Turning the fountain screws **in** reduces the flow of ink, while turning them **out** increases the flow. Continue to adjust the screws until an even film of ink covers the full length of the fountain roller.

The procedure with **can ink** is somewhat different. With an ink knife, remove and discard any skin that may have formed on the ink surface. Next, to remove the ink, scrape the surface with the ink knife, keeping the surface flat and smooth. Do not dig holes in the ink as this will cause the ink to dry out. Place the ink on the fountain roller, and turn the fountain roller knob to pull the ink from the ink knife. Additional ink may be added at different locations, Fig. 9-76.

Turn the ratchet control to the **number 4** position, Fig. 9-77. The ratchet control regulates the ink flow rate from the fountain to the inking rollers. The higher the number, the faster the flow.

Before turning on the duplicator, be sure the single-lever control is in the **off** postion. Allow the duplicator to run until all of the ink rollers are covered with a thin, even film of ink. While the duplicator is running, it may be necessary to readjust the fountain screws. Turn the duplicator off and return the ratchet control to zero.

UNIT 36 — TERMS FOR DISCUSSION AND REVIEW

dampening system	duplicator
inking system	molleton-covered
molleton system	roller
aquamatic system	fountain control
water rollers	knob
water fountain	ductor roller
fountain roller	fountain roller
knurled	ink fountain
immersed	ink ductor roller
fountain	fixed distribution
fountain solution	roller
ductor roller	distribution roller
molleton sleeve	auxiliary vibrator
oscillating roller	roller
form roller	fixed oscillating
non-image areas	roller
plate	night latch
ink form rollers	nonoperating side
ratio	hand wheel
water form roller	fountain liners
control knob	tube ink
single-lever control	fountain screws
plate cylinder	can ink
water fountain	ink knife
control lever	ratchet control
ductor roller	
contact lever	

FEEDING SYSTEM PREPARATION

To prepare the feeding system, first lower the paper feed table by pushing the **release lever** to the right and turning the **paper table crank** in a counterclockwise direction, Fig. 9-78. Lower the **table** about halfway.

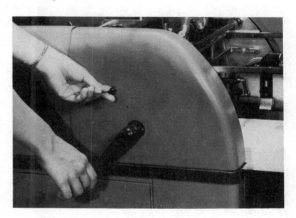

Fig. 9-78. Lower the feed table

The approximate position of the paper in the feeding magazine may be determined by placing a sheet of paper that is cut to size over the plate to be printed. The paper should be placed on the plate so that the image falls in the desired position. Measure the distance from the left plate edge to the left edge of the paper, Fig. 9-79.

Raise the **magazine guides' lock lever**, and set the **left guide** to this dimension. Using the **locating scale** on the paper magazine, set the dimension on the outer edge of the guide, Fig. 9-80. Place a single sheet of paper on the **paper supports**, and position the **right guide** at the right edge of the paper. A gap of approximately 1/8″ (3 mm) should appear between one side of

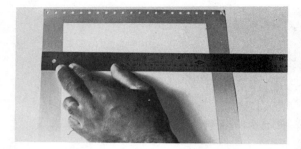

Fig. 9-79. Determining the approximate position of the paper in the feeding magazine by measuring the distance from the left side of the plate to the left edge of the paper

Fig. 9-80. Set the left guide

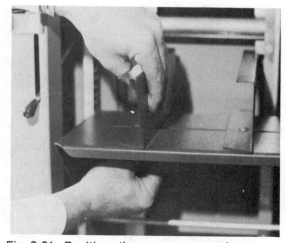

Fig. 9-81. Position the paper supports

Fig. 9-82. Place the paper in the paper magazine

the paper and the magazine guide. Push the lock lever down to lock the guides in position.

Loosen the wing nuts under the paper table, and position the paper supports so that they divide the distance between the guides in three equal sections, Fig. 9-81. Place the paper in the paper magazine, Fig. 9-82. (A stiff piece of cardboard that is slightly smaller than the paper should be on the bottom of the pile.) The paper should fit between the left and right guides and against the flanges.

Loosen the lock screws and position the **suction feet** one-quarter the distance in from each edge of the paper. The flat, flexible, protruding **sheet separators** should be positioned directly under each of the suction feet. To position the sheet separators, slide the brackets along the locating scale of the paper magazine. Allow the sheet separators to project over the edge of the paper approximately 3/16″ (5 mm). The sheet separators limit the height to which the blowers raise the paper and prevent the suction feed

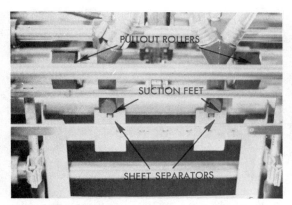

Fig. 9-83. Position the suction feet, sheet separators, and pullout rollers

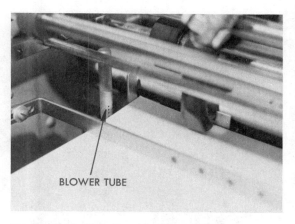

Fig. 9-84. Adjust the blower tubes

from picking up more than one sheet. The **pullout rollers** may be positioned on either side of the suction feet, Fig. 9-83.

Turn the hand wheel until the two suction feet are at their lowest point of travel. Raise the feed table by turning the crank clockwise until the top pile sheet is approximately ¼″ (6 mm) below the suction feet. Move the release lever to the left. This engages the automatic table-raising mechanism which maintains the proper pile height during duplicator operation.

Adjust the position of the **blower tubes** so that the upper holes are slightly above and pointed toward the paper pile, Fig. 9-84. During duplicator operation, air is forced through the blower tubes on each side of the pile to separate and float each sheet of paper to the suction feet.

The **paper height control bar** should just touch the top sheet of paper in the feed table. Turn the **paper height control** in the direction indicated to raise or lower the height control bar, Fig. 9-85.

With the paper positioned squarely between the side guides and against the sheet separators, move the **end guide** to the center of the trailing end of the paper, and tighten the wing nut. The left and right **paper side guides** should also be positioned and locked. The end and side guides should just clear the edges of the paper, Fig. 9-86.

Fig. 9-85. Adjust the paper height control

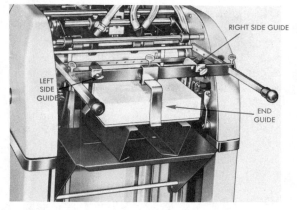

Fig. 9-86. Position the end and right and left side guides

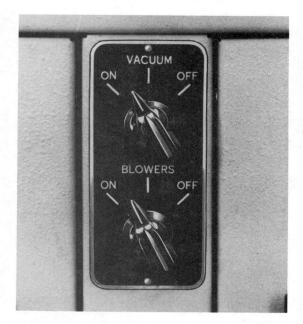

Fig. 9-87. Adjust the vacuum and blower controls

Turn on the vacuum switch, and adjust the blower and vacuum controls, Fig. 9-87. The blowers should be adjusted so that the air flutters the top few sheets. The vacuum must be strong enough to enable the suction feet to pick up the top sheet.

UNIT 37 — TERMS FOR DISCUSSION AND REVIEW

feeding system	suction feet
paper feed table	sheet separators
release lever	pullout rollers
paper table crank	hand wheel
table	automatic
feeding magazine	table-raising
plate	mechanism
image	blower tubes
magazine guides'	paper height
lock lever	control bar
left guide	paper height
locating scale	control
paper supports	end guide
right guide	paper side guides

UNIT 38

REGISTER BOARD SYSTEM PREPARATION

The register board system jogs the paper into position before it is fed into the printing unit. Accurate adjustment of the register board system assures that the image will be printed in exactly the same location on all sheets of paper. This is especially important when multicolor sheets are printed.

Begin preparing the register board system by setting the **jogger guide.** Turn the hand wheel of the duplicator until the jogger guide reaches its inward-most point of travel. Align the guide with the **graduate scale** on the register board, Fig. 9-88. This setting should be the same as that used when positioning the left paper guide in the paper magazine.

Turn on the vacuum switch, and snap the machine switch on and off, allowing one sheet of paper to be fed onto the register board. Run the sheet down the register

Fig. 9-88. Position the jogger guide

Fig. 9-89. Adjust the stationary guide

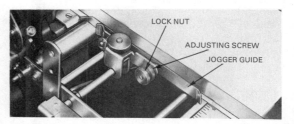

Fig. 9-90. Adjust the jogger guide so that it is parallel to the paper edge

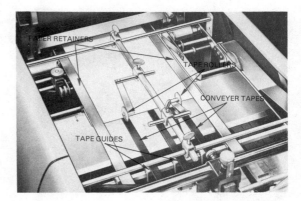

Fig. 9-91. Position the conveyor tapes, tape guides, paper retainers, and tape rollers

board until the jogger guide touches the edge at its inward-most position. The lead edge of the sheet should now be in contact with the stop fingers entering the printing unit. Move the **stationary guide** in so that the register spring is compressed approximately 1/16″ (2 mm) against the right edge of the paper, Fig. 9-89. The squareness of the jogger guide to the paper edge should be checked and adjusted if necessary. Loosen the lock nut and turn the adjusting screw so that the paper edge and jogger guide are parallel, Fig. 9-90.

Position the **conveyor tapes** evenly across the register board. This is done by adjusting the **tape guides** under the register board while the duplicator is stopped. When the duplicator is started, the tapes will conform to the position of the tape guides. The **paper retainers** are then positioned directly over the two outside conveyor tapes. This causes the paper to lie flat on the tapes. Position the **tape rollers** just off the trailing edge of the paper when it is fully jogged. The tape rollers ride on the conveyor tapes and help control the sheet, Fig. 9-91.

The final step in preparing the register board system is to adjust the **multiple-sheet detector**. Insert a 2″ (51 mm) strip of paper to be printed under the multiple-sheet detector with the duplicator running slowly. Turn the **adjusting knob** toward "lower" until the **deflector** opens. At this setting, the sheet will be deflected under the register board so it does not enter the registering

Fig. 9-92. Adjust the multiple-sheet detector

system. Turn the adjustment knob in the "raise" direction approximately two clicks so that the deflector closes. This will allow single sheets to pass, but will eliminate multiple-sheet feeding, Fig. 9-92.

UNIT 38 — TERMS FOR DISCUSSION AND REVIEW

register board
    system
jogs
printing unit
multicolor sheet
jogger guide
hand wheel
duplicator
align
graduate scale
left paper guide

paper magazine
stop fingers
stationary guide
conveyor tapes
tape guides
paper retainers
tape rollers
multiple-sheet
    detector
adjusting knob
deflector

DELIVERY SYSTEM PREPARATION

The delivery system receives and stacks the printed sheets. Two commonly used delivery systems are employed on offset duplicators: (1) the **chute delivery** and (2) the **chain delivery.**

PREPARING THE CHUTE DELIVERY

Run a sheet of paper through the printing system by turning the hand wheel with the duplicator **off.** (Refer to Fig. 9-93 for location of duplicator parts.) As the paper begins to enter the delivery system and before it passes under the **ejection rollers,** stop turning the hand wheel. The ejection rollers should be adjusted by sliding them

along the shaft so that they will ride in the left and right margins. Position the **ejection rings** on the outside of the ejection rollers for paper that has a downward curl and position them on the inside for paper that has an upward curl.

Before the paper is completely ejected, position the **side guides** of the **receiving tray** approximately ⅛″ (3 mm) from the edges of the sheet. Turn the hand wheel to eject the paper, and position the **paper stop** to allow the trailing edge of the paper to fall clear of the ejection unit. The sheets are deflected into the receiving tray by the **paper retainer.**

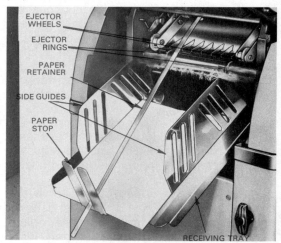

EJECTOR WHEELS
EJECTOR RINGS
PAPER RETAINER
SIDE GUIDES
PAPER STOP
RECEIVING TRAY

Fig. 9-93. Adjust the receiving tray guides

PREPARING THE CHAIN DELIVERY

The chain delivery system uses **gripper** bars to grip the sheet at the impression cylinder and deposit it into the automatic receding jogger-stacker. The gripper bars are mounted across two endless chains which run on either side of the delivery system. (Refer to Fig. 9-94 for location of duplicator parts described below.)

Turn the hand wheel, and run a sheet of paper through the duplicator. Stop the sheet just before it is released by the delivery gripper bar. Move the **stationary guide** until it just touches the edge of the

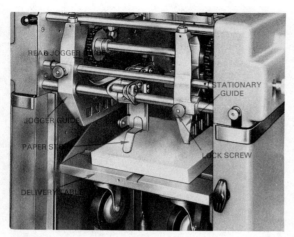

Fig. 9-94. Chain delivery

UNIT 40

OPERATION OF THE DUPLICATOR

Safety Note

Before starting the production phase of offset duplication, remove jewelry such as rings and watches. Loose clothing such as shirt sleeves and shirt tails should also be rolled up or tucked in.

After the duplicator systems have been prepared, the plate may be positioned on the plate cylinder. Turn the hand wheel until the lead pin bar becomes accessible. Hook the pin holes of the plate over the pins of the pin bar, Fig. 9-95. Hold the plate taut with the right hand, and turn the hand wheel counterclockwise to wrap the plate around the cylinder, Fig. 9-96.

Change hands and hold the tail end of the plate against the cylinder. Hold the plate in position, and align the pins of the pin bar with the holes of the plate. Allow the tail pin bar to spring back to its normal position,

sheet. Turn the hand wheel, and allow the sheet to fall on the **delivery table.** Continue to turn the hand wheel until the **jogger guide** is at its inward-most point of travel. Loosen the **lock screw,** and position the jogger guide so that it just contacts the sheet edge. Lock both guides in position.

The **rear jogger guide** can now be positioned so that it contacts the trailing edge and pushes the sheet forward until it contacts the **paper stop.** Be sure all locking screws are tightened after positioning the joggers and guides.

UNIT 39 — TERMS FOR DISCUSSION AND REVIEW

delivery system	paper stop
offset duplicator	paper retainer
chute delivery	gripper bars
chain delivery	impression
hand wheel	cylinder
ejection rollers	stationary guide
ejection rings	delivery table
side guides	jogger guide
receiving tray	rear jogger guide

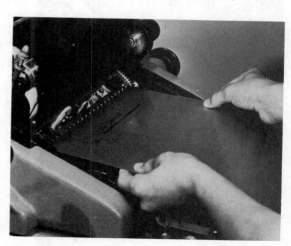

Fig. 9-95. Hook the lead end of the plate on the pin bar

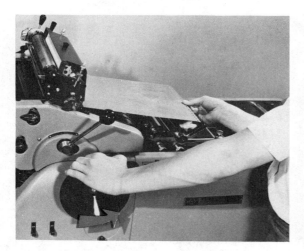

Fig. 9-96. Turn the hand wheel counterclockwise to wrap the plate around the cylinder

Fig. 9-98. Remove the gum from the surface of the plate

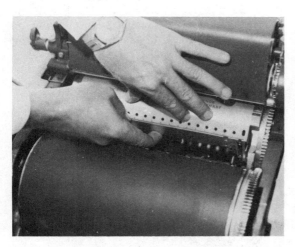

Fig. 9-97. Clamp the tail end of the plate

Fig. 9-97. Form the tail end of the plate to the end of the cylinder with your thumb.

The protective coating (gum arabic) that was applied earlier to preserve the plate must now be removed. Use a soft sponge or cotton pad dampened with fountain solution to wipe the entire plate surface while turning the hand wheel, Fig. 9-98. An alternate procedure is to remove the plate preserva-

tive before the plate is installed on the plate cylinder.

Turn the machine power switch to **on**, and adjust the variable speed control so that the duplicator is running slowly. With the single-lever control in the **off** position, turn the water and ink form roller control knobs to the **on** or horizontal position, Fig. 9-99. The form roller control knobs may be left in the **on** position during the duplicator run because the single-lever control will regulate the position of the form rollers.

Move the single-lever control to the **moist** position. This drops the water form roller into contact with the plate surface, Fig. 9-100. After several duplicator revolutions, move the single-lever control to the **ink** position to bring the ink form rollers into contact with the plate. Allow the image areas of the plate to pick up ink before moving the single-lever control to the **print** position. In the print position, the inked image from the plate will be offset to the rubber blanket.

Turn on the vacuum switch, and allow a few sheets to be printed. The duplicator should now be turned off, reversing the starting procedure; that is, (1) turn **off** the vacuum, (2) move the single-lever control to **off**, and (3) turn the machine switch **off**.

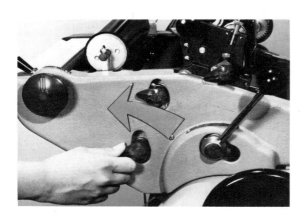

Fig. 9-99. Move the water and ink form roller control knobs to the **on** position

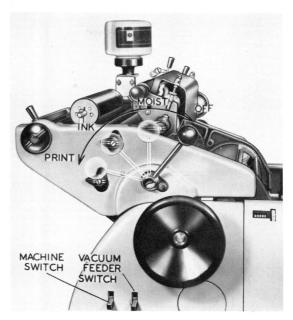

Fig. 9-100. Move the single lever control

Inspect the printed copy. It should be free of all background tone. Background tone is the result of an improper balance of water and ink on the plate, causing the non-image areas to print. This may be corrected either by increasing the amount of water being applied to the plate or by decreasing the ink flow. Adjust either the water or the ink fountain control lever. As a general rule, the duplicator should be operated with a minimum amount of water being applied to the plate and only enough ink to produce dark copy. When a proper balance is maintained, the printed copy will appear clear and dark and without background tone.

Check both the vertical and lateral copy position on the printed sheet. The **vertical positioning adjustment** is located on the nonoperating side of the duplicator, Fig. 9-101.

Turn the hand wheel until the cylinder lock screw is aligned with the vertical positioning knob. Push the control knob in and over the lock screw. Turn the control knob to loosen the lock screw, and continue to exert the inward push. Turn the hand wheel clockwise to raise the image and counter-

Fig. 9-101. Vertical positioning adjustment

clockwise to lower the image on the printed sheet. The graduated scale on the cylinder will aid in vertical positioning. Tighten the cylinder lock screw and release the control knob. Because the image position has been changed, it is necessary to clean the blan-

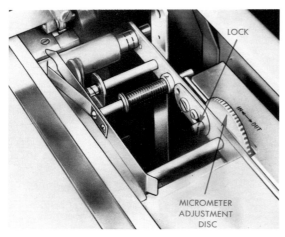

Fig. 9-102. Micrometer adjustment

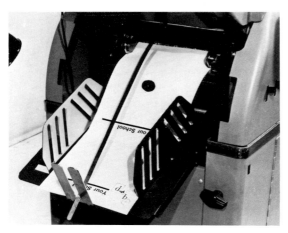

Fig. 9-103. Inspect the first few printed sheets

ket with a cloth dampened with blanket wash.

Lateral positioning adjustments may be made by resetting both the jogger guide and the stationary guide of the register board. The **micrometer adjustment wheel** on the stationary guide may be turned to make minor lateral adjustments, Fig. 9-102. It may be necessary to reposition the feed pile if a large adjustment is required.

After making all the necessary adjustments, start the duplicator and print several more sheets. These should also be in-spected, Fig. 9-103. Be sure the ejector rollers are not streaking the image area. Check to see that multiple sheets have been eliminated.

When satisfactory copy is being printed set the counter to 00000 and begin the run. During the production run, the operator must be continually checking the quality of the printed copy.

At the end of the production run and while the duplicator is still running, move the ink and water form roller control knobs to the **off** position. Allow several waste sheets to be printed to **run down** the ink supply on the plate and blanket. Turn off the vacuum, move the single-lever control to **off,** and stop the duplicator.

Remove the plate by releasing the tail pin bar and turning the hand wheel clock-wise. Lift the plate from the lead pin bar. Wipe the remaining ink from the plate, and coat the surface with gum arabic. Clean the blanket.

If the duplicator will not be used for several hours, drain the water fountain, and turn the night latch for the ink and water form rollers to the vertical position. The ink and water fountain controls and the ductor roller contact lever should also be moved to the **off** position.

UNIT 40 — TERMS FOR DISCUSSION AND REVIEW

production	vacuum switch
offset duplication	machine switch
plate	printed copy
plate cylinder	background tone
lead pin bar	water fountain
hand wheel	control lever
tail end	ink fountain
align	control lever
tail pin bar	vertical position
gum arabic	lateral position
fountain solution	vertical positioning
variable speed	adjustment
control	nonoperating side

single-lever
   control
water form roller
   control knob
ink form roller
   control knob
moist position
water form roller
ink position
ink form rollers
image areas
print position
rubber blanket

jogger guide
stationary guide
register board
micrometer
   adjustment
   wheel
ejector rollers
counter
run down
night latch
ductor roller
   contact lever

Fig. 9-104. Remove the water fountain roller, water fountain, and the ductor, oscillating, and form rollers

CLEANING THE DUPLICATOR

To prevent the ink from drying on the ink rollers or to change colors, the duplicator must be cleaned. Remove the water fountain roller, water fountain, ductor roller, oscillating roller, and form roller to prevent the dampening system from picking up ink during the cleaning operation, Fig. 9-104.

Using an ink knife, remove and discard the ink in the ink fountain. The fountain can then be removed and the liner removed, if used. If a fountain liner was not used, clean the ink from the fountain with a cloth dampened with cleaning solvent. The ink fountain roller may also be cleaned.

Attach a cleaner sheet to the plate cylinder following the same procedure as used for attaching an offset plate. Start the duplicator and adjust the speed control so that the duplicator is running at its slowest speed. Turn the ink form roller control knobs to the **on** position, leaving the single-lever control **off**. Use a squirt bottle or oil can filled with solvent to apply a small amount of solvent evenly across the distribution roller. Allow the duplicator to complete

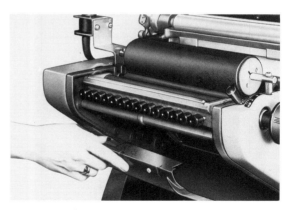

Fig. 9-105. Replace the drip pan

several revolutions to loosen the ink before turning the single-lever control to the **ink** position. The cleaner sheet will absorb the dissolved ink. It is usually necessary to run two or three cleaner sheets to clean the rollers. Do not discard any cleaner sheet because the other side may be used after another production run.

To complete the cleaning procedure, lift out the removable rollers. These may be wiped with a cloth and solvent to remove any remaining ink. Be sure to clean the roller ends. The stationary rollers should also be wiped with a cloth and solvent.

Safety Note

All cloths that have been used with solvent for removing ink should be placed in metal safety cans.

Replace the ink and water rollers, the ink fountain, and the water fountain. Replace the drip pan after it has been wiped clean of any ink and solvent drippings, Fig. 9-105. Turn the duplicator to the night latch position if it will not be used for several hours or longer.

UNIT 41 — TERMS FOR DISCUSSION AND REVIEW

ink	ink fountain roller
ink rollers	cleaner sheet
duplicator	plate cylinder
water fountain	offset plate
roller	speed control
water fountain	ink form roller
ductor roller	control knobs
oscillating roller	single-lever control
form roller	solvent
dampening system	distribution roller
ink knife	stationary roller
ink fountain	drip pan
fountain liner	night latch

UNIT 42

COLOR SEPARATION

UNDERSTANDING COLOR THEORY

Without light there is no color. White light is composed of all colors. This can be proven by directing a beam of white light through a prism. The prism separates the wavelengths that make up white light into individual colors, Fig. 9-106. This range of colors is known as the visible spectrum. The colors of the visible spectrum include violet, blue, green, yellow, orange, and red. Of these, blue, green, and red light are said to be **additive primary colors**. They are the only ones that cannot be made by mixing other colors. Also, when combined in the proper proportions, they produce white light.

When white light strikes a solid object, one of three things can happen: (1) all the wavelengths of light can be absorbed, (2) all the wavelengths of light can be reflected, or (3) some of the wavelengths can be ab-

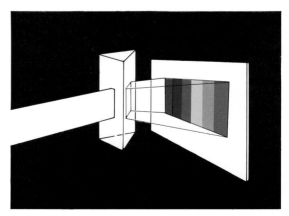

Fig. 9-106. A prism separates white light into the colors of the visible spectrum

sorbed and some can be reflected. If all wavelengths are absorbed, the object is said to be black. There are no wavelengths of any visible spectrum color being reflected to the eye of the observer. When all of the light wavelengths are reflected to the observer's eye, the object is said to be white. If the object absorbs some of the wavelengths and reflects some, the object is said to have the color of the combined reflected wavelengths. For example, a strawberry appears red because it absorbs all visible wavelengths except red. The red wavelength is reflected to the eye of the observer, Fig. 9-107A. With transparent objects, such as a glass of colored water, the same principle applies. Instead of being reflected, however, the light wavelengths that are not absorbed are merely allowed to pass through to the eye of the observer, Fig. 9-107B.

COLOR MIXING

As already stated, blue, green, and red light are the three **additive primary colors.** If three projectors were set up, each projecting one of the three additive primary light colors, white light would be produced where the three projections overlap, Fig. 9-108. Three additional colors would be seen in the projection. These are magenta, yellow, and cyan. Magenta is produced by a combination of red and blue light. Yellow is created by the overlapping of red and green light. Cyan is produced by mixing the green and blue light. These three colors are known as the **subtractive primary colors.** On a color wheel of additive and subtractive primary colors, green is the complement of magenta (blue and red), blue is the complement of yellow (red and green), and red is the complement of cyan (green and blue). When the complementary colors are mixed, the colors are neutralized. The result is white light.

The subtractive colors are created when white light interacts with a colorant such as ink, a dye, pigment, or a filter. When white light strikes a colorant, some of the

A. Color is reflected to the eye

B. Color is passed through to the eye

Fig. 9-107.

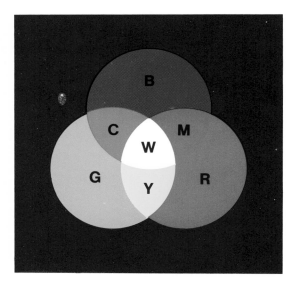

Fig. 9-108. When additive primary colors are combined, the subtractive primary colors are created

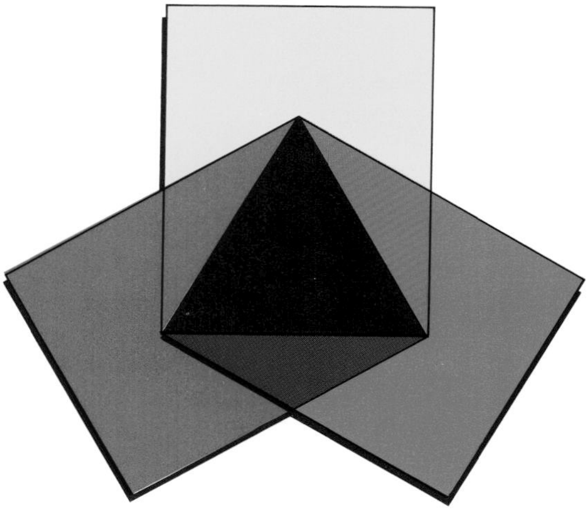

Fig. 9-109. When two subtractive primary colors overlap, an additive primary color is created

wavelengths are absorbed. The wavelengths that are not absorbed are seen by the human eye as the color. Because some of the wavelengths have been absorbed, the subtractive primary colors are not as bright as the original additive primary colors.

In **four color process printing**, three colors, plus black, can be printed to produce what appear to be all the colors of the visible spectrum. The three pigment colors are the subtractive primary colors of yellow, magenta, and cyan. Black is needed to provide additional detail and image definition.

When two primary subtractive colors overlap, a primary additive color is created, Fig. 9-109. A combination of magenta and yellow produces red. Magenta and cyan combine to form blue. Cyan and yellow produce green. Where all three subtractive primary colors overlap, black is produced. By varying the density or halftone dot percentages of the three printed colors, other colors can also be produced. For example, when equal amounts of yellow and cyan are combined, the resulting color is green. However, if more yellow density or pigment

is printed than cyan, the resulting color would be yellow-green.

For printing process color, four plates are required: one for each of the transparent inks used — yellow, magenta, and cyan — and one for black. Four negatives are required to make the four plates. The process of making the required negatives from a full color original is called **color separation**.

COLOR SEPARATION COPY

Color separations may be made from reflection copy or transparent copy. **Reflection copy** includes such items as color photographs, water colors, oil paintings or any other copy that has an opaque base. White light necessary for the separation exposure is directed toward the reflection copy. The light is reflected from the copy and passes through the necessary filters before it strikes the unexposed separation film. **Transparent copy** includes color slides or transparencies which have a positive image on a transparent base. The white exposure light for making these separations is directed through the transparent copy and the filters before striking the separation film, Fig. 9-110.

SEPARATION METHODS

Three methods commonly used for making color separations are: (1) direct screen, (2) indirect, and (3) electronic scanning. The direct screen method produces separations that are screened in one step. The indirect method is more complex as more steps are required to produce the screened separations. In the indirect method, the copy is first separated into continuous tone negatives. The continuous tone negatives are then converted to halftone positives. The halftone positives are used to produce the screened separation negatives, Fig. 9-111. Electronic scanners automatically analyze the copy and are capable of producing either continuous tone separations or screened halftone negative separations. The explanation that follows uses the direct separation method with reflection copy.

MAKING THE SCREENED SEPARATION NEGATIVES

One phase of color separation is referred to as **color correction**. To achieve high quality separations, the individual negatives must be color corrected to compensate for the impurities of the printing ink used. Color correction techniques include: (1) photographic masking, (2) electronic scanning, and (3) dot etching. Because each color correction technique adds complexity to the color separation procedure, they will not be presented in this text. Separations made with the color correction steps omitted are referred to as **pleasing color separations.**

Special consideration must be given to the type of halftone screens that are used when making color separation negatives.

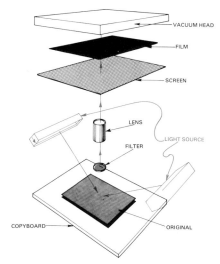

A. Camera set up for reflection copy

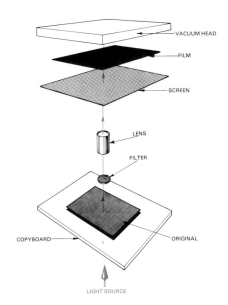

B. Camera set up for transparent copy

Fig. 9-110. Separation can be made from reflection and transparent copy

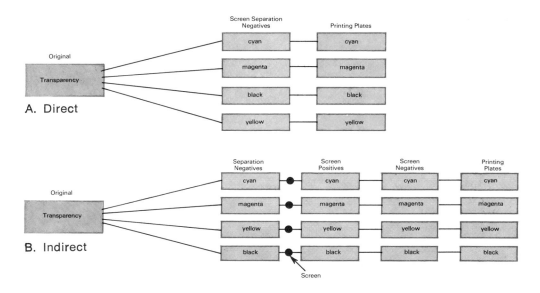

Fig. 9-111. Direct and indirect separation methods

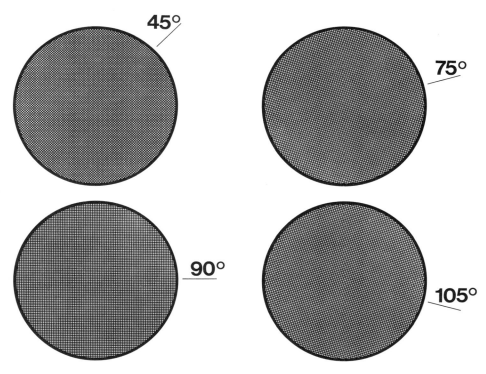

Fig. 9-112. Different screen angles are used for each of the color separation negatives

Fig. 9-113. A moiré pattern

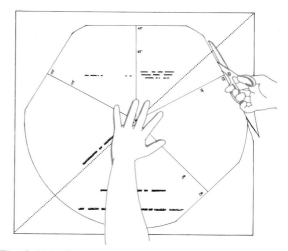

Fig. 9-114. One halftone screen can be cut to make a "circular" screen with the four required screen angles

Gray contact halftone screens should be used because their neutral color will not interfere with the separation filter action. A color screen would act as a filter.

Each of the four separation negatives should be made with a different halftone dot angle called a **screen angle**, Fig. 9-112. This permits the halftone dots of the individual negatives to print at different angles thus preventing the formation of a wavy pattern referred to as a **moiré pattern**, Fig. 9-113. One solution is to use a set of four separate halftone screens each screen having a different angle. Complete instructions for the use of the pre-angled screens are available from Kodak.

If only one screen is available, it can be cut into a "circular" shape with four straight edges on the perimeter. Each straight edge would be cut at one of the required screen angles of 105°, 75°, 90°, and 45°, Fig. 9-114. Using the "circular" screen requires the use of a guide edge. This would be located on the inside of the vacuum frame of the camera. The desired angle, straight edge of the screen, would be butted against the guide edge on the vacuum back for each of the four separations. For example, when making the cyan negative, the 105° screen straight edge would be butted against the vacuum back guide edge. The screen would be repositioned with the 75° straight edge against the guide edge when exposing the magenta negative.

Three registration marks should be positioned on the original copy. Place these in the nonimage areas in a triangular pattern. They will appear as transparent areas on each of the separation negatives. Their purpose is to aid in registration when stripping the negatives.

The original copy should then be positioned on the copy board of the camera. A gray scale and a set of color-control patches should be included on the copy board. (See Fig. 9-115.) The **gray scale** is useful in comparing density and density range on the separation negative. A **color block set** may be used to serve as a means of negative identification after the negatives have been processed. If exposed and processed correctly, the cyan color block will be the only one registered as a transparent area on the cyan negative. Likewise, the magenta block will register on the magenta negative and the yellow block will be transparent on the yellow negative. The **color-control patches** are useful in determining the accuracy or correctness of exposure and development. The chart in Fig. 9-116 will be helpful in color-control patch evaluation of the separation negative. Each

HALFTONE NEGATIVES

HALFTONE SCREEN ANGLES

SEPARATION FILTERS

BLUE 90°

GREEN  75°

RED  105°

ORIGINAL COPY
(PAINTING, TRANSPARENCY
OR COLOR PHOTO)

ALL THREE  45°

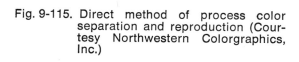
Fig. 9-115. Direct method of process color separation and reproduction (Courtesy Northwestern Colorgraphics, Inc.)

PLATE FOR EACH COLOR

PROGRESSIVE PROOFS

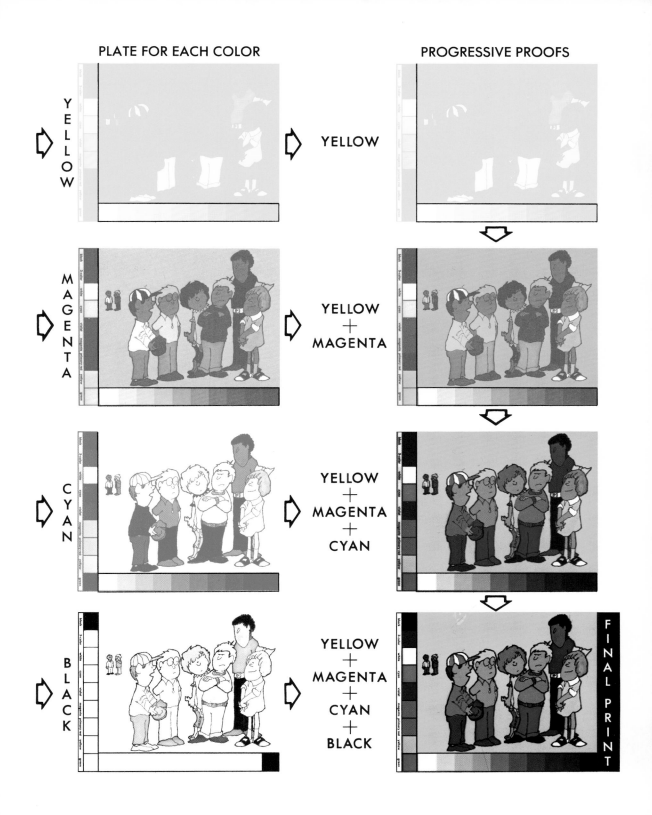

	BLACK	3 COLOR	WHITE	CYAN	VIOLET	MAGENTA	PRIMARY RED	YELLOW	GREEN
CYAN PRINTER	Transparent	Transparent	Solid	Transparent	Transparent	Solid	Solid	Solid	Transparent
MAGENTA PRINTER	Transparent	Transparent	Solid	Solid	Transparent	Transparent	Transparent	Solid	Solid
YELLOW PRINTER	Transparent	Transparent	Solid	Solid	Solid	Solid	Transparent	Transparent	Transparent
BLACK PRINTER	Transparent	Solid	Solid	Solid	Solid	Solid	Solid	Solid	Solid

Fig. 9-116. Wanted and unwanted color-control patches on "color corrected" color separation negatives

separation negative should register the "wanted" colors as transparent areas and the "unwanted" colors as solid or black areas. The transparent areas represent a printing surface on the offset plate. The solid or black areas will not register as a printing plate area.

The actual exposure time used for each of the separation negatives will be different. A series of test exposures may be required. As a general rule, the f/number used to produce black and white halftone negatives is satisfactory for producing color separation negatives.

Panchromatic film is used when making color separations. It is sensitive to all colors of light. If **orthochromatic film** were used, there would be no separation between the reds and the black. Orthochromatic film is insensitive to red light rays and registers red as black.

The first exposure when making color separations is to record the cyan of the original copy. The resulting negative is referred to as the cyan negative or the **cyan printer**. To make the cyan printer, a 105° angle screen is used over the film. Because green and blue make cyan, the light that is reflected from the original copy must pass through a complementary red filter. The red filter absorbs the green and blue light wave-

lengths but permits the red wavelengths to pass through the halftone screen and expose the film. Those areas exposed by the red wavelengths appear as black areas on the processed film. The green and blue (cyan) areas of the original copy are transparent.

After exposure, the cyan printer is developed by the time-temperature control method. No safelights may be used as the panchromatic film is sensitive to all light. Conditions should be constant for each piece of film processed. Fresh developer should also be used for each sheet of film processed.

At this point, the cyan printer should be evaluated by inspection of the color-control patches. The wanted colors of cyan, violet, and green should be transparent as well as the 3-color patch and the black patch. The unwanted colors should appear as black or solid patches.

Once the exposure time has been determined for the cyan printer using the red filter, the remaining separation exposure times can be computed. All filters that are used for color separation have a filter ratio number. The red (25-A) has a filter ratio of 1.0 while the green (58-B) has a filter ratio of 3.0. The blue (47-C5) has a ratio of 2.5. By multiplying the cyan printer exposure time by each of the other filter ratios, exposure times for use of the green and blue filters may be computed. For example, assume that the red filter exposure time for the cyan printer was 90 seconds. The exposure time when using the green filter would be 270 seconds and the blue filter would require a 225-second exposure time.

The second exposure in the color separation sequence is for the magenta printer. Red and blue make magenta. Therefore, for this exposure, a complementary green filter is used and a screen angle of 75°. The green filter absorbs the red and blue light wavelengths but allows the green wavelengths to pass through and expose the film. The processed film will be transparent in the red and blue (magenta) copy areas.

The third exposure is to produce the yellow printer. The screen angle should be 90°. The complementary blue filter is used which allows the blue light wavelengths to pass and expose the film. The red and green light wavelengths are absorbed by the filter. Because of this, the copy areas of red and green, which produce yellow, are not exposed on the film and remain as transparent areas.

The fourth exposure is for the black printer. This separation negative may be produced by partial exposure of the film through each of the previously used filters. The single exposure technique using a yellow or orange filter may also be used to make the black printer. The screen angle should be 45°.

The separation printers may be proofed using 3M Color Key before stripping and platemaking. Color Key is a light sensitive material. It is available in a variety of colors including yellow, magenta, cyan, and black. Each separation is exposed to the appropriate color of Color Key and processed. The individual sheets of Color Key are then taped in position on a bright white paper backing. When positioning the Color Key, observe the printing order of yellow on the bottom, then magenta, and then cyan, ending with black on the top. The assembled Color Key proofs will appear as a full color representation of the separations when printed.

The individual separations must be stripped into position on four separate masking sheets for making four separate plates. The triangular registration mark pattern may be used to assure stripping accuracy. When printing four color separations on the offset duplicator, each color should be printed in succession as soon as possible. This will ensure that the duplicator registration of the printed sheets will remain the same. Also, a better blending of colors will be reproduced if the ink is still wet when the next color is applied to the sheet.

UNIT 42 — TERMS FOR DISCUSSION AND REVIEW

wavelengths
prism
visible spectrum
additive primary
   colors
absorb
reflect
magenta
yellow
cyan
subtractive primary
   colors
complement
neutralize
filter
four color
   process printing
transparent inks
halftone dot
   percentage
density
negative
color separation
reflection copy
transparent copy
direct screen
   method
indirect screen
   method
electronic scanning

color correction
photographic
   masking
dot etching
pleasing color
   separations
halftone screen
gray contact
   halftone screen
magenta screen
screen angle
moiré pattern
circular screen
perimeter
registration marks
stripping
gray scale
color block set
color-control
   patches
cyan printer
magenta printer
yellow printer
panchromatic film
orthochromatic
   film
filter ratio
black printer
Color Key

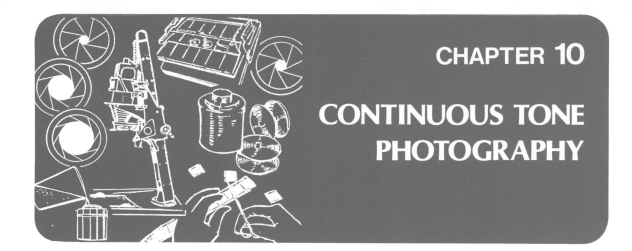

CHAPTER 10

CONTINUOUS TONE PHOTOGRAPHY

Continuous tone photography is both an image generation process and a production process in the graphic communications industry. Images are generated when a light-sensitive film is placed in a camera and an exposure is made. The light that was reflected from the subject being photographed passed through the camera lens and registered as a latent image on the film emulsion, Fig. 10-1. This method of image generation is called **continuous tone** because the film registers all gradations of tone from white to black. As you recall, Unit 11 described different types of cameras and explained how to make a good exposure.

After exposure, the film must be developed to reveal the latent image. The development chemistry that is used depends upon the type of film that was exposed. There are basically four different types of film. These include:

1. black and white negative film,
2. black and white positive or slide film,

Fig. 10-1. Photographic image generation

3. color negative film, and
4. color positive or slide film.

Negative films develop as a reverse image. That is, the black areas that are photographed appear as white areas on the

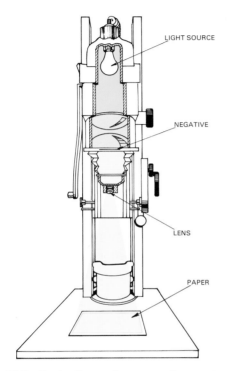

Fig. 10-2. Projection of a negative onto enlarging paper

film. Negatives are used to make photographic enlargements or prints. To produce an enlargement, the negative is placed in an enlarger between a light source and a lens. As the light passes through the negative and the lens, it is projected onto enlarging paper to produce the image, Fig. 10-2. The enlarging paper is then developed to bring out the image.

Positive films or **slides** develop as a positive image. In other words, the image appears exactly as the subject when it is photographed. To make the slides ready for viewing, they must be mounted in slide mounts so they can be inserted into a projector, Fig. 10-3. Slides are also known as **transparencies.** Units 43 and 44 which follow this chapter explain developing techniques for both negative and positive films.

Once the film has been developed, the production phase for continuous tone photography can be initiated. The **enlarger** is used for making photographic prints. The negative is placed in the enlarger between the light source and the lens. The light passes through the negative and the lens and projects the image of the negative onto the baseboard which holds the sensitized photographic paper. The process of making enlarged prints from negatives is called **projection printing.** On the other hand, a simple procedure termed **contact printing** produces photographic prints that are the same size

Fig. 10-3. Slides are projected for viewing

as the negatives. This process employs a contact printing frame positioned on the baseboard of the enlarger.

After exposure, the photographic paper must be developed through a series of four baths. It must then be dried with either a glossy or a matte finish. Units 45 through 49 provide necessary information on the production phase of continuous tone photography. (Do not confuse continuous tone photography with process photography which was described in Unit 31.)

UNIT 43

BLACK AND WHITE NEGATIVE ROLL FILM DEVELOPMENT

CHEMICALS

There are three required processing chemicals necessary for the development of black and white roll film negatives. These are, in order, (1) **developer,** (2) **stop bath** and (3) a **fixing bath.**

Developer is available in both liquid and dry concentrated form. Stock developer (full strength) may be used for film development; however, a working solution is generally prepared by diluting the stock solution with water according to the manufacturer's directions. All developer should be stored in labeled brown glass containers that are tightly sealed to prevent oxidation.

Stop bath is prepared by mixing 8 ounces (236.6 ml) of 28% acetic acid in 32 ounces (946.4 ml) of water. **Always add the acid to the water.** Stop bath should be stored in a bottle that will resist the action of the acid. Plain water may also be used as a stop bath.

Concentrated **fixer** is also available in liquid and dry forms. A hardener is sometimes added to the fixer to harden the film

emulsion. Consult the manufacturer's instructions when preparing the fixing solution.

LOADING THE DEVELOPING TANK

Developing tanks are light-tight containers that consist of a **tank,** a **reel** or an **apron,** and a **cover,** Fig. 10-4. The cover is designed with a built-in light trap that allows the processing chemicals to be poured in and out of the tank, but will not permit light to enter, Fig. 10-5. This makes it possible

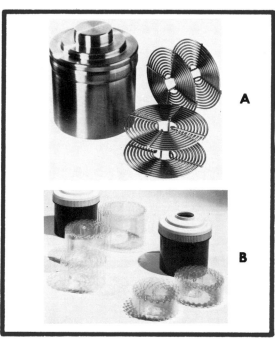

Fig. 10-4. Nikor developing tank and reels (part A) and Kodak roll film development tanks, covers, and aprons (part B)

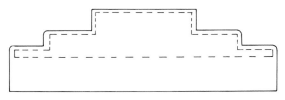

Fig. 10-5. Cross section view of developing tank cover

to process the film with the room lights on once the film has been placed in the tank and the cover secured in position.

Fig. 10-6. Hold the reel with the spiral ends to the right

Fig. 10-7. Attach the semiautomatic loader to the reel

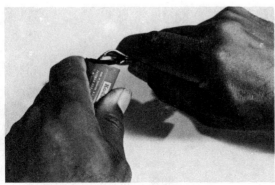

Fig. 10-8. Opening the film cassette

WITH A REEL

Film is held by developing reels having continuous spiral wire sides. To load the film, hold the reel in the left hand with the spiral wire ends pointing to the right, Fig. 10-6. (This procedure is reversed if you are left-handed.) The semiautomatic loader is placed over the outside of the reel so that the two discs of the loader snap into place on the center axis of the reel. The loading guide should be curved downward to the right of the reel, Fig. 10-7.

Films used for continuous tone photography are **panchromatic** which is sensitive to all light. Because of this, the loading operation must be carried out in **total** darkness.

Turn out the room lights, and remove the paper backing from the film. If 35mm film is being developed, there will be no paper backing. Simply open the **cassette**, and remove the film and spool. A bottle opener may be used to open the cassette, Fig. 10-8. The leader must be trimmed so that it is square.

Insert the film from right to left into the loading guide. The emulsion side of the film should be down or away from the curved surface of the loading guide, Fig. 10-9. Roll film curls in the direction of the emulsion side. Continue to push the film as far as possible into the open side of the center core of the reel, Fig. 10-10. Some reels are equipped with a clip to hold the film in place. Holding the semiautomatic loader by the outside bracket arms, begin turning the

Fig. 10-9. Start the film into the semiautomatic loader with the emulsion side down

reel in a counterclockwise direction. As the reel is turned, the film is wound into the spirals of the reel sides so that the film is not touching itself at any point, Fig. 10-11. This permits the processing chemicals to flow over both sides of the film. Continue to turn the reel until all the film has been wound. Remove the semiautomatic loader, place the loaded reel in the tank, secure the cover, and turn on the room lights.

WITH AN APRON

If an apron is used, the film and apron are rolled together. Hold the apron in the left hand so it curls to the right. The apron must be exactly the same width as the film. In **total** darkness, remove the film and hold it in the right hand so that it also curls to the right. Start the end of the film at the center loop of the apron, and roll the apron and film together. When the film has been completely rolled, place the apron and film in the developing tank. When the cover has been securely positioned, turn on the room lights.

AS SHEETS

Sheet film developing tanks, Fig. 10-12, must also be loaded in **total** darkness. The film is inserted into a sheet film developing holder which is then placed in the developing tank. With the cover securely in position,

the room lights may be turned on without exposing the film.

FILM DEVELOPMENT

To determine the correct development time, consult the data sheet for either the film or the developer. In either case, the temperature of the developer must be known before it is possible to determine the development time.

Begin the development sequence by pre-wetting the film with cool water. This helps to reduce air bubbles which will cause spots to appear on the negative. All liquids should be poured into the developing tank from a graduate. Hold the developing tank at a slight angle to allow the air to escape

Fig. 10-11. Turn the reel in a counterclockwise direction to load the film

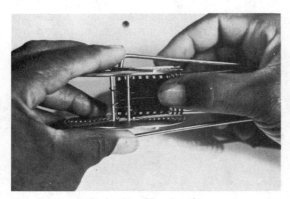

Fig. 10-10. Attach the film to the center core of the reel

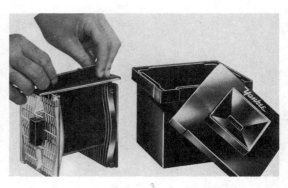

Fig. 10-12. Sheet film developing tank

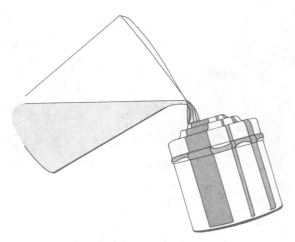

Fig. 10-13. Hold the tank at a slight angle when pouring in the chemicals

Fig. 10-15. Wash the film in running water

Fig. 10-14. GraLab Universal timer

as the liquid is poured into the tank, Fig. 10-13. Be sure to pour enough of each liquid into the tank to completely cover the film.

Pour the water from the tank, and pour in the developer. A timer such as the one in Fig. 10-14 may be used for accurate timing. During the development time, the tank should be agitated according to the manufacturer's recommendations. The developer causes a chemical reaction which makes the latent image become visible.

At the end of the development time, pour the developer into a container marked "Used Developer." It has not been exhausted and may be reused; however, a slightly longer development time will be required. Pour in the stop bath solution to stop or neutralize the action of the developer. The stop bath should remain in the tank for 1 to 2 minutes. Be sure to agitate the film in the tank during this time.

Pour the stop bath from the tank into the proper container. Fill the tank with fixing solution. Agitate the tank for 5 seconds at regular 60-second intervals. Leave the fixing solution in the tank for 7 to 10 minutes before returning it to its original container. The fixer removes the unexposed emulsion from the film.

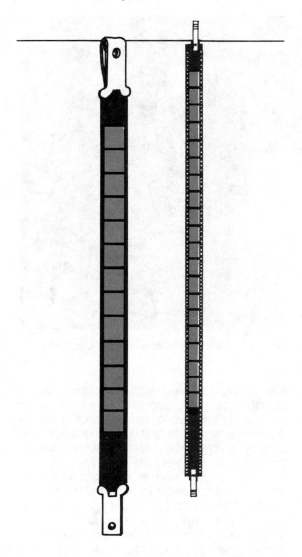

Fig. 10-16. Hang the film in a dust-free area
with a clip on the bottom

The cover of the developing tank may
now be removed. Place the tank under
running water that is approximately the same
temperature as was the developer. This is
called the "wash." Allow the film to rinse
for a minimum of 20 minutes to remove all
traces of the processing solutions, Fig.
10-15.

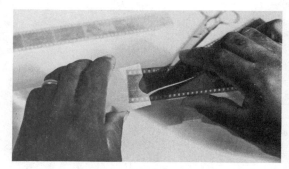

Fig. 10-17. Strips of negatives are stored in
glassine sleeves

At the end of the wash, the film may be
placed in a wetting agent bath such as
Kodak Photo-Flo for a minimum of 1 minute.
The wetting agent bath helps to eliminate
water streaks and spots when the film is
drying. Dry the film by hanging it in a dust-
free area. A clip at the bottom will prevent
the film from curling, Fig. 10-16. Glassine
sleeves are sometimes used for storage of
dried negatives. The negatives are cut into
strips and slipped into the sleeve which
protects them from being scratched and
collecting dust, Fig. 10-17.

UNIT 43 — TERMS FOR DISCUSSION AND REVIEW

processing chemicals
development
black and white roll
  film negatives
developer
stop bath
fixing bath
concentrated
stock developer
working solution
diluting
oxidation
acetic acid
hardener
developing tanks
light-tight
  container

continuous tone
  photography
panchromatic
sensitive
total darkness
cassette
leader
emulsion
counterclockwise
sheet film
  developing tank
data sheet
pre-wetting
graduate
timer
agitate
latent image

tank
reel
apron
cover
light trap
continuous spiral
  wire sides
semiautomatic
  loader

exhausted
neutralize
wash
wetting agent
  bath
water streaks
glassine sleeves

Fig. 10-18. Kodak C-22 Kit for processing color negatives

FILM DEVELOPING PROCESSES

COLOR NEGATIVE ROLL FILM

The procedure used for developing color negatives is very similar to that used for the development of black and white negatives. Color negative development, however, requires the use of different processing chemicals.

The Kodak C-22 Processing Kit is complete with all the necessary chemicals and instructions for developing color negatives, Fig. 10-18. The detailed kit instruction sheet should be carefully followed.

TRANSPARENCIES (SLIDES)

Transparencies, commonly referred to as "slides," are produced on reversal film. This film develops with a positive image. When the slide is placed between a light source and a projection surface, a positive image is projected, Fig. 10-19.

Black and white slides may be developed by using a Kodak Direct Positive Film Developing Kit, Fig. 10-20. Each kit contains all the necessary chemicals for processing several rolls of black and white

Fig. 10-19. Slides are projected for viewing

reversal film. Complete processing instructions are provided with each developing kit.

The Kodak E-3 and E-4 Processing Kit may be used for the development of **color slides,** Fig. 10-21. Each kit contains all the chemicals required for developing color slides, as well as processing instructions. Consult the instruction sheet for complete details regarding time and temperature of each processing step.

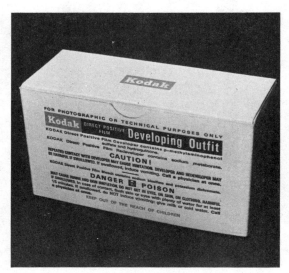

Fig. 10-20. Kodak Direct Positive Developing Kit for black and white transparencies (slides)

Fig. 10-22. Slides are cut into individual frames

Fig. 10-23. Seal the slide frames in slide mounts with a tacking iron

SLIDE MOUNTING

When dry, the developed reversal film is cut into individual frames, Fig. 10-22. The frames are then sealed in a slide mount so that they may be placed in a projector for viewing.

Handle the slide frame by the edges to prevent fingerprints from appearing on the slide. Place the slide frame squarely in the mount. The slide mount is then closed and sealed along all four edges with a warm tacking iron, Fig. 10-23.

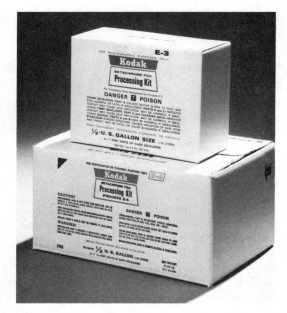

Fig. 10-21. Kodak E-3 and E-4 Color Slide Processing Kits

UNIT 44 — TERMS FOR DISCUSSION AND REVIEW

color negatives
development
black and white
   negatives
processing
transparencies
slides
reversal film
positive image

light source
projection surface
black and white
   slides
individual frames
slide mount
projector
tacking iron

UNIT 45

ORIENTATION TO ENLARGER

The enlarger is used for making photographic prints. The negative is placed in the enlarger between the light source and the lens. The light passes through the negative and the lens and projects the image of the negative onto the baseboard which holds the sensitized photographic paper, Fig. 10-24.

To be effective, all enlargers consist of (1) a light source, (2) a means of light distribution, (3) a negative carrier, (4) a lens, (5) a focusing device, (6) a means of changing the distance between the lens and the paper, and (7) a baseboard.

Refer to Fig. 10-25 for the location of the parts of an enlarger which are described in the remainder of this unit. The light source is generally an electric light bulb which may be clear or frosted. The bulb is

positioned inside a light-tight box called the **lamphouse.** To distribute the light evenly over the negative, a set of two plano-convex condensers may be used. The condensers are positioned in the **condenser housing,** with the convex sides facing each other.

The negative carrier, which holds the negative in position, is placed in the enlarger at the **film stage.** The **lens** projects the image onto the **baseboard.** The baseboard supports the enlarger and also serves as a flat surface for positioning the photographic **easel.** The **focusing knob** changes the dis-

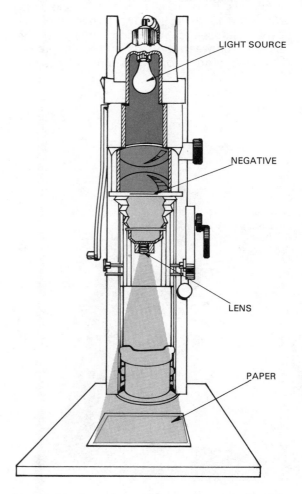

Fig. 10-24. An enlarger is used to make photographic prints

tance between the lens and the negative, making it possible to project sharp, clear images. To vary the size of the projected image, the **hand crank** is turned. The hand crank raises or lowers the entire projection assembly, changing the distance between the lens and the baseboard.

Other operating points may vary with the enlarger being used. The **lifting lever** (which cannot be seen in Fig. 10-25) opens the film stage so that the negative carrier may be inserted. The **bellows** is a collapsible light-tight structure that channels the light rays from the film stage to the lens. When the focusing knob is turned, the bellows collapses or expands, changing the distance between the lens and the negative. The **lens stage** holds the lens in position

under the bellows. On some enlargers, a **lens turret** which holds three lenses is used, each lens having a different magnification power. The **red filter** swings in place between the lens and the photographic paper on the baseboard. With the red filter in place, the image may be projected (for a short period of time) without exposing the paper. This enables the operator to make final positioning adjustments with the image projected onto the paper.

Some enlargers are equipped with **automatic resetting timers**. The operating controls for focusing, exposing, and raising and lowering the projection assembly are sometimes located at the front edge of the baseboard, Fig. 10-26.

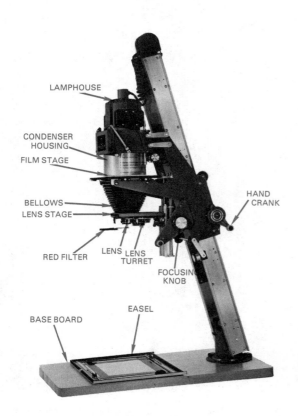

Fig. 10-25. Parts of an enlarger

Fig. 10-26. Beseler CB7-FRST enlarger

UNIT 45 — TERMS FOR DISCUSSION AND REVIEW

enlarger	film stage
photographic prints	easel
negative	focusing knob
light source	hand crank
lens	projection
baseboard	assembly
sensitized	lifting lever
photographic paper	bellows
negative carrier	lens stage
focusing device	lens turret
lamphouse	magnification
plano-convex	red filter
condensers	automatic resetting
condenser housing	timer

UNIT 46

CHEMICAL PREPARATION FOR BLACK AND WHITE PRINTS

The development of exposed black and white photographic papers requires four processing baths. These are, in left to right sequence: (1) **developer,** (2) **stop bath,** (3) **fixing bath,** and (4) **running water,** Fig. 10-27. Since the individual trays should be prepared before any prints are made, this unit should be studied carefully before attempting to do either contact or projection printing as explained in Units 47 and 48.

Developer. The developer is available in a concentrated liquid or dry chemical form. To prepare a stock solution, follow the manufacturer's mixing recommendations. The stock developer should be stored in a brown glass container with a tight stopper to prevent oxidation. A working developer solution is usually prepared by diluting the developer with water. The developer-water ratio may vary with different types of paper. The recommended temperature of the tray developer solution is between 68° and 72° F (20° and 22° C).

Stop bath. This is also referred to as "short stop." Stop bath is usually prepared by adding 1½ ounces (44.4 ml) of 28 percent acetic acid to 32 ounces (946.4 ml) of water.

Safety Note

When preparing stop bath, **always add the acid to the water.**

Commercially prepared stop bath, called Indicator Stop Bath, comes in a concentrated liquid form. It must be mixed with water to prepare a working solution. Indicator Stop Bath is a straw yellow in color, but turns purple when it is exhausted, at which time it must be discarded.

Fig. 10-27. Processing chemicals for black and white photographic paper

Fixer. The same fixing solution that was used during the processing of black and white negatives may be used for black and white prints.

Running water. The last required processing step is washing the processed prints. This may be done by placing them in a tray of running water or in a print washer. Fresh water should be continually supplied to the prints during the washing step.

Each of the three trays (developer, stop bath, and fixer) should be filled to a depth of approximately ¾″ (19 mm). The size of the tray should be slightly larger than the largest print to be made.

One pair of developing tongs is used in the developer only. Do not place them in the stop bath as they will carry stop bath to the developing solution and neutralize the developer. A second pair of tongs may be used for the stop bath and fixing solutions.

UNIT 46 — TERMS FOR DISCUSSION AND REVIEW

development	working developer
exposed	solution
photographic paper	dilute
developer	short stop
stop bath	Indicator
fixing bath	Stop Bath
running water	exhausted
contact print	negatives
projection print	prints
stock solution	developing tongs
oxidation	neutralize

UNIT 47

CONTACT PRINTING

Contact prints are made by placing film negatives in direct contact with the photographic paper in a contact printing frame. The frame is then positioned on the baseboard of an enlarger. During exposure, the light passes through the negative and exposes the light-sensitized emulsion of the photographic paper. The exposed paper is then processed. Contact printing produces photographic prints that are the **same size** as the negatives.

Two types of contact printing frames are generally employed. The contact printing frame in Fig. 10-28 consists of a glass front and spring-loaded back which applies pressure to hold the negative and paper in tight contact. When loading this type of contact printing frame, place the negative, emulsion side up, on the glass. The photographic paper is then placed emulsion side down on the negative. The emulsion side of a negative is the dull side, while the emulsion side of photographic paper is generally the glossy side.

The gang contact printing frame in Fig. 10-29 consists of a glass top which is hinged to a backing plate covered with sponge rubber. On the inside of the glass, negative guides hold the negatives in place. With the contact printing frame opened, the negatives are inserted with the emulsion side face up, Fig. 10-30. The photographic paper is placed on the sponge rubber backing with the emulsion side up, and the frame is locked closed.

Contact prints are always made with the emulsion side of the negative in direct contact with the emulsion side of the paper — **emulsion to emulsion.** Photographic negatives and paper should be handled by the edges with clean, dry hands.

Before loading the contact printing frame, clean the glass to remove all dust and fingerprints. The negatives should also be dusted on both sides before they are inserted into the contact printing frame. Place the negatives in the contact printing frame with the emulsion side up by sliding them under the negative guides. On the enlarger, the lens and condenser lenses should also be checked that they are dust-free.

Place the contact printing frame on the enlarger baseboard, and turn the enlarger on manually. The position of the contact printing frame should be adjusted so that the projected light just surrounds the entire frame,

Fig. 10-31. It may be necessary to raise or lower the projection assembly.

Turn the lens ring to a middle f-stop number, Fig. 10-32. The f-stop regulates the size of the lens aperture which determines the amount of light that will pass through the lens. The f-stop range of most enlarger

Fig. 10-29. Paterson contact printer, 35mm model

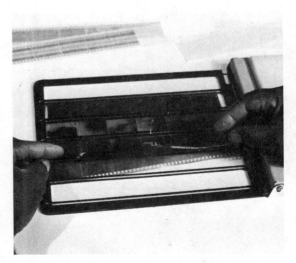

Fig. 10-30. Place the negatives in the gang contact printer with the emulsion up

Fig. 10-28. Contact printing frame

lenses is f/2.8, f/4, f/5.6, f/8, f/11, and f/16. The higher the f-stop number, the smaller the lens aperture, Fig. 10-33. After positioning the contact printing frame and adjusting the f-stop, turn off the enlarger.

Before opening the photographic paper, turn off the room lights and turn on the safelights. The safelight filter used may vary for different paper emulsions. Check the manufacturer's safelight recommendations for the photographic paper that is being used.

Open the package of photographic paper, and remove one sheet. This sheet should be cut into **test strips** approximately 1″ (25.4 mm) wide. The test strips will be used for determining the basic exposure time. Return all but one test strip to the package. Be sure the package is tightly closed to prevent accidental exposure of the paper.

Place one test strip on the sponge rubber backing with the emulsion side up. Close and lock the contact printing frame.

Expose the first test strip for exactly 10 seconds. After exposure, immerse the test strip in the developer. Gently rock the tray to agitate the developing solution. Develop the test strip for exactly 1½ minutes before placing it in the stop bath. Use tongs to keep your hands free of chemicals. The stop bath stops or neutralizes the action of the developer. Leave the test strip in the stop bath for a minimum of 30 seconds with continuous agitation. When using resin coated paper, leave the test strip 5 to 10 seconds in the stop bath. Transfer the test strip to the fixing bath using a second set of tongs. The test strip should be left in the fixer for a minimum of 2 minutes before it can be inspected under white light. The test strip should, however, remain in the fixing bath for a total of 8 to 10 minutes. When using resin coated paper, the total fixing time is only 2 to 3 minutes.

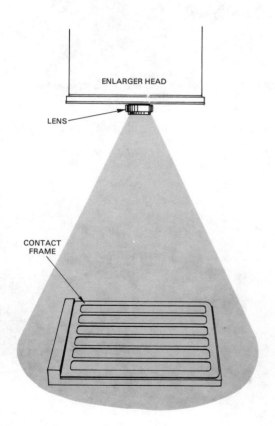

Fig. 10-31. The projected light should encompass the entire contact printing frame

Fig. 10-32. Set the lens to a middle f-stop

If the test strip appears too light, the exposure time must be lengthened. Conversely, the exposure time must be shortened if the test strip print is too dark, Fig. 10-34. Make the necessary time adjustments, and expose another test strip. Be sure the f-stop, developing time, and developer temperature remain the same for the second test strip. When a satisfactory test strip has been obtained, repeat the process, making a full-size contact print, Fig. 10-35.

Fig. 10-33. Enlarger lens f-stops

UNIT 47 — TERMS FOR DISCUSSION AND REVIEW

contact prints
film negatives
photographic paper
contact printing
  frame
baseboard
enlarger
light-sensitive
  emulsion
dull side
glossy side
gang contact
  printing frame
emulsion to emulsion

lens
condenser lens
projection
  assembly
lens ring
f-stop
lens aperture
safelights
test strip
basic exposure
  time
agitate
neutralize
resin coated

BLACK AND WHITE PROJECTION PRINTING

Enlarged prints can be made from negatives by a process called **projection printing**. The size of the enlargement is governed by the distance between the enlarger lens and the photographic paper on the baseboard. As the lens is raised, the

A. Too light — not enough exposure

B. Too dark — too much exposure

Fig. 10-34. Test strips are made to determine the correct exposure

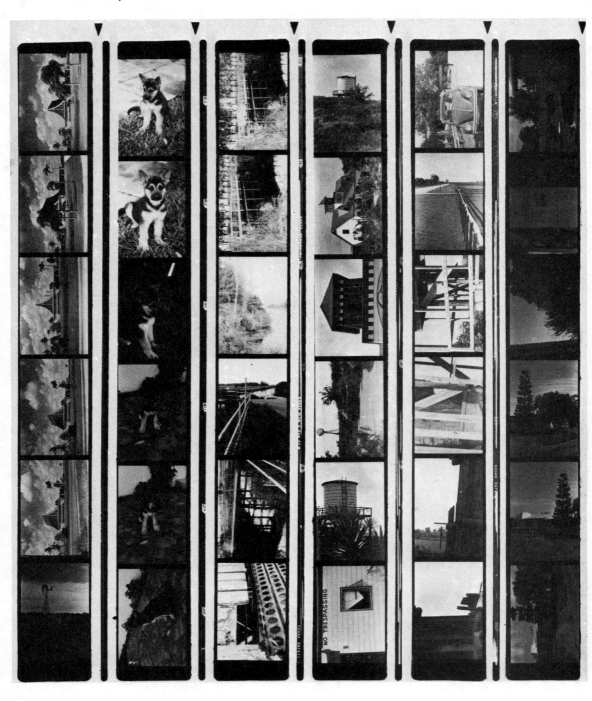

Fig. 10-35. Full-sized contact print

projected light and image are spread over a wider area, thereby increasing the size of the print, Fig. 10-36.

The negative to be enlarged should be dusted on both sides with a negative brush. Any dust that remains on the negative will appear as a white spot on the print. Place the negative in the negative carrier with the emulsion side down, Fig. 10-37. It is sometimes helpful to position the negative in the negative carrier upside down; that is, with the bottom of the negative to the top of the

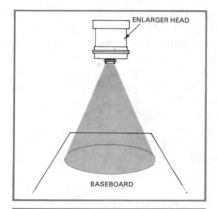

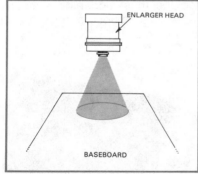

Fig. 10-36. The size of the projected image can be controlled by raising and lowering the enlarger head

Fig. 10-38. Insert the negative carrier into the film stage

Fig. 10-37. Place the negative in the negative carrier with the emulsion side down

Fig. 10-39. Unwanted portions of the negative may be cropped out of the projection

negative carrier. When projected, the image will then appear right side up on the easel. Using the lifting lever, open the enlarger film stage, and insert the negative carrier, Fig. 10-38.

With the negative carrier in position, turn off the room lights, and turn on the safelights. Turn the enlarger on manually, and open the lens to its widest f-stop. Position the paper easel to be used on the baseboard, and focus the image on the easel. It is sometimes helpful to use a strip of enlarging paper on the easel when you are focusing. If the projected image is too small, raise the projection assembly and refocus the image. Lower the projection assembly if the image is too large.

Sometimes printing the entire projected negative image area is not necessary nor desirable. After the contact print is inspected, it may be found that only a portion of the negative is desirable as a finished print. The projection assembly may be raised or the easel moved to **crop** out those areas that are unwanted in the enlargement, Fig. 10-39.

With the image sharply focused on the easel, close down the lens f-stop until the fine detail just begins to disappear, but remains visible. Turn off the enlarger.

Factors that determine the best exposure time are: (1) the brightness of the light source, (2) the distance between the lens and the paper, (3) the lens aperture, (4) the negative density, (5) the developing solution strength, and (6) the type of paper being used. Because of these variables, it is impossible to provide a standard exposure time. Therefore, a test strip must be made to determine the exposure time to be used.

Remove one sheet of photographic paper from the package, and cut it into test strips approximately 1″ (25.4 mm) wide. Return all but one test strip to the package. Be sure to close the package tightly.

Position the test strip on the easel, emulsion side up. Using a black cardboard mask, cover approximately three-quarters of the test strip, and make a 5-second exposure, Fig. 10-40. Before making the second test exposure, move the mask to uncover an additional one-quarter of the test strip. Repeat the 5-second exposure. Continue this procedure until the entire test strip has been exposed. The test strip will have been exposed for 20 seconds at the first step, 15 at the second, 10 at the third, and 5 seconds at the last step. Process the test strip in the same manner as used when contact prints are processed.

The test strip is inspected under white light and the exposure time selected that produced the most acceptable results, Fig. 10-41. Use this exposure time for making the enlargement.

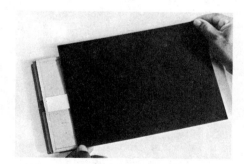

Fig. 10-40. Cover all but a small portion of the test strip

| 20 | 15 | 10 | 5 |

Fig. 10-41. Photographic test strip

Fig. 10-42. Position a full sheet of paper in the easel

Position a full sheet of photographic paper squarely in the easel, Fig. 10-42. Many easels have positioning guides which automatically allow for a uniform white border on all sides of the enlargement. Borderless prints may be made by using double-sided masking tape to form a rectangular pattern on a piece of glass. The pattern should be slightly smaller than the paper being used. The paper is then pressed down along all four edges.

Process the enlargement by following the same steps as used for the test strip: developer, stop bath, fixer, and wash. The image should be fully developed between 1½ and 2 minutes. The print should be washed for a minimum of one hour to remove all traces of processing chemicals. Resin coated paper requires a 5-minute maximum final wash time. Hypo clearing agent, when used according to the manufacturer's recommendations, may be used to shorten the wash time. A print that has not been sufficiently washed may turn yellow when it is dried.

UNIT 48 — TERMS FOR DISCUSSION AND REVIEW

prints
negatives
projection printing
enlargement
enlarger lens
photographic paper
baseboard
negative brush
white spots
negative carrier
emulsion side
easel
lifting lever
enlarger film stage
safelights
f-stop
focus

projection
  assembly
crop
lens aperture
negative density
developing
  solution
test strip
cardboard mask
double-sided
  masking tape
developer
stop bath
fixer
wash
hypo clearing
  agent

UNIT 49

PRINT FINISHING

Photographic prints may be dried with either a **glossy** (shiny) or a **matte** (dull) finish. If a glossy finish is desired, the print must be made on photographic paper that may be dried with a glossy finish. The three most common drying techniques use (1) ferrotype plates, (2) photographic blotters, and (3) electric dryers. Resin coated paper requires special care.

FERROTYPE PLATES

Ferrotype plates are usually made of brass or steel with a highly polished chromium-plated surface. To produce a glossy finish, remove the prints from the wash and allow them to drain to shed any excess water. Soak the prints in a glossing solution; then place face down on the polished surface of the ferrotype plate and cover with a blotter. Pass a print roller or squeegee over the blotter to assure tight contact between the ferrotype plate and the print, Fig. 10-43. The prints will fall off when they are dry if the ferrotype plates are stood on edge.

Fig. 10-43. Rolling a print onto a ferrotype plate

PHOTOGRAPHIC BLOTTERS

Photographic blotters may be used for drying prints with a matte finish. Place the well-drained prints between blotters and allow them to dry, Fig. 10-44. Photographic blotters are available in both roll and sheet forms.

ELECTRIC DRYERS

Prints may be dried with either a glossy or a matte finish on electric dryers of many types, Fig. 10-45. To produce a glossy finish,

Fig. 10-44. Place prints in a photographic blotter roll

Fig. 10-45. Beseler 1620 Universal Dryer

soak the washed print in a gloss solution before it is placed face up on the apron. This brings the face of the print in contact with the polished, heated drum which acts as a ferrotype plate. Matte finishes are produced by placing the washed print face down on the apron.

RESIN COATED PAPER

Resin coated paper (R. C. paper) should not be dried using any of the previous methods. Because of the resin coating, the paper absorbs very little water. After the final wash, the excess water on the surface of the print may be blotted or

Fig. 10-46. Commercial 200 Dry Mounting Press

sponged off. The paper should be placed on a clean surface and allowed to air dry. A fan may be used to circulate the air over the surface of the paper to speed the drying process.

DRY MOUNTING

Dry mounting is a process of mounting prints on a backing board using dry mounting tissue rather than paste, glue, or cement. Dry mounting tissue is a thin sheet of paper coated on both sides with an adhesive. The tissue is placed between the print and the mounting board and positioned in the dry mounting press, Fig. 10-46. A combination of heat and pressure bond the print to the mounting board.

The dry mounting press must be preheated. As a general rule, a temperature between 225° and 275° F (107° and 135° C) is suitable for most dry mounting.

Attach a sheet of dry mounting tissue (slightly larger than the print) to the back of the print to be mounted. The tissue may be tacked in the center of the print with a tacking iron, Fig. 10-47. Trim the tissue and the print at the same time to assure exactness in size.

Place the print and tissue in the desired location on the mounting board. The corners of the print are lifted to tack the tissue to the mounting board with the tacking iron, Fig. 10-48. This will prevent the print from moving from position.

Fig. 10-47. Tack the tissue to the back of the print with a tacking iron

Fig. 10-48. Tack the tissue and print into position on the mounting board

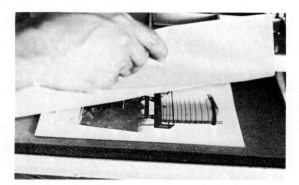

Fig. 10-49. Cover the face of the print with a clean sheet of paper

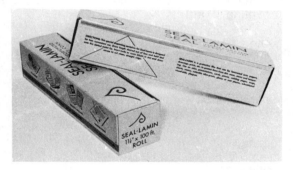

Fig. 10-50. Laminating film may be used to protect the surface of prints

Fig. 10-51. Applying clear plastic spray to protect the surface of a print

Place the mounting board, with the print face up, on the bed of the preheated dry mounting press. To prevent any dust on the platen from getting on the face of the print, cover the face with a clean sheet of paper, Fig. 10-49. Close the dry mounting press, and observe the flashing timing light. It flashes at a rate of once per second when the press is closed. The required mounting time will vary from 5 to 60 seconds, depending upon the thickness of the mounting board and print. Carefully remove the mounted print, and allow it to cool under a weight to prevent curling.

A clear laminating film may be mounted over the print to protect the surface. Laminating film is available for use with the dry mounting press in both gloss and matte finishes, Fig. 10-50. Clear plastic spray may also be applied to prints to preserve and protect the surface, Fig. 10-51.

UNIT 49 — TERMS FOR DISCUSSION AND REVIEW

glossy
matte
ferrotype plates
photographic
    blotters
electric dryers
glossing solution
roller or
    squeegee
dry mounting

backing board
dry mounting
    tissue
adhesive
tacking iron
resin coated
    paper
laminating film
clear plastic
    spray

11 CHAPTER

Office Copying and Office Duplicating

Schools and businesses need fast, less expensive ways of printing. Office copying and office duplicating machines have been designed to do this job.

Office copying machines produce copies of the original **without an intermediate image carrier**. They generally use a **toner**, which is a fine powder, rather than an ink to produce the image, Fig. 11-1. The original image can be prepared by a variety of processes. Strike-on and technical illustrating are the two most commonly used. When office copiers are used to produce larger quantities, automatic collators reduce assembly time, Fig. 11-2.

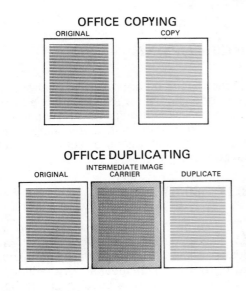

Fig. 11-1. Office copying and office duplicating

Fig. 11-2. 3M VHS-R copier with collator

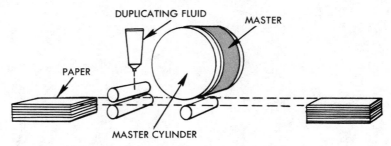

Fig. 11-3. Operation of the spirit duplicator

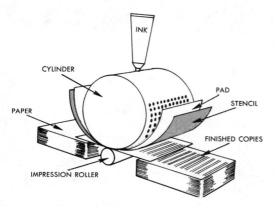

Fig. 11-4. Operation of the mimeograph duplicator

or made electronically. The stencil is positioned on the outside of the mimeograph
cylinder. As the paper is fed through the
machine, the impression roller presses it
against the stencil on the cylinder. The ink
flows from inside the cylinder through the
stencil pad and the image openings to make
the image impression on the paper. The
printed copies are then ejected from the
machine and stacked, Fig. 11-4.

UNIT 50

Two office duplicating processes are
known as **spirit duplication** and **mimeograph duplication**. The spirit duplication
process is technically a planographic
process. A flat image carrier is used. The
paper spirit master has a carbon image. It
is placed on a master cylinder which rotates.
Paper being fed into the machine is
moistened by vapors of duplicating fluid.
The moistened paper makes contact with
the master. The image is formed when a
small amount of carbon is dissolved and
transferred to the paper, Fig. 11-3.

The mimeograph duplication process
uses a direct-plate stencil. This can be
considered a screen process printing technique. Images are pressed into the stencil
coating. They may be typed, made by hand,

OFFICE COPYING

Office copiers are used to reproduce
original documents for offices, schools, or
businesses. This is a quick and easy method
of copy reproduction with a minimum cost.
Following are descriptions of some types of
office copiers.

XEROX 3600 III

The Xerox 3600 III is often referred to
as an electrostatic copier, Fig. 11-5. It reproduces copies from original documents
by **xerography** which means ''dry writing.''
Instead of ink, a **toner** is used to create be-
image. Electrostatic forces are created be-

tween the original and the copy paper. This causes the toner to be attracted to the copy paper in the image areas. A schematic drawing is shown in Fig. 11-6 and is explained as follows:

The original document is placed face down on the curved platen (1). The position of the original on the platen determines the position of the copy image. The reflected light from the original is measured by a photo cell which signals the lens (2) to open or close depending upon the light. The oscillating mirror (3) scans the original document and reflects the image through the lens to the fixed mirror (4). The fixed mirror reflects the image to the selenium drum (5) which receives a positive charge from the charge corotron (6). The positive charge on the drum is in the same pattern as the reflected image. In other words, only the image areas receive a positive charge. Toner (7), which is negatively charged, is then poured between the drum and the electrode (8). As opposites attract, the toner is attracted to the positively charged image areas on the drum. The copy paper input unit (9) stores the copy paper which is always maintained at the proper feed level by an automatic elevator. The image transfer occurs as the positively charged copy paper passes under the drum (10). The paper is then transported to the fusing lamp and reflector (11) where the toner is heated and fused to the paper. Where there is no image, the toner does not fuse to the paper. Any excess toner is brushed away by the copy brush (12). Copies are stacked in the output tray (13) at a rate of one per second.

Fig. 11-5. Xerox 3600 III electrostatic copier

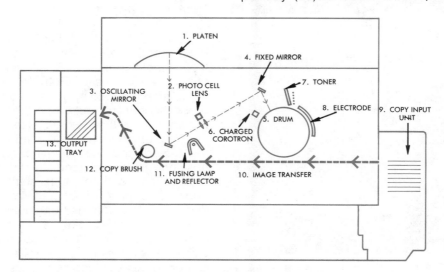

Fig. 11-6. Xerox 3600 III schematic

Fig. 11-7. A. B. Dick 695 dry copier

Fig. 11-8. IBM Copier II

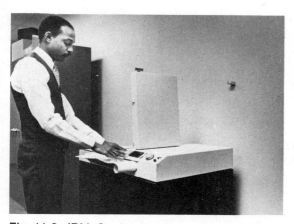

Fig. 11-9. IBM Copier II with **rolled document holder**

A. B. DICK 695 DRY COPIER

The A. B. Dick 695 Dry Copier shown in Fig. 11-7 is a tabletop **direct electrostatic** copier. It reproduces exact size copies (no reduction). This copier uses rolls of bond-like copy paper. It is available in a variety of widths to match different original sizes. Because the copy paper is in a roll, originals of varying lengths may be copied without trim waste and without changing paper sizes. The copy length control is adjusted to the desired length for the copies to be made.

The original is placed face down on the platen of the copier using the copy size markings as a guide. The platen cover is then replaced and the countdown dial is set. It is possible to produce four copies per second.

During the copying operation, the copy paper receives a positive electrical charge in the same areas as the image of the original. The magnetic toner has a negative charge and adheres to the positively charged areas. Thus the image of the original is re-created on the copy paper. The darkness of the reproduction copy is controlled by adjusting the contrast dial.

IBM COPIER II

The IBM Copier II, Fig. 11-8, is a **direct electrostatic** copier which is roll fed. Either IBM General Bond or IBM Watermark Bond paper may be used. Both **letter size** and **legal size** copies may be produced. Depress the selector button on the copier control panel for the desired size.

The original copy is placed in the document feed and the machine automatically positions it on a flatbed. In this way, copy registration is kept consistent for each original. Copies of documents, halftones, drawings, low-contrast originals, oversized originals, thick books, and three-dimensional originals can be produced. The IBM Copier II also features a rolled document holder for use in copying maps and architectural drawings, Fig. 11-9.

Copies are produced every 2.4 seconds. The machine can be set to produce a limited number of copies or to copy continuously. The IBM Copier II also has a copy darkness control to produce copies darker than the original.

3M "SECRETARY" II

The 3M "Secretary" II is an **indirect electrostatic** copier, Fig. 11-10. The image of the original is projected onto a photoconductive exposure drum which transfers the image to the paper. The image areas of the original copy have a positive electrical charge on the exposure drum.

During the development stage, negatively charged toner is transferred from a magnetic developing roller to the positive latent (invisible) image on the drum. Positively charged copy paper makes contact with the drum and the image is transferred to the paper. The toner is then heated by an infrared light source to create a permanent bond between the toner and the paper.

The 3M "Secretary" II copier accepts sheet, book, or three-dimensional originals.

Fig. 11-10. 3M "Secretary" II

It will produce copies at a rate of 10 per minute. A variety of paper sizes and kinds (including color stock, bond paper, and letterheads) are automatically fed from a sheet cassette cartridge. A fold-down by-pass system permits manual feeding of special stock, such as offset plates, address labels, overhead projection transparencies, ledger stock, and computer sheet size stock. Copies may be made on both sides of the paper.

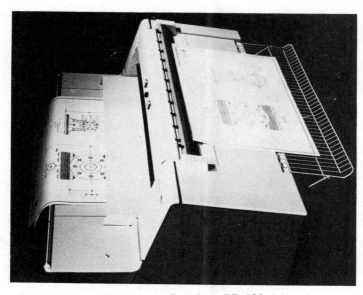

Fig. 11-11. Bruning PD-160

BRUNING PD-160 COPIER

The Bruning PD-160 Copier uses a pressure diazo process. It is primarily used for copying architectural drawings, Fig. 11-11. Original architectural drawings are generally prepared on a translucent paper, such as drafting vellum. When the original drawing is fed into the machine, an exposure light shines through it. Those areas of the copy paper that receive exposure light are broken down chemically. When the copy paper is developed by activator applied under pressure, the areas that did not receive exposure light form the image of the original. A variable speed control permits the regulation of the copy contrast.

UNIT 50 — TERMS FOR DISCUSSION AND REVIEW

office copying
reproduction
original
Xerox 3600 III
xerography
toner
electrostatic
schematic drawing
curved platen
reflected light
photo cell
lens
oscillating mirror
fixed mirror
selenium drum
positive charge
charge corotron
image
negatively charged
electrode
copy paper
   input unit
copy paper

automatic elevator
image transfer
fusing lamp
   and reflector
fused
copy brush
output tray
direct electrostatic
   copier
documents
halftones
drawings
rolled document
   holder
indirect
   electrostatic
   copier
projected
photoconductive
   exposure drum
pressure diazo
   process
translucent

OFFICE DUPLICATING

Office duplicating systems are used by many businesses for communication purposes. They are less expensive to purchase and operate than high quality printing equipment. The machines are easy to operate and do not require a dedicated operator. Spirit and mimeograph duplicating are frequently used for low volume duplication. (For information on more complex duplicating systems, refer to Chapter 9, "Planographic Printing.")

SPIRIT DUPLICATING

Spirit masters usually consist of three separate sheets: (1) **the paper master**, (2) a **tissue paper** protecting sheet, and (3) an **aniline dye carbon sheet**. The color of the carbon sheet used determines the color of the reproduced copy. Green, red, black, blue, or purple carbons can be purchased. Spirit masters are available in high-performance, long-run grades as well as economical short-run grades.

PREPARING THE MASTER

The spirit duplicating master may be **drawn, handwritten, or typed**. The first step in preparing a spirit master is to remove the sheet of tissue paper. As the image is prepared on the master, the exerted pressure transfers a deposit of carbon to the back of the master, forming a reverse image. One master may be used to reproduce several colors at one time by using different color carbons during preparation.

To prepare a drawn or handwritten master, place the master, carbon side up, on a hard, smooth surface. (Preliminary

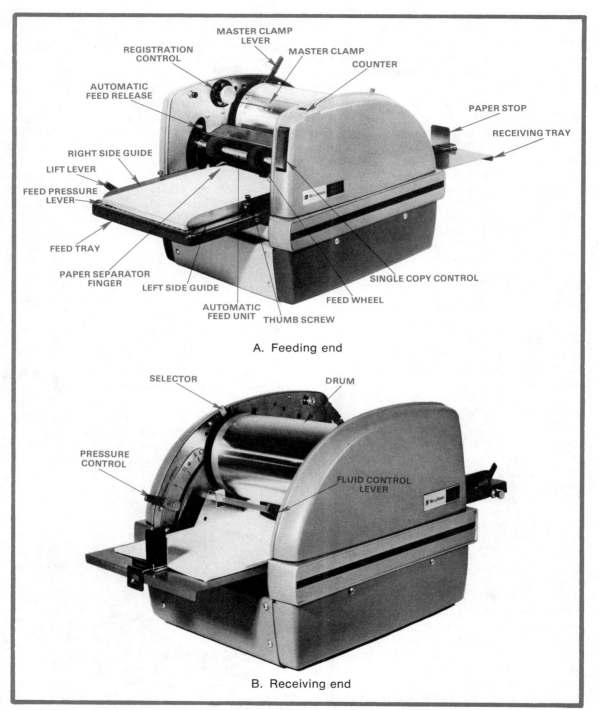

A. Feeding end

B. Receiving end

Fig. 11-12. Ditto Model D-31 spirit duplicator

sketches or tracings can be lightly drawn on the master before the tissue paper is removed.) Using a ball-point pen, hard lead pencil, or stylus, draw or write directly on the master surface. Apply just enough pressure to produce the desired line thickness.

When a spirit master is typed, the back of the master must contact the carbon side of the carbon paper. To produce a sharp, clear image, clean the typewriter keys before typing.

To correct errors, erase the carbon deposit with an ink eraser. Then tear off an unused portion of the carbon paper and place it over the error. Make the correction. A razor blade or knife may also be used to carefully scrape the carbon from the back of the master. Try to avoid any damage to the master.

USING A SPIRIT DUPLICATOR

The operating control points for the Ditto Model D-31 spirit duplicator are labeled in Fig. 11-12. The location of these controls may vary with the type of machine being used.

To prepare the spirit duplicator for production, first check the duplicator fluid level. Next prime the wick if the machine has not been used for a prolonged period of time. To do this, engage the **fluid control lever**, and turn on the machine. Allow the machine to run for 25 to 30 revolutions without feeding paper. Then feed a sheet of paper by pressing the **single copy control**. The wick is properly primed if light streaks appear across the sheet. If the sheet is excessively wet, adjust the **fluid control** and feed several sheets of paper to absorb the excess fluid.

To load the **feed tray**, move the **lift lever** toward the **drum**. Raise the **automatic feed unit**, and lower the feed tray. Align the **left side guide** with the number on the feed tray that corresponds to the size paper being used. Place the front edge of the paper against the **paper separator fingers**, Fig. 11-13. Move the **right side guide** to the edge of the paper and then back off slightly.

When the adjustment is correct, the sheets will feed consistently during production. Lock both side guides in position by tightening the **thumbscrews**.

Position the **feed wheels** about ¾" (19 mm) inside each side guide. Then set the **feed pressure lever** according to the weight of the paper being used. Lightweight papers require a low-pressure setting, while a high-pressure setting must be used for heavyweight papers.

To attach the spirit master, move the **master clamp** lever to the open position. Align either edge of the master with the calibrations on the drum that correspond to the calibrations on the feed tray, Fig. 11-14.

Insert the master into the clamp with the paper portion of the master in contact with the drum and the carbon sheet on top. Then tear off the carbon sheet to expose the prepared master image. Make certain the master lies flatly and squarely on the drum to prevent wrinkles during production. Close the master clamp.

The **receiving tray** is then adjusted by sighting along the edge of the master. Position the side guides between ¹⁄₁₆" and ⅛" (2 mm and 3 mm) from the edges of the master. Set the **selector** to the size paper that is being used, and adjust the **paper stop** position according to paper size.

Fig. 11-13. Loading the feed tray

Fig. 11-14. Inserting the spirit master

Fig. 11-15. Vertical positioning registration control

The **pressure control** (with its low, medium, medium high, or high settings) regulates the amount of pressure that presses the paper against the surface of the master. To produce the maximum number of copies from one master, first set the pressure control to low. Then, as the brightness of the copies begins to disappear, increase the pressure setting. A medium pressure setting is satisfactory for most duplicator production.

The amount of duplicating fluid used on a production run depends largely upon the size of the paper being used. Set the fluid control lever to your paper size. Then press the **automatic feed release** to lower the feed unit to the operating position.

To check image placement before the production run, use the single copy control to feed a few sheets of paper. Check the position of the copy, and adjust the feed tray side guides to regulate side positioning. For vertical positioning, adjust the **registration control,** Fig. 11-15. Set the **counter** to zero and begin the production run.

At the completion of the production run, turn the motor off, release both the pressure control and fluid control levers, and remove the master. Spirit masters may be stored for future use by placing a clean sheet of paper against the carbon side to protect the image.

MIMEOGRAPH DUPLICATION

Mimeograph stencils accept typed, handwritten, or drawn images. They are available in three- or four-part assemblies. Both assemblies have (1) a **backing,** (2) a **typing cushion,** and (3) a **stencil sheet**. Included in the four-part assembly is a **typing film** which covers the stencil sheet, Fig. 11-16.

The stencil sheet has a fibrous base tissue which is coated on both sides. When the image is prepared, the coating is pushed aside by the pressure of typewriter keys or stylus, leaving the fibrous base tissue exposed. During the mimeograph duplication process, the ink will pass through the fibrous tissue wherever the coating has been pushed aside.

The typing cushion is placed between the stencil sheet and the backing. It softens the pressure of the typeface when the image is prepared by typing. The hard, smooth surface of the backing provides a uniform base on which to prepare the stencil.

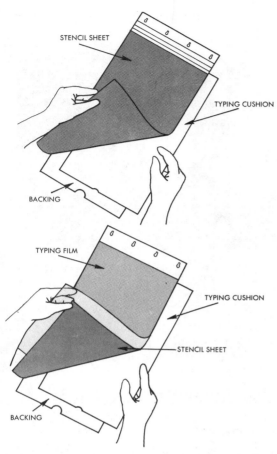

Fig. 11-16. Parts of a mimeograph stencil

TYPING A MIMEOGRAPH STENCIL

The first step in preparing to type a mimeograph stencil is to clean the typewriter keys. Then move the ribbon selector lever to the **white** or **stencil** position. In this position, the typewriter keys will not strike the ribbon, but will make direct contact with the stencil sheet. Better stencils are made in this manner.

Place the typing cushion between the stencil sheet and the backing with the white side up. Insert the stencil assembly into the typewriter so that the typing will be done either on the stencil sheet (three-part assembly) or on the typing film (four-part assembly). Using the numbered lines and paper-size outlines, position the stencil and set the desired margins.

Strike the typewriter keys firmly. As the typeface strikes the stencil sheet, the coating is pushed aside, Fig. 11-17. After typing a few words, inspect the stencil. If the letters are not clear, a firmer typing stroke is necessary.

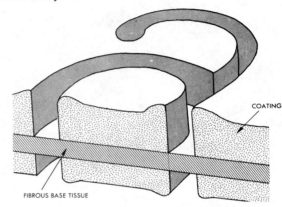

Fig. 11-17. Enlarged view of a mimeograph stencil that has been struck by a typewriter key

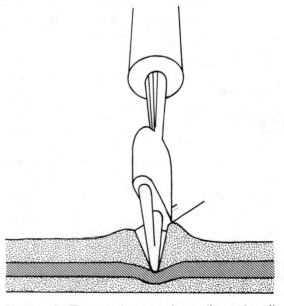

Fig. 11-18. The stylus pushes the stencil coating aside

A typing error may be corrected by using **correction fluid**. This is brushed over each letter of the error in a thin coating. Allow the correction fluid to dry between 30 seconds and 1 minute. The stencil will then be ready to receive the typed correction.

HANDWRITING OR DRAWING A MIMEOGRAPH STENCIL

When a mimeograph stencil is to receive a handwritten or drawn image, a writing plate should be inserted between the cushion and the backing. A handwriting guide sheet with horizontal guide lines may be inserted under the stencil sheet. Use it as a guide to write evenly across the stencil and to keep lines equally spaced. Or a drawing may be placed under the stencil sheet for tracing.

A roll-point stylus should be used for handwriting or drawing a stencil. The width of the point and the pressure applied will determine the width of the lines when reproduced. Keep the stylus nearly straight up and write or draw slowly, applying downward pressure, Fig. 11-18. Inspect the stencil by holding it up to the light.

ELECTRONIC SCANNER

Mimeograph duplicating stencils may also be prepared by electronic-scanning devices, Fig. 11-19. The original copy is placed in the scanner on the left-hand side of the drum. A blank stencil is wrapped around the right-hand side of the drum. During operation, an electric eye scans the original copy as it rotates. Electrical impulses are sent to a stylus which burns the image into the stencil.

Fig. 11-19. A. B. Dick 590 stencilmaker

Fig. 11-20. A. B. Dick mimeograph duplicator

USING THE MIMEOGRAPH DUPLICATOR

The mimeograph duplicator in Fig. 11-20 is used to show the location of many of the major operating points.

To prepare for production, turn the **hand wheel** until the **tail clamp** of the **cylinder** comes into view. Pull the tail clamp away from the cylinder, and pick up the tail end of the protective ink pad cover, Fig. 11-21. Close the tail clamp and turn the hand wheel, pulling the ink pad cover away from the cylinder until the **head clamp** can be seen. Open the head clamp and completely remove the ink pad cover.

Holding the tail end of the stencil, attach the head end, backing sheet up, to the opened head clamp, Fig. 11-22. Close the clamp. Separate and tear off the stencil backing sheet. Next, pull the stencil smoothly over the ink pad by turning the hand wheel. Then clamp the **tail end**.

To load the **feed table**, push the **feed table lowering button**. Adjust the **left guide rail** to the width of the paper being used,

referring to the positioning scale on the feed table. Place not more than one-half ream of paper on the feed table against the left guide rail. Position it as far forward as possible under the corner separators. Adjust the **right guide rail** so that it just touches the edge of the paper.

Position the **feed rollers** between 1/4" and 1/2" (6 mm and 13 mm) inside each side guide rail. Set the **receiving tray** according to the scale markings for the size paper used. The **back stop** should allow the paper to fall clear of the delivery mechanism.

Make certain the **feed lever** is in the **off** position. Then raise the feed table by turning the **feed table raising knob.** The table will automatically stop at the proper height for feeding paper.

Start the duplicator, and allow several sheets of paper to run through. Stop the machine, and check the position of the duplicated copy. If the copy position must be changed laterally (side to side), adjust the position of the feed table, guide rails, feed rollers, and paper. Remember that the paper and not the stencil is being moved.

To change the vertical placement of the copy (top to bottom), loosen the **raise-lower locking clamp** on the cylinder, and make the necessary adjustment, Fig. 11-23. Many duplicators also have an angular adjust-

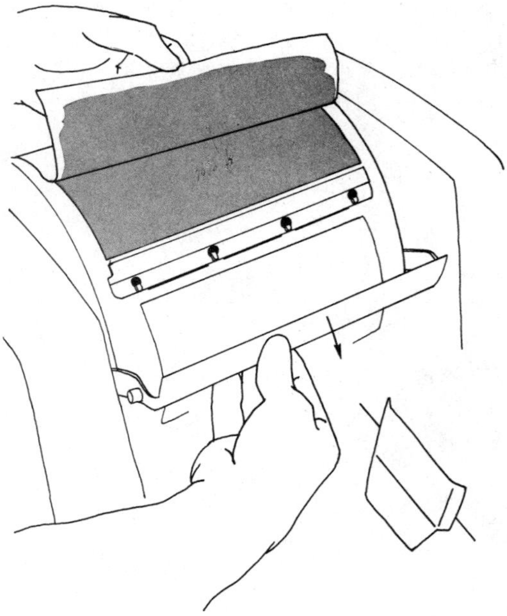

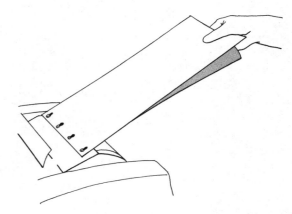

Fig. 11-21. Raise the tail clamp to remove the protective ink pad cover

Fig. 11-22. Attach the head end of the stencil to the head clamp

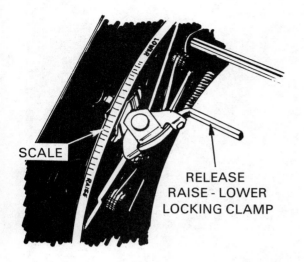

SCALE

RELEASE
RAISE - LOWER
LOCKING CLAMP

Fig. 11-23. Use the raise-lower lock to adjust
copy position

Place a cover on the cylinder to protect the ink pad. Use the same procedure as for attaching a stencil. Position the protective cover smoothly over the cylinder. Then close the tail clamp. Run about five sheets of paper through the duplicator to seal the protective cover.

ment lever. Adjustments can be made to straighten the copy on the paper.

Unclear or spotty duplicated copy generally indicates that the duplicator must be re-inked. To do this, turn the cylinder until the ink cap is up. Remove the ink cap and insert the measuring rod into the cylinder. IIf the measuring rod indicates "refill," screw the tube of ink into the filler hole and squeeze the tube. Do not overfill the cylinder. Remove the ink tube and replace the ink cap. If the ink pad is dry, turn the cylinder once to ink the pad.

After making the necessary adjustments, set the **counter** to zero and begin production.

At the end of the production run, press the outside of a file folder against the stencil. The image transferred to the folder will aid in identifying the stencil for future use. (This step is not necessary if the stencil is to be discarded.)

Remove the stencil (tail end first), and place it inside the folder, ink side up. Close the folder, and rub the surface to seal the stencil inside. The file folder will absorb the ink and clean the stencil. Before filing, open the folder and turn the stencil over.

UNIT 51 — TERMS FOR DISCUSSION AND REVIEW

office duplicating
dedicated operator
spirit duplicator
mimeograph duplicator
spirit masters
paper master
aniline dye
  carbon sheet
reverse image
preliminary
stylus

Spirit machine:

duplicator fluid
fluid control lever
single copy control
wick
feed tray
lift lever
drum
automatic feed unit
side guides
paper separator
  fingers
thumbscrews
feed wheels
feed pressure
master clamp
master clamp lever
receiving tray
selector
paper stop

pressure control
automatic feed
  release
registration control

Mimeograph machine:

mimeograph
stencil
backing
typing cushion
stencil sheet
typing film
electronic-
  scanning
hand wheel
tail clamp
cylinder
head clamp
feed table
guide rails
feed rollers
receiving tray
back stop
feed table
  raising knob
feed lever
laterally
raise-lower
  locking clamp
spotty copy
counter

V SECTION

FINISHING, BINDING, AND PACKAGING

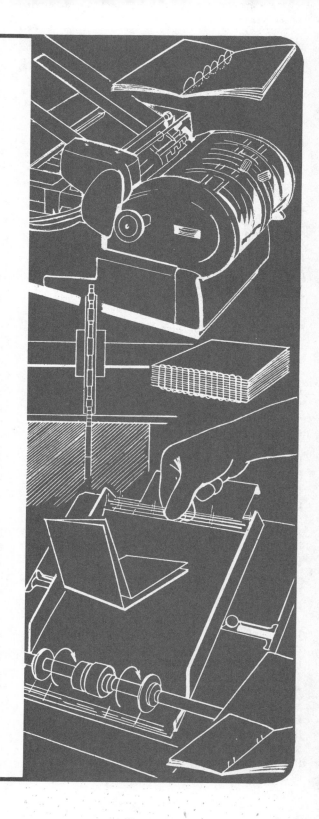

A printed product generally requires additional work before it is ready for distribution. This includes various types of **finishing, binding** and **packaging** operations. These are the final steps in the graphic communications reproduction process.

Simple printed products, such as business cards, envelopes, and letterheads, may only require a packaging operation before they can be distributed. Other products, such as books, magazines, and catalogs, may require finishing and/or binding before they are packaged for distribution.

The type of product and its purpose usually determine the operations that must be performed in finishing, binding, and packaging. These operations are generally established during the message analysis stage of product development.

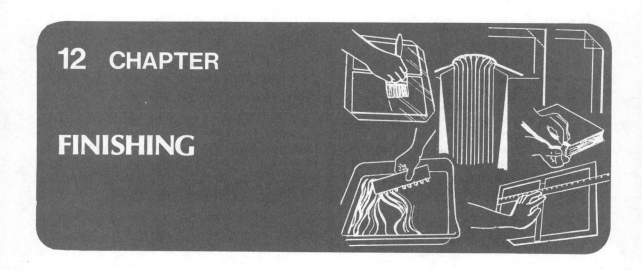

12 CHAPTER

FINISHING

Not all printed products require both finishing and binding operations before they are packaged. Many products require only one operation before distribution.

In most cases, the finishing operations are performed before product binding. For example, the finishing operation of drilling must be performed before binding the sheets for a ring notebook. However, there are occasions when certain finishing op-erations must take place after the product has been bound. If the sheets are to be bound by a spiral bind, they are generally drilled after they are bound. The type of product binding sometimes dictates whether the finishing operation comes **before** or **after** actual binding. The specifications for finishing are usually considered during the message analysis stage of product development.

UNIT 52

MISCELLANEOUS FINISHING OPERATIONS

SCORING

Scoring is a process used to crease paper (without cutting) at the folding point. It is done so that the fold may be made easily and smoothly. Heavy papers such as cardboard display boxes and folders are usually scored.

Scoring may be done either by (1) letterpress (relief) or (2) offset. In letter-press, a steel scoring rule with a round edge is locked in the chase. Usually, the rollers are removed to prevent cutting. Sufficient packing is placed under the draw-sheet to allow the scoring rule to crease the paper.

Some offset duplicators may have a scoring attachment on the delivery end of the machine. The scoring is done using three wheels, Fig. 12-1. The two wheels on the bottom (form rollers) provide a channel for the scoring wheel to crease the paper. Some paper folders may have a similar set of rollers and wheels for scoring.

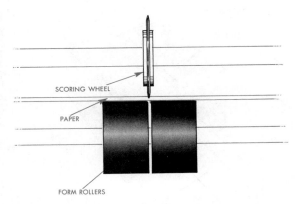

Fig. 12-1. Offset scoring wheel

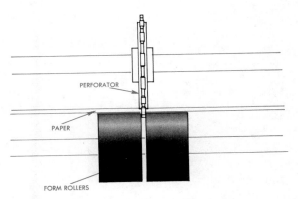

Fig. 12-3. Offset perforating wheel

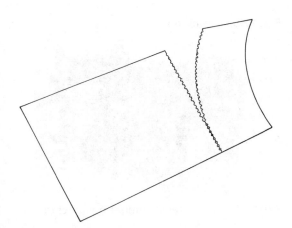

Fig. 12-2. Perforated sheet

PERFORATING

Perforating is much the same as scoring. In this process, however, small slits are cut in the paper so that it will tear easily, Fig. 12-2.

When perforating is done on the letterpress, the perforating rule is locked in a chase and positioned in the press bed. The rollers should be removed to prevent the perforating rule from cutting the rollers. A sheet metal plate is then placed over the platen. It serves as a cutting surface. Grippers may be used to prevent the paper from sticking to the perforating rule after the impression.

Perforating may also be done on some offset duplicators with the same attachment as that used for scoring. As the paper feeds out of the delivery end, a perforating wheel cuts in the direction the sheet is moving. The perforating wheel runs between two wheels (form rollers) that provide a cutting surface, Fig. 12-3.

Many folding machines may also be equipped with perforating wheels. The folds in sheets are sometimes perforated to allow trapped air to escape. This will prevent wrinkles when the sheet is folded.

SLITTING

Slitting is the operation of cutting a sheet into two pieces. As a sheet is delivered by the offset duplicator, it is cut by a slitting wheel that runs between two rollers, Fig. 12-4. Slitting may also be done on some folding machines.

DIE CUTTING

Die cutting is the process used for cutting paper to regular and irregular designs. It is basically a letterpress operation.

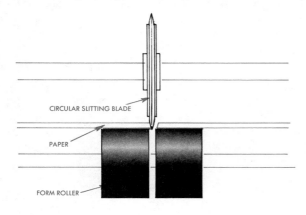

Fig. 12-4. Offset slitting wheel

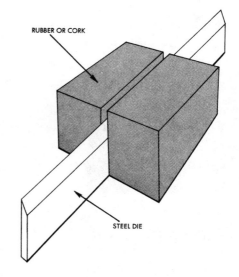

Fig. 12-5. Die cutter

The die is made by forming the steel cutting rule into the desired shape and mounting it on a wood backing. Sponge rubber or cork that is slightly higher than the cutting rule is glued around the rule. The rubber or cork causes the paper to spring away from the rule after the cut has been made, Fig. 12-5.

For die cutting on the platen press, the die is locked in a chase and placed in the press bed. The rollers are then removed. A piece of sheet metal is placed over the platen to provide a cutting surface.

NUMBERING

Consecutive numbering of tickets or other printed items is done on the letterpress. The numbering machine, Fig. 12-6, is locked in the chase with the type form. As each impression is made, the numbering head presses down to print the number. When the pressure is relaxed, the numbering head rises again and the number is changed. Numbering attachments may also be positioned on some offset duplicators.

EMBOSSING

Embossing, generally considered a letterpress operation, produces a raised design on the paper. In this process, the

Fig. 12-6. Letterpress numbering machine

paper is pressed between the embossing **die** and the **counter** (makeready), Fig. 12-7. The embossing die is usually made of brass or bronze. It has an **intaglio image** that may be produced by hand engraving or etching.

With the die in position in the press bed, the counter is formed by placing soft papier-mâché over the platen. The die is pressed into the papier-mâché. The resulting counter has a relief (raised) image that matches the intaglio (recessed) image of the die. The nonembossing areas are then cut away from the papier-mâché makeready.

Fig. 12-7. Embossing die and counter

Fig. 12-8. General Binding Corporation laminator

LAMINATING

Laminating printed pages, cards, and pictures is one method of protecting their surfaces. The laminator seals material between layers of plastic, Fig. 12-8. Heat and pressure are generally used to bond the plastic to the material being laminated. Sometimes an adhesive is used.

APPLYING GUMMED HOLLAND

Gummed Holland is a cloth tape. It can be used to cover the sewing thread or wire stitching and the back of a book if a soft cover has been specified for the binding. Gummed Holland is available in a wide variety of colors and widths. The application of gummed Holland is done after the binding of the materials.

Select the desired width and color. Cut a piece of gummed Holland that is slightly longer than the book. Using a straightedge, mark the position of the gummed Holland

Fig. 12-9. Attach the gummed Holland to the cover

on the front cover. It should extend the same distance over the front and back covers.

Fig. 12-10. Using a round cornering machine

Fig. 12-11. Paper drill round cornering attachment

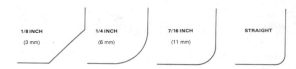

Fig. 12-12. Cuts made with the paper drill cornering attachment

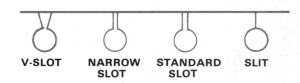

Fig. 12-13. Cuts made with the paper drill slitting and slotting attachment

Moisten the gummed side of the gummed Holland with a damp sponge. Attach it to the front cover, Fig. 12-9. Turn the book over, and stretch the gummed Holland across the back before attaching it to the back cover. Crease the edges to assure good contact. Allow the gummed Holland to dry before trimming the exposed edges.

ROUND CORNERING

Often the specifications for printed products, such as business cards and tickets, require that corners be rounded. Since the usual cutting operations would not round the corners, it must be done as a separate process.

A round cornering machine can round the corners in a variety of radii. This is done by a simple interchange of the cutting edge. The card is placed on the table against two right-angle side guides. The handle is then pressed down and the corner is rounded, Fig. 12-10. The card is then turned and the next corner is rounded. This operation is repeated for each corner.

Round cornering may also be done by using a cornering attachment on the paper drill, Fig. 12-11. (See Unit 55 for operation of the paper drill.) The round cornering attachment can be adjusted to cut round corners of various sizes as well as straight cuts, Fig. 12-12.

Slitting and slotting attachments are also available for some paper drills. A variety of slits and slots can be cut. These may be necessary to permit easy removal and replacement of sheets in loose-leaf binders, Fig. 12-13.

UNIT 52 — TERMS FOR DISCUSSION AND REVIEW

scoring	numbering head
crease	embossing
folding point	embossing die
letterpress	counter
offset	intaglio image
scoring rule	hand engraving
locked	etching
chase	papier-maché
packing	relief
drawsheet	laminating
offset duplicators	adhesive
delivery end	gummed Holland
paper folders	sewing thread
perforating	wire stitching
perforating rule	round cornering
press bed	packaging
platen	distribution
grippers	round cornering
perforating wheel	machine
slitting	radii
die cutting	right angle
die	paper drill
platen press	slotting
numbering	loose-leaf binder
impression	

FOLDING PAPER

One or several folding operations may be involved in preparing a printed product. This depends upon the type of printed product and the number of images printed on the sheet to be folded. In book printing, for instance, a single sheet of paper is printed on both sides with several pages on each side. The folding operation folds the sheet into a **signature**, Fig. 12-14.

Fig. 12-14. A single sheet of paper may be folded to form a signature which is trimmed to make pages

TYPES OF FOLDS

All paper folds may be classified as either (1) **parallel folds** or (2) **right angle folds**. **Parallel folds** are made by folding the paper two or more times in such a way that each fold runs parallel to the others. **Right angle folds** have at least one fold that is at a right angle to the others.

Here are some of the most common folds, Fig. 12-15:

1. The **single fold** may be used wherever a sheet must be folded once. The fold may be made to either equal or unequal page sizes.
2. The **parallel letter fold** is used for folding letters that are to be placed in envelopes for mailing.
3. The **accordian fold**, often used for advertising brochures, is made by a series of parallel folds.
4. The **panel** or **gate fold** is also a parallel fold. It usually has two panels that fold toward each other overlapping the center leaf. Each edge is aligned with the fold line of the opposite panel. This type of fold is often used for a six-page brochure.

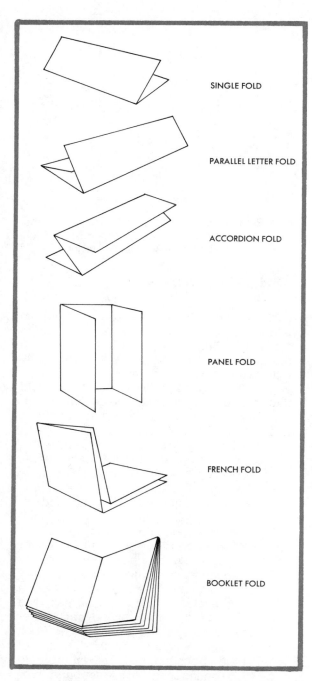

SINGLE FOLD

PARALLEL LETTER FOLD

ACCORDION FOLD

PANEL FOLD

FRENCH FOLD

BOOKLET FOLD

Fig. 12-15. Some of the common paper folds

5. The **French fold** is an example of right angle folding. The sheet is first folded in half on one dimension and then folded a second time at a right angle to the first fold. Announcements and greeting cards are often folded in this manner.
6. The **booklet fold** is used for folding one large sheet of paper into a multipage booklet or signature. A 16-page signature is made by folding a single sheet three times.

TYPES OF FOLDERS

Folding machines are classified as either (1) **knife folders** or (2) **buckle folders**. The **knife folder** uses a thin blade in its folding process. First, a sheet of paper is positioned according to registration guides for accurate folding. Then, the knife folder uses the thin blade to push the paper between the pair of rollers which make the fold, Fig. 12-16.

On the **buckle folder**, the position or location of the fold is determined by the fold plate setting. As the paper is fed into the folder, it passes into the fold plate. When the end of the paper strikes the fold plate stop, the paper buckles at a predetermined point. A pair of fold rollers, which are rotating toward each other, then grasps the paper at the buckle and creases the paper, Fig. 12-17.

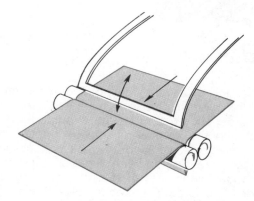

Fig. 12-16. Action of the knife folder

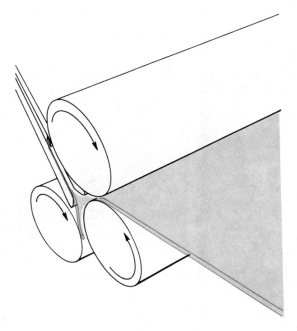

Fig. 12-17. Action of the buckle folder

Paper folders are available in a wide variety of sizes to meet folding needs. The tabletop folder, Fig. 12-18, is limited to single and double parallel folding. Larger folders, Fig. 12-19, are capable of folding 32-page signatures by using a series of parallel and right angle folds.

FOLDER OPERATION

The following description for folder operation applies only to tabletop folders producing a single or double parallel fold, Fig. 12-20. Some folders are equipped with a fold chart which gives the fold plate settings for standard folds. In other cases, the fold plate settings may be determined by measuring the folds. Make the first fold manually. Then measure the distance from the fold to the edge of the paper farthest from the fold. This is the **upper fold plate** setting, Fig. 12-21. Make the second fold, and measure the distance from fold to fold. This is the **lower fold plate** setting, Fig. 12-22.

Fig. 12-18. XHD tabletop folder

Fig. 12-19. Large floor model Baumfolder

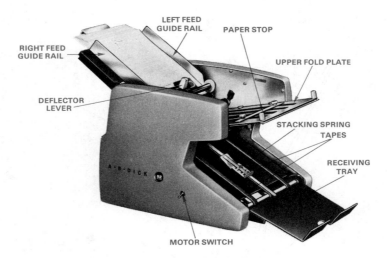

Fig. 12-20. A. B. Dick tabletop paper folder

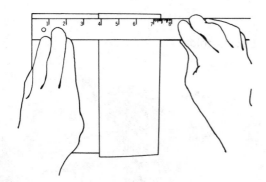

Fig. 12-21. Measure the first fold

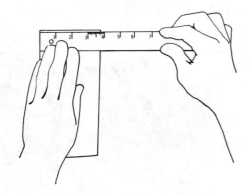

Fig. 12-22. Measure the second fold

To set the upper fold plate, loosen the paper stop knobs. Position the paper stop so the scribe marks align with the first fold dimension. The lower fold plate is set by aligning the lower edge of the paper stop with the dimension of the second fold.

If just one fold is being made, only the upper fold plate is used. Move the **deflector lever** to the **on** position. This prevents the paper from entering the second fold plate. In the **off** position, the paper is allowed to enter the lower fold plate where the second fold is made.

Position the left side guide rail of the feeding table for the width of the paper being folded. Place a single sheet of paper on the feed table against the left guide rail. Move the right guide rail up to the edge of the paper, and then back it off slightly to prevent binding the paper. Align the two guide rollers with the inner edges of the guide rails, Fig. 12-23.

ADJUSTING THE FEEDING SYSTEM

The feeding system must be adjusted for the thickness of the paper being folded. Turn the adjusting knob until a small gap appears between the feed roller and the

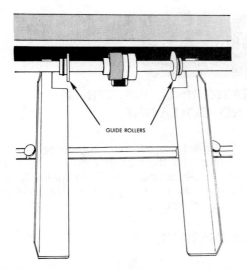

Fig. 12-23. Position the guide rollers

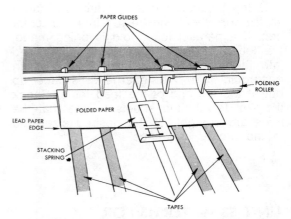

Fig. 12-25. Position the stacking spring and paper guides

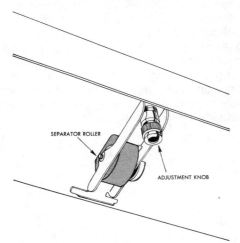

Fig. 12-24. Adjust the feeding system

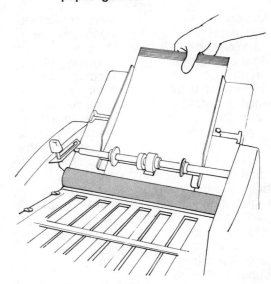

Fig. 12-26. Load the feed table

separator roller, Fig. 12-24. Turn on the folder, and place a single sheet of paper on the feed table between the separator roller and feed roller. Hold the paper between your thumb and finger and turn the adjusting knob until the sheet is pulled from your hand.

Safety Note

Turn the folder to **off** position prior to checking the feeding system further.

After the folder is in the **off** position, check the feeding system by placing a folded sheet on the receiving tray tapes with one edge evenly touching the folding roller, Fig. 12-25. Position the stacking spring in the center of the paper so that the first step is resting on the lead edge of the paper. Position the two outside paper guides about 1″ (25.4 mm) in from the edges of the paper. The other two paper guides should be evenly spaced across the sheet.

Jog the paper to be folded, and fan it so the top sheet will be fed into the folder first. If a parallel letter fold is being made, the letterhead should be face up and fed into the machine first, Fig. 12-26. For an accordian fold, the letterhead is face up but at the tail end of the feed table. Check the first few folded sheets to see that the folds are straight, of the desired size, and in the proper sequence.

UNIT 53 — TERMS FOR DISCUSSION AND REVIEW

folding
signature
parallel fold
right angle fold
single fold
parallel letter fold
accordian fold
panel fold or
   gate fold
French fold
booklet fold
knife folder
buckle folder
registration guides
fold plate
fold plate stop
fold roller
table top folder
upper fold plate

lower fold plate
deflector lever
left side
   guide rail
feeding table
right side
   guide rail
guide rollers
feed roller
adjusting knob
separator roller
receiving
   tray tapes
stacking spring
outside
   paper guides
jog
fan

GATHERING, INSERTING AND COLLATING

Printed pages and signatures must be assembled in their proper sequence before they can be bound. The three methods used for assembly are (1) gathering, (2) inserting, and (3) collating.

GATHERING

Gathering is the process of assembling signatures in proper sequence, one on top of the other, to form a book. In the case of eight-page signatures, the first eight-page signature (pages 1 through 8) is placed on top of the second signature (pages 9 through 16), Fig. 12-27. Gathering is the most commonly used method of assembling book signatures. It may be done either manually or automatically.

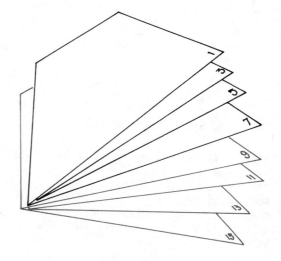

Fig. 12-27. Assemblying signatures in their proper sequence is known as gathering

MANUAL GATHERING

In manual gathering, the various stacks of signatures are placed in proper sequence on long tables. An operator walks along the table, removing one signature from each stack and placing it in assembled order with other signatures. Revolving circular tables may also be used. The table, driven by an electric motor, slowly revolves with the signatures stacked in their proper sequence. As the table turns, the seated operator removes one signature from each stack and assembles the signatures into a book, Fig. 12-28. The use of the revolving table in gathering permits several workers to sit at the table.

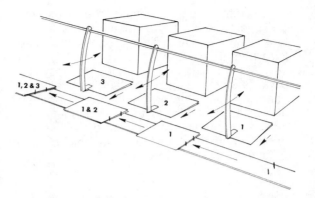

Fig. 12-29. Automatic gathering machine

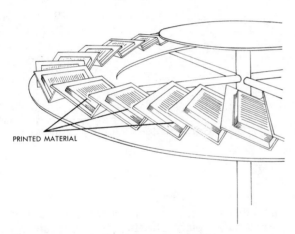

Fig. 12-28. A rotating gathering table

Fig. 12-30. Placing one signature inside another is called inserting

AUTOMATIC GATHERING

Fully automatic gathering machines are used for the assembly of signatures in mass production printing operations. The signatures from each printing are placed in a pocket. (Each pocket holds several signatures.) As the gathering machine advances from one pocket station to the next, a signature from each pocket is fed to a conveyor. One type of feeding mechanism is the **swing arm gathering system**. An arm removes one signature from the bottom of the pocket (so that the pocket can continue

to be loaded from the top) and places it on top of the previously gathered signatures on the conveyor, Fig. 12-29. A signature is deposited on the conveyor at each pocket station every time the machine advances. Once the gathering machine is in full operation, a complete set of signatures is leaving the final pocket with each advance of the machine.

INSERTING

When a product will have a thickness of less than ½″ (13 mm) folded or less than

¼″ (6 mm) open, sometimes the signatures are best assembled by placing one signature inside another. This process is called **inserting**, Fig. 12-30.

As with gathering, inserting may be done either manually or automatically. In hand inserting, the first signature is opened at the center fold and the next signature is inserted. Inserting machines do the same thing automatically. Some machines also bind the inserted signatures.

COLLATING

The operation of arranging individual sheets into sequential order is called **collating**. This form of assembly is used mainly for loose-leaf and mechanical binding. Collating may be done by hand or with the use of machines. In the manual operation, separate piles of each sheet are positioned in sequence along the edge of a table. The operator moves from pile to pile, taking a sheet from each, and stacking the collated material for further processing.

To keep pace with the demands of collating printed materials, several types of collating machines have been developed. Following are descriptions of some of these.

Fig. 12-31. Gathermate-8 electric collator

GATHERMATE 8

The Pitney Bowes Gathermate 8, Fig. 12-31, is a semiautomatic eight-station, tabletop collator. The eight bins or stations allow sets of two to eight sheets to be collated. Each of the eight stations will hold 1¼″ (32 mm) of paper ranging from 5″ x 8″ (127 mm x 203 mm) to 11″ x 17″ (279 mm x 432 mm) in most common weights and finishes.

If more than eight sheets must be collated, the collating must be done in sections. The sections must then be combined or married. For example, if 15 sheets are to be collated, the collating would be done in sections of eight sheets and seven sheets. The two sections would be married to form the finished 15-sheet collated product.

The sheets are placed in the bins in ascending order starting at the top. When activated, the feed roller on top of each of the eight stacks is pushed forward. This movement pushes the top sheet of each stack forward. This permits the operator to remove the collated sheets and stack them in the receiving tray on the front of the machine. When the operator removes the first eight sheets, the machine is automatically activated and the action of the feed rollers begins again. The sections are generally cross-stacked so that later they may be bound or combined with other sections.

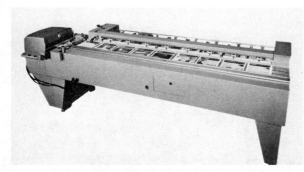

Fig. 12-32. GBC Automatic 8 collator

Fig. 12-33. Thomas Rotomatic 50-station collator

GBC AUTOMATIC 8 COLLATOR

The GBC Automatic 8 Collator, Fig. 12-32, is capable of collating sheets into sets ranging from two to eight pages. A variable speed control can be adjusted to collate between thirty and fifty sets per minute.

The individual page stacks are inserted into the feeding stations in ascending order starting at the delivery end of the collator. During operation, the feed rollers push the top sheet of each stack onto the conveyor. If a sheet is missed or a feeding station runs out of paper, the collator will automatically shut off. The conveyor then delivers the pages to the jogging area. Here, the set is formed and the pages are jogged.

Next, the set may be punched or stapled automatically. The sets are then cross-stacked in the receiving tray.

THOMAS ROTOMATIC

The Thomas Rotomatic 50-station collator and stitcher, Fig. 12-33, can be programmed to collate and stitch any number of sheets up to fifty. It will accommodate sheet sizes ranging from 7¼″ x 8″ (184 mm x 203 mm) to 11″ x 14″ (305 mm x 356 mm). Each bin has a capacity of 1¾″ (44 mm) of paper. Various weights and stock finishes may be collated at one time with no required machine adjustments.

The sheets are placed in the rotary bin in sequential order for collating. The Rotomatic is programmed by a series of push buttons which control the delivery of the paper in each of the sections. Stations may be activated or bypassed by the push-button programming.

During operation, sheets are removed from the bins, collated, and delivered to the automatic jogger-stitcher. The stitcher may also be activated or bypassed automatically by programming. The sections are then stagger-stacked in the delivery tray.

The Rotomatic automatically stops when a sheet is missed or a double sheet is detected. The collating speed may be adjusted to reach a maximum of 25,000 sheets per hour. A running count of the number of collated sets is maintained by a five-digit counter.

DIDDE-GLASER GATHER-ALL

The Didde-Glaser Gather-All collator, Fig. 12-34, combines the operations of collating, stitching, folding, and trimming into one machine. It is primarily designed for book and pamphlet production.

The stacks of individual sheets are first placed into each feeding station. One sheet from each stack is removed as a chain conveyor passes underneath each feeding station. The collated set is then held in register and moved to the center stitching

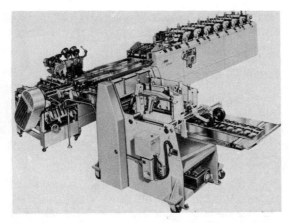

Fig. 12-34. Didde-Glaser Gather-All collator

unit. Here, two wire staples are inserted along the center line of the set. The set is then folded at the center line. The three-knife trimmer trims the three open sides of the book or pamphlet.

UNIT 54 — TERMS FOR DISCUSSION AND REVIEW

signature
assembled
sequence
bound
gathering
inserting
collating
mass production

swing arm
  gathering system
loose-leaf binding
mechanical binding
married
cross-stacked
stitch
rotary bin

UNIT 55

DRILLING PAPER

When a printed product is to have a loose-leaf binding (for instance, if the sheets are to be placed in a ring notebook), holes

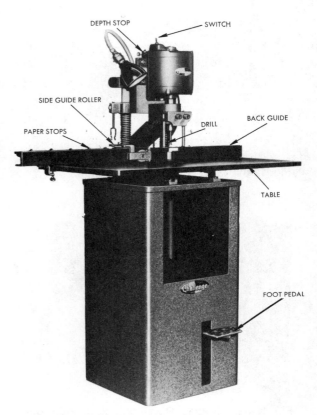

Fig. 12-35. Foot-operated paper drill

are drilled in the paper with a paper drill, Fig. 12-35. This is done on the flat table surface of the drill.

PRINCIPLES OF OPERATION

In the following paragraphs, refer again to Fig. 12-35 for the location of the parts described. The **drill** is a hollow, sharpened tube which rotates during the drilling operation. The round beads drilled from the paper are forced up through the drill and are caught by a receptacle on the back of the paper drill. The diameter of the hole is determined by the size of the drill used. Large paper drills may have more than one drill for gang drilling, Fig. 12-36.

Fig. 12-36. Gang paper drill

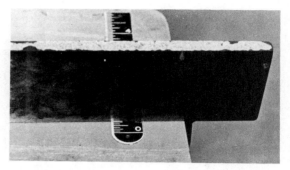

Fig. 12-38. Set the back fence according to the measuring scale on the table

Fig. 12-39. Set the paper stops on the paper stop rod

Fig. 12-37. Replacing the hardwood cutting block

old cutting block is removed by reaching under the table and pushing up on the block. The new cutting block is then placed in the recess.

The **back guide** or **back fence** regulates the drilling location of the holes from the edge of the paper. Adjust it according to the measuring scale on each end of the table, Fig. 12-38. Loosen the thumbscrews on each end of the back guide and slide the guide either toward or away from the drill.

The **paper stops** determine the location of the holes along the edge of the paper. Set the paper stops on the paper stop rod according to the measurement scale, Fig. 12-39.

The **side guide roller** is moved from one stop to the next along the paper stop rod. As the side guide roller makes contact

The **depth stop** regulates the drill's depth of cut. The drill should pass through all the sheets of paper and just make contact with the hardwood **cutting block**. The cutting block is recessed into the surface of the **table** directly under the drill and must be replaced periodically, Fig. 12-37. The

Fig. 12-40. Position the paper against the side guide roller

Fig. 12-42. Waxing the drill

Fig. 12-41. Hand-operated paper drill

with each paper stop, the paper is in position to be drilled, Fig. 12-40.

Depressing the **foot pedal** allows the drill to pass through the paper. Just before the rotating drill makes contact with the paper, the **pressure foot** automatically clamps the paper to the table. Some paper drills are hand-operated. They require the operator to lower the drill to the paper using a hand lever near the top of the machine, Fig. 12-41.

OPERATING THE PAPER DRILL

Safety Note

All adjustments on the paper drill must be made while the machine is turned **off.**

Jog the paper to the side to be drilled, and place it on the table against the back guide and the side guide roller. Most paper drills can easily drill a stack of paper between ½″ (13 mm) and 1″ (25.4 mm) high at one time.

Safety Note

Before operating the paper drill, remove all jewelry, such as rings and watches. Only one person should operate the machine at one time.

Turn on the paper drill, and carefully touch a wax stick to the rotating drill, Fig. 12-42. This will lubricate the drill and prevent burning. The wax stick should be used periodically when a large amount of drilling is done.

With the paper in position and the side guide roller against the first paper stop,

Fig. 12-43. Move the side guide roller and paper to the paper stop when drilling each hole

step down on the foot pedal in one smooth, even motion. When the drill reaches the

bottom of the paper stack, release the pressure, and allow the drill to withdraw slowly from the drilled hole. Move the side guide roller and paper to the next stop, and repeat the drilling operation, Fig. 12-43.

When all the papers have been drilled, turn off the paper drill and remove all scraps of paper.

UNIT 55 — TERMS FOR DISCUSSION AND REVIEW

loose-leaf binding
ring notebook
paper drill
gang drilling
drill
depth stop
cutting block
table

back guide or
   back fence
paper stops
side guide roller
foot pedal
pressure foot
jog
wax stick

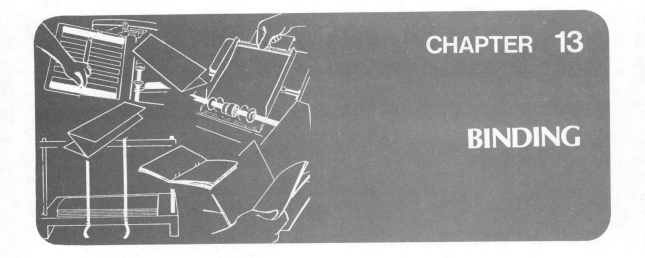

CHAPTER 13

BINDING

Binding is the process of fastening individual sheets or signatures together. There are eight commonly used methods of binding in the graphic communications industry, Fig. 13-1. Seven of these methods are detailed in Unit 56 and include:

1. Saddle sewing.
2. Side sewing.
3. Saddle stitching.
4. Side stitching.
5. Adhesive binding.
6. Mechanical binding.
7. Loose-leaf binding.
8. Smythe sewing. (See Unit 57.)

Each binding method has characteristics that are more suitable than other methods for any given product. The nature and purpose of the product play an important part in the selection of the binding method. The selection of the bindery method is usually decided upon at the message analysis stage of product development.

Before most printed products can be bound, special finishing operations such as (1) scoring, (2) perforating, (3) slitting, (4)

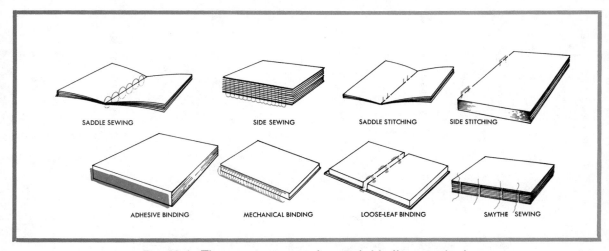

SADDLE SEWING   SIDE SEWING   SADDLE STITCHING   SIDE STITCHING

ADHESIVE BINDING   MECHANICAL BINDING   LOOSE-LEAF BINDING   SMYTHE SEWING

Fig. 13-1. The most commonly used binding methods

die cutting, (5) numbering, (6) embossing, and (7) laminating may have to be performed. Some printed products will not require any of these operations, while other products may require one or more before they can be bound. Unit 52 explains these finishing operations in detail.

In addition, the printed product may require additional prebinding operations such as (1) folding, (2) gathering, (3) inserting, (4) collating, or (5) drilling. Units 53 through 55 describe these fully.

The floor plan for a typical commercial printing firm is shown in Fig. 13-2. Notice the size relationship between the bindery section and the preparatory and presswork departments.

METHODS OF BINDING

After the individual sheets or signatures have been assembled, they are fastened together by binding. There are several different methods, each involving special procedures. The binding method used often depends upon the nature and purpose of the printed material.

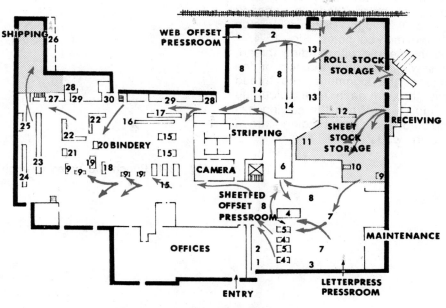

Equipment layout and workflow
Deseret News Press, Salt Lake City, Utah

1—General storage area	13—Pre-web press staging area	24—Mailing machine
2—Ink storage	14—Web offset press	25—Shrink wrapping
3—Perfector press	15—Folder	26—Covered shipping dock
4—One-color press	16—Perfect binder	27—Shipping office
5—Two-color press	17—Hot melt attachment	28—Men
6—Four-color press	18—Paper drill	29—Women
7—Pre-press staging area	19—Three-knife trimmer	30—Bindery office
8—Off-press staging area	20—Sewing machine	
9—Paper cutter	21—Embossing press	
10—Board cutter	22—Stitcher-trimmer	
11—Central stores area	23—Wrapping-packaging tables	
12—Shelves for paper storage		

Fig. 13-2. Floor plan for typical commercial offset-letterpress printing firm

SADDLE SEWING

Saddle sewing is limited to brochures, pamphlets, and other short publications that are made up from one signature. In this method, **binding thread** is sewn through holes punched in the center fold of the signature, Fig. 13-3. The pages lie flat when opened. If a soft paper cover is used, it may be sewn together with the signature pages.

To saddle sew manually, open the signature to the middle of the folded pages, and mark the position for punching the holes. The first holes to be marked should measure ½″ (13 mm) from the top and the bottom edges of the pages. Divide the remaining distance into sections between ⅝″ and 1″ (16 mm and 25.4 mm) apart. Mark the location of all holes. Place the opened signature in a V trough. Using a scratch awl, punch the marked holes, Fig. 13-4.

Thread the needle with binding thread, and begin sewing at either the top or the bottom edge of the signature. The thread should pass through each hole twice, up and down, Fig. 13-5. When the sewing has been completed, pull the binding thread tight and tie the ends.

SIDE SEWING

Side sewing is a method of binding single printed sheets or signatures. In this fastening method, **binding thread** is passed through drilled holes in the binding margin, Fig. 13-6.

Although industrial processes are automated, side sewing can be done in the

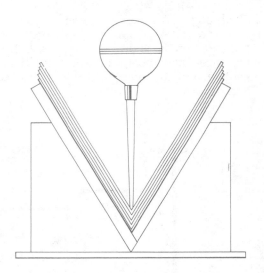

Fig. 13-4. Punch the holes through the center fold

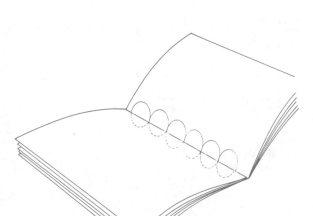

Fig. 13-3. Saddle sewing

Fig. 13-5. Saddle sewing method

school laboratory. Assemble the materials to be side sewn. Place a blank sheet of paper at the front and back of the assembly to protect the pages. (For this illustration, assume that signatures are being bound as a book.) Jog the materials to the binding margin side. Clamp the side opposite the binding margin side with a hand clamp. Place the drill jig in position on the binding vise, and insert the material so that the binding margin side of the paper is even with the top of the drill jig. Place the material so that the holes at the top and bottom ends of the paper will be drilled at equal distances in from the edge, no closer than ½" (13 mm), Fig. 13-7.

Drill 1/16" (2 mm) holes at each point provided on the drill jig, Fig. 13-8. An ordinary hand drill may be used. The holes must extend all the way through the materials to be bound. To prevent damage to the paper, use light drilling pressure and keep the drill turning freely.

After the holes have been drilled, remove the drill jig. Do not remove the drilled materials from the vise. Fold back the two blank protective sheets at the front and the back of the book. Select binding thread that is long enough to completely sew (up and back) the length of the printed material. Begin sewing at either end of the book. Pass the needle through the first hole in the direction it was drilled. Always push the needle in the same direction for each hole, coming across the back each time. Sew from one end of the book to the other. Then return to the starting point where the thread is pulled tight and tied. Tie the loose end, across the back, to the thread first passed through the hole, Fig. 13-9. The sewing should be in a crisscross pattern across the back of the book, Fig. 13-10.

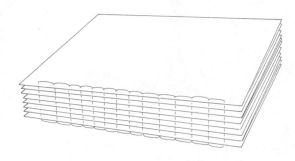

Fig. 13-6. Side sewing

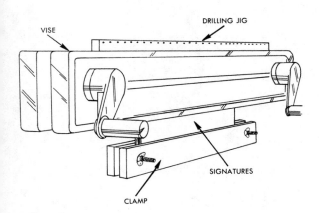

Fig. 13-7. Clamp the assembled signatures in the drilling jig

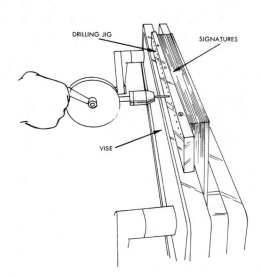

Fig. 13-8. Drilling the holes

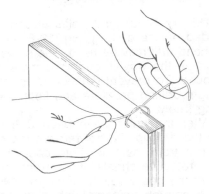

Fig. 13-9. Tie the sewing thread across the back of the book

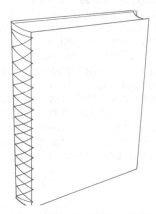

Fig. 13-10. Crisscross pattern of a side sewn book back

Fig. 13-11. Saddle stitching

SADDLE STITCHING

In **saddle stitching, wire staples** are the fastening device. The staples pass from the back side, through the assembled pages at the center fold, Fig. 13-11. The cover can be included in the binding.

The foot-powered stapler, as well as specially designed deep-throat staplers, can be used for saddle stitching, Fig. 13-12.

Fig. 13-12. Foot-powered stapler set for saddle stitching

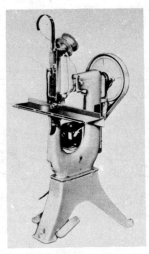

Fig. 13-13. Bostitch 19E stitcher

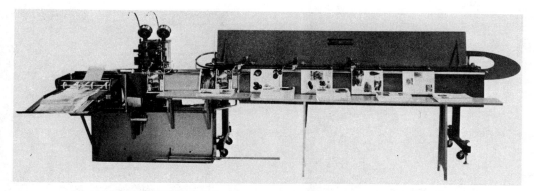

Fig. 13-14. Rosback Auto-Stitcher and Gathering Saddle

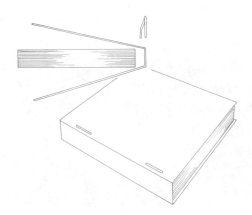

Fig. 13-15. Side stitching

Some stitchers form their own staples using a continuous wire roll, Fig. 13-13. Saddle stitching may also be done on large machines that assemble and stitch the folded sheets, Fig. 13-14.

Saddle stitching is used for short publications that must lie flat when opened, such as brochures and some magazines. A binding margin of at least ½" (13 mm) is required. Saddle stitching should not be used for printed materials with more than 140 pages (70 sheets).

SIDE STITCHING

The **side stitching** method of fastening is generally used for binding single printed pages where no fold is required. A **wire staple** passes through the pages in the binding margin on the left side, Fig. 13-15. The binding margin should be at least ¾" (19 mm). Materials fastened by side stitching have a tendency to close if they are not held open.

The foot-powered stapler can be used for side stitching by adjusting the position of the stapling saddle, Fig. 13-16. Some collators, as well as other machines, automatically side stitch materials as they are assembled.

Fig. 13-16. Foot-powered stapler set for side stitching

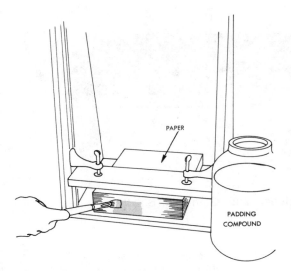

Fig. 13-17. Applying padding compound to form an adhesive binding

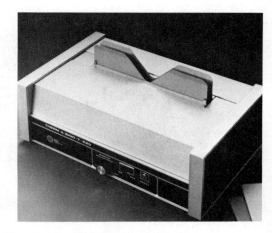

Fig. 13-18. GBC Therm-A-Bind

ADHESIVE BINDING

Adhesive binding, sometimes referred to as **perfect binding**, is used for such graphic products as telephone books, catalogs, and some magazines. The pages to be bound by an **adhesive** must be jogged to the binding edge. If there are folded pages along the binding edge, the folds must be trimmed off to expose the back edge of each sheet to the adhesive since no sewing or stitching is used. The jogged pages are then clamped or weighted and the adhesive is applied, Fig. 13-17. A piece of **super**, which is an open-weave, gauze-like cloth, can be imbedded in the adhesive along the binding edge to give added strength. A second coat of adhesive is then applied. A cover may also be attached by pressing it against adhesive that is still wet. After drying, the three remaining edges may be trimmed on the paper cutter.

Adhesive binding is an inexpensive fastening method. It is used for such items as notepads and school tablets so that sheets can be easily removed. Adhesive-bound pages lie flat when opened.

Fig. 13-19. Punching operation for **plastic** comb binding

The GBC Therm-A-Bind, Fig. 13-18, uses heat to adhesive bind materials and apply a wraparound cover in the same operation. The sheets are first assembled in their proper order and jogged to the binding edge. They are then placed in a cover which has adhesive material on the backbone. The sheets inside the cover are placed in the Therm-A-Bind. Heat causes the adhesive to soften, and the sheets become attached to the cover. A secure bond between the binding edges of the sheets and the backbone of the cover forms as the adhesive cools.

Fig. 13-20. Inserting the pages in the expanded plastic comb binder

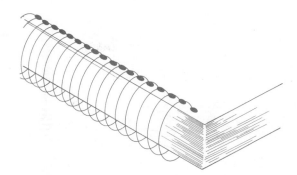

Fig. 13-21. Wire spiral binding

MECHANICAL BINDING

Mechanical binding is another method of fastening individual sheets together. The two most commonly used methods of mechanical binding are (1) the plastic comb binder and (2) the wire spiral binder.

In the **plastic comb binding** method, the pages are first punched a few sheets at a time, Fig. 13-19. The comb is then placed over fingers and separated so that the sheets may be placed over the comb tongues, Fig. 13-20. When all of the pages have been placed in it, the comb is allowed to close by releasing the tension. The comb, with the pages, is then removed from the fingers.

Plastic combs are available in a variety of colors and in sizes from 3/16″ to 2″ (5 mm to 51 mm) in diameter. Plastic comb bindings are used on manuals and catalogs. The pages lie flat when they are opened.

Wire spiral binding is done by threading a continuous coil of wire through holes that are punched in the binding margin, Fig. 13-21. Mechanical bindings do not permit the addition of pages.

LOOSE-LEAF BINDING

Loose-leaf binding methods permit the addition or removal of pages because the binding device can easily be opened

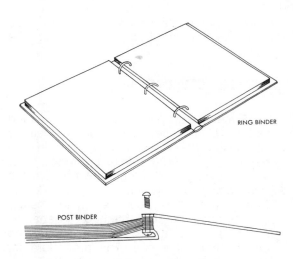

RING BINDER

POST BINDER

Fig. 13-22. Loose-leaf binding methods

and closed. The two commonly used loose-leaf binding methods are (1) the post binder and (2) the ring binder, Fig. 13-22.

The **binding posts** have a screw thread. They are inserted through holes drilled in the binding margin of the paper. Binding posts are available in a variety of lengths, making it possible to bind any number of pages. Pages fastened together by binding posts have a tendency to close when not held open.

Ring binders are used on standard notebooks. The sheets are drilled where needed to fit the rings of the binder. Ring binders have two, three, or more **rings**. The

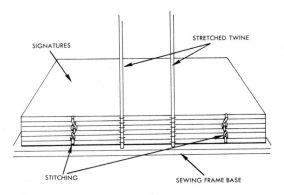

SIGNATURES

STRETCHED TWINE

STITCHING

SEWING FRAME BASE

Fig. 13-23. Smythe sewn book

drilled paper is placed on the binding rings which are snapped closed to hold the sheets.

SMYTHE SEWING

Smythe sewing is a binding method used to saddle sew individual signatures and to sew the signatures together in one operation, Fig. 13-23. It is also referred to as **center sewing** and **loom sewing**. Smythe sewn book pages lie flat when opened. The **binding thread** may be seen in the center of each signature. This method is generally used in the production of a hard covered book such as this one. The procedure for Smythe sewing is described in Unit 57.

UNIT 56 — TERMS FOR DISCUSSION AND REVIEW

signature
assembled
binding
saddle sewing
binding thread
V trough
scratch awl
side sewing
binding margin
jog
hand clamp

stitches
wire roll
side stitching
stapling saddle
collator
adhesive binding
perfect binding
super
backbone
mechanical
    binding

drill jig
binding vise
hand drill
back
crisscross
saddle stitching
wire staple
center fold
foot-powered
    stapler
deep-throat
    stapler

plastic comb
    binder
wire spiral
    binder
loose-leaf
    binding
binding post
ring binder
drilled
Smythe sewing
center sewing
loom sewing

UNIT 57

HAND CASING A BOOK

To hand case a book, first assemble the individual signatures in their proper sequence so that they may be fastened together. The Smythe sewing method is generally used because in one operation the individual signatures are saddle sewn and the signatures are sewn together.

Place a piece of **binder's board** on the top and the bottom of the assembled signatures. Jog the signatures and the binder's board to the top and back of the book. With the top and the back edges held flush, insert the signatures and the binder's board into the **binder clamp**. Allow the back edge to extend about ½" (13 mm) above the clamp. Tighten the clamp to hold the book securely in position.

Measure in 1" (25.4 mm) from the top and bottom of the book. Using a T-square, draw a line across the back at both points, Fig. 13-24. Divide the remaining distance between these two marks into three **equal** sections, and draw two additional lines across the back of the book. (If the book is over 10" (254 mm) in length, the distance should be divided into four equal sections.)

Cut a **saw kerf** at each end of the four lines across the back. A back saw may be used, Fig. 13-25. The saw kerfs should be just deep enough to cut through the inner-most center fold of each signature.

Remove the signatures and binder's board from the clamp, and place the **last** signature in the center of the base of the sewing frame. Stretch two pieces of soft twine between the base and the horizontal support at the top of the sewing frame. Be certain it is in line with the two center saw kerfs, Fig. 13-26.

Thread a needle with the binding thread, and begin sewing at the saw kerf nearest the **bottom** of the signature. This kerf is known as the "bottom kettle stitch kerf." Insert the needle from the back of the signature so that it comes out in the center fold. Leave 2″ to 3″ (51 mm to 76 mm) of thread extending out of the kerf. Follow the center fold of the signature to the first twine cord. Pass the needle out through the signature, around the cord, and back to the inside of the signature. Following the center fold, sew around the second twine cord and bring the needle out of the back edge at the kerf nearest the top of the signature, the "top kettle stitch kerf," Fig. 13-27.

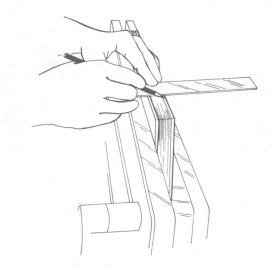

Fig. 13-24. Mark the position for cutting the kerfs

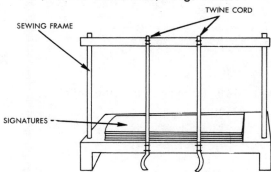

Fig. 13-26. The twine is stretched so that it is aligned with the two center kerfs

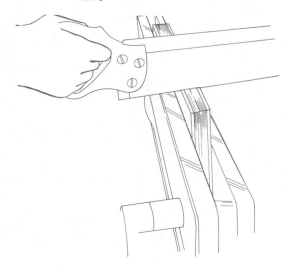

Fig. 13-25. Cut the kerfs in the back of the book

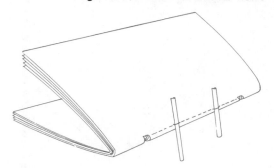

Fig. 13-27. Sewing the signature in the sewing frame

The next to the last signature is placed on top of the last signature in the sewing frame. When adding signatures, be sure the heading of each signature is at the same end. Pass the needle through the back of the second signature and repeat the sewing operation. At the bottom kettle stitch kerf, pull the thread tight and tie the loose end so that the two signatures are held together.

Position the third signature, and follow the same sewing procedure as used for the first two. Bring the needle out the back of the signature at the top kettle stitch kerf. Use the **kettle stitch** to tie the signatures together at both the top and the bottom kerfs. It is made by passing the needle under the thread, between the two previous-ly sewn signatures at the kerf, before starting to sew the next signature, Fig. 13-28. Continue to sew the remaining signatures. Cut the thread after the kettle stitch has been made for the last signature.

To remove the Smythe sewn book from the sewing frame, cut the twine cord. Leave a length of approximately 1″ (25.4 mm) of each cord extending beyond the front and back of the book, Fig. 13-29.

After the twine has been trimmed, place the book in a vise so that the kettle-stitched edge is flush with the jaws. The twine should not be clamped in the vise. To protect the book pages, the vise jaws should be lined with pieces of binder's board. Apply a thin coat of padding compound (adhesive) to the back of the book, Fig. 13-30. This provides added strength and bonds the sewing thread to the back of the book.

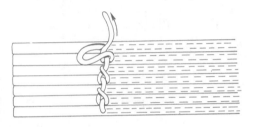

Fig. 13-28. Forming the kettle stitch

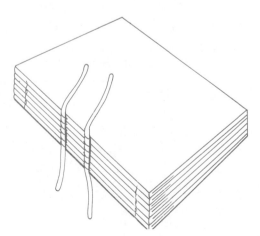

Fig. 13-29. Cut the twine cord, and remove the book from the frame

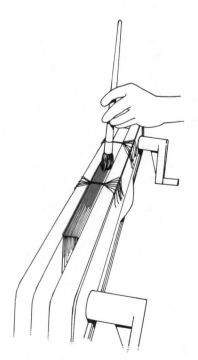

Fig. 13-30. Coat the book back with padding compound

ENDSHEETS

The paper used for endsheets generally is heavier than that used for the book pages. Each of the two endsheets is folded in half. One half is attached to the inside of either the front or back cover. The other half is glued to the respective front or back page of the book by a narrow strip of glue adjacent to the fold. Each endsheet, when folded in half, should be the same size as a page of the book.

DECORATING THE ENDSHEETS

The endsheets in some books are plain, unprinted paper, while others may have a decorative pattern. One method of producing a freely created pattern of colors on endsheets is by a process known as **marbelizing.**

To marbelize paper, fill a shallow tray with about 1″ (25.4 mm) of water. In a separate container, dissolve printer's ink in solvent. (A separate container must be used for each color of ink.) Using a small spatula, drop small quantities of the dissolved ink on the surface of the water, Fig. 13-31. The ink and the solvent mixture will float on the surface. Several different colors may be used at one time to produce a variety of color patterns.

When the paper is placed on the surface of the water, the ink pattern is transferred to the paper. To vary the pattern and to blend or intermix color areas, the surface may be combed using a wooden stick with a row of protruding finishing nails, Fig. 13-32.

As each sheet is removed from the tray, place it on a layer of newspaper to absorb the water. Do not stack the marbelized sheets because the wet ink will cause the sheets to stick together.

A fresh supply of ink must be placed on the surface of the water with each sheet being dipped. To clean the water when another color is desired, draw an absorbent paper, such as a paper towel, over the water to pick up the remaining ink. When dry, the sheets may be pressed by placing them between two sheets of kraft paper and using a warm clothes iron.

APPLYING THE ENDSHEETS

Fold the selected endsheet paper in half. Place a sheet of paper or cardboard

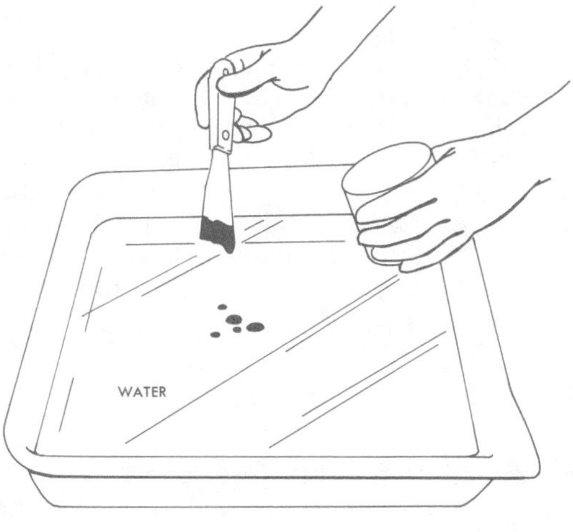

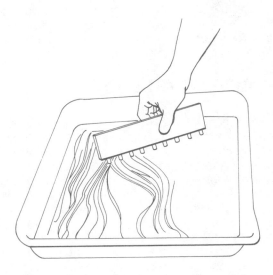

Fig. 13-31. Drop the dissolved ink on the surface of the water

Fig. 13-32. Comb the surface to develop ink patterns

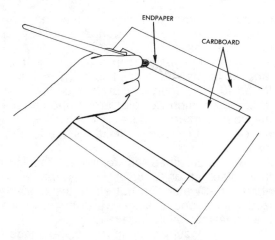

Fig. 13-33. Apply glue to the endsheets

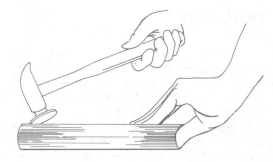

Fig. 13-34. Rounding the bound book edge

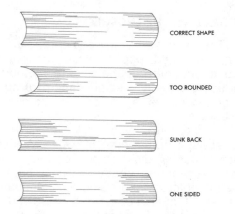

Fig. 13-35. The book back should be rounded to a slight curve

over the endsheet so only the ¼″ (6 mm) portion to receive the glue is exposed. Apply glue to this exposed folded edge of the endsheet, Fig. 13-33. Attach the endsheet to the **first page** of the bound book so that it is flush with the book back. Do not glue the ends of the cord under the endsheet. Repeat the same procedure for the second endsheet, applying it to the **last page** of the bound book.

Allow the glue to dry. Then trim the three unbound book edges beginning with the fore edge (opposite the bound edge). Trim the bottom edge next, and the top last.

ROUNDING THE BOOK

The thickness of the binding thread creates a swelling at the back of the book. To make up for this, the back is rounded. The process of rounding the book gives a slight concave shaping of the fore edge. The backs of books that have been bound by side stitching, saddle stitching, side sewing, or saddle sewing should not be rounded.

Place the book to be rounded on the flat surface of a workbench. Press the fore edge with the thumb in approximately the center. At the same time, pull the side of

the book with the fingers, Fig. 13-34. Using a backing hammer, gently tap the back edge into shape. Turn the book over and repeat this process. To make an evenly rounded back, the rounding operation should be done gradually. It may be necessary to turn the book over several times. Only a slight curve or round is necessary, Fig. 13-35.

BACKING THE BOOK

Backing the book is a process that helps provide for the flexibility of the book and the permanence of the rounded back. In this operation, a groove is formed along the spine on both the front and back sides

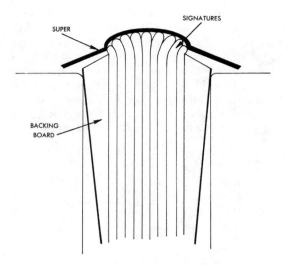

Fig. 13-36. Position of the bound signatures for backing

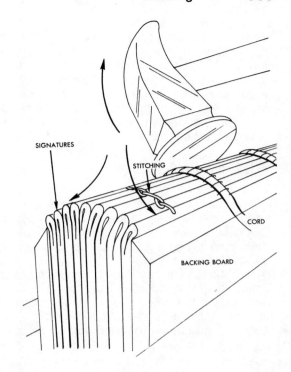

Fig. 13-37. Backing a book

Fig. 13-38. Position the headbands

of the book. Also, the rounded back is further shaped to permit fitting the binder's board which is used for the cover.

Place the rounded book between backing boards with the rounded back pointing up, Fig. 13-36. Leave the back edge extending above the top edge of the backing boards from $\frac{3}{16}''$ to $\frac{1}{4}''$ (5 mm to 6 mm), depending upon the size of the book and the thickness of the binder's board to be used for the cover.

Begin backing the book by striking glancing blows with a backing hammer. Work from the center of the back out toward each side along the full length of the book so that the back edge is forced out over the backing boards, Fig. 13-37.

ATTACHING SUPER AND HEADBANDS

After completing the backing operation, apply a coat of padding cement to the back. Cut a piece of **super** about $\frac{1}{2}''$ (13 mm) shorter than the book, but wide enough to extend over both edges $1\frac{1}{2}''$ (38 mm). (Super is an open-weave cloth that will give added strength to the back.) While the padding cement is still wet, position the super in the center of the back.

Headbands are pieces of cloth that are fastened to the back. They serve only to improve the appearance of the finished book. From the headband material, cut two pieces that are exactly the same width as the book and about ½" (13 mm) long. Position the headbands in the still wet padding cement so that the colored or finished edges are facing the fore edge of the book, Fig. 13-38. Allow the padding cement to dry. Then apply a second coat over the super and headbands.

FULL CASINGS

A book casing is made by folding covering material over binder's board covers. Begin by measuring the size of the book to determine the size of the binder's board to be cut for the cover. The length of the binder's board is obtained by measuring the actual length of the book from top to bottom and adding the amount of overhang desired at both the top and bottom. In some instances, the amount of overhang on each of the three exposed edges of the book is equal to the thickness of the binder's board being used. However, the standard overhang is ⅛" (3 mm) on each edge, Fig. 13-39. Cut two pieces of binder's board to exactly the same length.

Determine the width of the binder's board by measuring the distance from the groove formed by backing to the fore edge of the sheet. Cut one piece of binder's board to this width, and label it "front." Repeat the same procedure for the back cover binder's board and label it "back." Both covers should be the same width. (If the book has not been backed, subtract ⅛" (3 mm) from

Fig. 13-40. Measure the distance across the back of the book

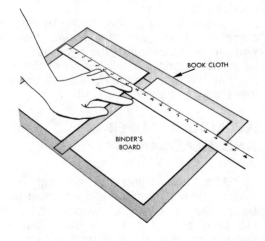

Fig. 13-41. Position the binder's boards on the covering material

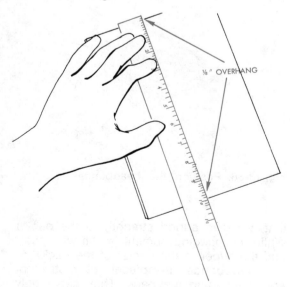

⅛" OVERHANG

Fig. 13-39. Measure the book to determine the size of the cover (⅛" = 3 mm)

the actual width when measured from the back to the fore edge.) When the covers are pulled over the fore edge to form the overhang, the joint along the back of the book will be formed.

Now measure the distance around the back of the book. Place both the front and back binder's board covers on the book so they are tightly secured against the groove. Wrap a strip of paper about 1″ (25.4 mm) wide around the back. Mark the paper at the point where it meets the binder's board on both the front and the back, Fig. 13-40. This is the **lining strip** dimension. Cut a piece of binder's board equal to this size. It will be used only temporarily to guide the positioning of the front and back covers.

Measure the width and length of the three pieces of binder's board: **front cover**, **lining strip**, and **back cover**. Cut a piece of covering material that is 2″ (51 mm) wider and 2″ (51 mm) longer than the width and length of these combined pieces.

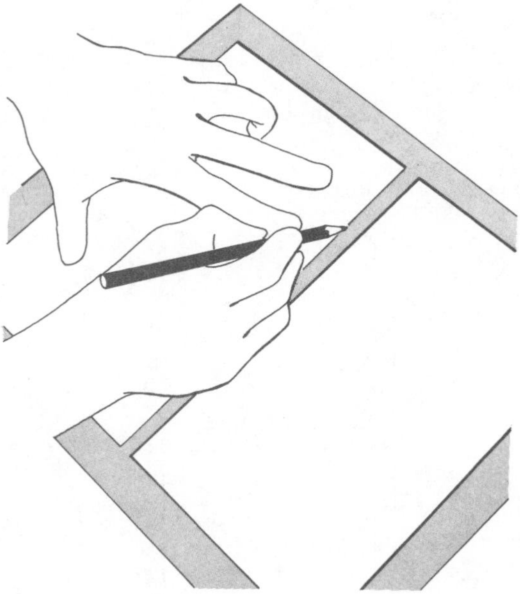

Position the three pieces of binder's board on the back of the covering material allowing a 1″ (25.4 mm) margin on each of the four sides, Fig. 13-41. Carefully remove the lining strip. It is no longer needed.

Some book casings, as in the case of loose-leaf notebooks, are made with a binder's board strip that **does** run up the back of the book. The width of this strip is determined by measuring the width of the back plus the width of the two covers. A 5/16″ (8 mm) space must be left between each cover and the strip for the back, to allow for the hinge joint. The spring binding rings are riveted into the back strip.

Outline the front and back covers (and back strip, if used) on the back of the covering material with a pencil, Fig. 13-42.

Two types of corners may be formed when the covering material is folded over the covers: (1) the nicked corner and (2) the library corner. For a **nicked corner**, mark the four corners of the covering material at 45° angles about ⅜″ (10 mm) away from the corner of the binder's board. Trim off the corners, Fig. 13-43. The **library corner** requires no trimming, but tends to be more bulky than the nicked corner.

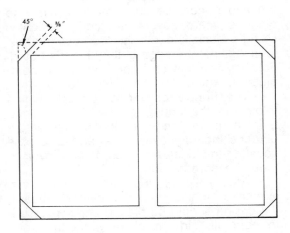

Fig. 13-42. Outline the binder's board location on the covering material

Fig. 13-43. Trim the corners at 45° angles when making the nicked corner (⅜″ = 10 mm)

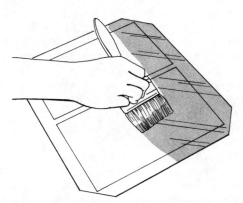

Fig. 13-44. Spread the paste over the back (inside) of the covering material

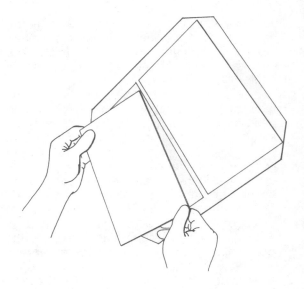

Fig. 13-45. Position the binder's board on the covering material

To affix the covering material to the binder's board covers, place the covering material on several layers of newspaper on a flat surface. Apply bookbinding paste to the back (inside) surface, Fig. 13-44. Cover the entire area, being careful not to leave any lumps of paste.

Using the pencil marks as guides, place the front and back binder's board covers in position, Fig. 13-45. (If a backing strip is used, it should also be positioned at this time.)

To form the **nicked corner**, fold the top and bottom covering material over the binder's board covers, stretching it tightly. Using a bone folder, push the covering material against the edge of the binder's board. Fold in the edge covering material to complete the nicked corner, Fig. 13-46.

The **library corner** is formed by first folding in the corner of the covering material at a 45° angle to the corner of the binder's board cover. The edges of the covering material are then folded over to form the corners, Fig. 13-47.

After the covering material has been stretched tightly over the binder's board, the casing should be placed under pressure to hold all folds in place while the book binding paste is drying.

The completed casing may now be printed by hot stamping or screen process

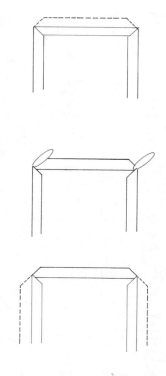

Fig. 13-46. Forming a nicked corner

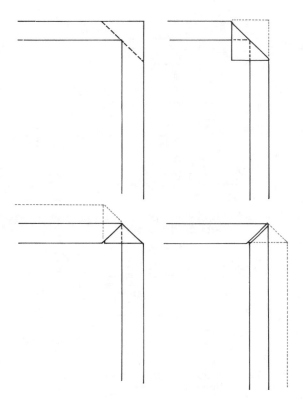

Fig. 13-47. Forming a library corner

Fig. 13-48. Hot stamping press

printing. (Screen process printing was presented in Chapter 7 and the units that follow it.)

HOT STAMPING THE CASING

Hot stamping is a process that uses foil of various colors to transfer type on die images to wood, plastic, paper, cloth, and leather surfaces by means of heat and pressure. The process is used not only for decorating book covers but on napkins, stationery, key cases, billfolds, playing cards, and for imprinting on luggage and briefcases as well.

The three fundamentals of hot stamping are (1) **heat,** (2) **pressure,** and (3) **dwell.** The hot stamping press, Fig. 13-48, has an electrical circuit which heats the type. The heated type melts the foil as **downward pressure** is applied to the material being stamped. The length of **time** the hot type and foil are in contact with the material is referred to as "dwell."

The image that is to be imprinted may be composed by hand-set type. Linotype and Ludlow slugs, as well as solid brass dies, may be used. Brass type is recommended for all-around stamping, since it has long-wearing qualities and works equally well on both soft and hard materials. Standard lead type may also be used. However, after use, it is unsatisfactory for other purposes.

Compose the necessary type in a composing stick with a slug on each side of the line or lines. Transfer the composed type to the center of the typeholder with the nicks pointing up. Using the tilt lock handle, lower the pallet so that the face of the type is pointing toward the base of the press. Lock the pallet in position.

Select the desired color and width of foil to be used. Place it on the spindle on the left side of the press. The foil should be ¼″ (6 mm) wider than the point size of the type being used. Feed the foil, bright side up, through the guides, under the type, and between the rollers on the right-hand side of the press.

Place the material to be stamped on the bed of the press, using the horizontal guidelines for positioning. Adjust the guides to assure positioning accuracy.

Turn on the electrical switch, and allow the type to heat for 10 minutes. Many hot stamping presses have a low, medium, and high temperature. A medium temperature of 250° F (121° C) is recommended for general-purpose stamping. Several test stampings should be made to check positioning, the amount of pressure necessary, and the length of time the type should be held in contact with the material. The test stamping should be done on scraps of the same material as that to be stamped.

When the best pressure and dwell have been decided on, place the material to be stamped in position, and bring down the handle of the press. Without moving the material, check the foil deposit. If inadequate, repeat the stamping operation. Advance the foil before making each successive imprint.

At the completion of the stamping operation, clean the typeface with a soft cloth while the type is still hot. Turn off the press, and allow the type to cool before it is distributed.

CASING IN A BOOK

"Casing in" a book is the process of **fastening the casing to the book.** Begin by placing the casing around the book to be sure it fits properly. Fold the covering around the back and into the backing grooves. Align the overhang on the three exposed edges. Place the opened casing (with the book still in the fitted position) on a flat surface. Fray the ends of the cord, and fan them out over the endsheets. Fold

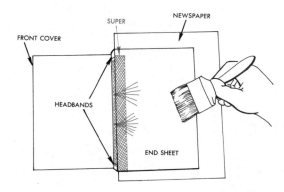

Fig. 13-49. Applying paste to the book to attach the cover

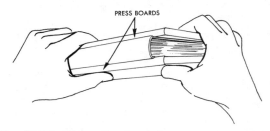

Fig. 13-50. Place the book between two press boards for pressing

the super over the frayed ends. Before applying the paste, slip a sheet of newspaper under the endsheet to protect the book pages. Apply a coat of paste over the super, frayed cord ends, and entire area of the endsheet, Fig. 13-49. Remove the newspaper and close the cover, making contact at the hinge end first. Turn the book over and repeat this process for attaching the back endsheet to the back cover.

After the endsheets have been glued, the book must be **pressed.** Insert a sheet of wax paper between each endsheet and the book. Place the book between two press boards that are larger than the book. The rounded edge of each press board should be fitted into the grooves on the front and back covers, Fig. 13-50. Place the book and the press boards under pressure in a standing press for as long as 24 hours if possible. After pressing, remove the wax paper sheets, and clean off any excess glue.

UNIT 57—TERMS FOR DISCUSSION AND REVIEW

hand casing
assemble
signatures
sequence
Smythe sewing
saddle sewing
binder's board
jog
binder clamp
T-square
saw kerf
back saw
sewing frame

backing hammer
backing
groove
super
headbands
padding cement
book casing
lining strip
loose-leaf binder
nicked corner
library corner
book binding
    paste

binding thread
bottom kettle
    stitch kerf
top kettle
    stitch kerf
kettle stitch
padding compound
endsheets
marbelizing
printer's ink
solvent
spatula
fore edge
rounded (rounding)
concave
side stitching
side sewing

hot stamping
screen process
    printing
dwell
hot stamping
    press
handset type
foil
Linotype
Ludlow
brass type
composing stick
slug
typeholder
nicks
casing in

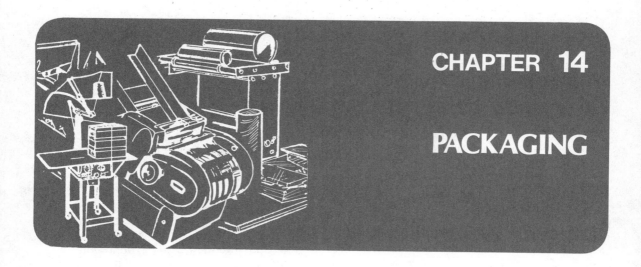

CHAPTER 14

PACKAGING

Graphic communications are packaged in a variety of ways for distribution to the message receiver. The packaging technique must be suited to the product, and is generally considered during the message analysis stage of product development.

A large proportion of the printed communication products are distributed by direct mail — that is, by the postal service. Products to be distributed by direct mail may be packaged in several ways. Large companies, for instance, often employ automatic folding and inserting machines for the distribution of such products as advertising pamphlets, flyers, and invoices, Fig. 14-1.

Fig. 14-1. Model 3300-FH folding and inserting machine

The Addresser Printer for addressing envelopes, Fig. 14-2, is often employed by large companies which distribute graphic communications by mail; it proves to be particularly valuable when the mailing list remains constant for each mailing. Individual embossed data plates contain the name and address of each message receiver. The data plates are inserted into a feed hopper and feed automatically to the print station where the address is printed on the product. After printing, the plate is ejected into a receiving stacker.

The automatic mail inserting machine relieves the time-consuming task of collating and inserting products into envelopes for mailing. The machine shown in Fig. 14-3 automatically collates and inserts printed products into envelopes from up to six insert feeders. This machine can also seal the envelopes and stamp them with postal charges.

Gummed address labels are sometimes applied to products to be distributed by direct mail. As the printed communication is fed into the machine, prepared gummed address labels are stripped from their backing and applied to the product, Fig. 14-4.

Periodical publications (such as magazines) may be prepared for distribution by direct mail by the simple application of a gummed address label. Some publications, however, are packaged in a wrapped band before they are addressed and mailed, Fig. 14-5.

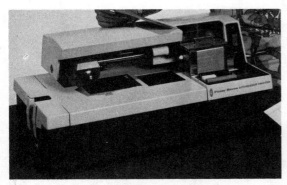

Fig. 14-2. Model 7200 Addresser Printer

Fig. 14-4. Multimatic automatic label applicator

Fig. 14-3. Model 3130 automatic inserter

Fig. 14-5. Direct mail magazine packaging

Printed products, as well as other types of products, may be packaged in a plastic film. The product is simply wrapped with plastic which conforms to the size and shape of the product. Once the plastic has been tightly stretched, heat is applied which seals the plastic wrapping, Fig. 14-6. If a plastic-wrapped product is to be distributed by direct mail, the plastic used must be strong enough to withstand handling without tearing; the address label generally is placed underneath the plastic coating since the packaging is waterproof.

In the shrink packaging system, a transparent film medium is wrapped around the product and then heated. With the application of heat, the film shrinks and conforms to the exact size and shape of the product, Fig. 14-7. Shrink packaging, which can be used for packaging printed products as well as many other manufactured products, provides a durable, protected package, while permitting the product to be seen.

Another packaging technique is to insert and seal the printed communication products in bags. This also provides a protective coating and permits the product to be easily viewed by the prospective customer, Fig. 14-8.

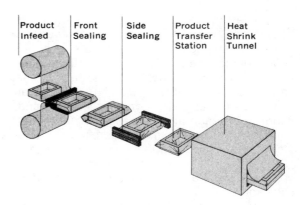

Fig. 14-7. How shrink packaging works

Fig. 14-6. Plastic film packaging

Fig. 14-8. Plastic bag packaging

Printed products such as newspapers are often tied in bundles for distribution to central locations and further distribution.

Fig. 14-9. Model F-16 Pak-Tyer

The automatic Pak-Tyer, Fig. 14-9, can be used not only for tying printed products, but also any size and shape of bundle, box, or package including those for cut flowers, vegetables, fabrics, and laundry.

Specially constructed boxes and cartons are also employed for packaging printed products, Fig. 14-10.

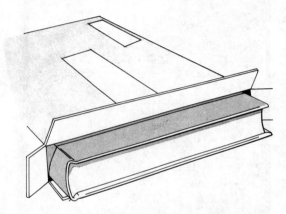

Fig. 14-10. Packaging of single copies of books

SECTION VI

OVERVIEW

Throughout this textbook we have seen how the graphic communications industry functions from the original need to communicate to the distribution of the finished product. We have studied the areas of Design, Character Generation, Preproduction and Production, and Bindery, Finishing, and Product Distribution.

Graphic communications' plants range in size from the very small to the very large which employ many people. The following are only a sampling of career opportunities in the field of graphic communications.

Sales
Management
Personnel
Ink manufacturing
Paper manufacturing
Production
Layout
Technical illustrating
Secretary
Telephone operator
Accountants
Research personnel
Marketing
Professional photographers
Conservation management —
    forrest service
Teachers
Editors
Science — research, chemistry

CHAPTER 15

INTRODUCTION TO GRAPHIC COMMUNICATION CAREERS

"While students are in high school," Mr. Jackson said to his class, "they should select subjects that will help them develop some knowledge and skills to prepare them for the world of work. This is an important part of career planning. Do any of you have an idea of what you'd like to do? You know, you'll have over 40 years of working life after high school."

The class moaned.

"John? What subjects do you want to take while in high school?"

John replied with hesitancy, "I don't know. Business courses, I guess."

"Why business courses, John?"

"Oh, my father owns an insurance agency. He thinks this would be a good place for me to work after I graduate."

"You don't sound very happy about it," said Mr. Jackson. "Is that what you really want to do?"

John's face brightened. "What I really like is photography. I'm good at it, too. But you can't make much of a living at that."

Mr. Jackson turned to the class. "What do you think? Do you have any advice for John?"

Tom raised his hand. "I think John is crazy not to want to go in with his dad. What a set-up! I wish my father had a business waiting for me."

"I don't agree," said Mary. "It's more important to like what you do. Work should be what you like, not what you have to do. I don't think John should go into business with his father if he doesn't want to."

Bob raised his hand. "I think it's possible to do what you enjoy and still make a good living," he said. "John, have you looked into the opportunities in photography?"

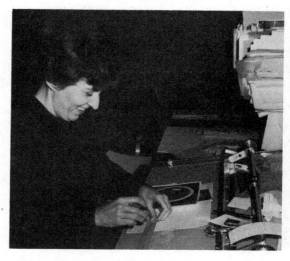

Fig. 15-1. "Work should be what you like, not what you have to do."

Fig. 15-2. It took years of careful planning to construct this rocket. It takes planning to construct a career, too.

Fig. 15-3. Each person is unique in interests, needs, and abilities.

"Well, not really," John replied.

"That's one of the three steps in good career planning," said Mr. Jackson.

"I've never heard of them," said John. "What are they?"

"The three steps are knowledge of self, knowledge of career opportunities, and testing," said Mr. Jackson.

"How do they work?"

"Well, first you must know **yourself.** You must know what kind of a person you are, what you like, what you don't like. John, you enjoy photography, for instance. The next step is to gain knowledge about career opportunities that you think fit you. What jobs are available in photography? When you see a certain area that interests you, **try it out. Test it by getting a summer or part-time job.** Perhaps become involved in a school work program. Try the job on for size, and see if it fits."

"I'm going to do that," John thought as he gathered his books for his next class. "Maybe I really can have a career in photography and make a good living too."

John is now on his way to planning his future career. He is going to start at the beginning — **with himself.** He will find that there is more to himself than he imagined. John, like all of us, is a sum total of four abilities: physical, mental, social, and emotional. These abilities play different roles of importance in different people. One person likes to work with things, another with ideas. Some people are not happy being alone. Others can only work alone. Certain types of people do their best when under pressure. Other people to do well must be free from pressure. We are all **unique!** The important thing for us is to know and understand ourselves.

After John learns about himself, he can form a job concept. Using the knowledge and the abilities of his own physical, mental, social, and emotional make-up, he can decide what career may be best for him. He can also determine what kind of working conditions will best suit him.

Now that John has some idea who he is and what he wants from a job, he is ready

Fig. 15-4. Exploring career opportunities is one of the steps in good career planning.

Fig. 15-5. "Designing is an important graphic art used in the production of nearly all products."

to explore career opportunities. He is going to make the career fit him.

While looking, John might see a particular area that appeals to him. He is ready for the third step. He should test the job by doing it or work in the environment of the job such as a photography store, lab, or printing company. Taking a summer or part-time job or enrolling in a school work program could mean the beginning of an interesting, life-long career.

This chapter will introduce you to some of the people who have careers in the graphic communications industry. As you meet them you might, like John, suddenly say to yourself, "That could be me!"

PEOPLE WHO DESIGN

Look around you. Just about everything you see was designed by someone, such as, the chair you are sitting in, the book you are holding, the table, the lamp, the rug. Designing is an important graphic art used in the production of nearly all products, Fig. 15-5.

People who design are expressing an idea visually. In graphic arts, the idea is conveyed to the consumer in a printed communication. This requires skill in arranging words, sentences, pictures, lines, and colors. The artist who designs the printed communication uses various images to convey the message. Some images are generated by the artist's own skill — freehand or technical art and lettering. To complete the design, however, the skill of the photographer for a picture or skill of the typesetter for a block of type may be needed.

People design food packages such as boxes, cans, bottles, and dairy containers. The shape of the package and the label on it help to sell the product inside, Fig. 15-6. Think of your favorite cereal, for example. What does the illustration on the box say about the cereal? How does it say it?

Designers work for department stores. They design advertisements to be used in newspapers and magazines. They create the displays for the store windows.

Publishing and printing firms employ people who design. Book covers and illustrations need both freehand and drafting talents. Photographs must be retouched, and charts and maps must be drawn.

Fig. 15-6. Often, the first contact the consumer has with a product is through its package. The design must make a good impression.

Fig. 15-7. "A great deal depends on the skills of clerical workers."

What else do people design? How about wallpaper, greeting cards, record album covers, wrapping paper, clip art, calendars, floor tile, coloring books, neckties, signs? What other products can you think of that need the talents of people who design?

PEOPLE IN THE OFFICE

In the graphic communications industry as in other fields, the office is an idea and fact center. Ideas are conceived, written, and projected into the processes of production. Facts are obtained and stored until needed. The purpose underlying both functions is to help make the work or product better understood by the consumer. A wide variety of talents is needed to achieve that goal.

Some people in the office write. **Advertising writers** communicate the value and purpose of a product or service to the consumer. **Technical writers** combine scientific knowledge with writing skill to help people understand technical subjects. **Copy editors** deal with the writing of other people. They check manuscripts to see that the ideas are communicated successfully. They also check for grammar and writing style.

Clerical people are fact people. The facts that they handle must be accurate if the graphic enterprise is to operate smoothly. **Secretaries** take facts through dictation, mail, or phone. Either they or **typists** organize the facts on paper. **File clerks** and **computer programmers** store the facts. A great deal depends on the skills of clerical workers, Fig. 15-7.

Another person in the office is the **estimator**. This person determines how much it will cost to produce a product in terms of material, machines, and human labor. The estimator must know the costs of operating machines and paying salaries and benefits, as well as the cost of materials in order to estimate the prices for customers.

Fig. 15-8. Customers depend on sales representatives.

There are many careers in the office. Each one is important to the success of the graphic communications business.

PEOPLE IN SALES

The sales representative stands between the producer and the consumer, offering the personal product called "service." Dependability, efficiency, and honesty as well as a special talent for working with people are required. This service is a main link from producer to consumer, Fig. 15-8.

Sales representatives in the graphic communications industry sell various commodities. They **sell other people's labor**. They might sell the services of designers or writers to a company that needs such services.

Sales representatives **sell machine time**. For example, when representing a printing company, the services of the printing machines can be sold to other companies. One customer may be a publishing company which has arranged for the writing and illustrating of a book but does not have the facilities to print the book. Orders can also be taken for the printing of stationery, business cards, and other items.

Sales representatives **sell space**. Newspapers and magazines that have space for advertisements hire people to sell that space in the publication to businesses.

Sales representatives **sell products**. Sometimes they sell a graphic art product to another graphic art business, as, for instance, paper, ink, clip art, photographs, and many other graphic materials. They may sell such products as books to school systems and bookstores.

Sales representatives **sell channels of communications**. They see that a line of communication is available between the producer and a particular group such as farmers, doctors, people in business, engineers, and others. An individual or group can use the existing mail lists to send information to other interested consumers. Being able to identify special groups of consumers is a valuable product for a sales representative.

PEOPLE IN THE PRODUCTION OF PRODUCTS OR SERVICES

Do you like to make things happen? That's what people in the production of products and services do. They make things happen through organizing people. They make things happen through the operation of machines. They make things happen by getting the finished product to the consumer. These are action people!

Meet the **production manager** who guides the work through the production process and makes things happen on time.

The **plant manager** understands and organizes people and machines.

The **plant engineer** watches equipment and technique to see that the operation works smoothly. If it doesn't, the engineer must find out why.

Layout people organize art, illustration, and copy which are then presented to the printer who arranges for stripping, plate-

making, presswork, and binding, as specified for the product.

In some kinds of printing, the **camera operator** makes things happen by photographing the work to be printed. The **stripper** arranges the negative films and strips them to size. The **platemaker** can then expose the sheets onto offset plates.

Photoengraving also makes things happen. In this process, the **etcher, finisher,** and **proofer** all play a part in turning the original idea into reality.

People and machines make the finished product happen. The **typesetter** turns copy into type. The **press operator** turns the type into product. The **binder** packages the product. Trucks, trains, and planes take the product to the consumer.

The product has happened. But other people are needed so that the process can start all over again for other productions in graphic arts. Buyers purchase new materials for people and machines. Storekeepers organize and maintain the graphic arts materials until they are needed.

Fig. 15-9. The production manager and the press operator are both action people who make the finished product happen.

Fig. 15-10. Getting the product to the consumer is a final, and important, step in production.

PEOPLE WHO RESEARCH AND DEVELOP PRODUCTS OR SERVICES

Related closely to the graphic communications industry are the many specialized careers in research and development of products or services. **Researchers** bring widely used skills into the industry. New printing techniques are continually being explored by this group of specialists. Other researchers are developing new machines to do the work. Foresters do research in wood and pulp. This contributes to paper technology. Chemists do research to find new or better ways to develop products, Fig. 15-11. A researcher in marketing finds out how well a product will sell, what the consumer wants, and what the consumer thinks of the product. This contributes to the graphic communications industry by providing information that will later be considered during the planning of a communication product.

The actual production of paper is, of course, an essential and basic part of the graphic communications industry. Many different skills are needed to process a tree to paper. Let's follow one tree and see how many jobs touch it.

The forester selects the trees to be cut for paper production, Fig. 15-12, and plans for the planting of new trees to replace them. A logger is needed to cut down the tree. The heavy-machinery operator often loads the log onto a truck, and the trucker takes the log to the mill, Fig. 15-13. That's four different occupations already! At the mill, the operator of a barker machine strips the log. A chipper machine cuts the log into chips. The chips are taken by the digester machine and reduced to pulp. The pulp, after being bleached, goes into the paper machine. Seven occupations needed to produce pulp. And the process is not over! Papermaking involves various kinds of techniques depending on the purpose the paper will serve. It therefore requires the knowledge and ability of skilled individuals, Fig. 15-14. A paper-cutting machine operator has a job to do. The paper might be sent to a corrugating machine or envelope machine. Can you think of any other skills that might affect the log's journey into paper?

Fig. 15-11. The chemist's research is an important part of industry progress.

Fig. 15-12. Among other things, a forester decides when a tree is ready to be cut.

Fig. 15-14. This paper is the result of the talents of many people.

Fig. 15-13. Each one of these occupations is essential to bring a tree from the forest to the mill.

These are only a few of the people who share in the research and development of products or services in the graphic communications industry.

Certainly, the skill of **managers** is essential to the industry's progress, Fig. 15-15. A manager's skill of organizing people to produce a product or service, added to a knowledge of the graphic communications industry, makes this job vital.

Lastly, some of the most important people in the graphic communications industry do not work for the industry at all! They work for banks, Fig. 15-16. They specialize in financing graphic communication enterprises such as the research and development of products and services. These banking specialists know a great deal about the graphic communications industry, of course, and through their knowledge they help others manage the growth and success of different businesses.

HOW YOU CAN ENTER

Several weeks had passed since Mr. Jackson first presented the three steps to career planning to John and the rest of the class. Had his advice helped John, he wondered.

Fig. 15-15. The manager is an organizer of "people power."

Fig. 15-17. Completion of school — and the beginning of a career.

Fig. 15-16. Banks such as this one finance many different graphic communication businesses.

"I think so," said John. "I really thought about myself — what kind of a person I am physically, mentally, socially, and emotionally. Photography was still my big interest, so I looked at careers in that field. I found an area that really appealed to me. It has the variety, security, working conditions, and human contact I need. But I want to learn more about the area. And how do I find a job when I'm ready to test it?"

"You can learn more about your field right here in school," Mr. Jackson answered. "You can take classes in the subject. If you feel you need to know more later on, you can go to a junior college or university. Or you can go right to work."

"How do I find a job?"

"There are a lot of ways. You can find a job through an employment agency, a state employment office, or newspaper ads. You can go to the business itself and apply for work. The counselor at school also can help you. Another good way is to talk to someone who works in the field you are interested in."

"That's what I'm going to do," said John. "It's really something to know that you can do what you enjoy and still have a career. It just takes a little planning."

INDEX